Hot Gimmick

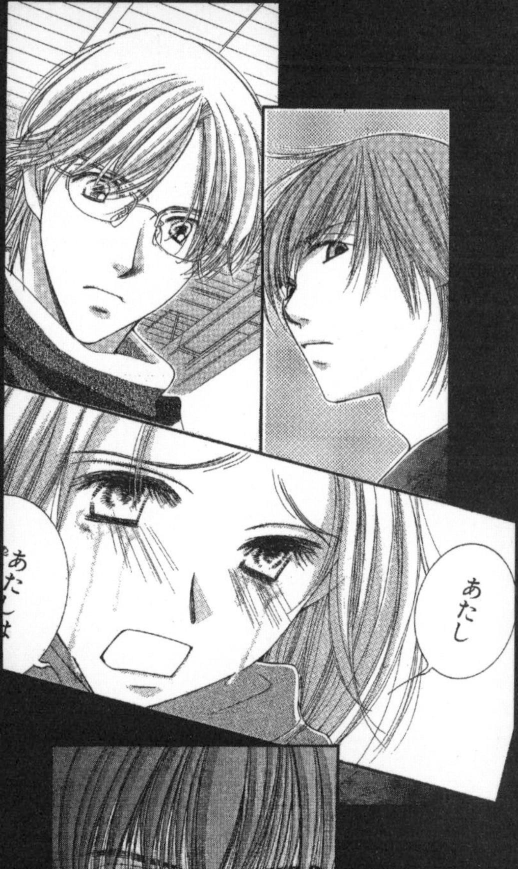
あたし
あたしは

vol.3

MIKI AIHARA

HOT GIMMICK
CONTENTS

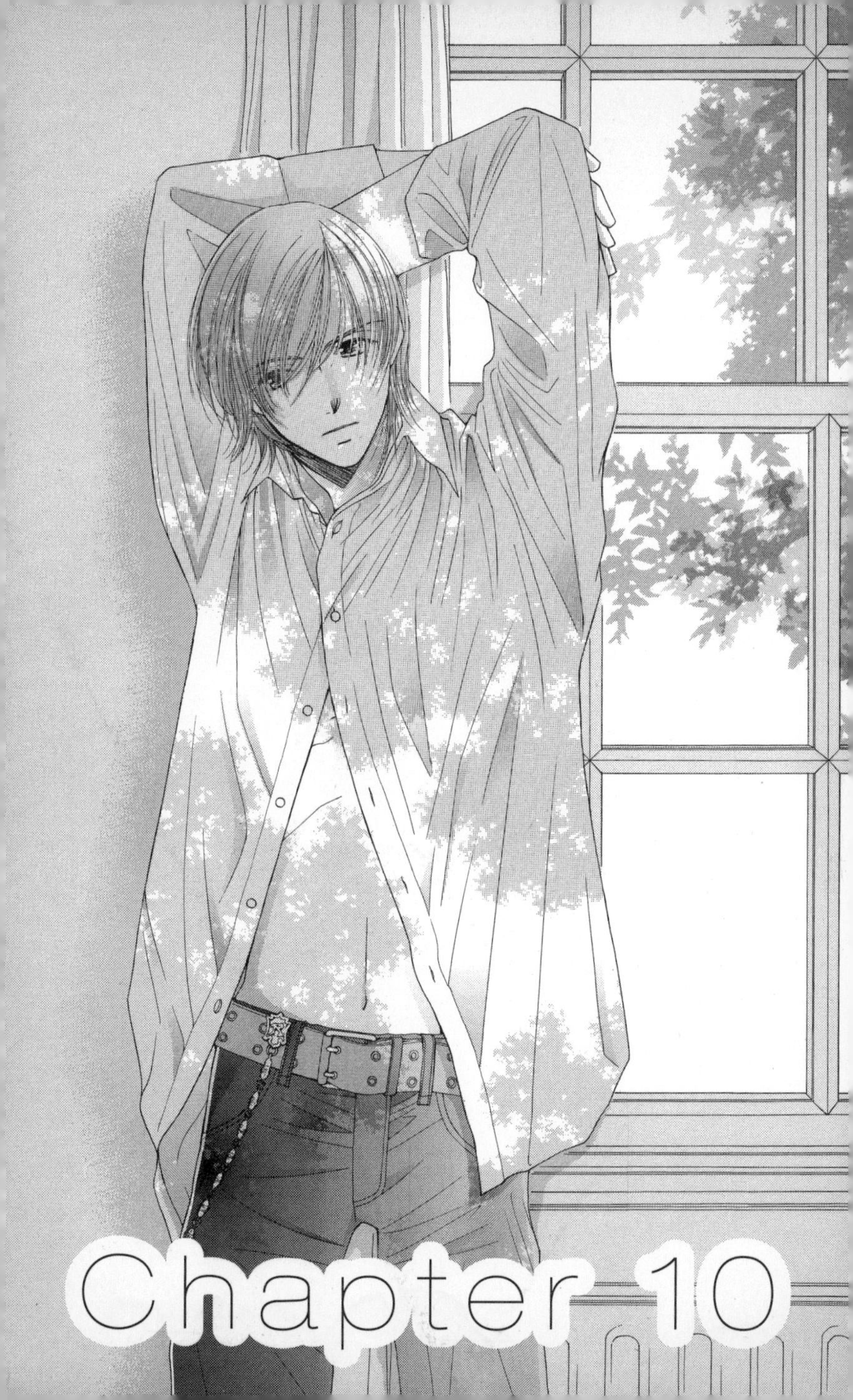
Chapter 10

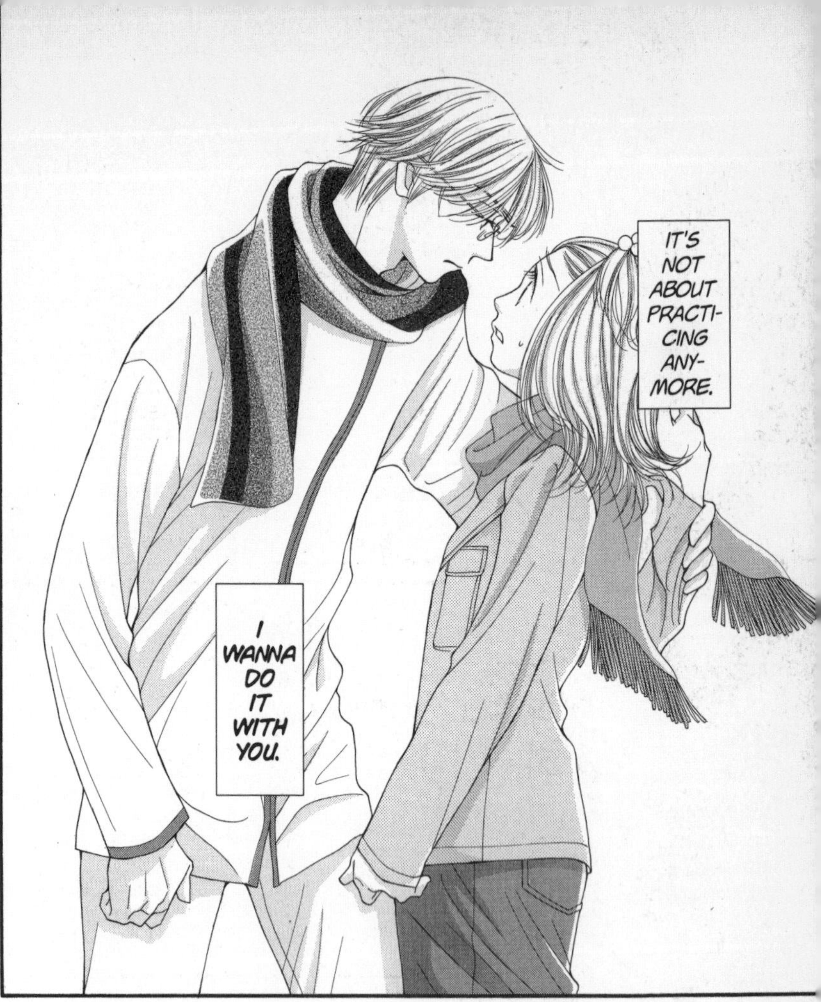
IT'S NOT ABOUT PRACTICING ANYMORE.
I WANNA DO IT WITH YOU.

hot gimmick

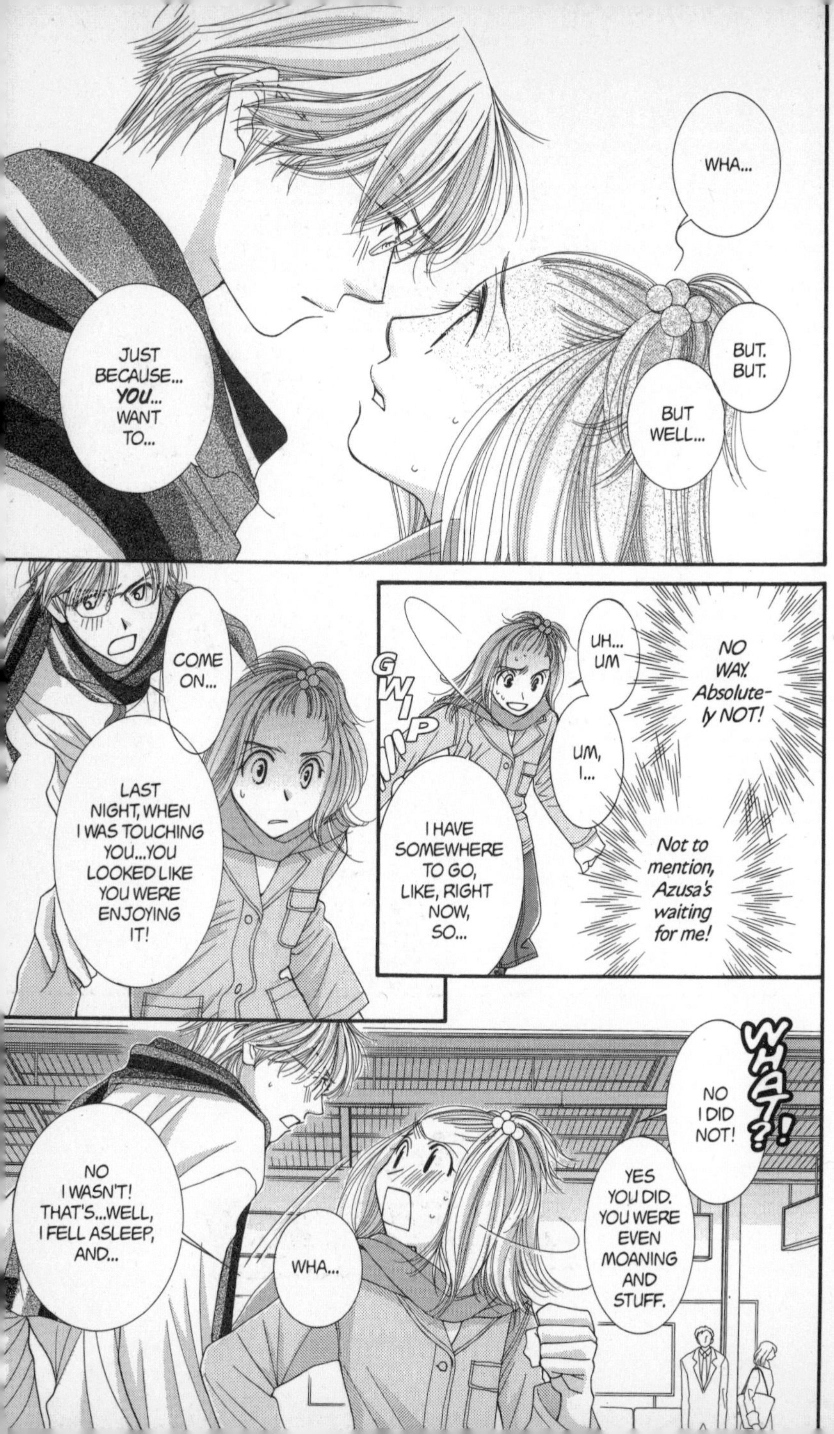
WHA...
BUT. BUT.
BUT WELL...
JUST BECAUSE... ***YOU***... WANT TO...
NO WAY. Absolutely NOT!
UH... UM
GWIP
UM, I...
Not to mention, Azusa's waiting for me!
I HAVE SOMEWHERE TO GO, LIKE, RIGHT NOW, SO...
COME ON...
LAST NIGHT, WHEN I WAS TOUCHING YOU...YOU LOOKED LIKE YOU WERE ENJOYING IT!
WHAT?!
NO I DID NOT!
YES YOU DID. YOU WERE EVEN MOANING AND STUFF.
WHA...
NO I WASN'T! THAT'S...WELL, I FELL ASLEEP, AND...

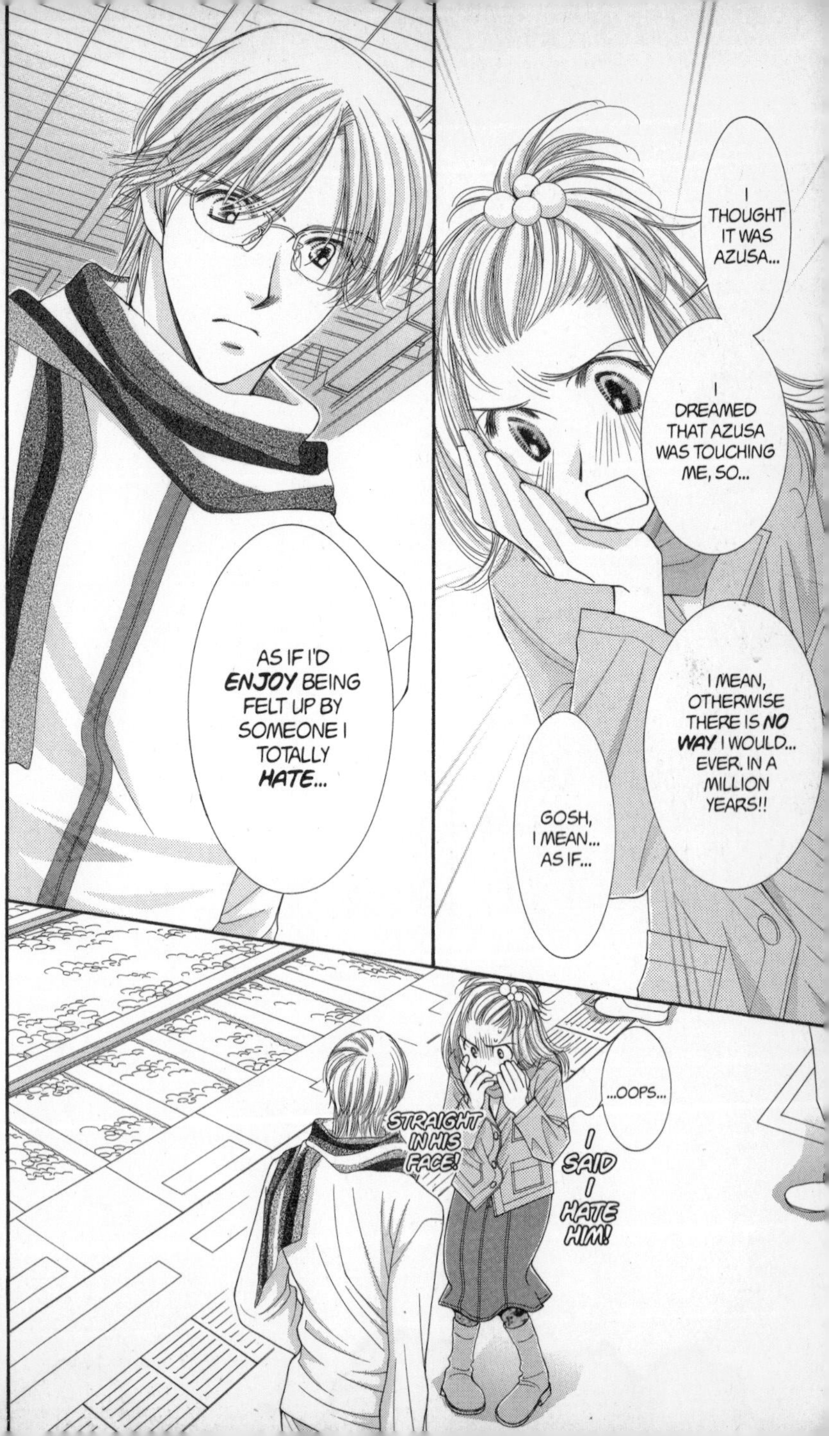
I THOUGHT IT WAS AZUSA...
I DREAMED THAT AZUSA WAS TOUCHING ME, SO...
I MEAN, OTHERWISE THERE IS **NO WAY** I WOULD... EVER. IN A MILLION YEARS!!
GOSH, I MEAN... AS IF...
AS IF I'D **ENJOY** BEING FELT UP BY SOMEONE I TOTALLY **HATE**...
...OOPS...
I SAID I HATE HIM!
STRAIGHT IN HIS FACE!

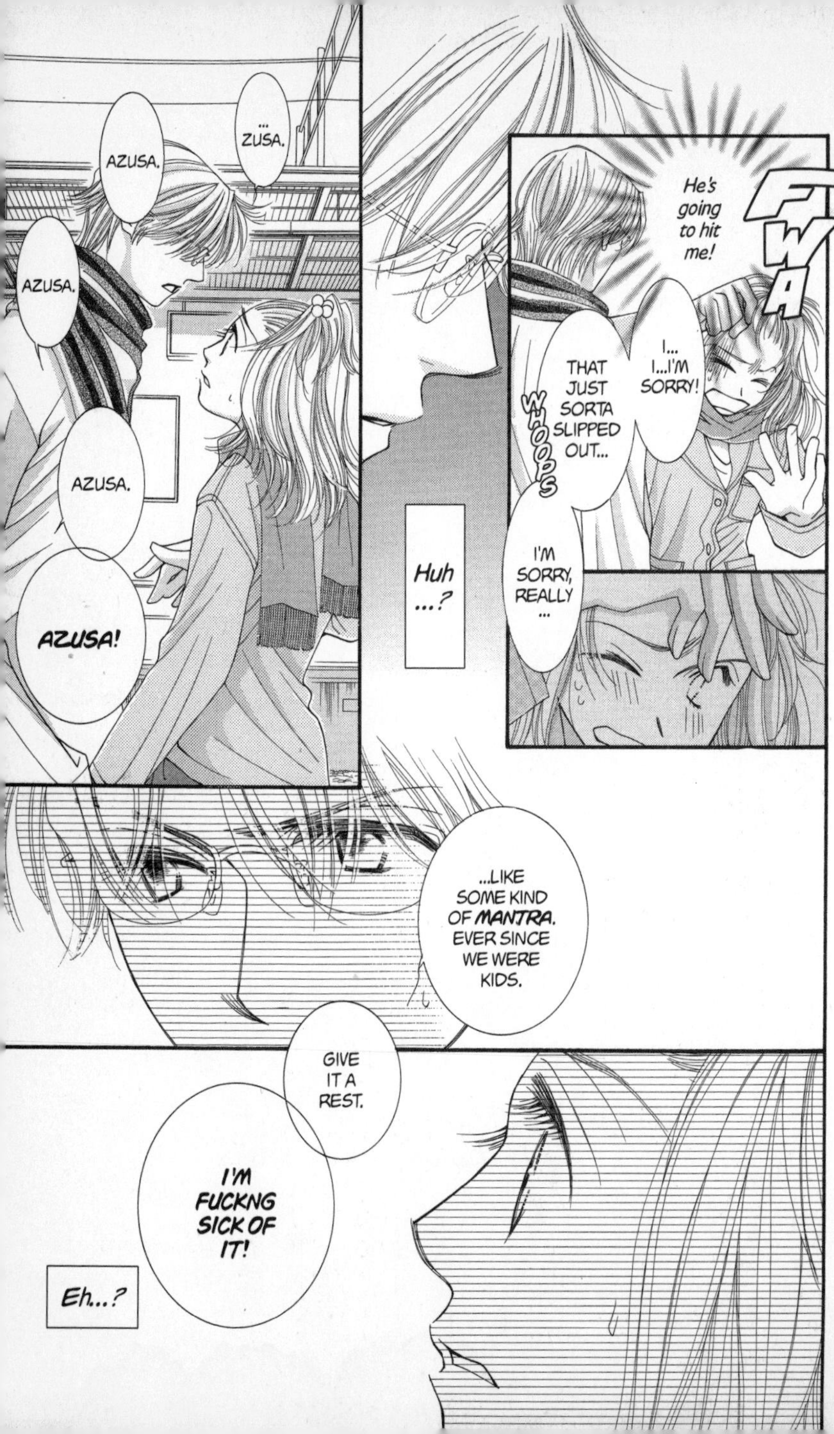
FWA
He's going to hit me!
I... I...I'M SORRY!
THAT JUST SORTA SLIPPED OUT...
WHOOPS
I'M SORRY, REALLY ...
Huh ...?
... ZUSA.
AZUSA.
AZUSA.
AZUSA.
AZUSA!
...LIKE SOME KIND OF *MANTRA*. EVER SINCE WE WERE KIDS.
GIVE IT A REST.
I'M FUCKNG SICK OF IT!
Eh...?

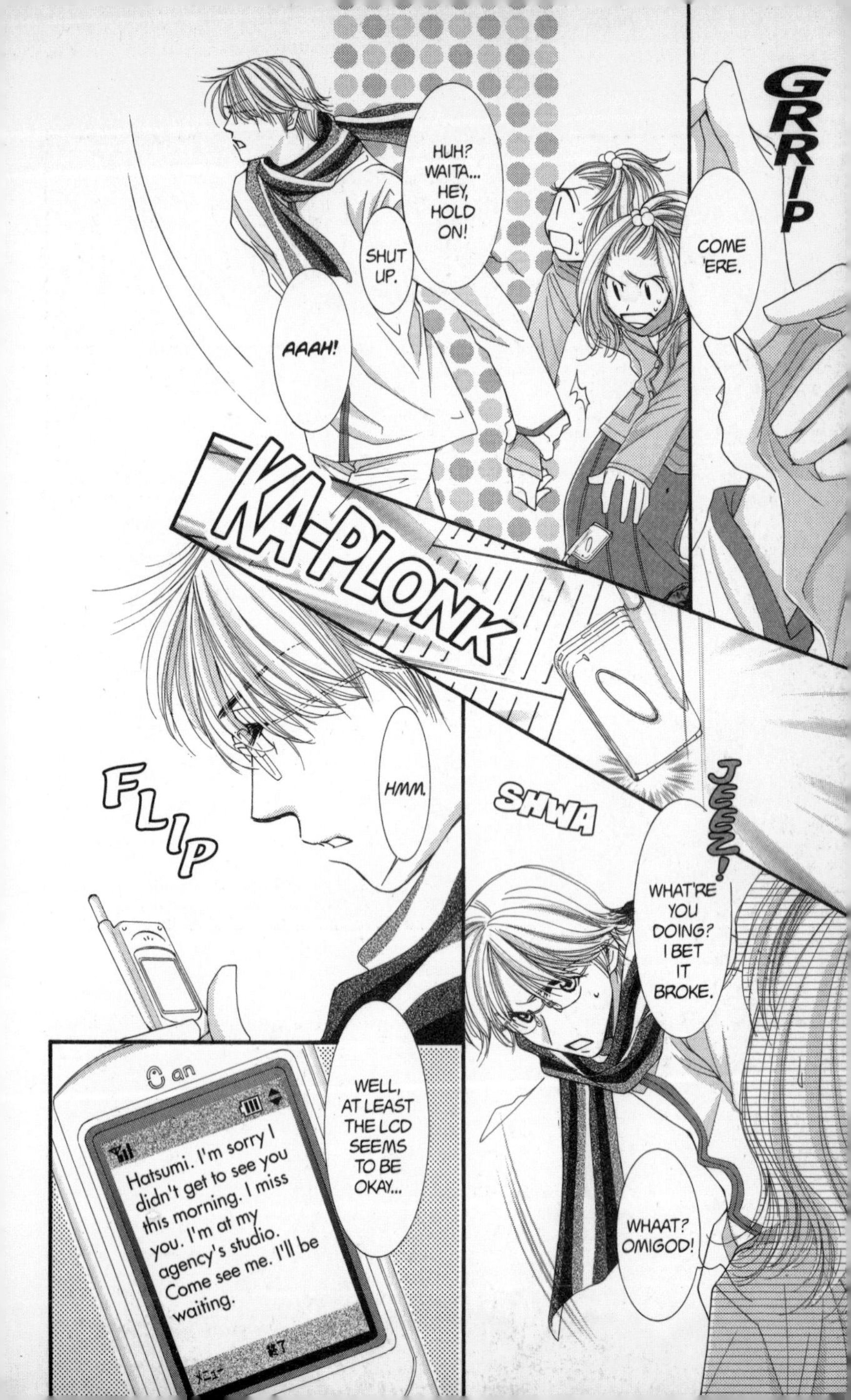
GRRIP
COME 'ERE.
HUH? WAITA... HEY, HOLD ON!
SHUT UP.
AAAH!
KA-PLONK
SHWA
JEEZ!
WHAT'RE YOU DOING? I BET IT BROKE.
WHAAT? OMIGOD!
HMM.
FLIP
WELL, AT LEAST THE LCD SEEMS TO BE OKAY...
Hatsumi. I'm sorry I didn't get to see you this morning. I miss you. I'm at my agency's studio. Come see me. I'll be waiting.

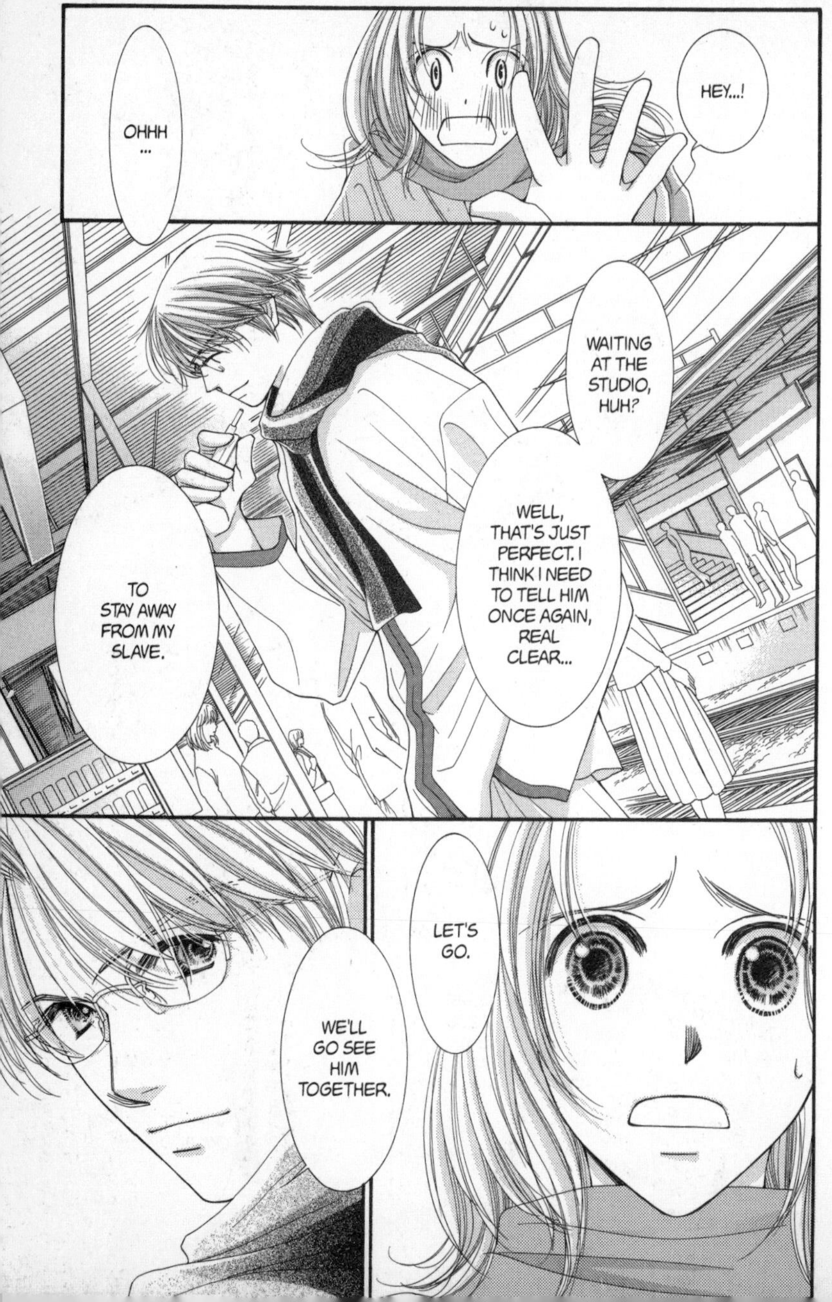
HEY...!
OHHH ...
WAITING AT THE STUDIO, HUH?
WELL, THAT'S JUST PERFECT. I THINK I NEED TO TELL HIM ONCE AGAIN, REAL CLEAR...
TO STAY AWAY FROM MY SLAVE.
LET'S GO.
WE'LL GO SEE HIM TOGETHER.

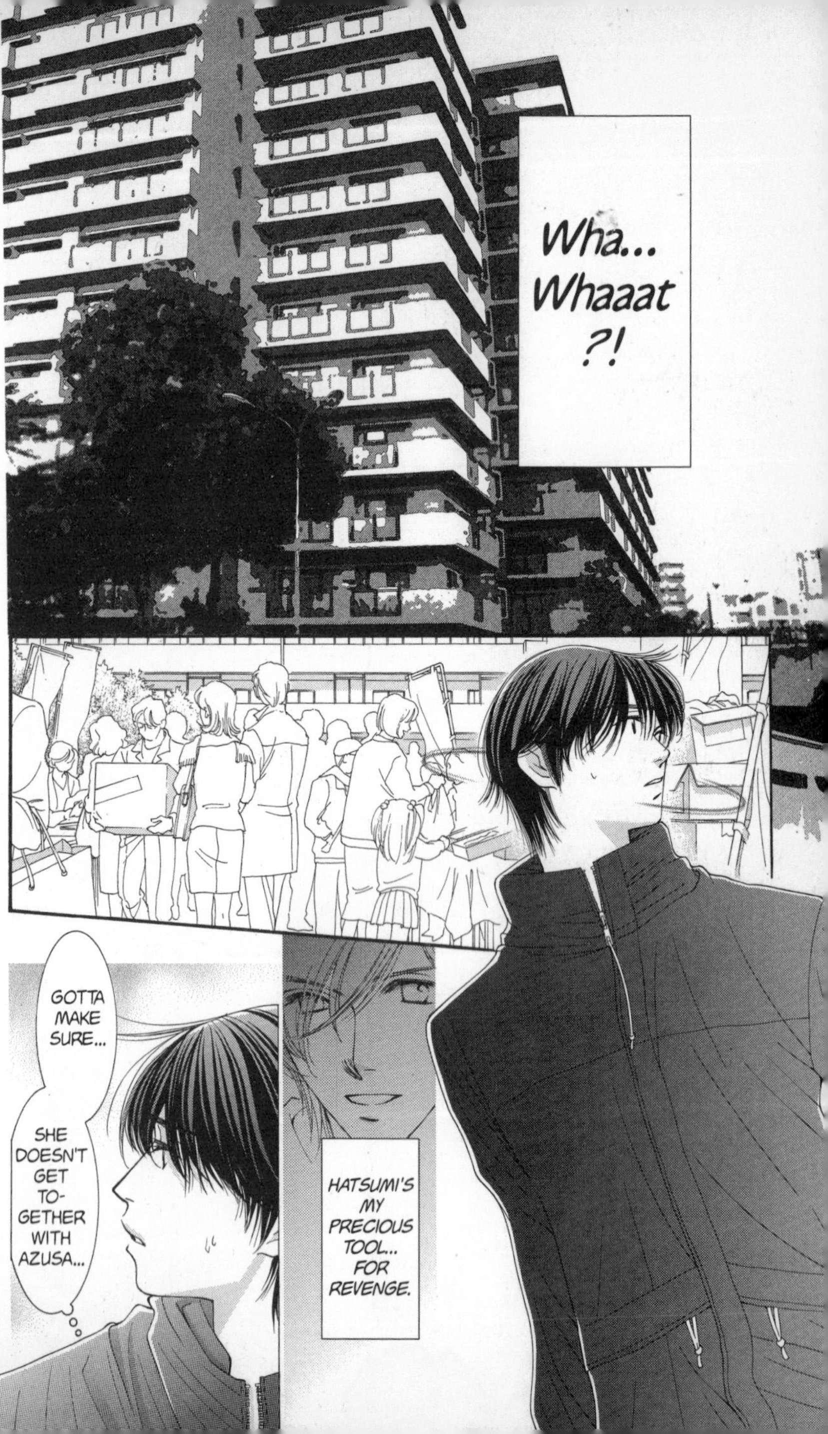
Wha... Whaaat ?!
HATSUMI'S MY PRECIOUS TOOL... FOR REVENGE.
GOTTA MAKE SURE...
SHE DOESN'T GET TO-GETHER WITH AZUSA...

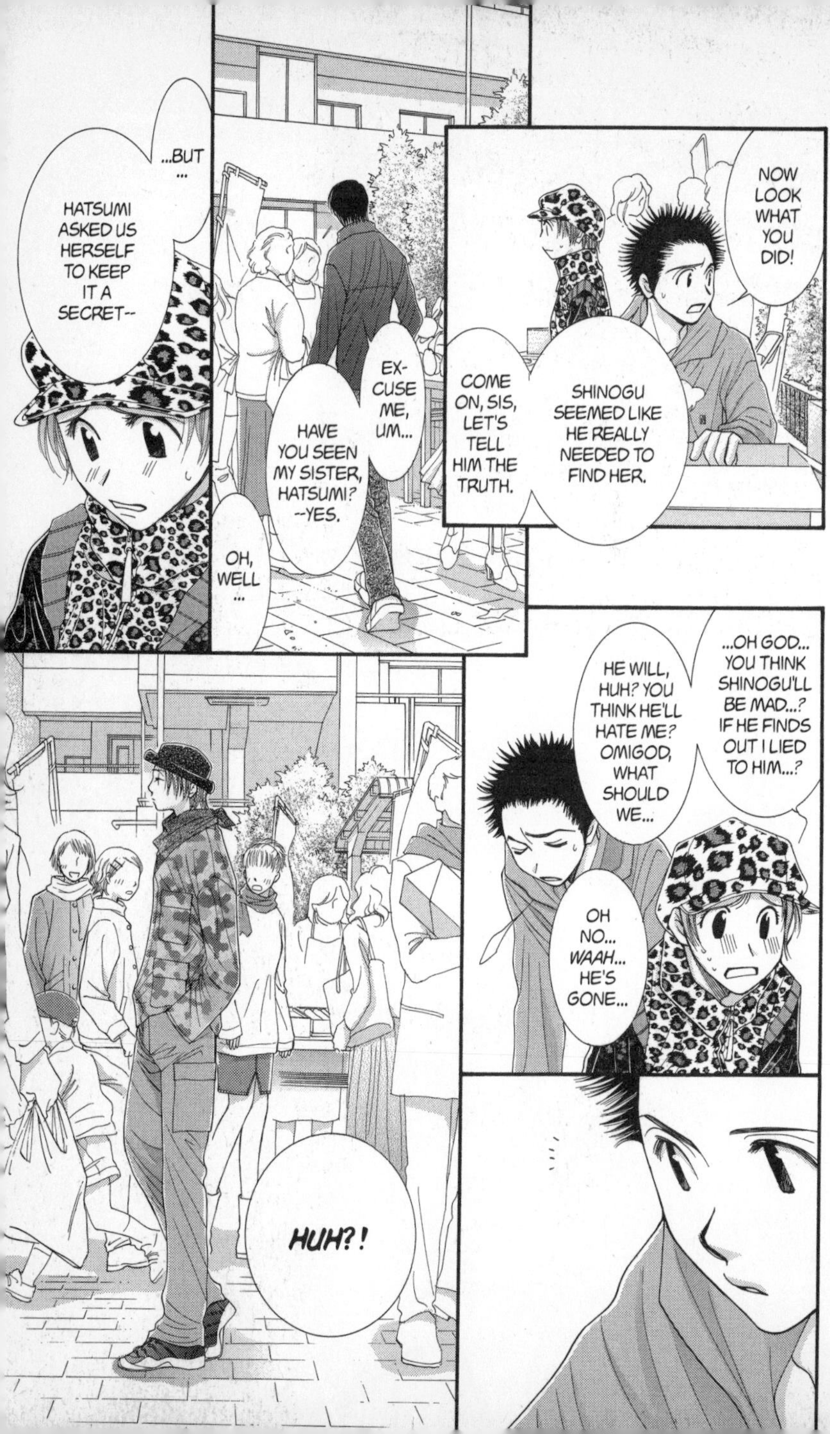
NOW LOOK WHAT YOU DID!
SHINOGU SEEMED LIKE HE REALLY NEEDED TO FIND HER.
COME ON, SIS, LET'S TELL HIM THE TRUTH.
EX-CUSE ME, UM...
HAVE YOU SEEN MY SISTER, HATSUMI? --YES.
OH, WELL ...
...BUT ...
HATSUMI ASKED US HERSELF TO KEEP IT A SECRET--
...OH GOD... YOU THINK SHINOGU'LL BE MAD...? IF HE FINDS OUT I LIED TO HIM...?
HE WILL, HUH? YOU THINK HE'LL HATE ME? OMIGOD, WHAT SHOULD WE...
OH NO... WAAH... HE'S GONE...
HUH?!

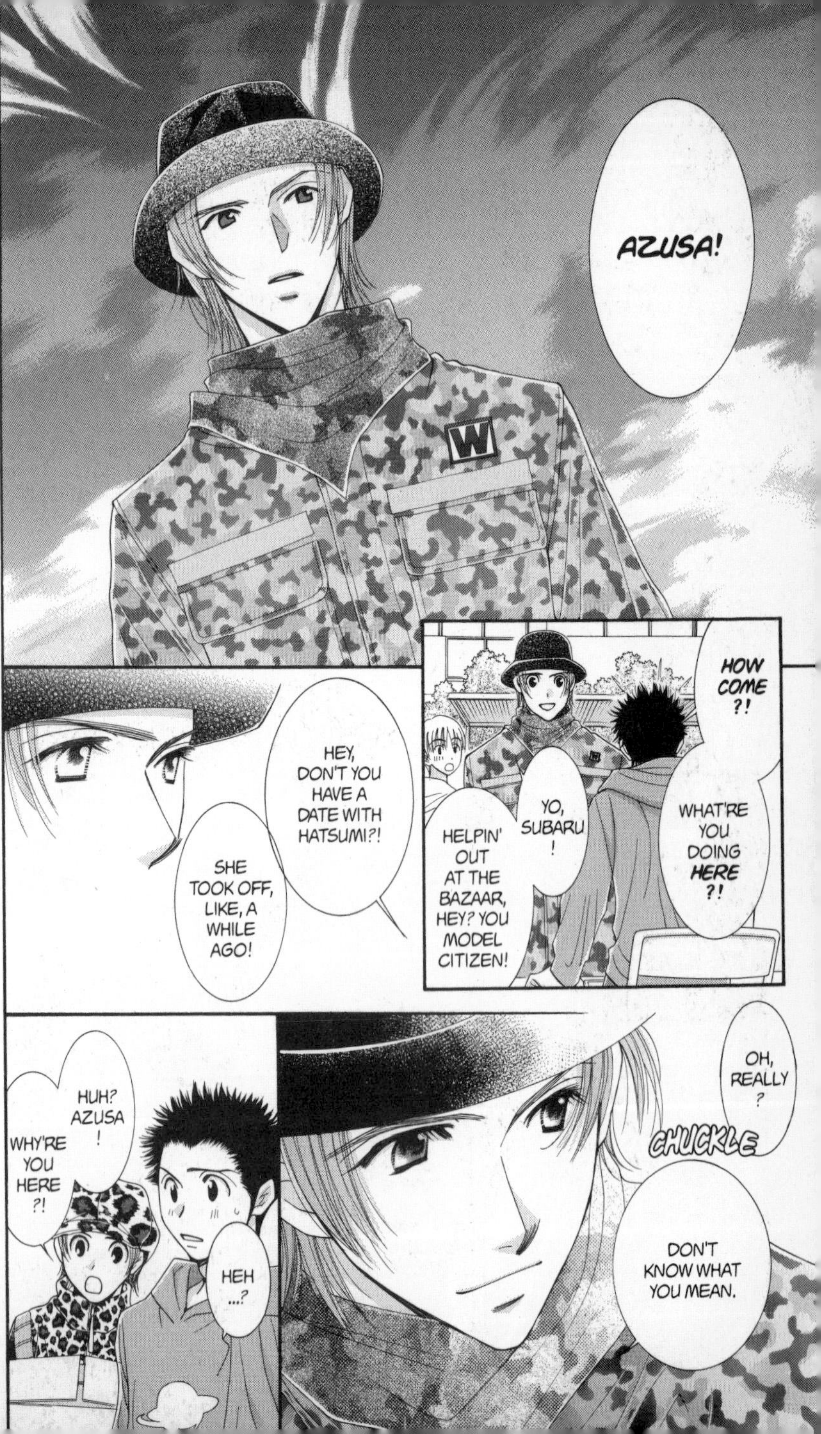
AZUSA!
HOW COME?!
WHAT'RE YOU DOING HERE?!
YO, SUBARU!
HELPIN' OUT AT THE BAZAAR, HEY? YOU MODEL CITIZEN!
HEY, DON'T YOU HAVE A DATE WITH HATSUMI?!
SHE TOOK OFF, LIKE, A WHILE AGO!
OH, REALLY?
CHUCKLE
DON'T KNOW WHAT YOU MEAN.
HUH? AZUSA!
WHY'RE YOU HERE?!
HEH...?

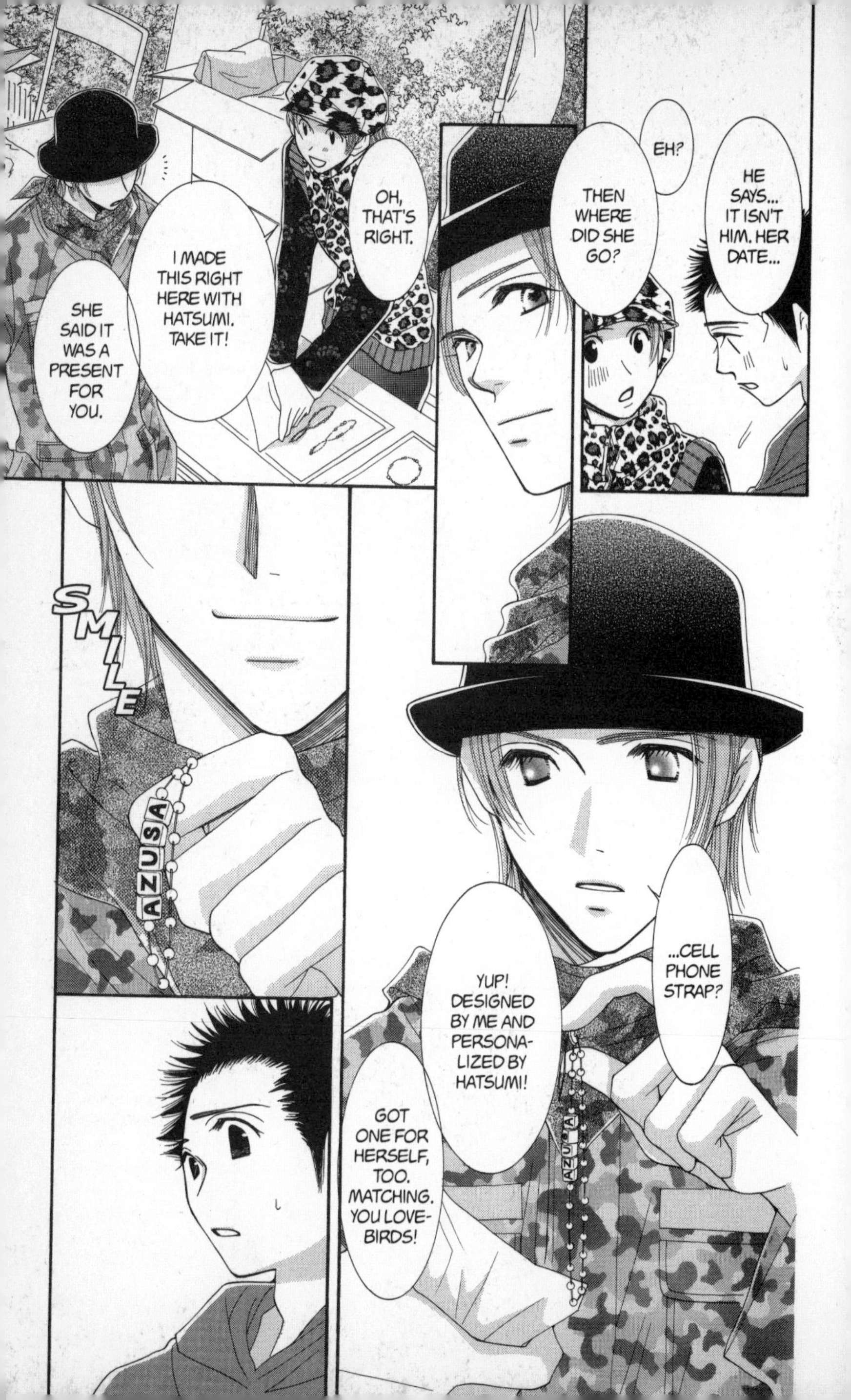
HE SAYS... IT ISN'T HIM. HER DATE...
EH?
THEN WHERE DID SHE GO?
OH, THAT'S RIGHT.
I MADE THIS RIGHT HERE WITH HATSUMI. TAKE IT!
SHE SAID IT WAS A PRESENT FOR YOU.
...CELL PHONE STRAP?
YUP! DESIGNED BY ME AND PERSONALIZED BY HATSUMI!
GOT ONE FOR HERSELF, TOO. MATCHING. YOU LOVEBIRDS!
AZUSA
SMILE
AZUSA

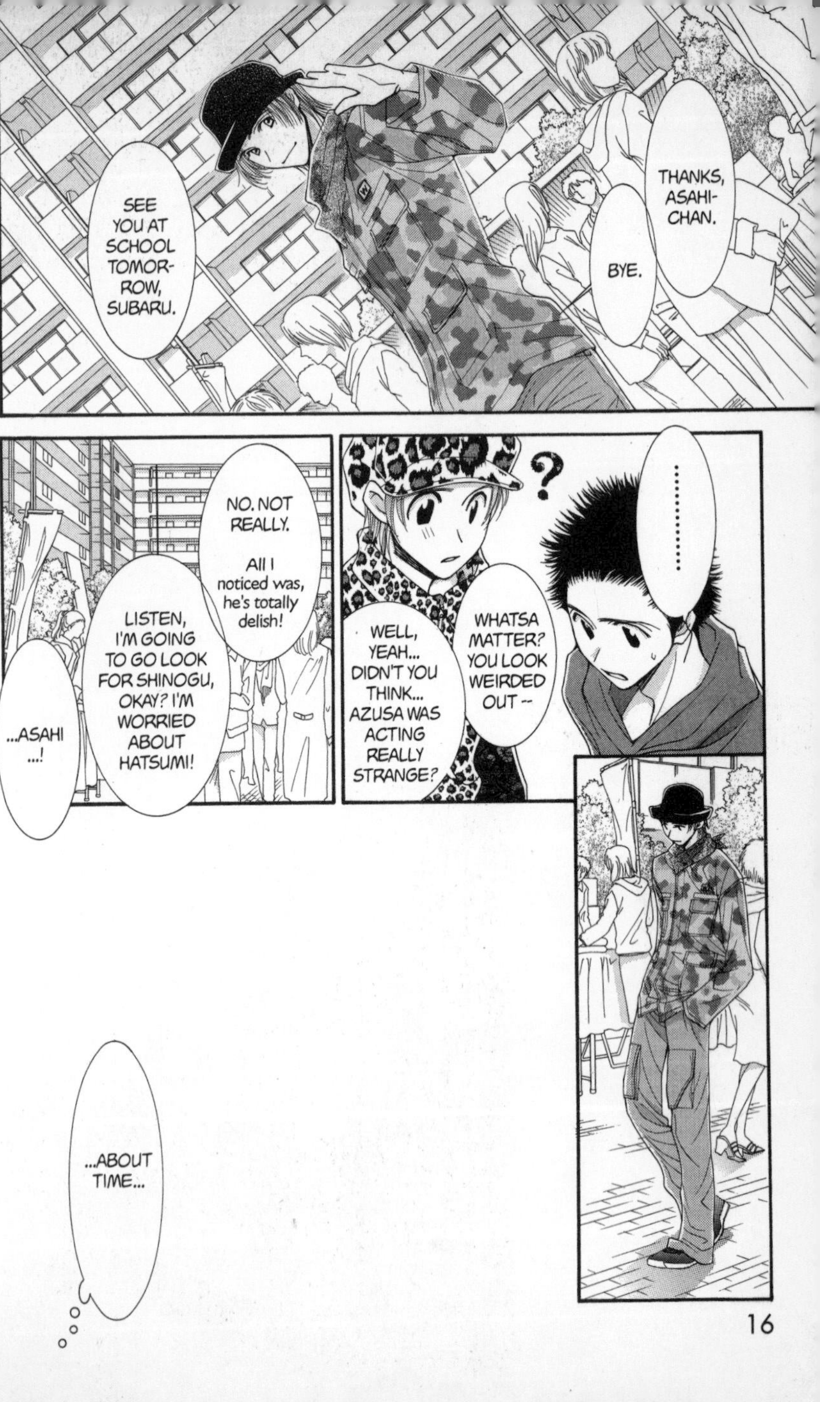
THANKS, ASAHI-CHAN.
BYE.
SEE YOU AT SCHOOL TOMOR-ROW, SUBARU.
......
?
WHATSA MATTER? YOU LOOK WEIRDED OUT --
WELL, YEAH... DIDN'T YOU THINK... AZUSA WAS ACTING REALLY STRANGE?
NO. NOT REALLY.
All I noticed was, he's totally delish!
LISTEN, I'M GOING TO GO LOOK FOR SHINOGU, OKAY? I'M WORRIED ABOUT HATSUMI!
...ASAHI ...!
...ABOUT TIME...

hotgimmick

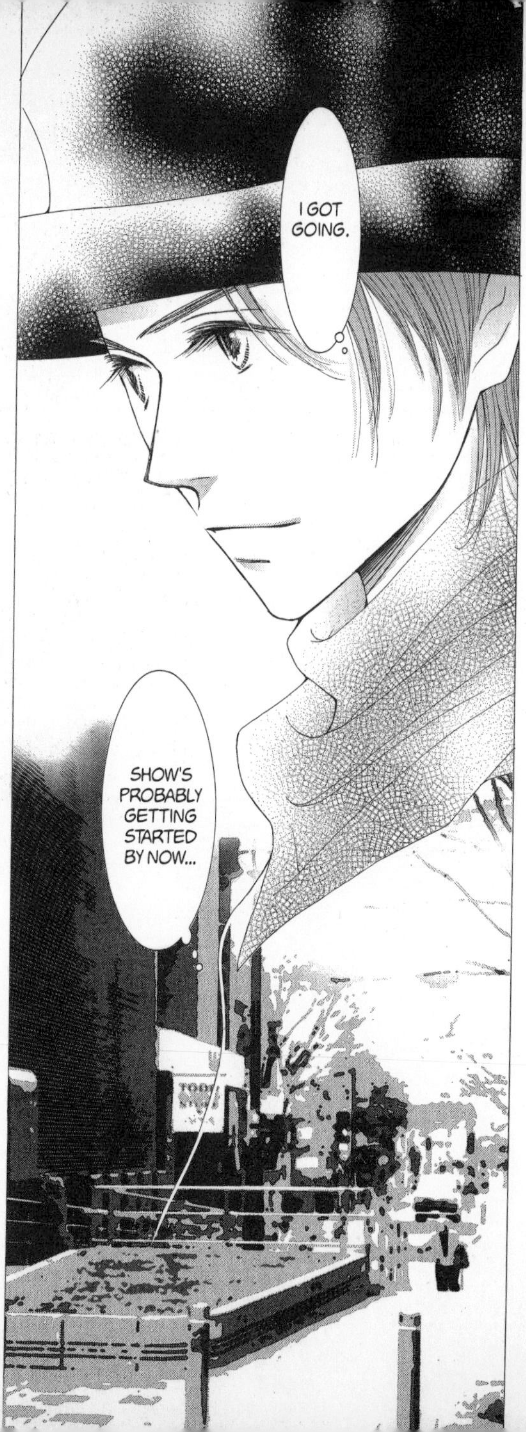
I GOT GOING.
SHOW'S PROBABLY GETTING STARTED BY NOW...

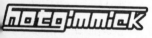

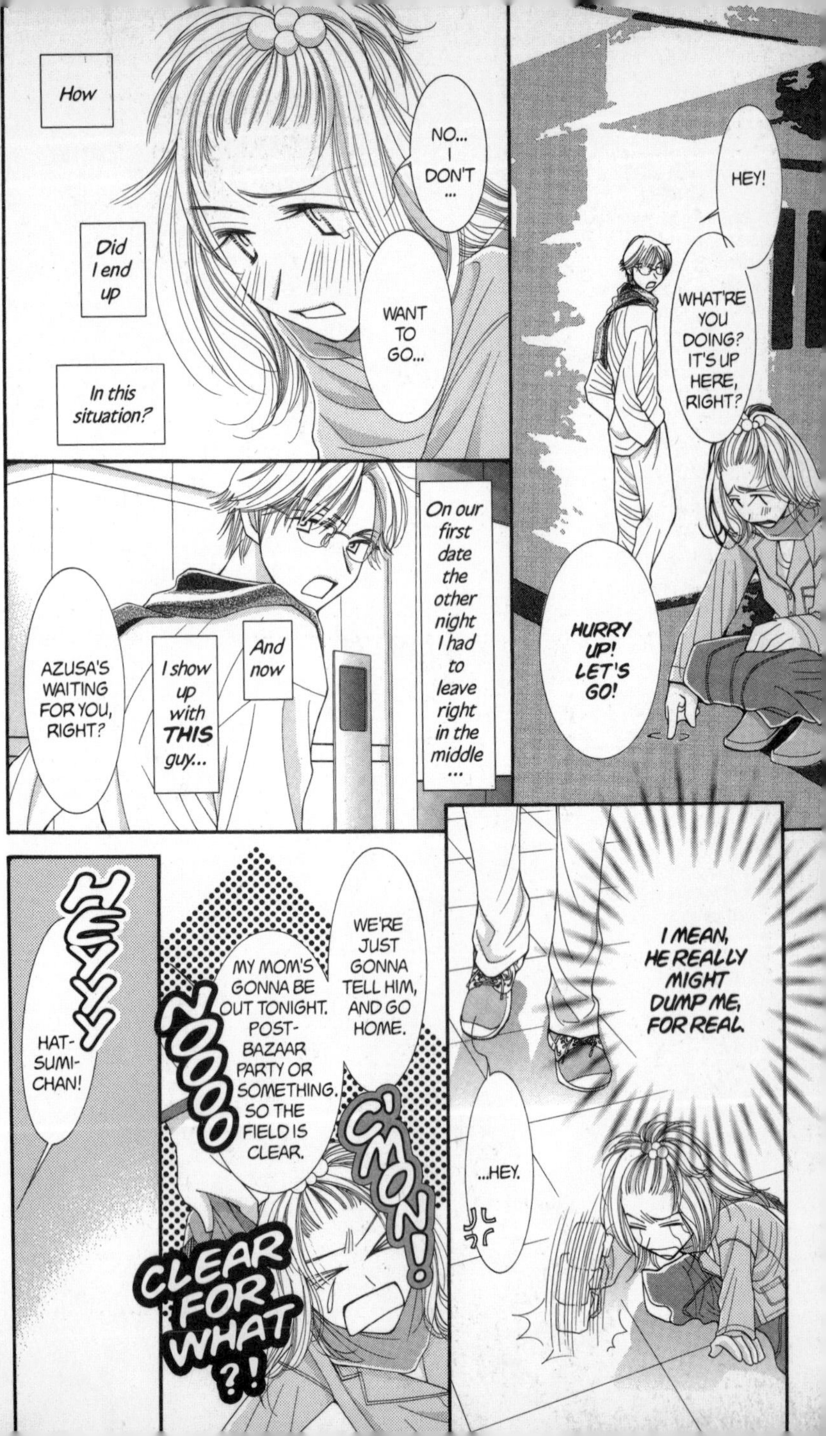
HEY!
WHAT'RE YOU DOING? IT'S UP HERE, RIGHT?
HURRY UP! LET'S GO!
NO... I DON'T ...
How
WANT TO GO...
Did I end up
In this situation?
On our first date the other night I had to leave right in the middle ...
And now
I show up with THIS guy...
AZUSA'S WAITING FOR YOU, RIGHT?
I MEAN, HE REALLY MIGHT DUMP ME, FOR REAL.
...HEY.
HEYYY
HAT-SUMI-CHAN!
WE'RE JUST GONNA TELL HIM, AND GO HOME.
MY MOM'S GONNA BE OUT TONIGHT. POST-BAZAAR PARTY OR SOMETHING. SO THE FIELD IS CLEAR.
NOOOO
C'MON!
CLEAR FOR WHAT?!

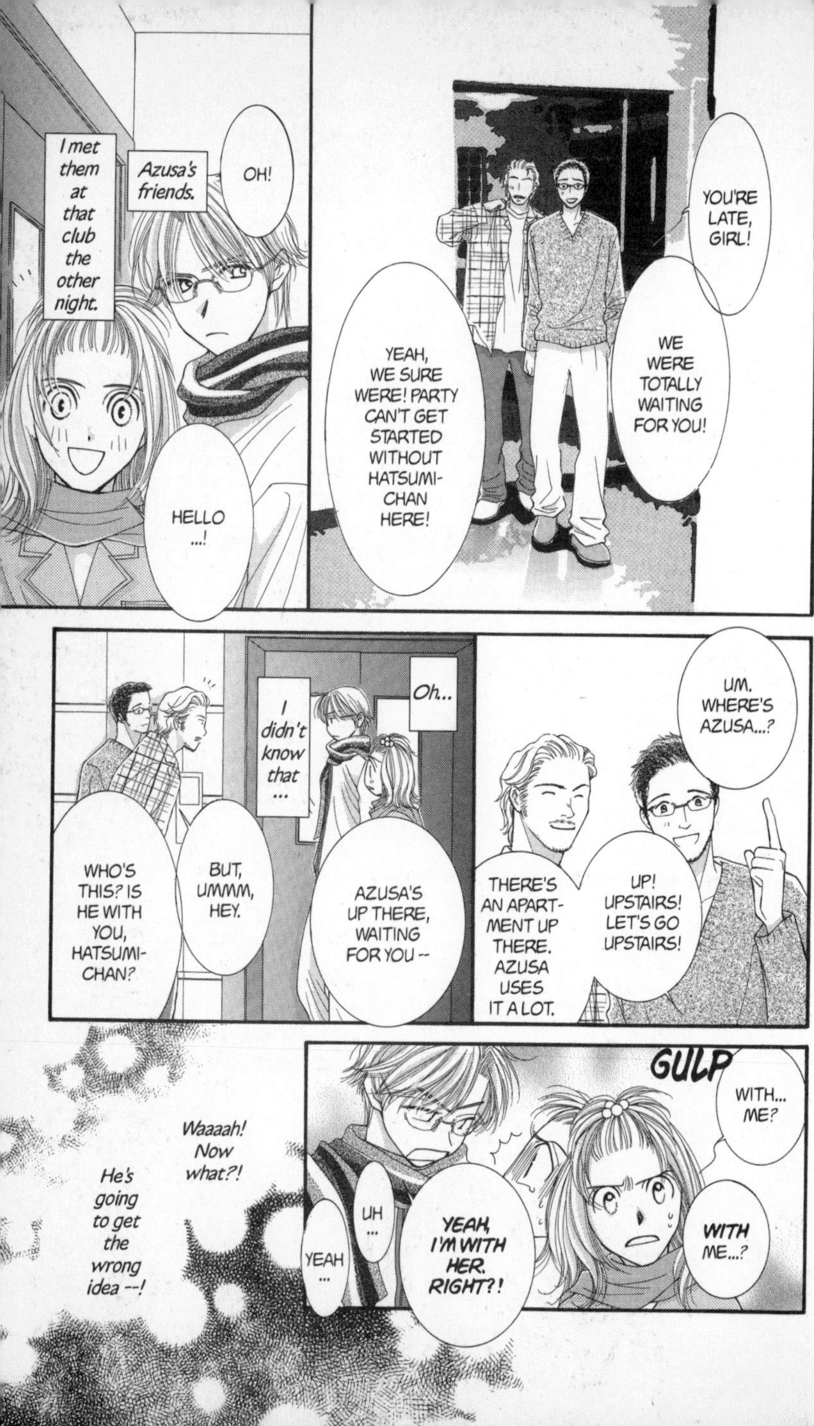
YOU'RE LATE, GIRL!
WE WERE TOTALLY WAITING FOR YOU!
YEAH, WE SURE WERE! PARTY CAN'T GET STARTED WITHOUT HATSUMI-CHAN HERE!
OH!
Azusa's friends.
I met them at that club the other night.
HELLO ...!
UM. WHERE'S AZUSA...?
UP! UPSTAIRS! LET'S GO UPSTAIRS!
THERE'S AN APARTMENT UP THERE. AZUSA USES IT A LOT.
Oh...
I didn't know that ...
AZUSA'S UP THERE, WAITING FOR YOU --
BUT, UMMM, HEY.
WHO'S THIS? IS HE WITH YOU, HATSUMI-CHAN?
GULP
WITH... ME?
WITH ME...?
YEAH, I'M WITH HER. RIGHT?!
UH ...
YEAH ...
Waaaah! Now what?!
He's going to get the wrong idea --!

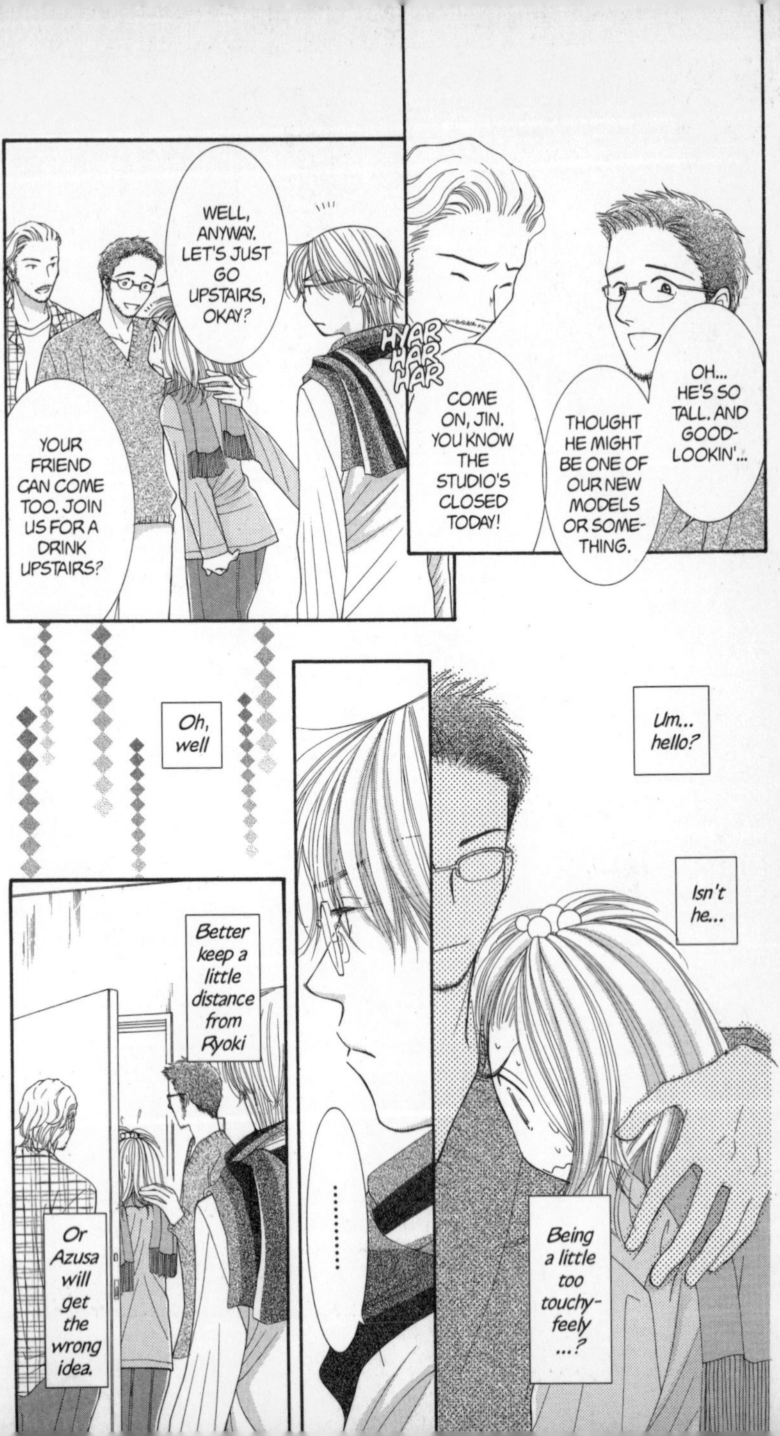
OH... HE'S SO TALL. AND GOOD-LOOKIN'...
THOUGHT HE MIGHT BE ONE OF OUR NEW MODELS OR SOME-THING.
HYAR HAR HAR
COME ON, JIN. YOU KNOW THE STUDIO'S CLOSED TODAY!
WELL, ANYWAY. LET'S JUST GO UPSTAIRS, OKAY?
YOUR FRIEND CAN COME TOO. JOIN US FOR A DRINK UPSTAIRS?
Um... hello?
Isn't he...
Being a little too touchy-feely ...?
....
Oh, well
Better keep a little distance from Ryoki
Or Azusa will get the wrong idea.

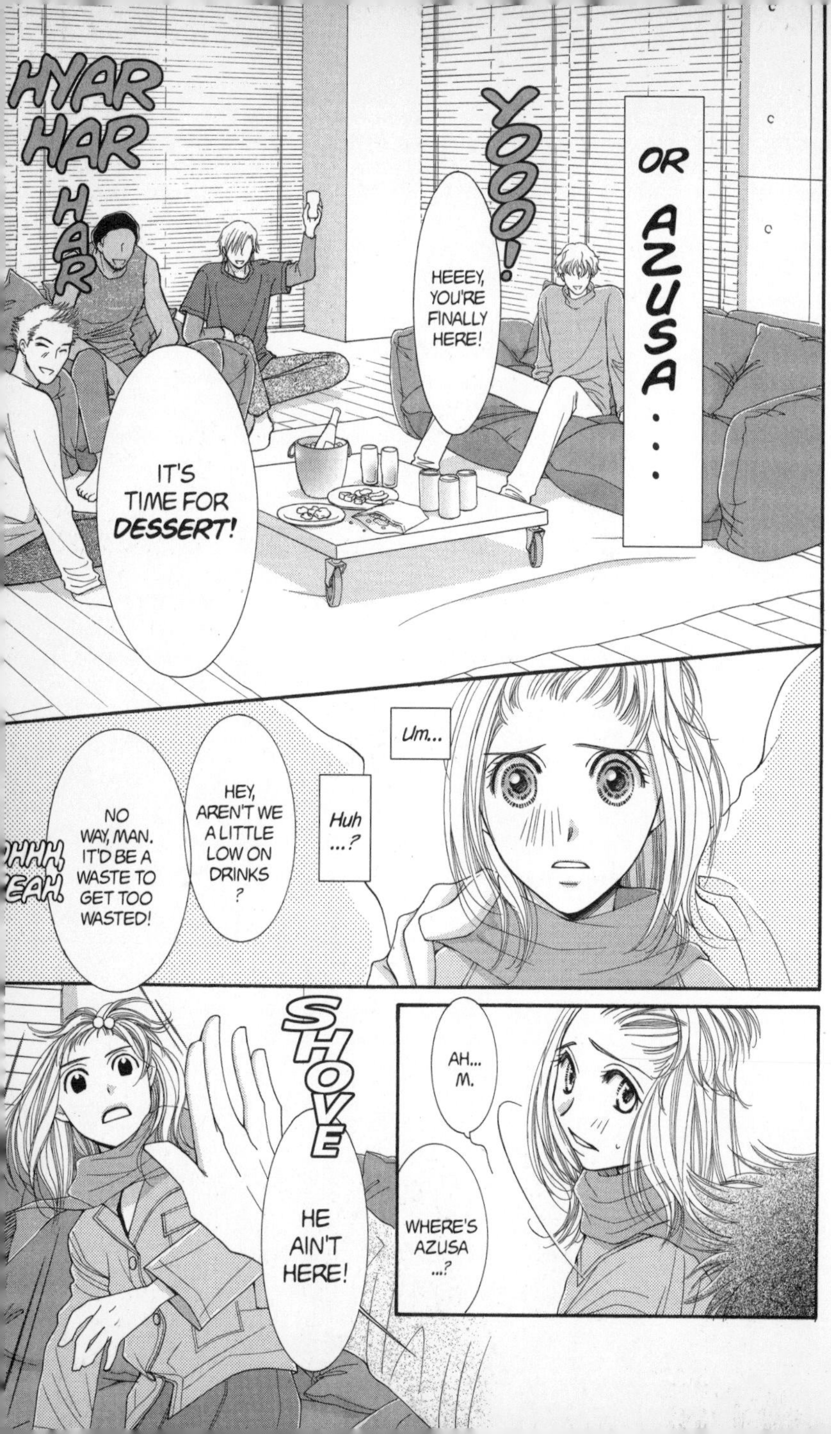

OR AZUSA...
YOOOO!
HEEEY, YOU'RE FINALLY HERE!
HYAR HAR HAR
IT'S TIME FOR DESSERT!
Um...
Huh ...?
HEY, AREN'T WE A LITTLE LOW ON DRINKS ?
NO WAY, MAN. IT'D BE A WASTE TO GET TOO WASTED!
HHH, EAH.
AH... M.
WHERE'S AZUSA ...?
SHOVE
HE AIN'T HERE!

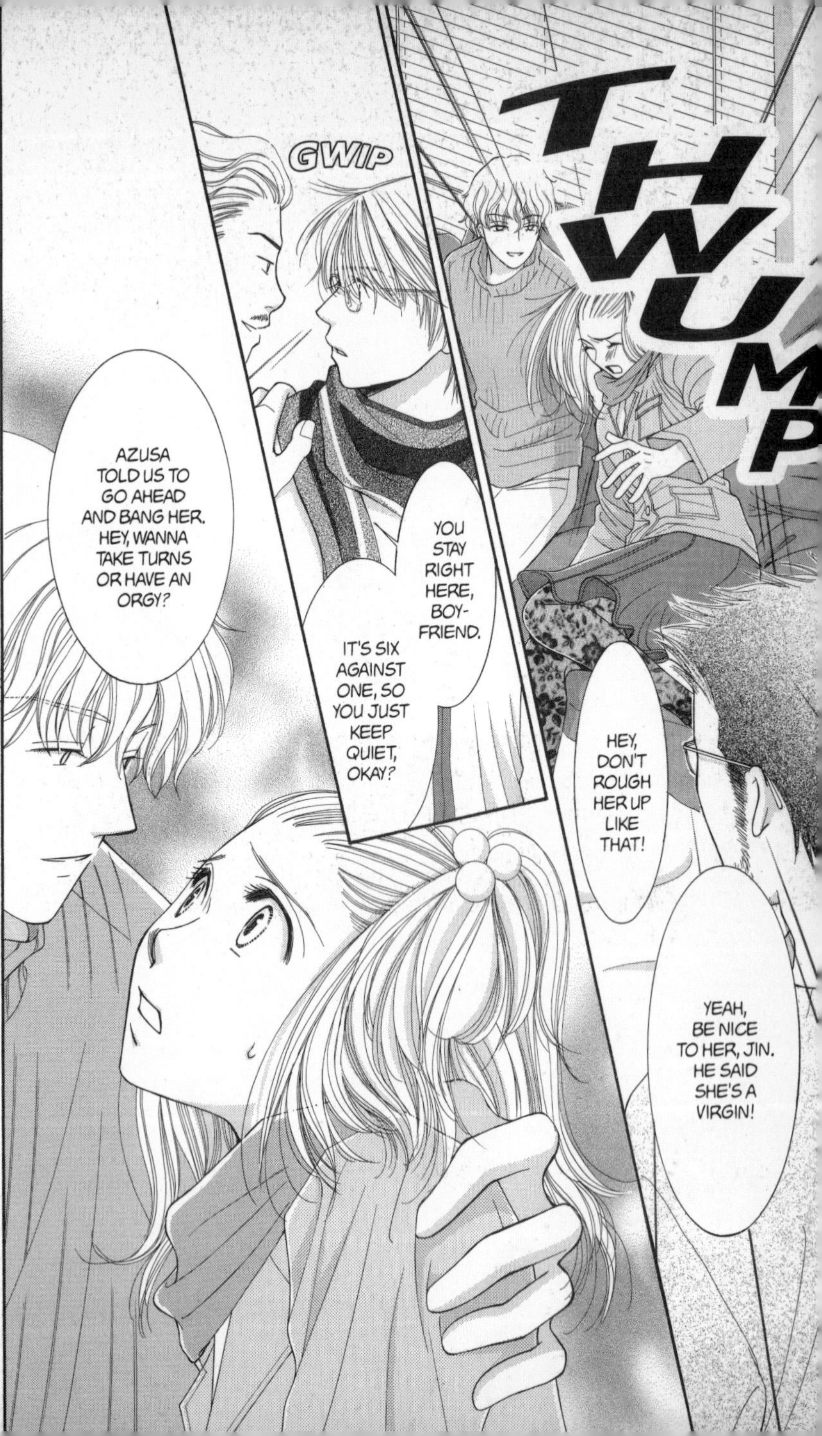
THWUMP
HEY, DON'T ROUGH HER UP LIKE THAT!
YEAH, BE NICE TO HER, JIN. HE SAID SHE'S A VIRGIN!
GWIP
YOU STAY RIGHT HERE, BOY-FRIEND.
IT'S SIX AGAINST ONE, SO YOU JUST KEEP QUIET, OKAY?
AZUSA TOLD US TO GO AHEAD AND BANG HER. HEY, WANNA TAKE TURNS OR HAVE AN ORGY?

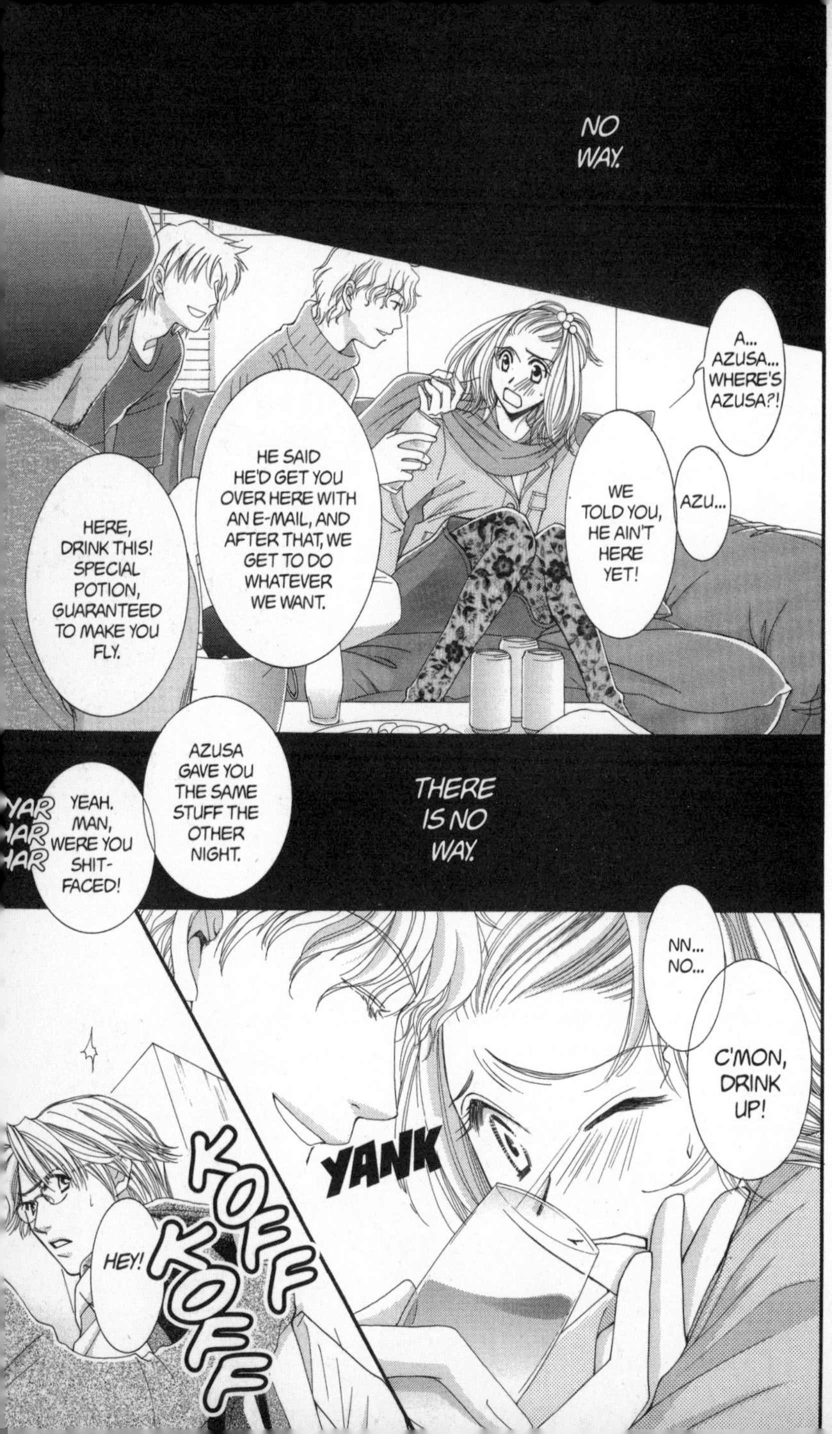
NO WAY.
A... AZUSA... WHERE'S AZUSA?!
AZU...
WE TOLD YOU, HE AIN'T HERE YET!
HE SAID HE'D GET YOU OVER HERE WITH AN E-MAIL, AND AFTER THAT, WE GET TO DO WHATEVER WE WANT.
HERE, DRINK THIS! SPECIAL POTION, GUARANTEED TO MAKE YOU FLY.
THERE IS NO WAY.
AZUSA GAVE YOU THE SAME STUFF THE OTHER NIGHT.
YEAH. MAN, WERE YOU SHIT-FACED!
YAR HAR HAR
NN... NO...
C'MON, DRINK UP!
YANK
KOFF KOFF
HEY!

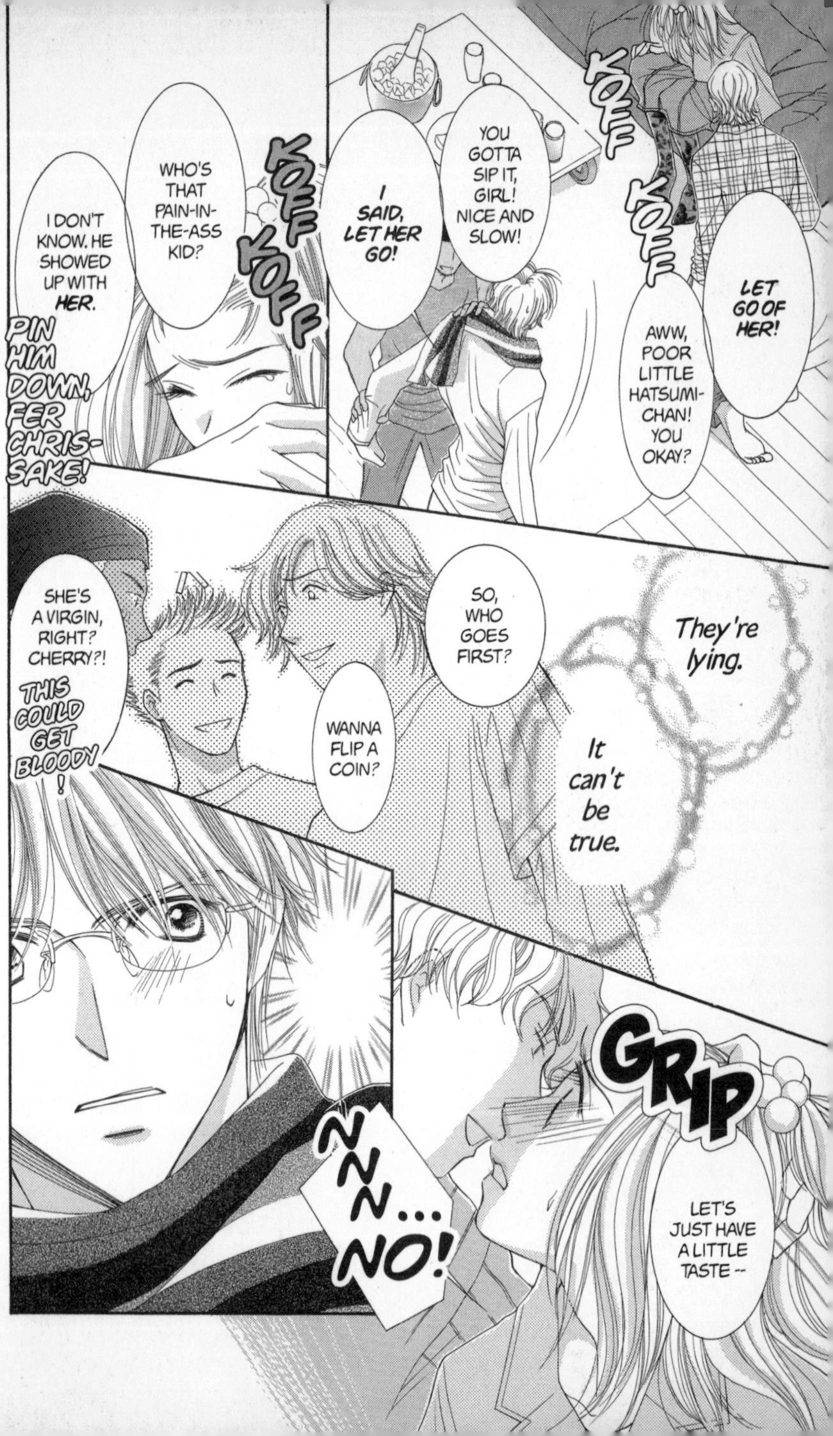
KOFF KOFF
LET GO OF HER!
AWW, POOR LITTLE HATSUMI-CHAN! YOU OKAY?
YOU GOTTA SIP IT, GIRL! NICE AND SLOW!
I SAID, LET HER GO!
KOFF KOFF
WHO'S THAT PAIN-IN-THE-ASS KID?
I DON'T KNOW. HE SHOWED UP WITH HER.
PIN HIM DOWN, FER CHRIS-SAKE!
They're lying.
It can't be true.
SO, WHO GOES FIRST?
WANNA FLIP A COIN?
SHE'S A VIRGIN, RIGHT? CHERRY?!
THIS COULD GET BLOODY!
GRIP
LET'S JUST HAVE A LITTLE TASTE --
NNN... NO!

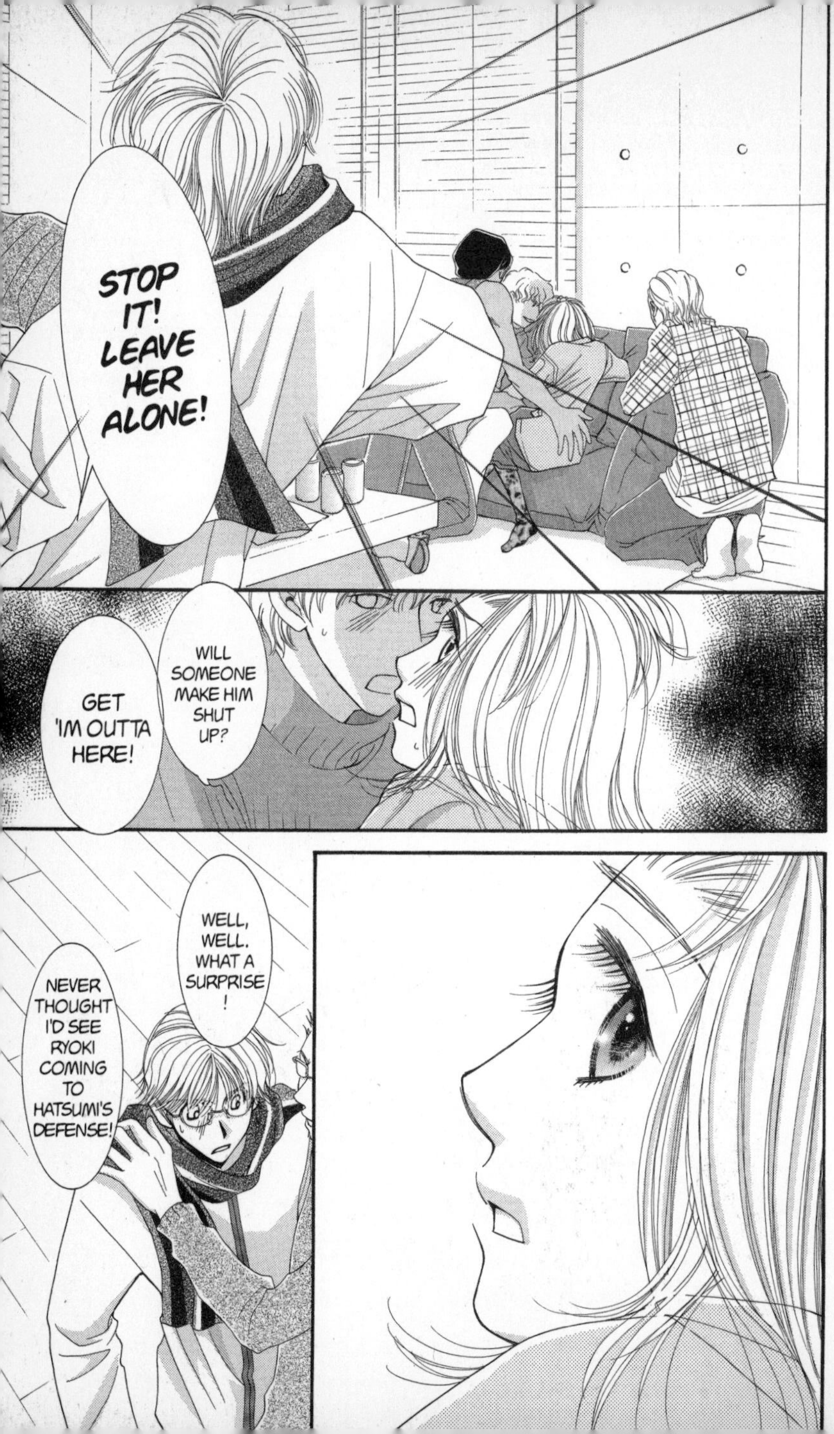
STOP IT! LEAVE HER ALONE!
WILL SOMEONE MAKE HIM SHUT UP?
GET 'IM OUTTA HERE!
WELL, WELL. WHAT A SURPRISE!
NEVER THOUGHT I'D SEE RYOKI COMING TO HATSUMI'S DEFENSE!

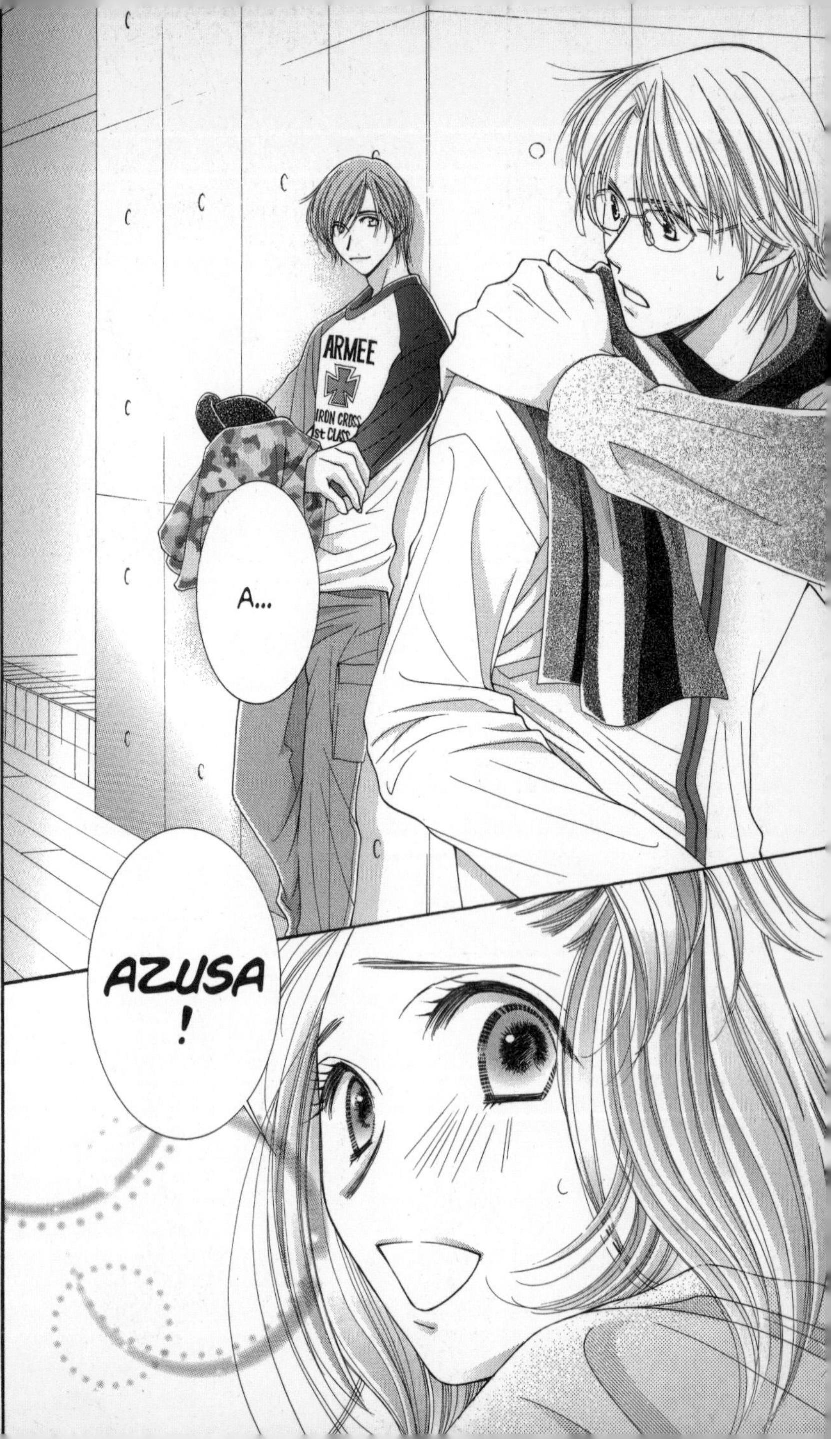
A...
AZUSA!
ARMEE
IRON CROSS
1st CLASS

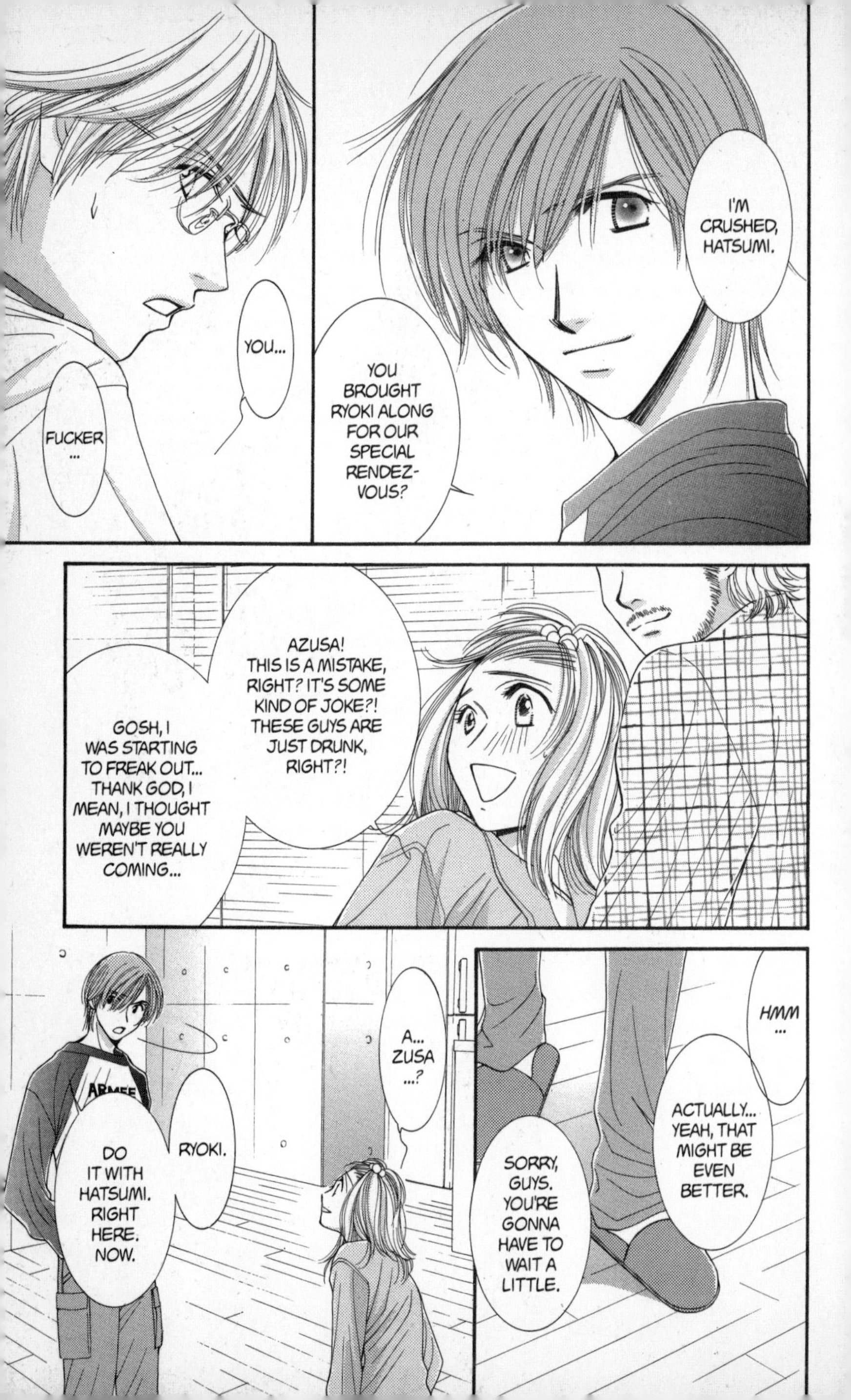
I'M CRUSHED, HATSUMI.
YOU BROUGHT RYOKI ALONG FOR OUR SPECIAL RENDEZ-VOUS?
YOU...
FUCKER ...
AZUSA! THIS IS A MISTAKE, RIGHT? IT'S SOME KIND OF JOKE?! THESE GUYS ARE JUST DRUNK, RIGHT?!
GOSH, I WAS STARTING TO FREAK OUT... THANK GOD, I MEAN, I THOUGHT MAYBE YOU WEREN'T REALLY COMING...
HMM ...
ACTUALLY... YEAH, THAT MIGHT BE EVEN BETTER.
SORRY, GUYS. YOU'RE GONNA HAVE TO WAIT A LITTLE.
A... ZUSA ...?
RYOKI.
ARMEE
DO IT WITH HATSUMI. RIGHT HERE. NOW.

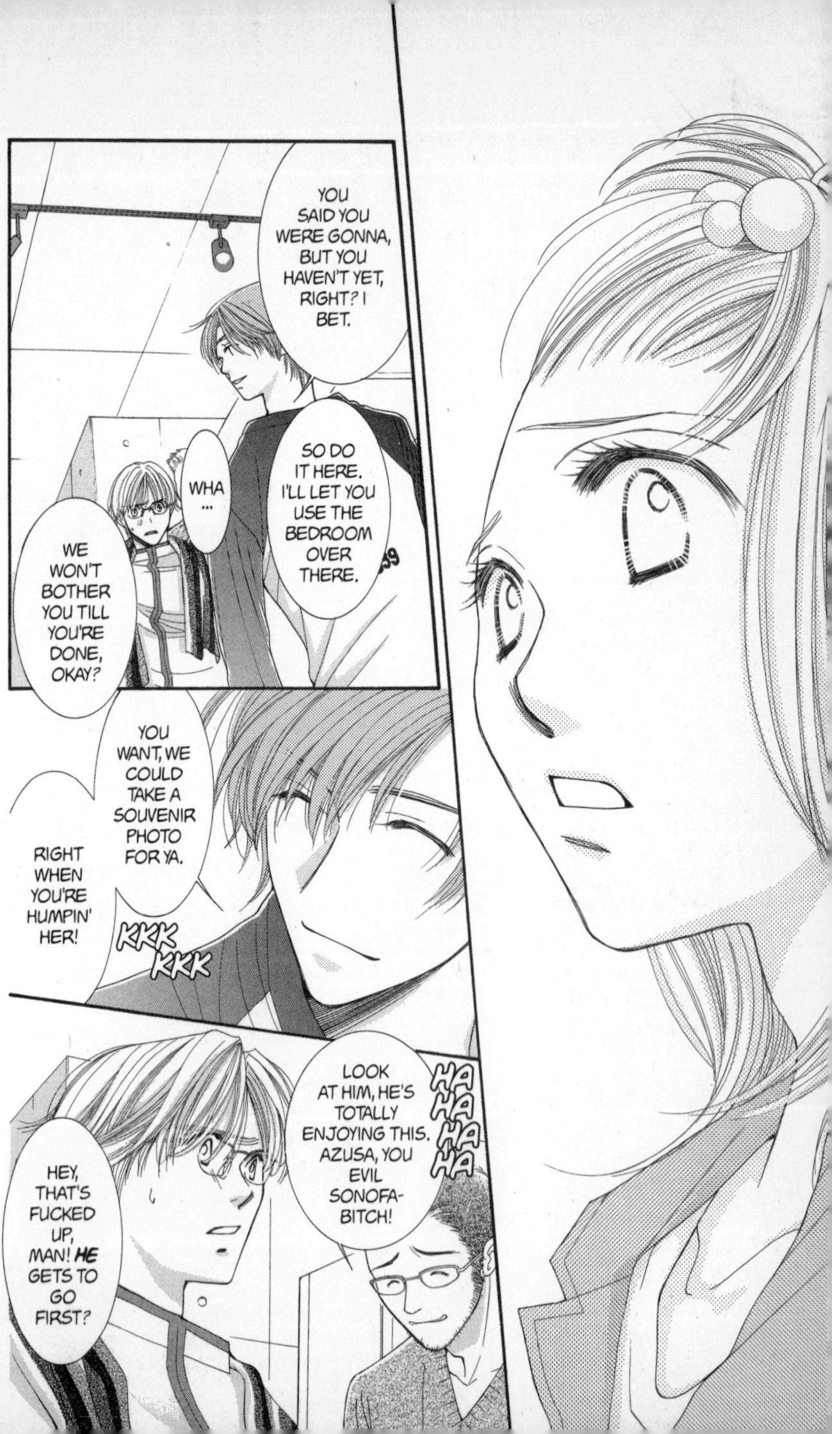
YOU SAID YOU WERE GONNA, BUT YOU HAVEN'T YET, RIGHT? I BET.
SO DO IT HERE. I'LL LET YOU USE THE BEDROOM OVER THERE.
WHA ...
WE WON'T BOTHER YOU TILL YOU'RE DONE, OKAY?
YOU WANT, WE COULD TAKE A SOUVENIR PHOTO FOR YA.
RIGHT WHEN YOU'RE HUMPIN' HER!
KKK KKK
HA HA HA HA
LOOK AT HIM, HE'S TOTALLY ENJOYING THIS. AZUSA, YOU EVIL SONOFA-BITCH!
HEY, THAT'S FUCKED UP, MAN! **HE** GETS TO GO FIRST?

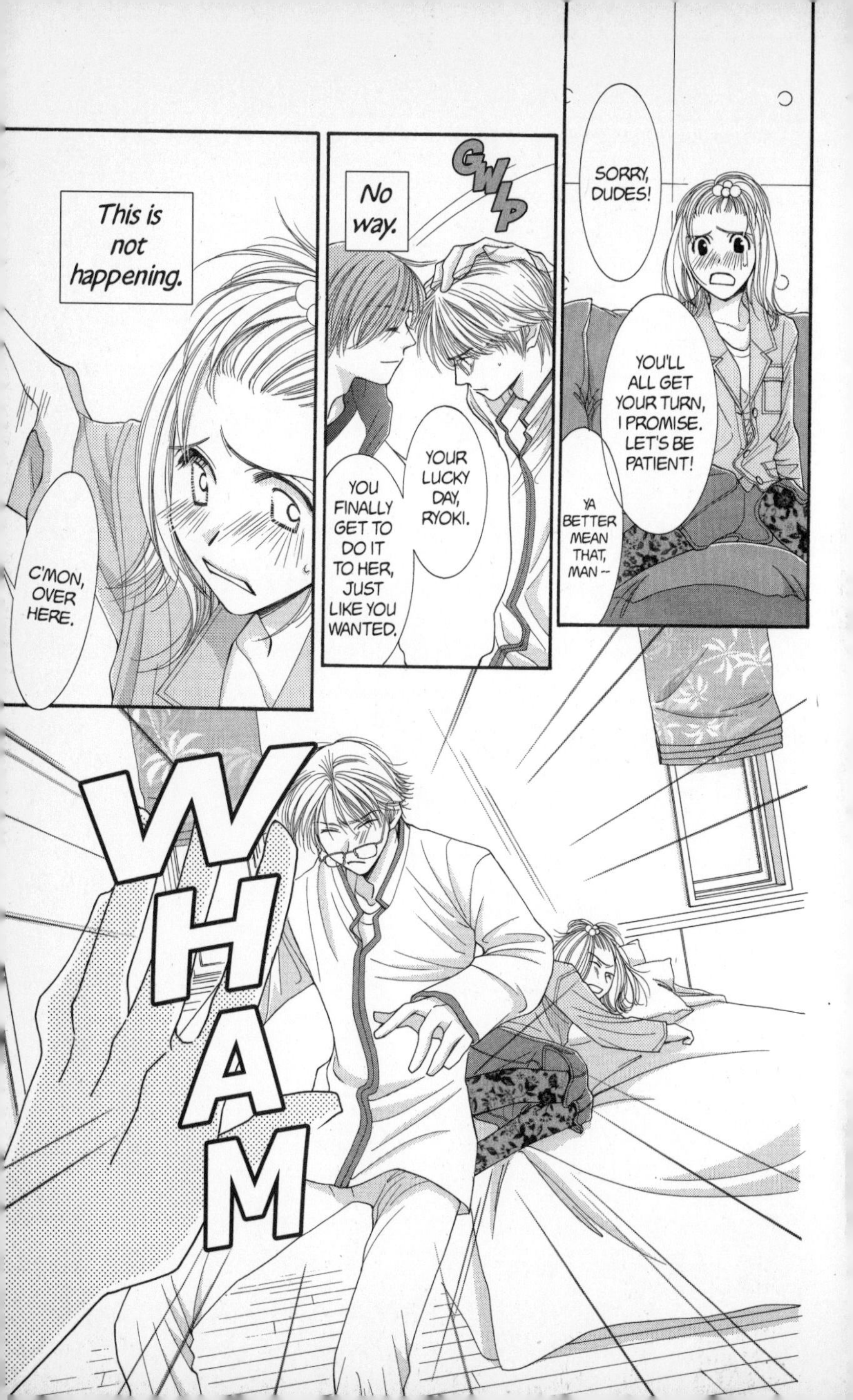
SORRY, DUDES!
YOU'LL ALL GET YOUR TURN, I PROMISE. LET'S BE PATIENT!
YA BETTER MEAN THAT, MAN --
GWIP
No way.
YOUR LUCKY DAY, RYOKI.
YOU FINALLY GET TO DO IT TO HER, JUST LIKE YOU WANTED.
This is not happening.
C'MON, OVER HERE.
WHAM

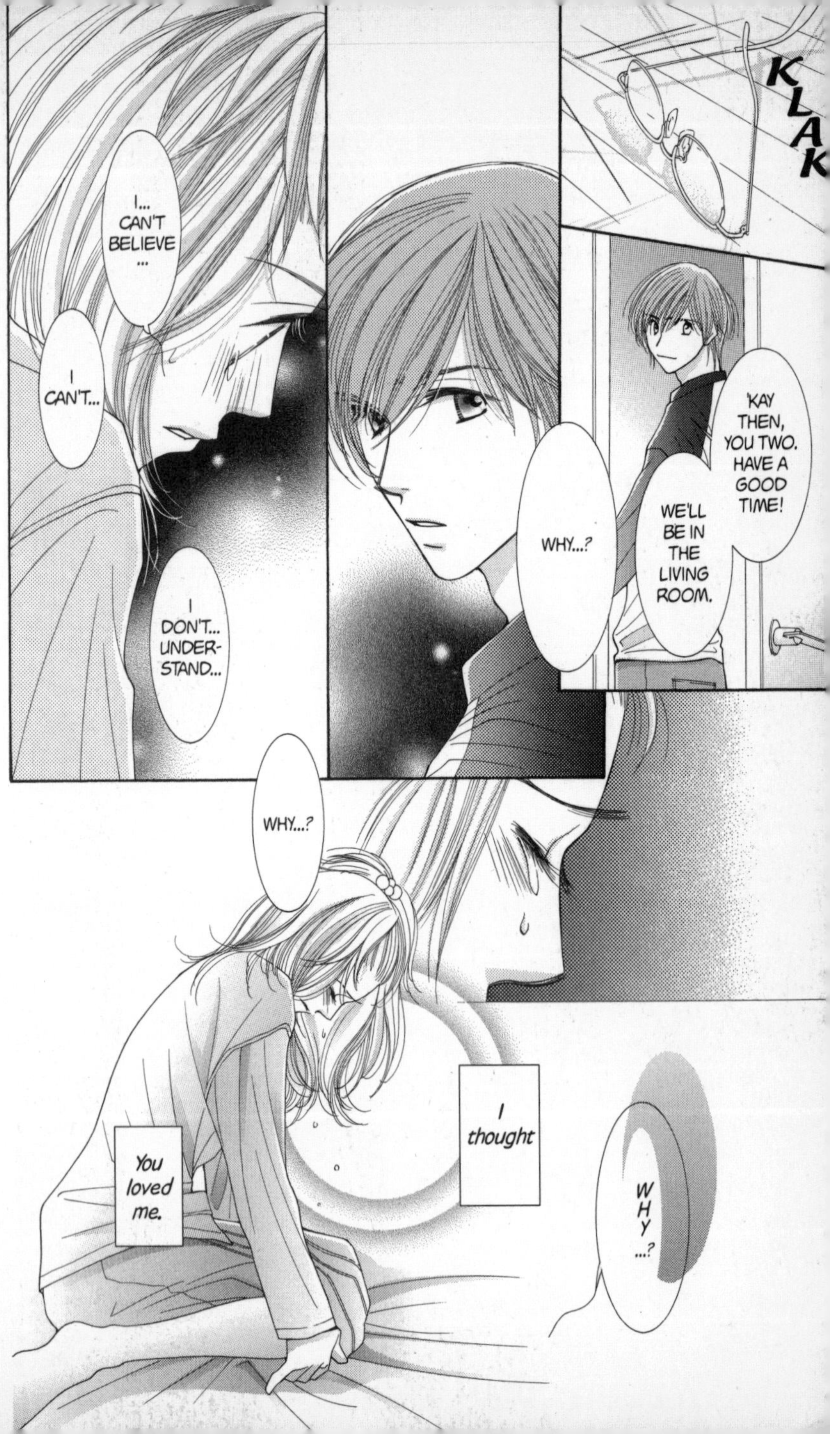
KLAK
'KAY THEN, YOU TWO. HAVE A GOOD TIME!
WE'LL BE IN THE LIVING ROOM.
WHY...?
I... CAN'T BELIEVE ...
I CAN'T...
I DON'T... UNDER-STAND...
WHY...?
WHY ...?
I thought
You loved me.

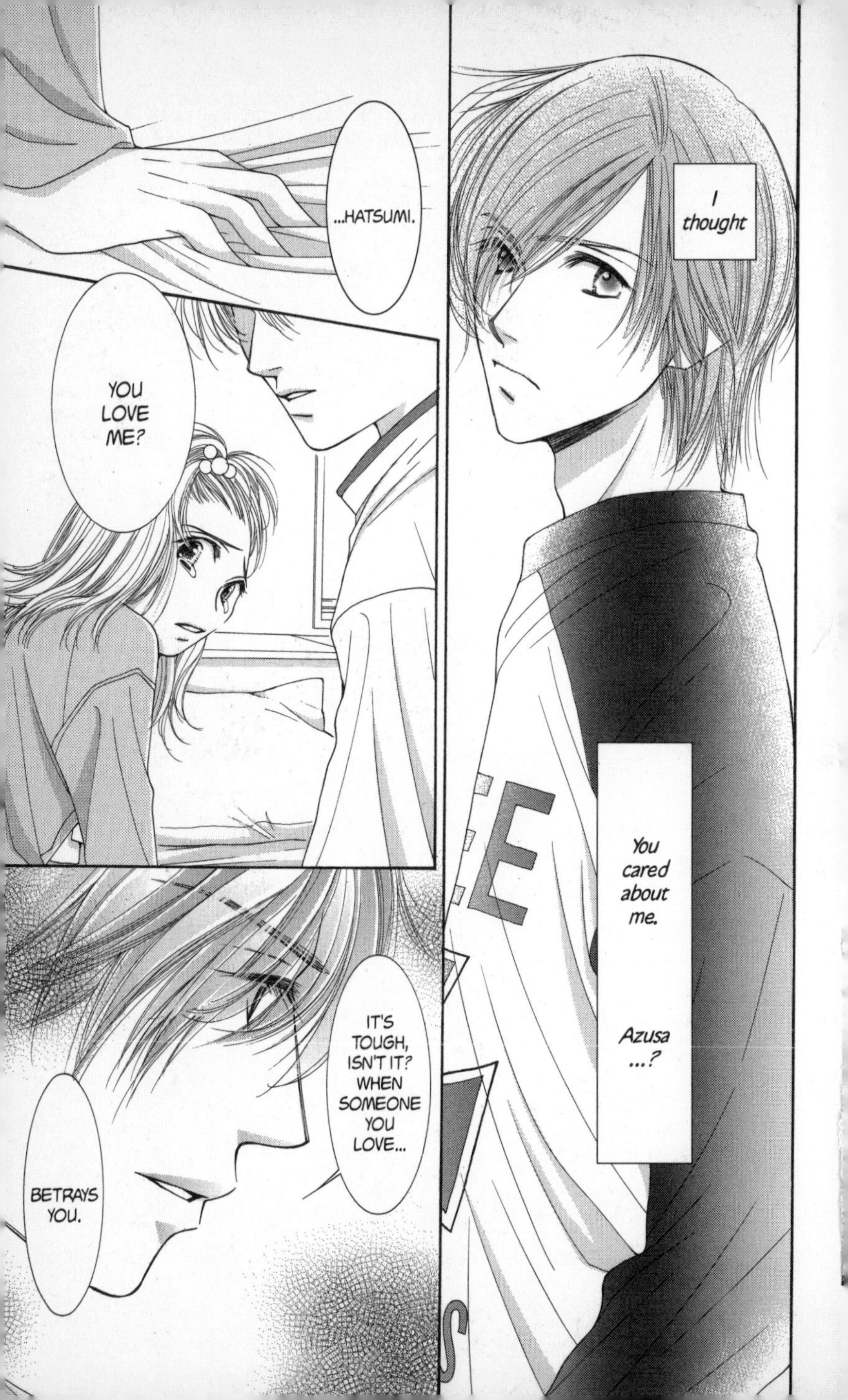
I thought
You cared about me.
Azusa ...?
...HATSUMI.
YOU LOVE ME?
IT'S TOUGH, ISN'T IT? WHEN SOMEONE YOU LOVE...
BETRAYS YOU.

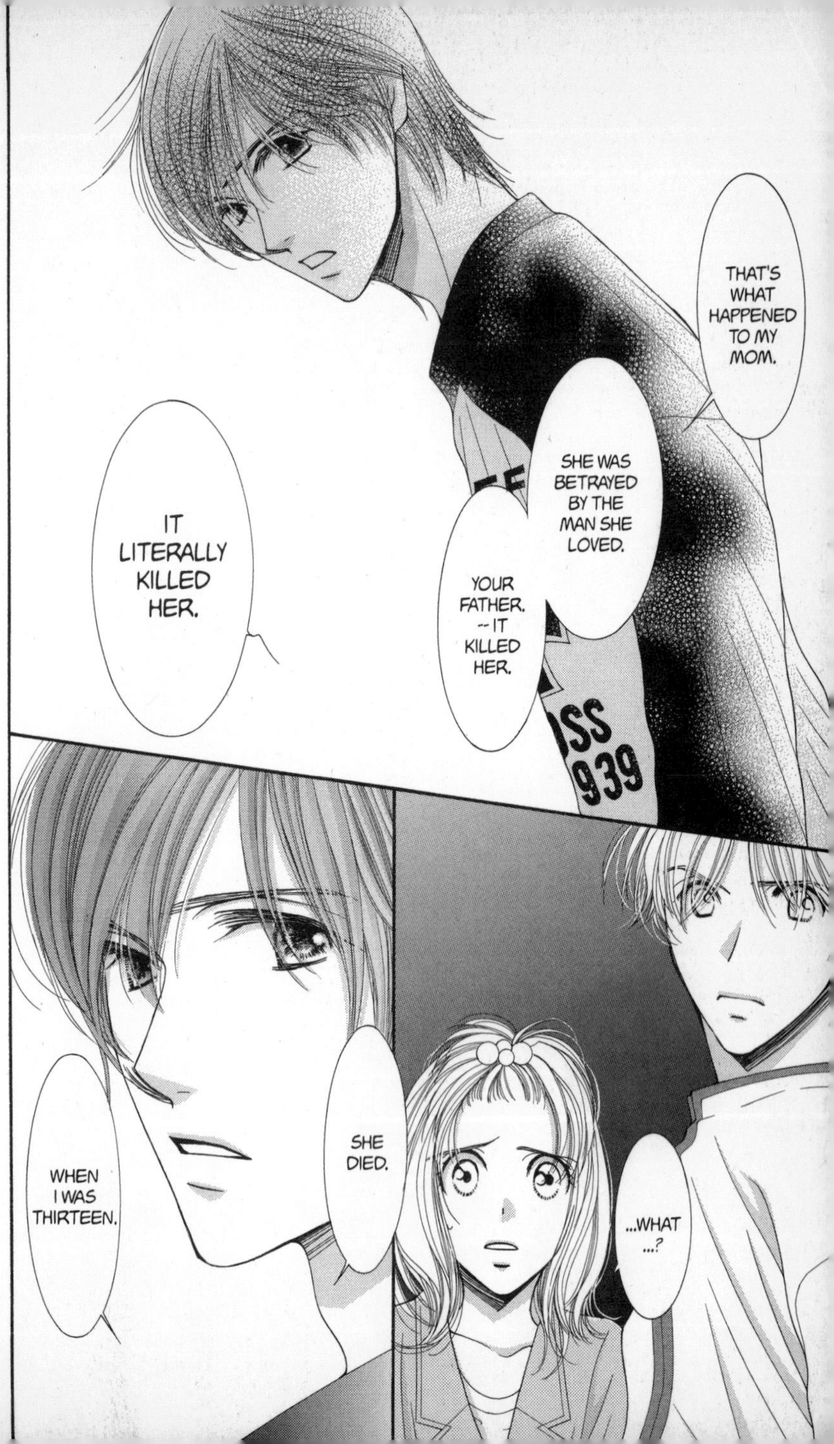
THAT'S WHAT HAPPENED TO MY MOM.
SHE WAS BETRAYED BY THE MAN SHE LOVED.
YOUR FATHER. --IT KILLED HER.
IT LITERALLY KILLED HER.
...WHAT ...?
SHE DIED.
WHEN I WAS THIRTEEN.

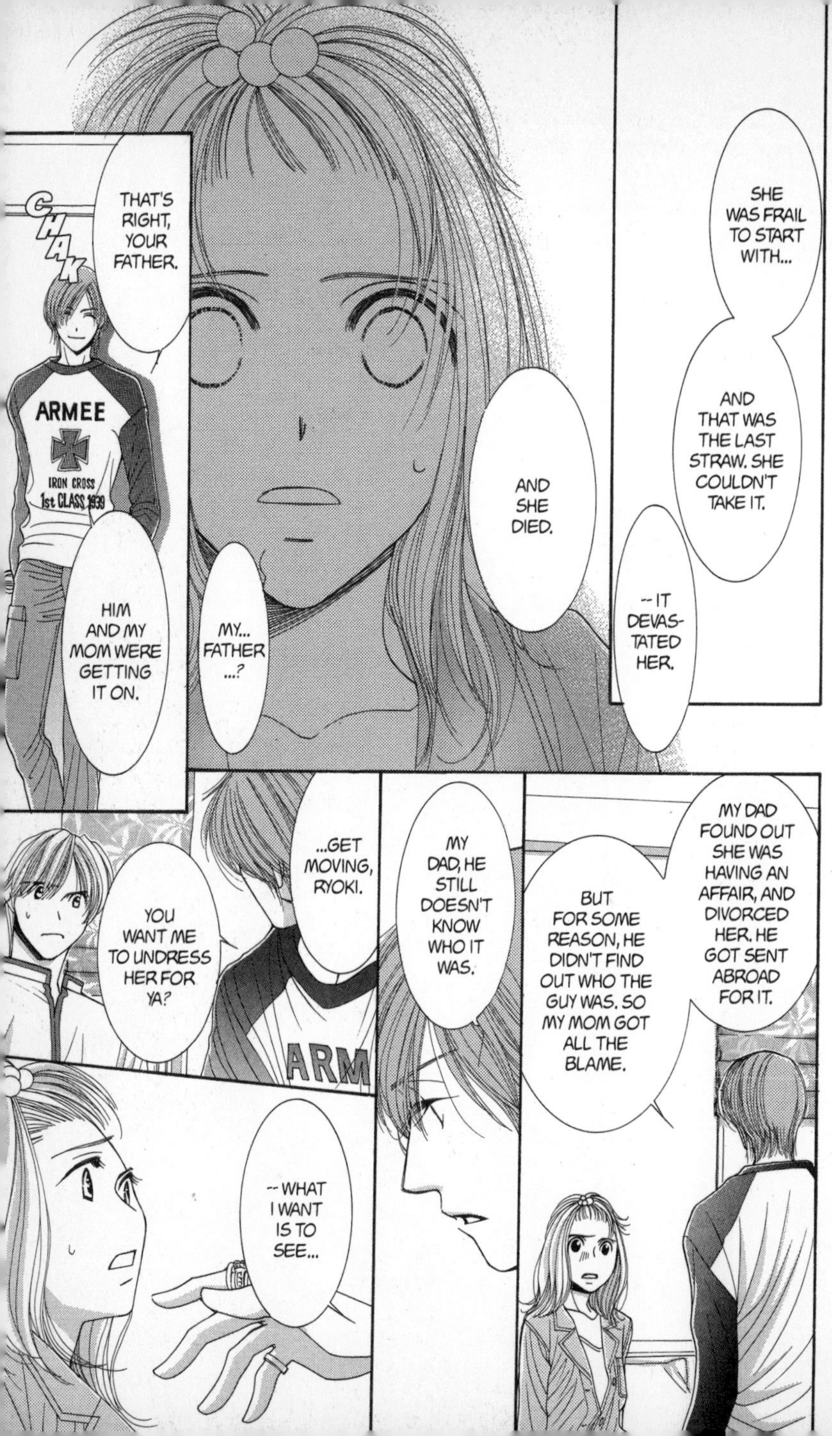
SHE WAS FRAIL TO START WITH...
AND THAT WAS THE LAST STRAW. SHE COULDN'T TAKE IT.
--IT DEVASTATED HER.
AND SHE DIED.
MY... FATHER ...?
THAT'S RIGHT, YOUR FATHER.
CHAK
HIM AND MY MOM WERE GETTING IT ON.
ARMEE
IRON CROSS
1st CLASS 1939
MY DAD FOUND OUT SHE WAS HAVING AN AFFAIR, AND DIVORCED HER. HE GOT SENT ABROAD FOR IT.
BUT FOR SOME REASON, HE DIDN'T FIND OUT WHO THE GUY WAS. SO MY MOM GOT ALL THE BLAME.
MY DAD, HE STILL DOESN'T KNOW WHO IT WAS.
...GET MOVING, RYOKI.
YOU WANT ME TO UNDRESS HER FOR YA?
ARM
--WHAT I WANT IS TO SEE...

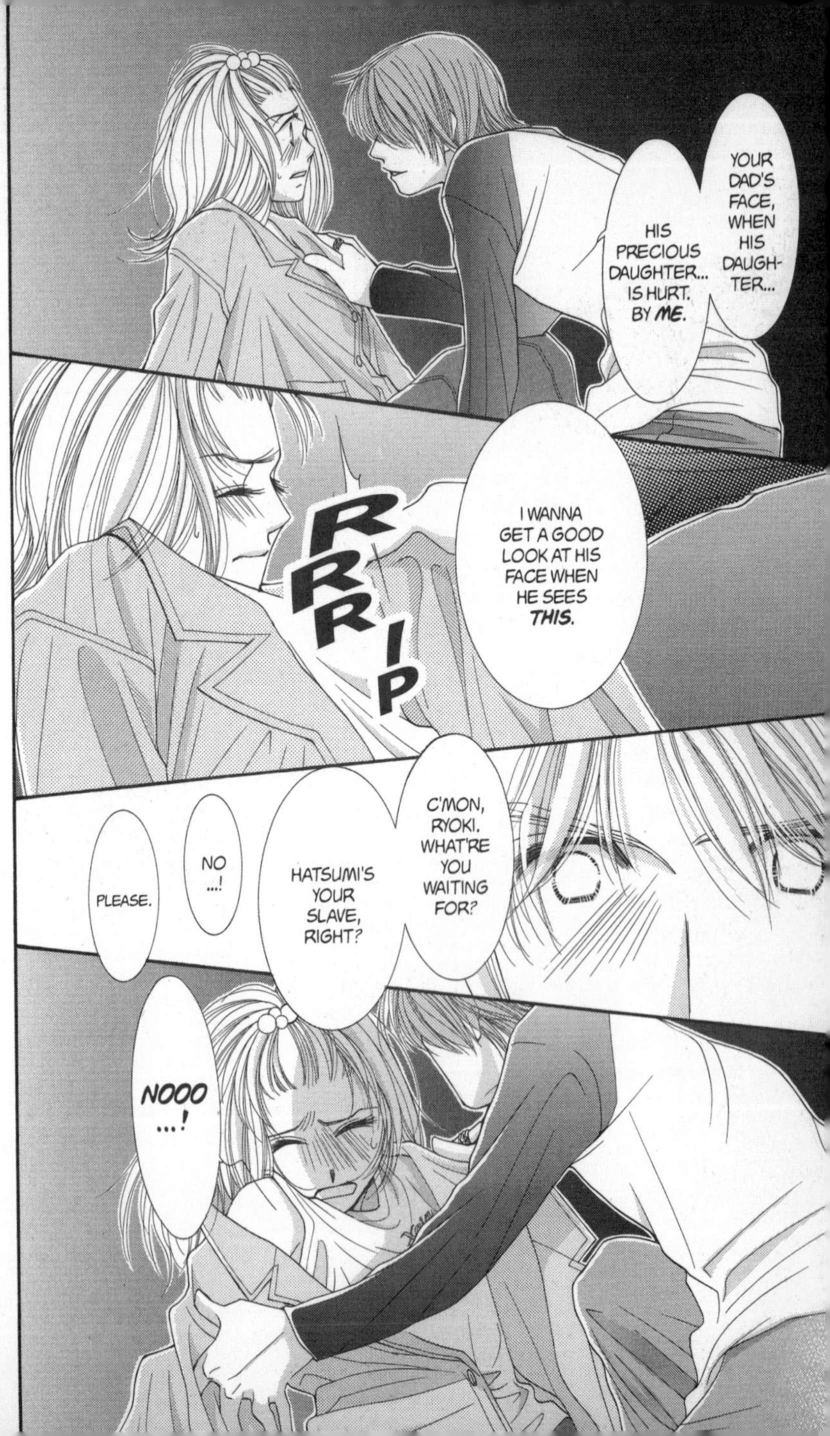
YOUR DAD'S FACE, WHEN HIS DAUGHTER...
HIS PRECIOUS DAUGHTER... IS HURT. BY ME.
I WANNA GET A GOOD LOOK AT HIS FACE WHEN HE SEES THIS.
RRRIP
C'MON, RYOKI. WHAT'RE YOU WAITING FOR?
HATSUMI'S YOUR SLAVE, RIGHT?
NO ...!
PLEASE.
NOOO ...!

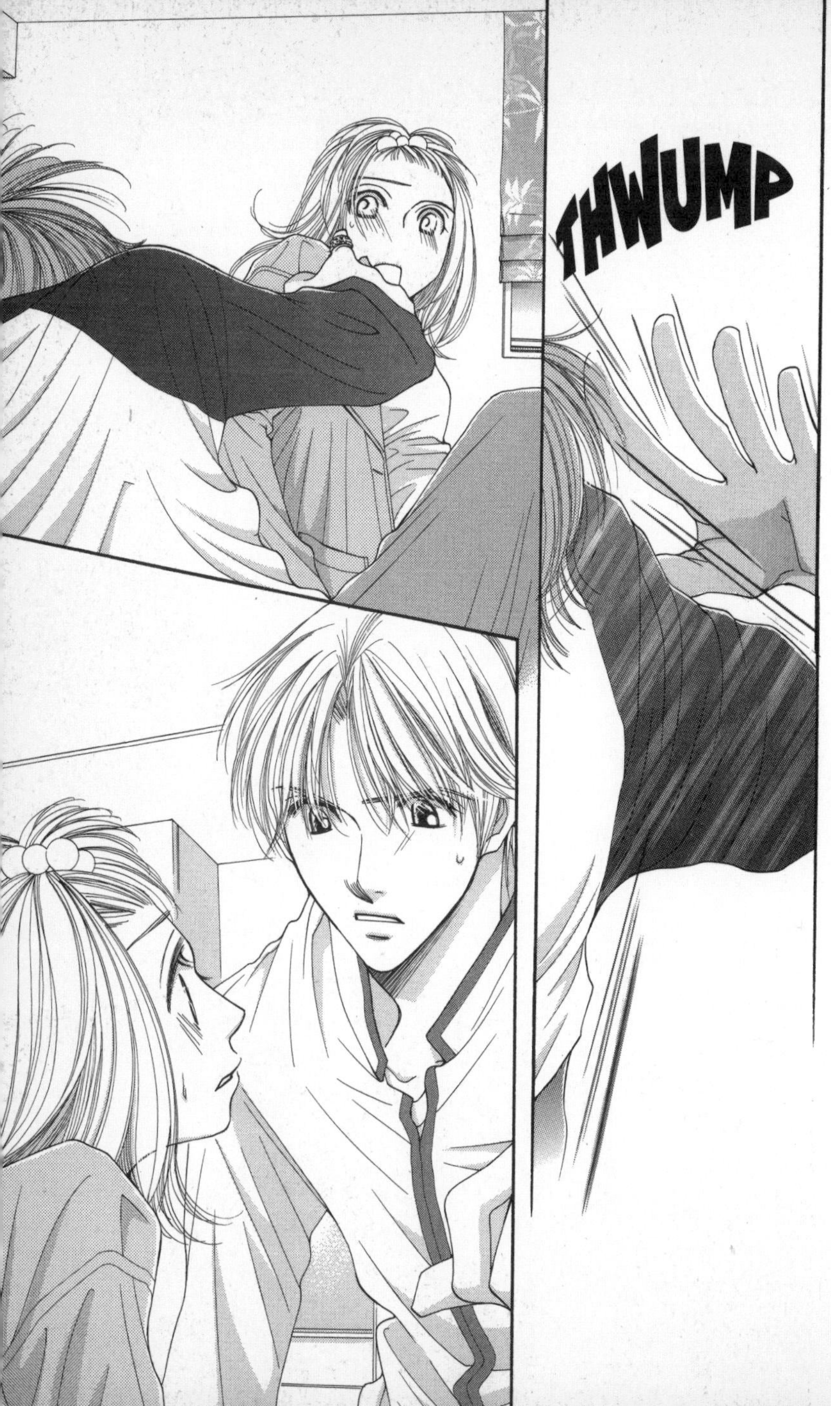
THWUMP

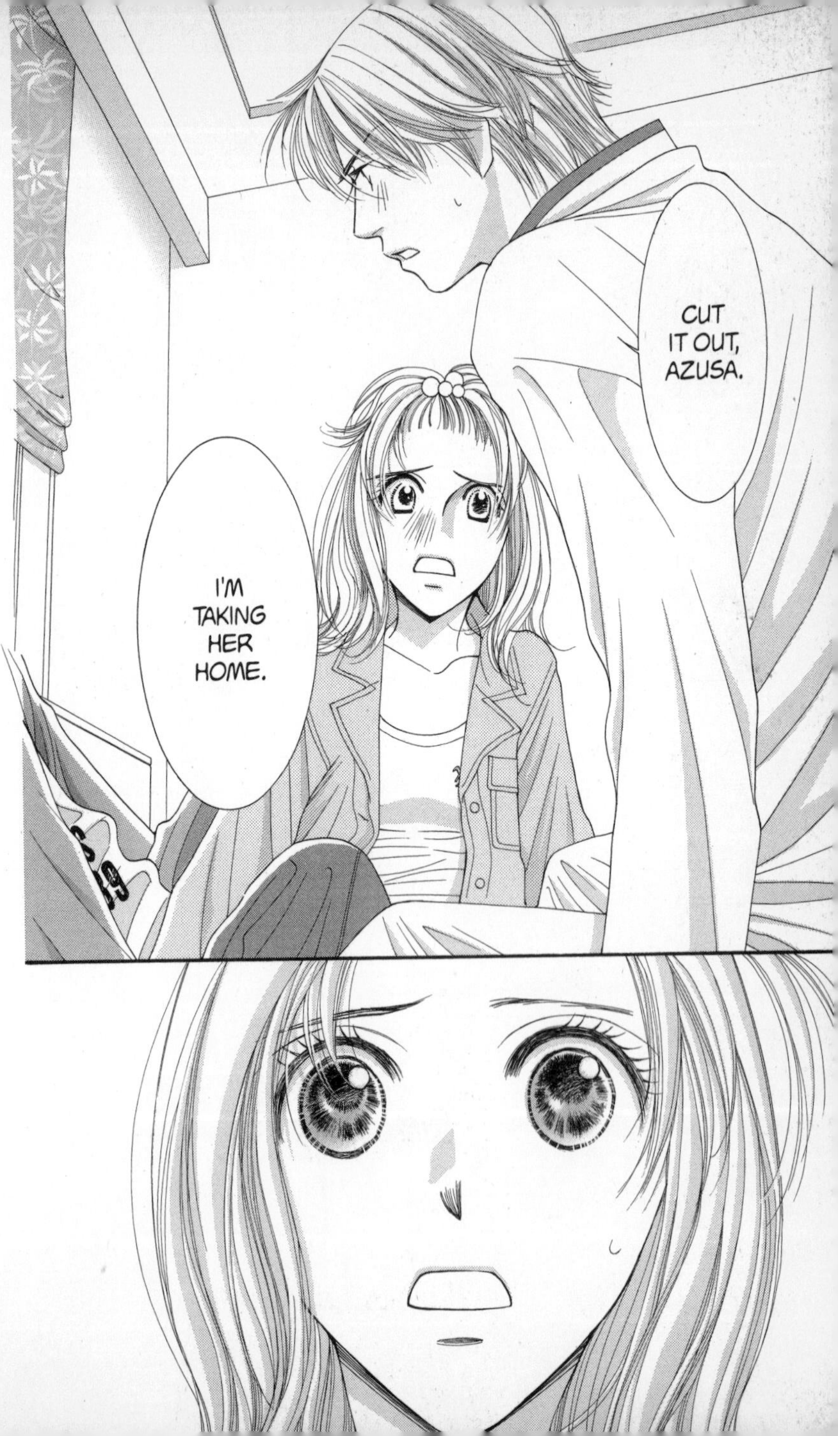
CUT IT OUT, AZUSA.
I'M TAKING HER HOME.

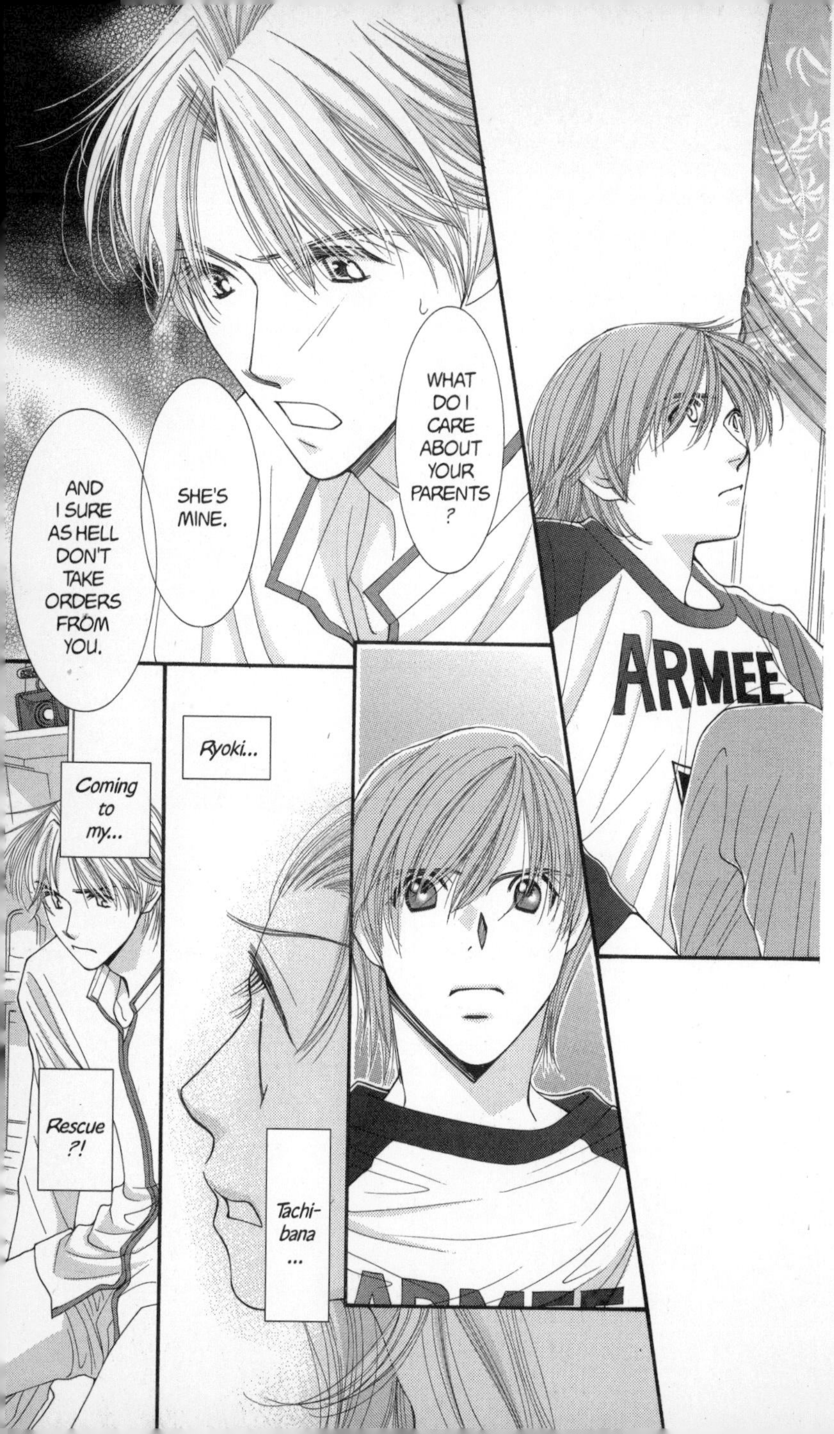
ARMEE
WHAT DO I CARE ABOUT YOUR PARENTS?
SHE'S MINE.
AND I SURE AS HELL DON'T TAKE ORDERS FROM YOU.
Ryoki...
Tachi-bana...
Coming to my...
Rescue?!

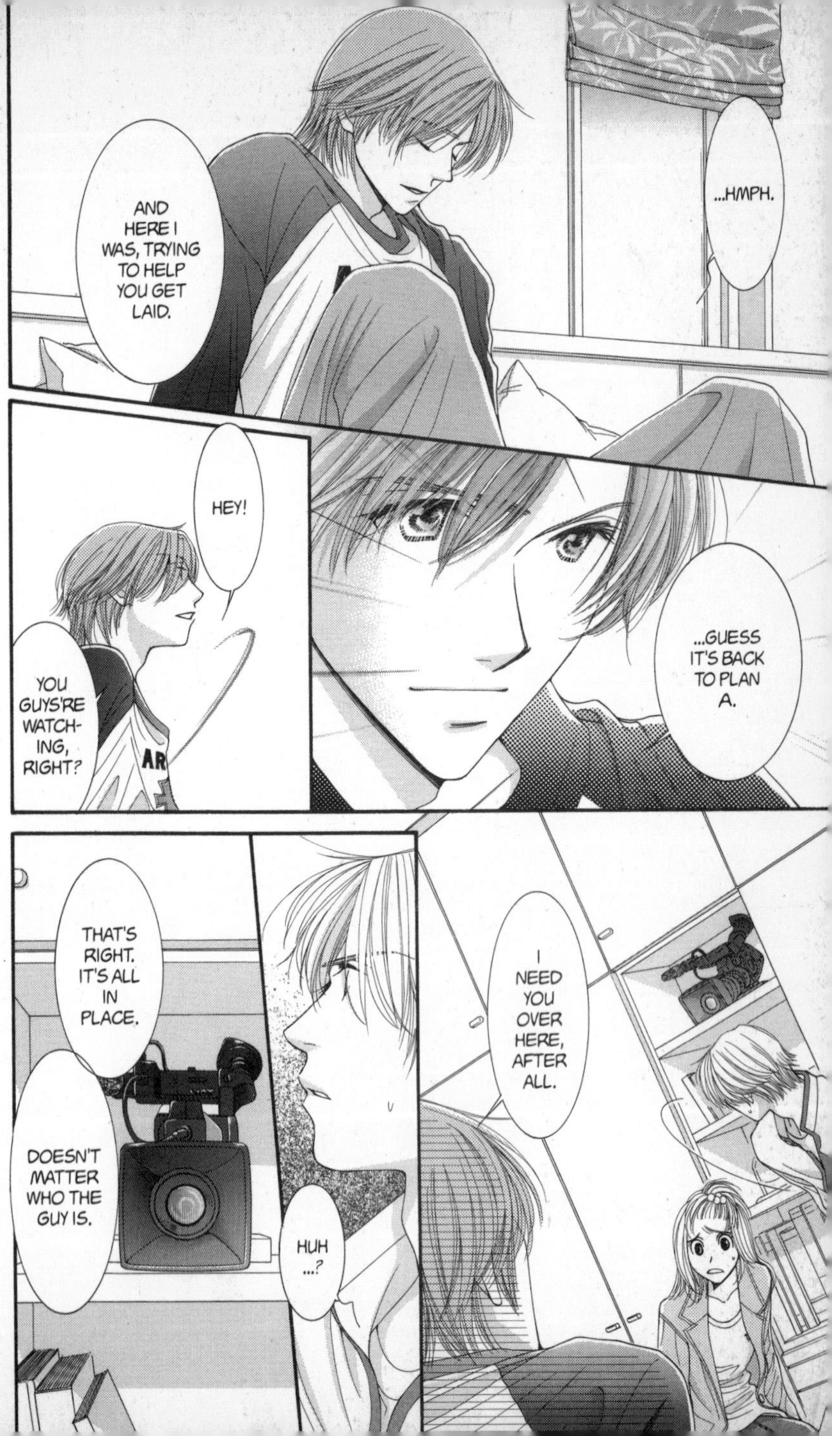
...HMPH.
AND HERE I WAS, TRYING TO HELP YOU GET LAID.
...GUESS IT'S BACK TO PLAN A.
HEY!
YOU GUYS'RE WATCHING, RIGHT?
I NEED YOU OVER HERE, AFTER ALL.
HUH ...?
THAT'S RIGHT. IT'S ALL IN PLACE.
DOESN'T MATTER WHO THE GUY IS.

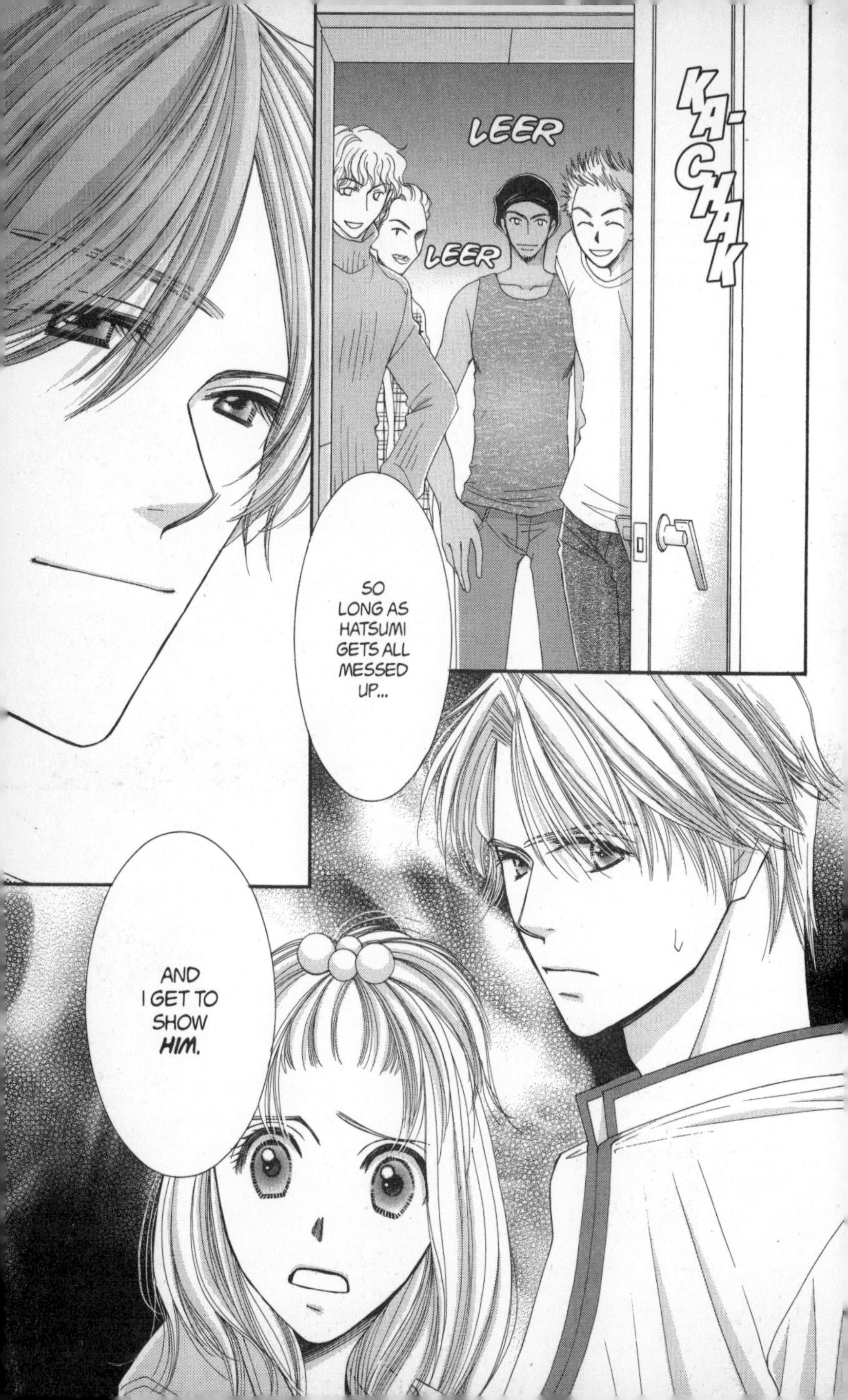
KA-CHAK
LEER
LEER
SO LONG AS HATSUMI GETS ALL MESSED UP...
AND I GET TO SHOW **HIM.**

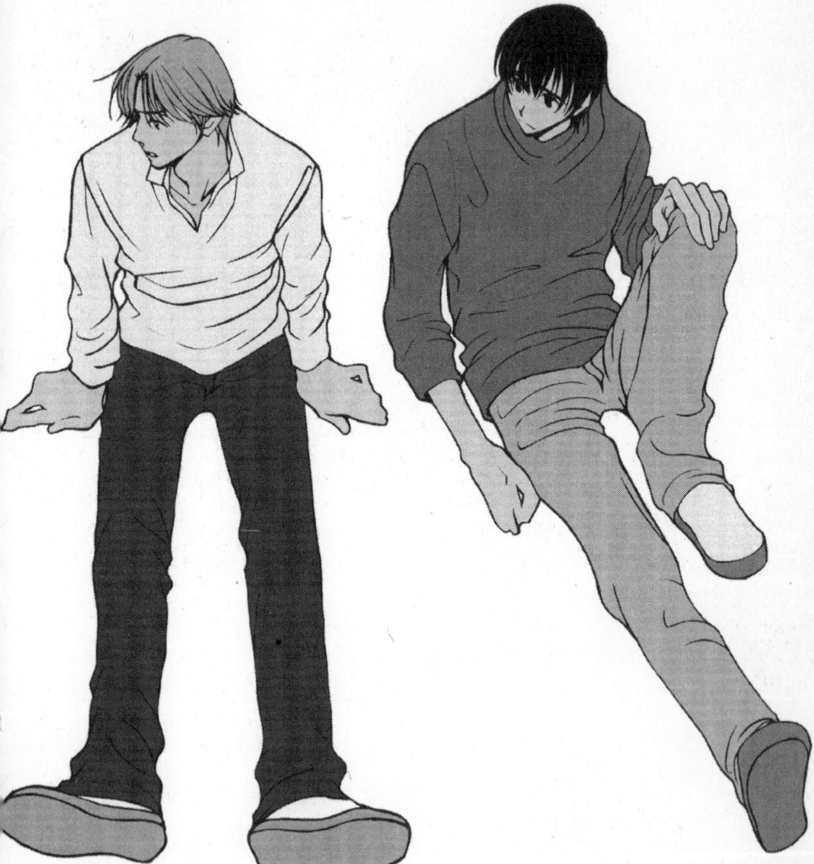

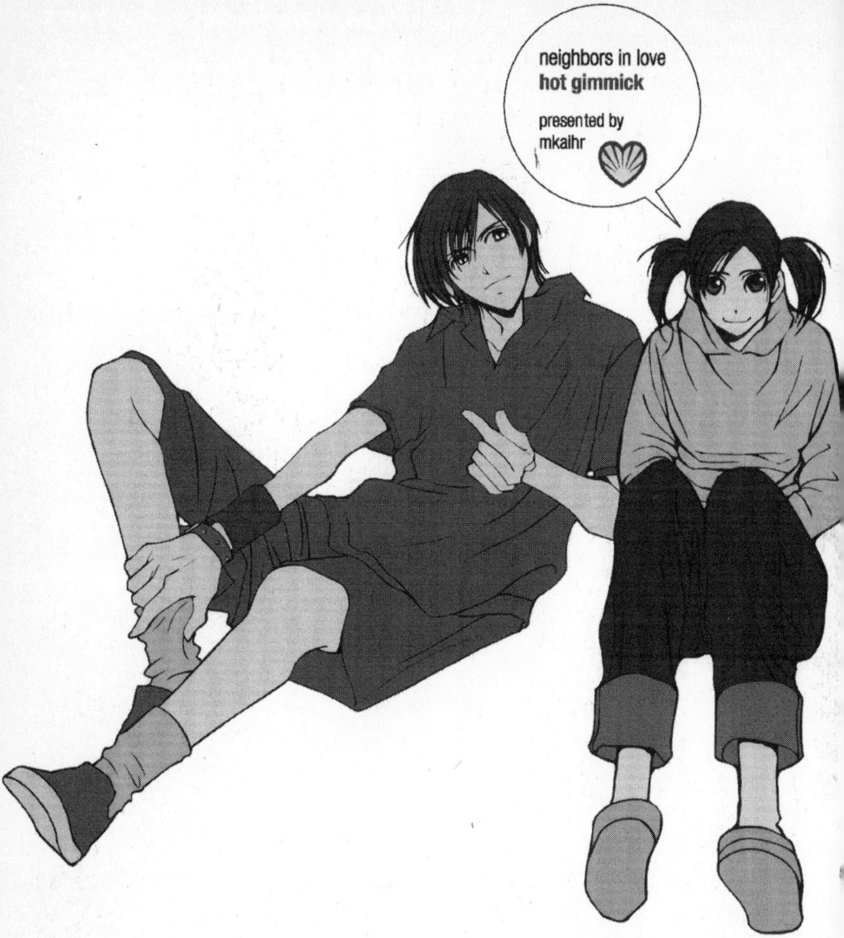
neighbors in love
hot gimmick
presented by
mkaihr

Chapter 11

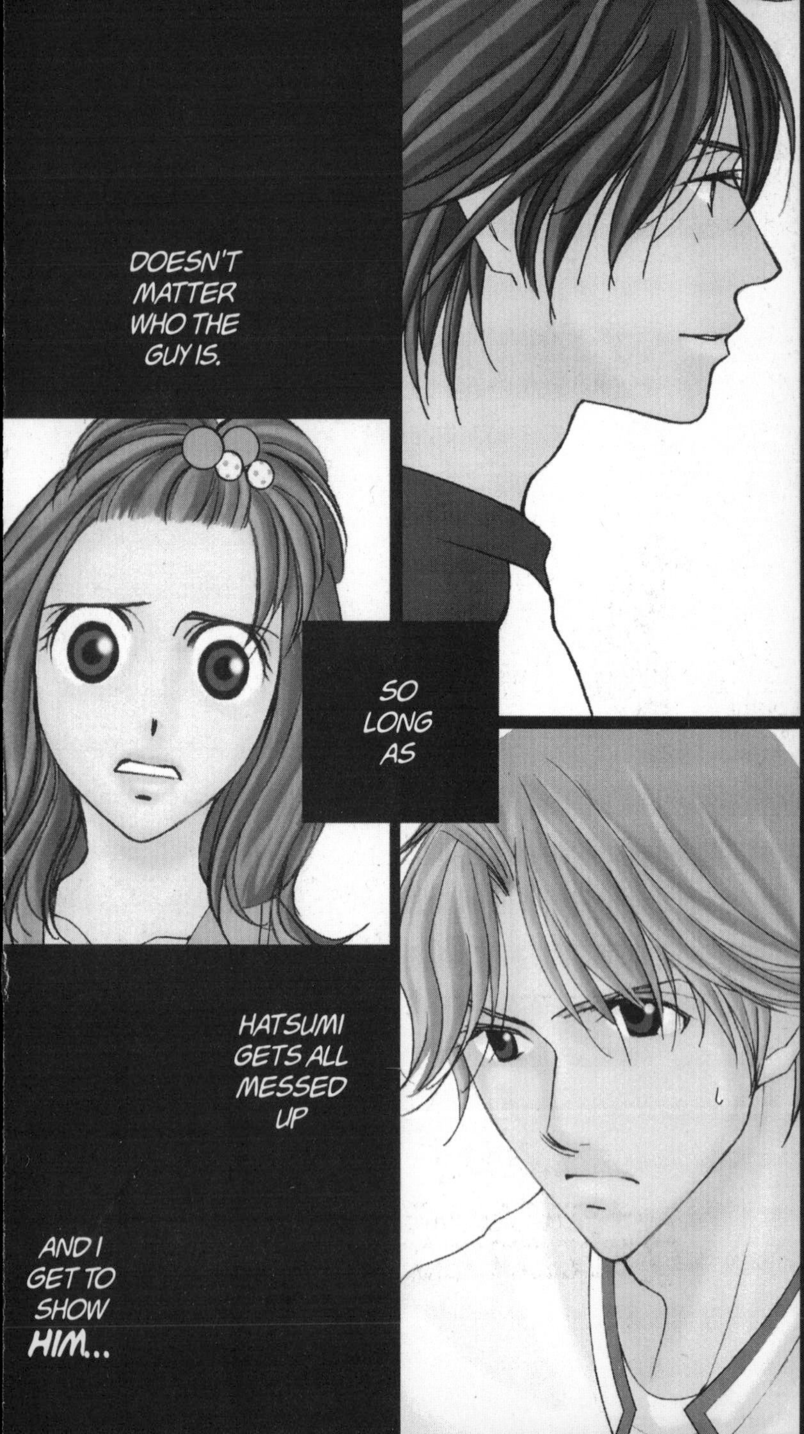
DOESN'T MATTER WHO THE GUY IS.
SO LONG AS
HATSUMI GETS ALL MESSED UP
AND I GET TO SHOW **HIM**...

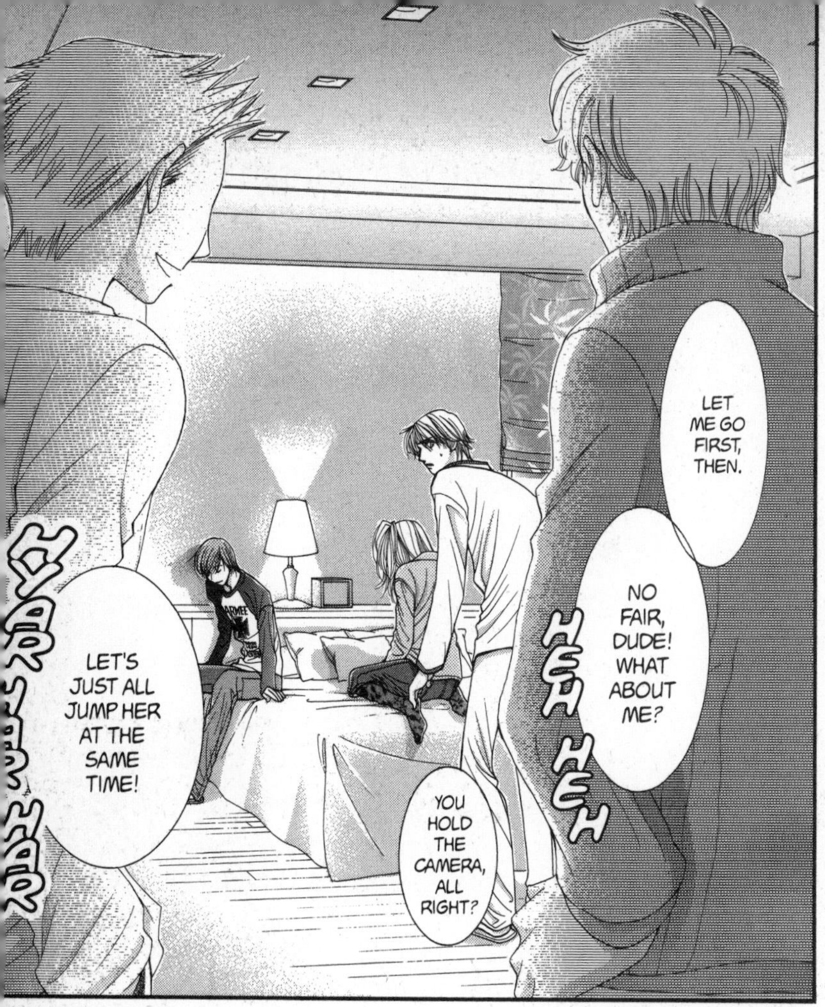
LET ME GO FIRST, THEN.
NO FAIR, DUDE! WHAT ABOUT ME?
HEH HEH
YOU HOLD THE CAMERA, ALL RIGHT?
LET'S JUST ALL JUMP HER AT THE SAME TIME!

hot gimmick

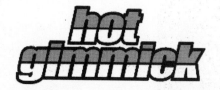

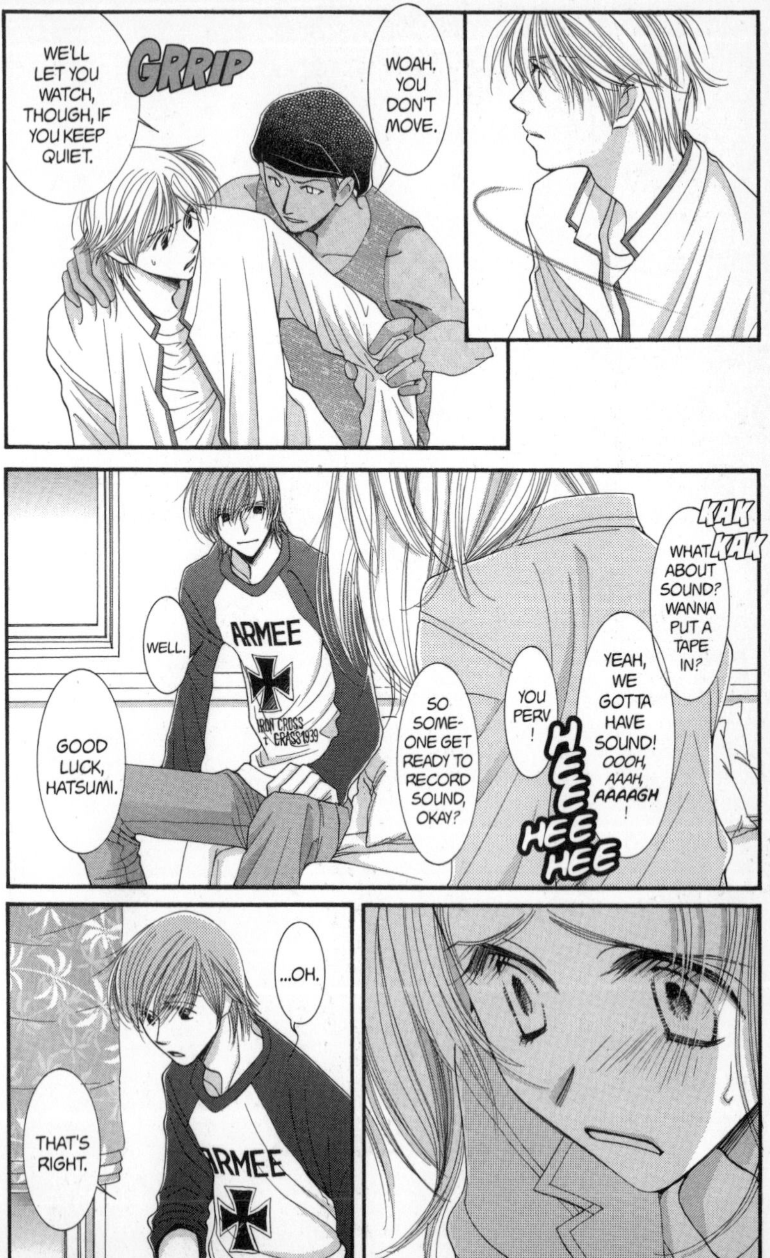
WOAH. YOU DON'T MOVE.
GRRIP
WE'LL LET YOU WATCH, THOUGH, IF YOU KEEP QUIET.
KAK KAK
WHAT ABOUT SOUND? WANNA PUT A TAPE IN?
YEAH, WE GOTTA HAVE SOUND! OOOH, AAAH, AAAAGH!
YOU PERV!
HEE HEE HEE
SO SOMEONE GET READY TO RECORD SOUND, OKAY?
WELL.
GOOD LUCK, HATSUMI.
...OH.
THAT'S RIGHT.
ARMEE
IRON CROSS 1st CLASS 1939

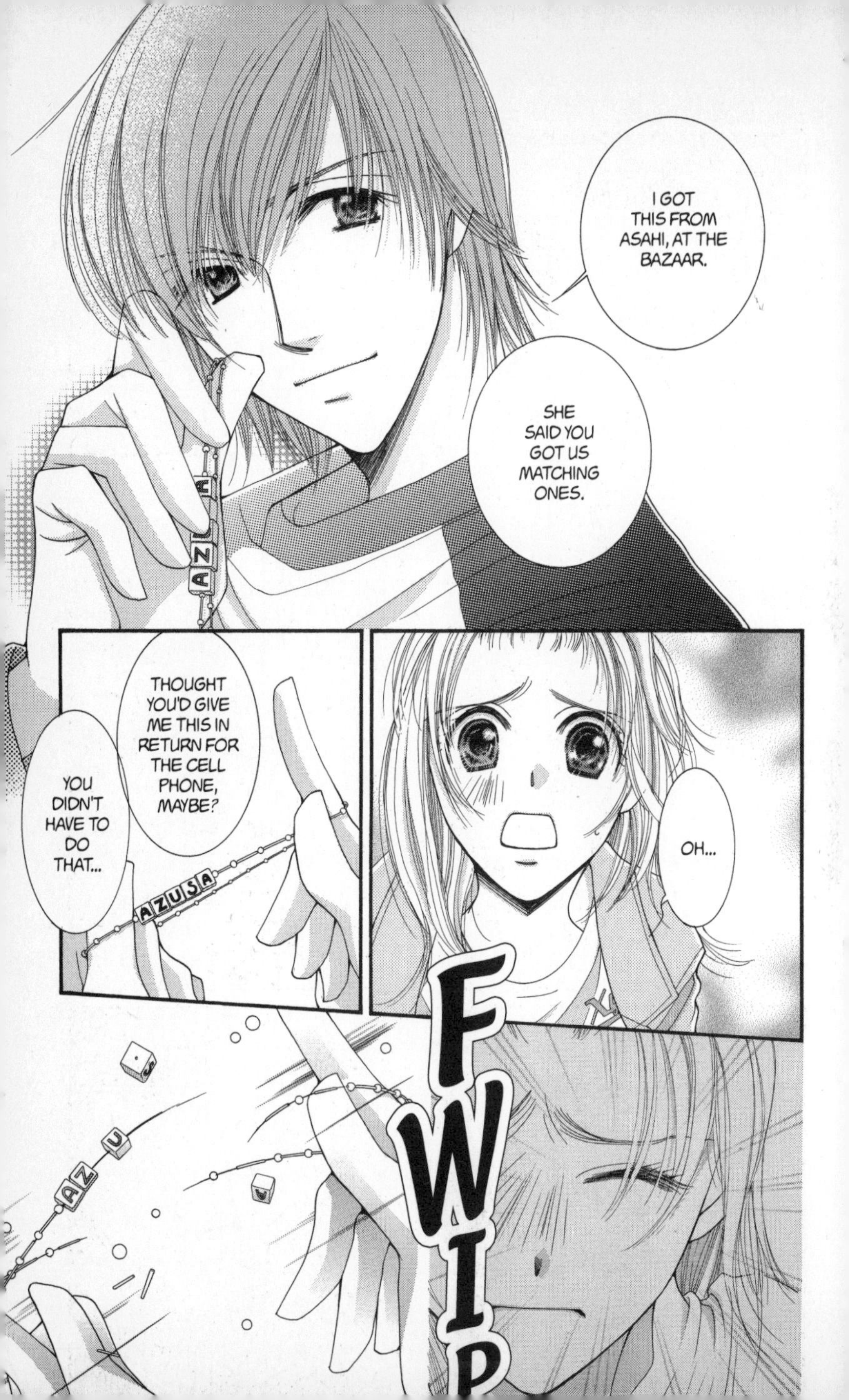
I GOT THIS FROM ASAHI, AT THE BAZAAR.
SHE SAID YOU GOT US MATCHING ONES.
OH...
THOUGHT YOU'D GIVE ME THIS IN RETURN FOR THE CELL PHONE, MAYBE?
YOU DIDN'T HAVE TO DO THAT...
FWIP

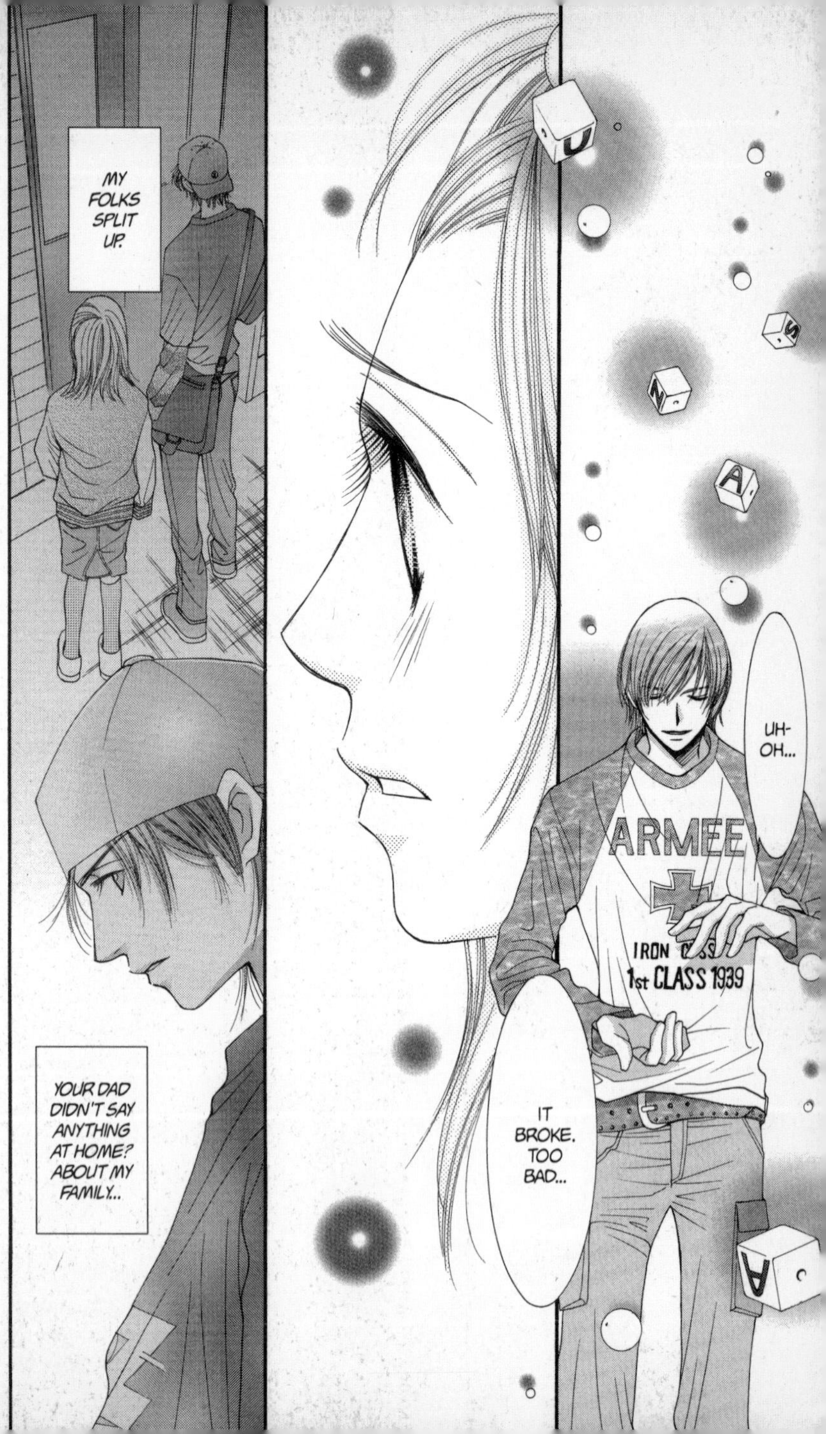
UH-OH...
ARMEE
1st CLASS 1939
IT BROKE. TOO BAD...
MY FOLKS SPLIT UP.
YOUR DAD DIDN'T SAY ANYTHING AT HOME? ABOUT MY FAMILY...

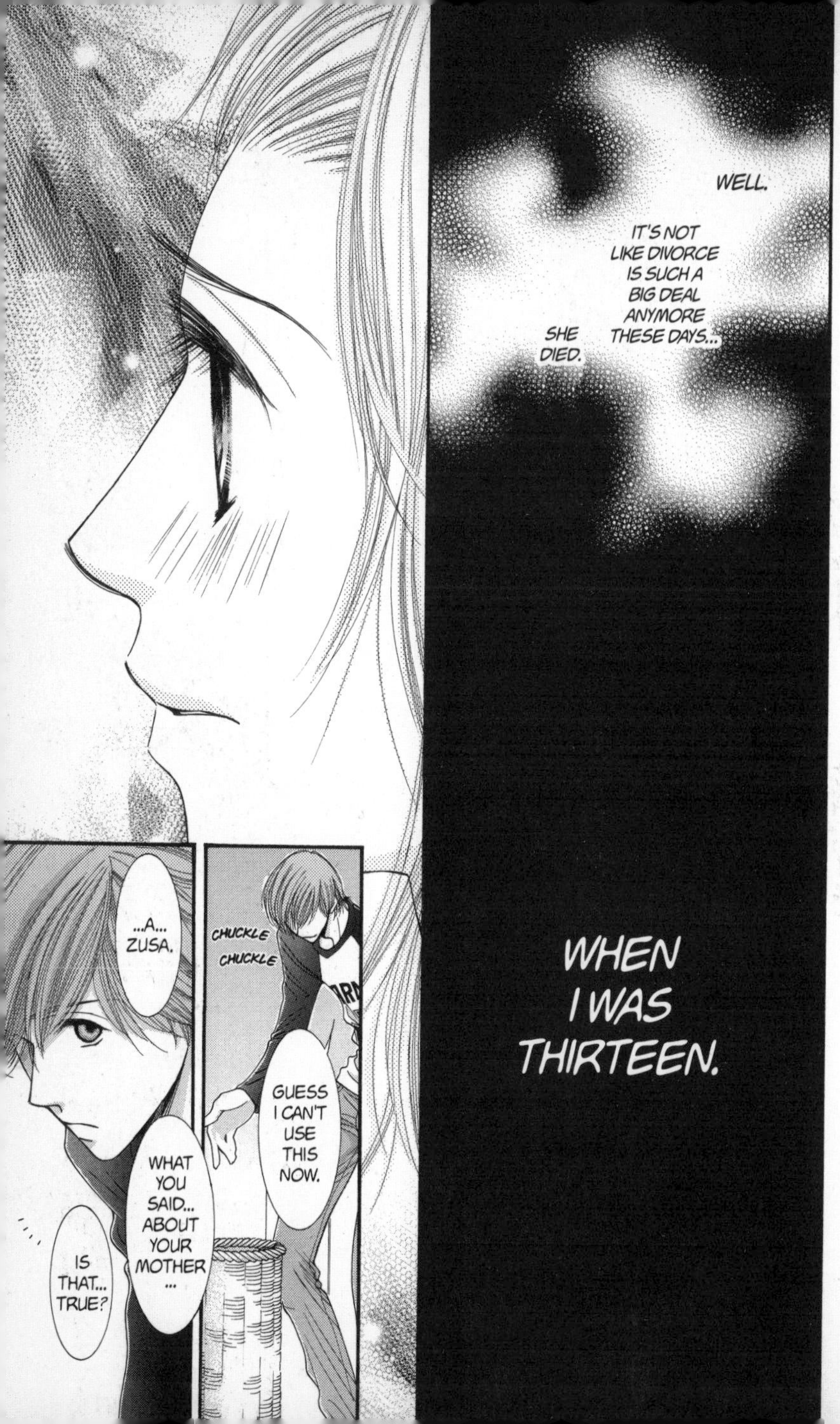
WELL.
IT'S NOT LIKE DIVORCE IS SUCH A BIG DEAL ANYMORE THESE DAYS...
SHE DIED.
WHEN I WAS THIRTEEN.
CHUCKLE CHUCKLE
GUESS I CAN'T USE THIS NOW.
...A... ZUSA.
WHAT YOU SAID... ABOUT YOUR MOTHER ...
IS THAT... TRUE?

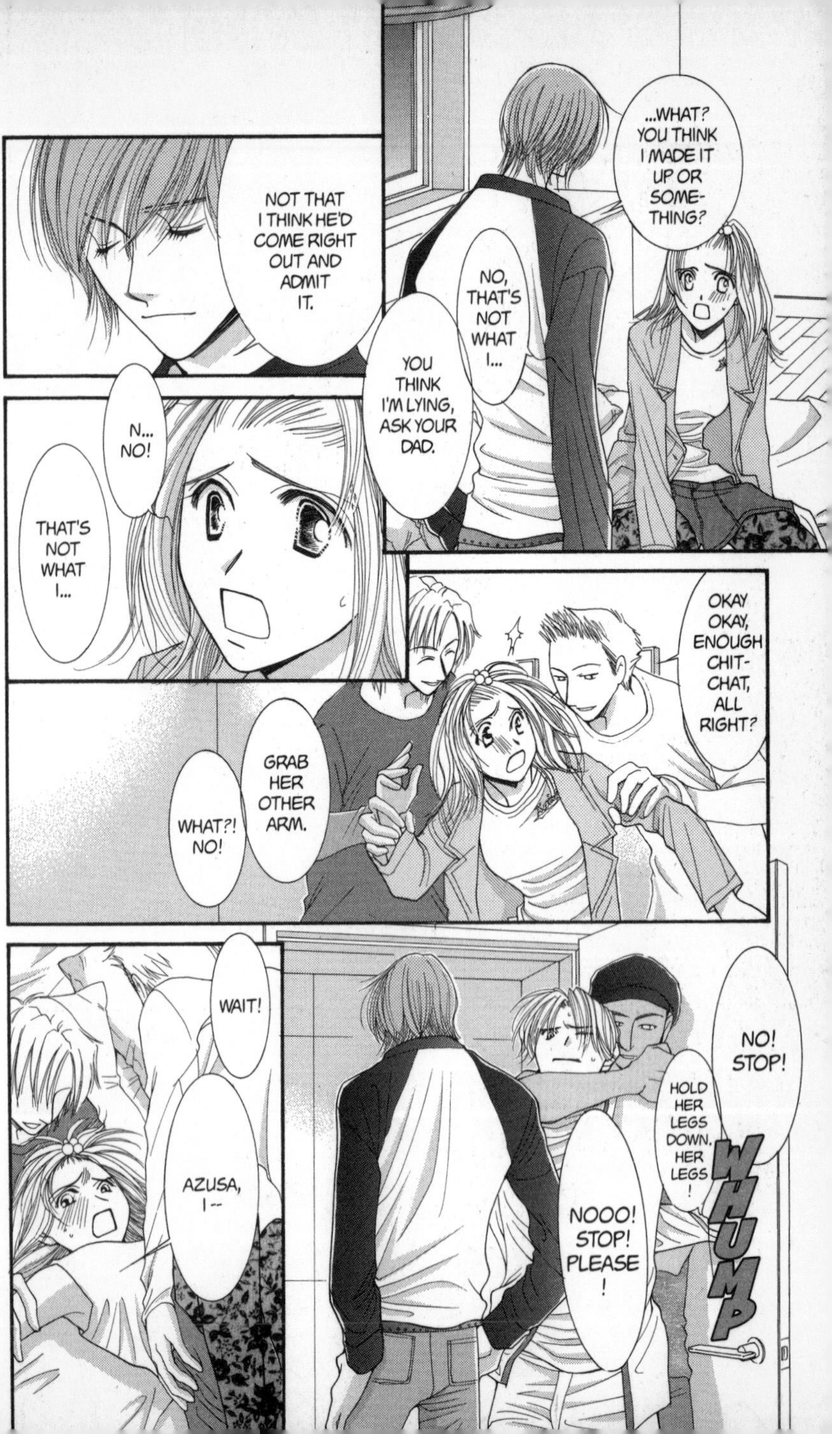

...WHAT? YOU THINK I MADE IT UP OR SOMETHING?
NO, THAT'S NOT WHAT I...
YOU THINK I'M LYING, ASK YOUR DAD.
NOT THAT I THINK HE'D COME RIGHT OUT AND ADMIT IT.
N... NO!
THAT'S NOT WHAT I...
OKAY OKAY, ENOUGH CHIT-CHAT, ALL RIGHT?
GRAB HER OTHER ARM.
WHAT?! NO!
NO! STOP!
HOLD HER LEGS DOWN. HER LEGS!
WHUMP
NOOO! STOP! PLEASE!
WAIT!
AZUSA, I--

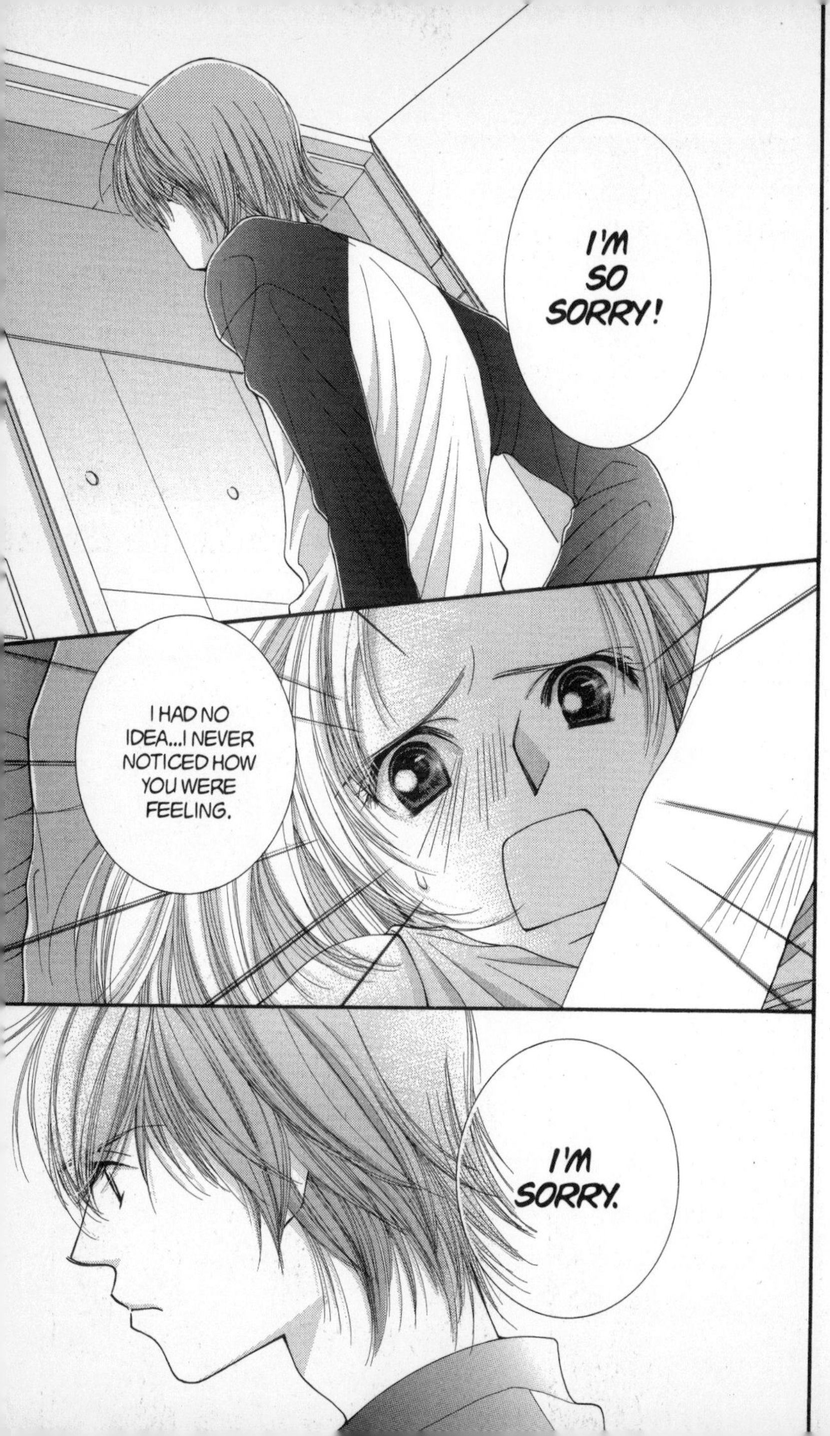
I'M SO SORRY!
I HAD NO IDEA...I NEVER NOTICED HOW YOU WERE FEELING.
I'M SORRY.

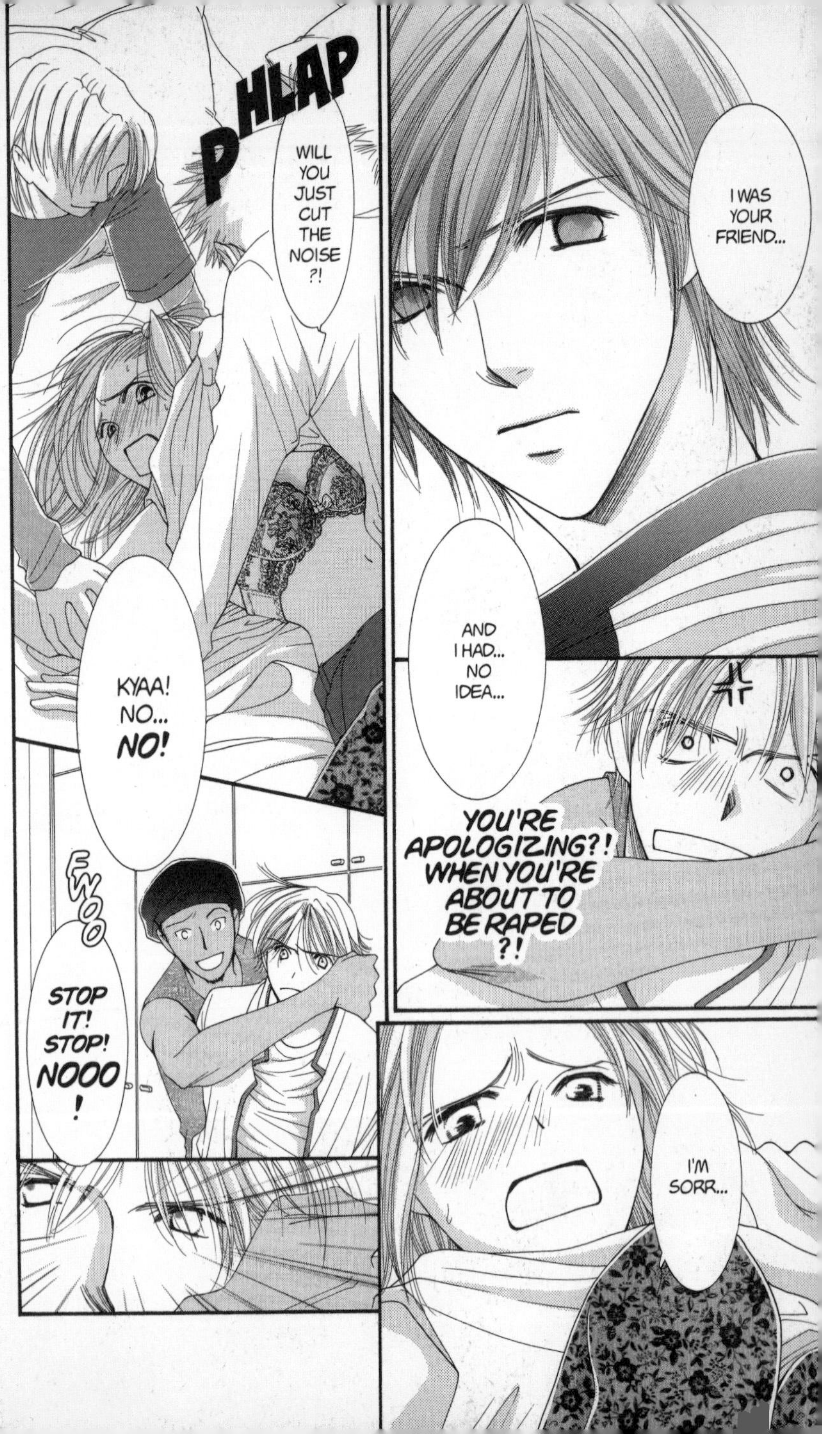
I WAS YOUR FRIEND...
AND I HAD... NO IDEA...
YOU'RE APOLOGIZING?! WHEN YOU'RE ABOUT TO BE RAPED?!
I'M SORR...
PHLAP
WILL YOU JUST CUT THE NOISE?!
KYAA! NO... NO!
FWOO
STOP IT! STOP! NOOO!

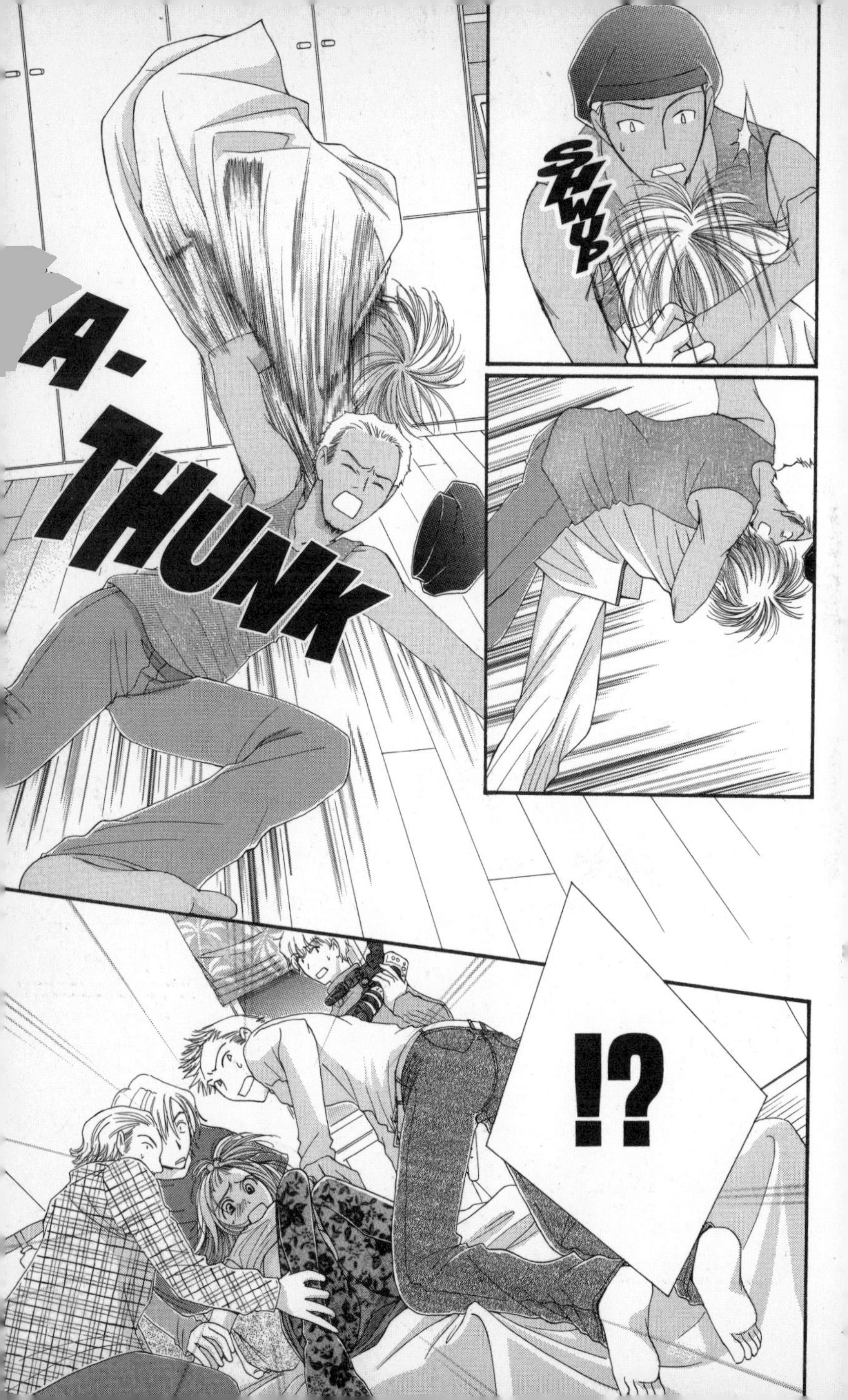
SHWUP
A-THUNK
!?

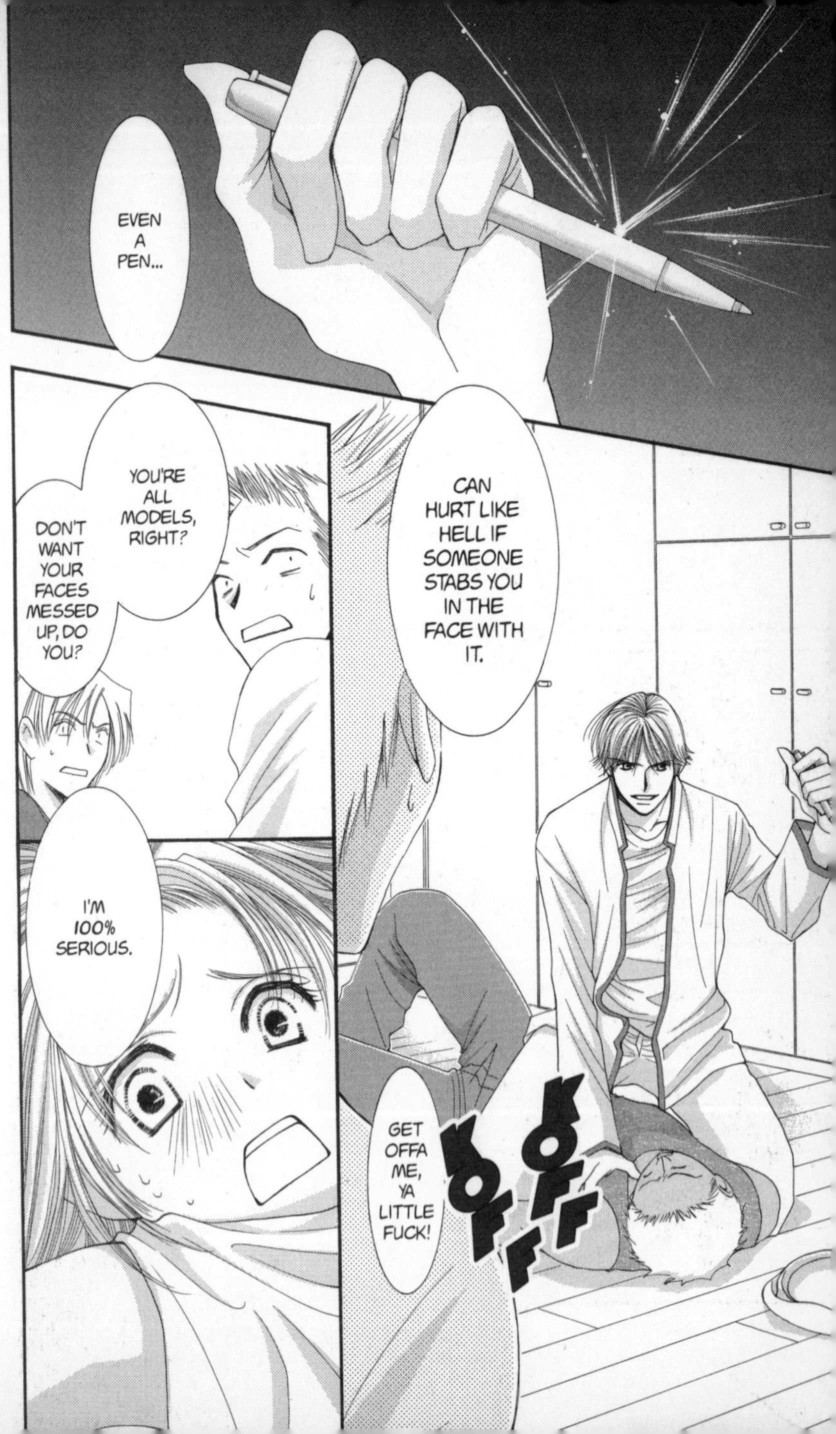
EVEN A PEN...
CAN HURT LIKE HELL IF SOMEONE STABS YOU IN THE FACE WITH IT.
KOFF
KOFF
GET OFFA ME, YA LITTLE FUCK!
YOU'RE ALL MODELS, RIGHT?
DON'T WANT YOUR FACES MESSED UP, DO YOU?
I'M 100% SERIOUS.

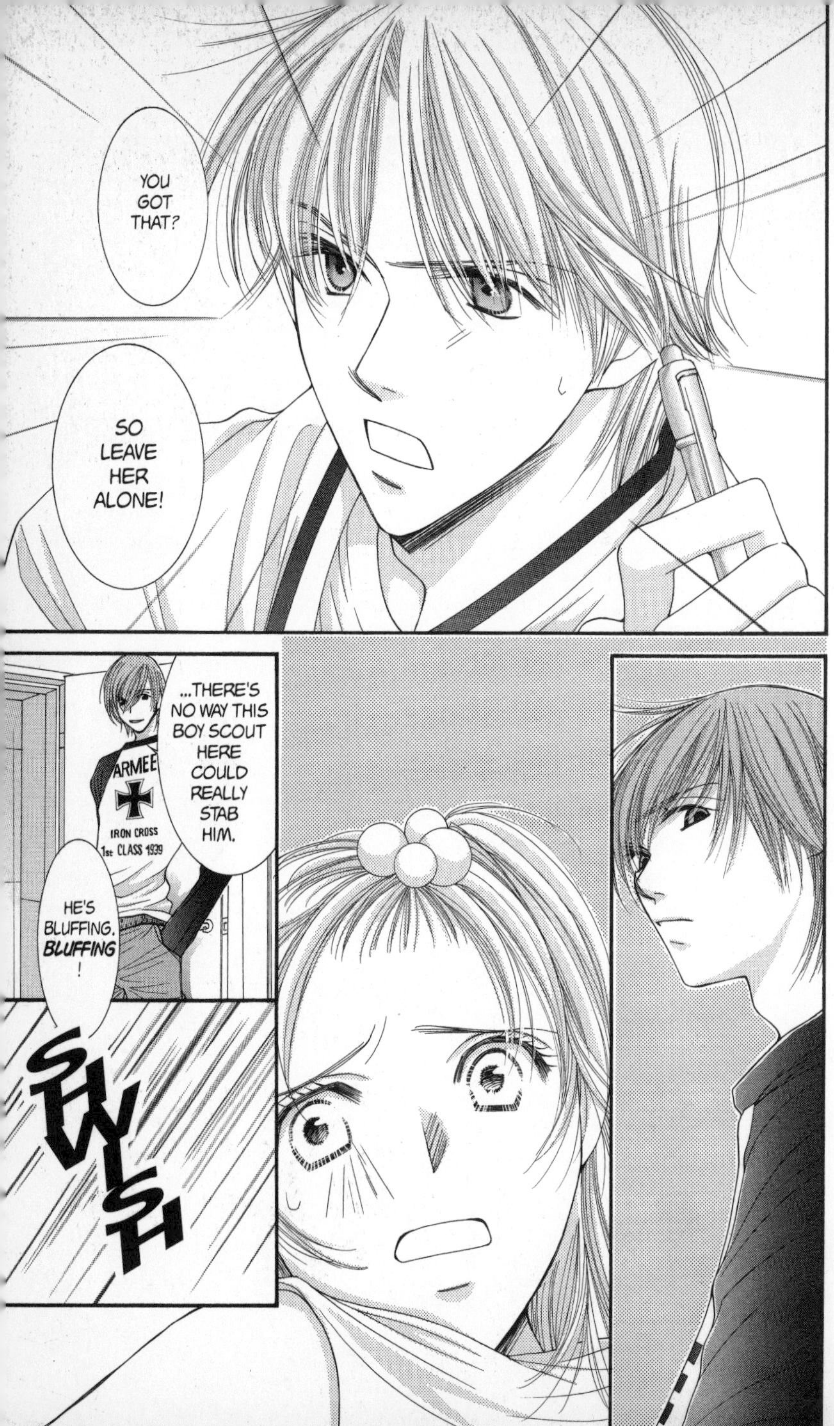
YOU GOT THAT?
SO LEAVE HER ALONE!
...THERE'S NO WAY THIS BOY SCOUT HERE COULD REALLY STAB HIM.
HE'S BLUFFING. BLUFFING!
ARMEE
IRON CROSS 1st CLASS 1939
SWISH

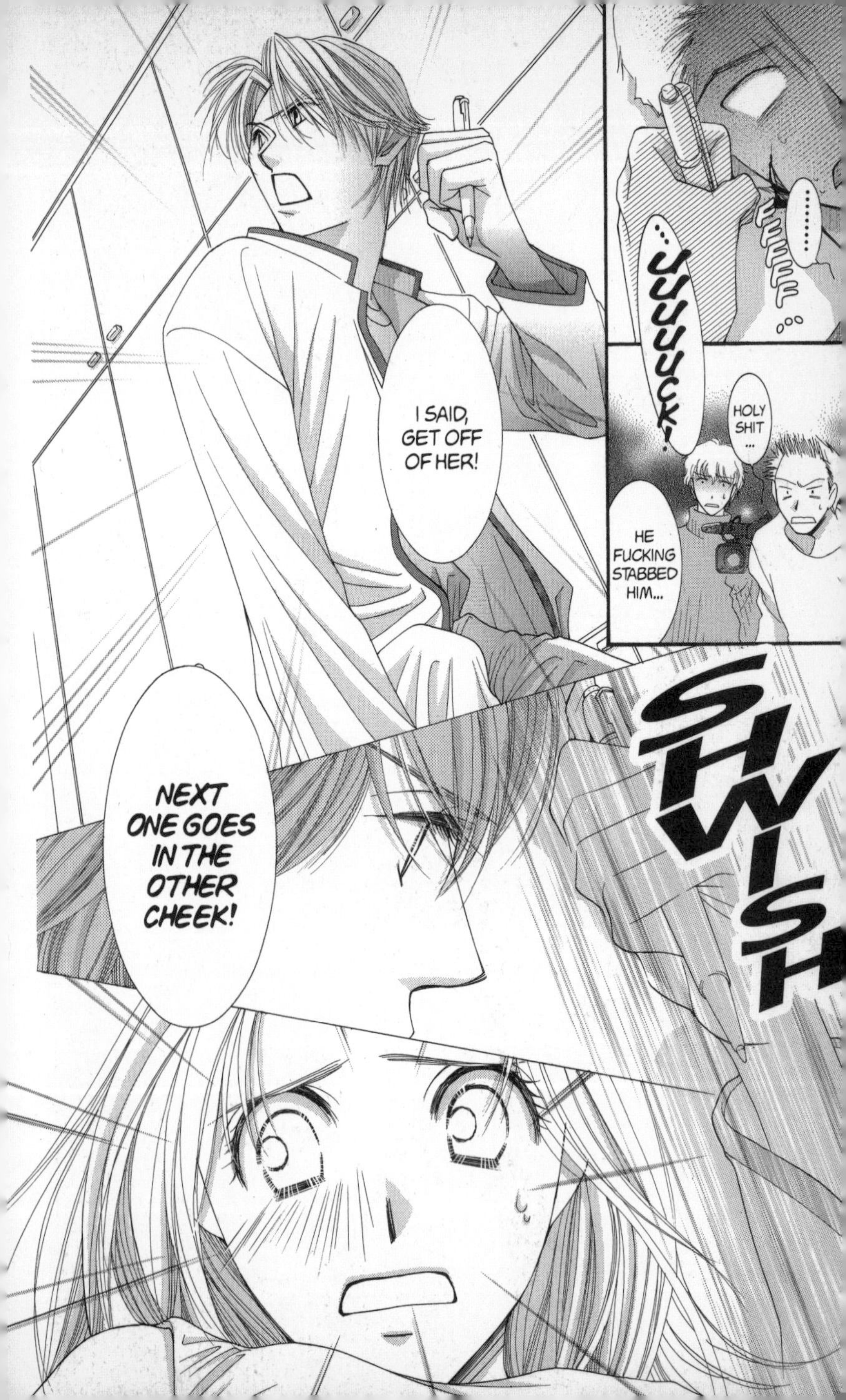
......
FFFFF ooo
...JUUUUUCK!
HOLY SHIT ...
HE FUCKING STABBED HIM...
I SAID, GET OFF OF HER!
SHWISH
NEXT ONE GOES IN THE OTHER CHEEK!

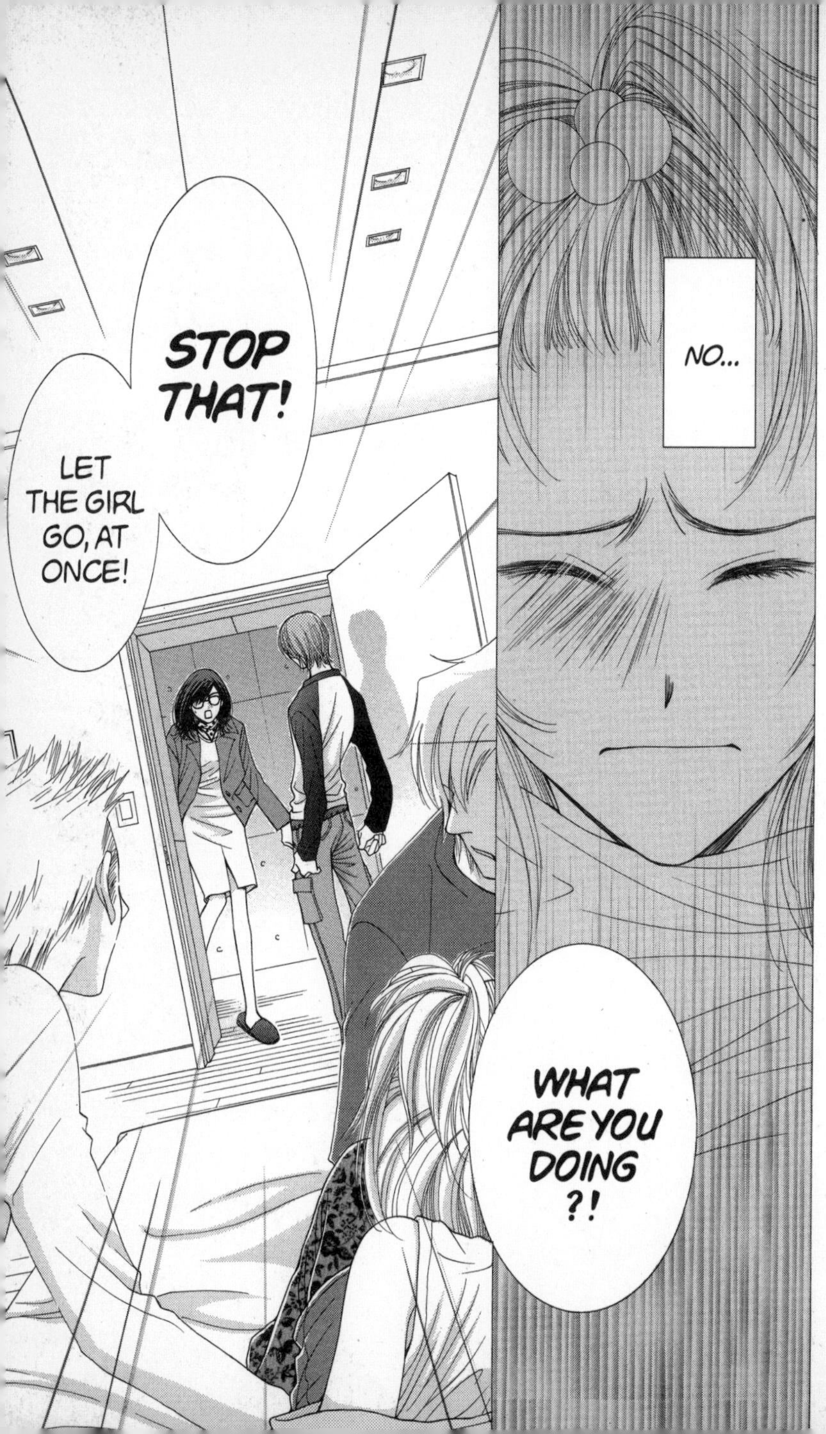
NO...
WHAT ARE YOU DOING?!
STOP THAT!
LET THE GIRL GO, AT ONCE!

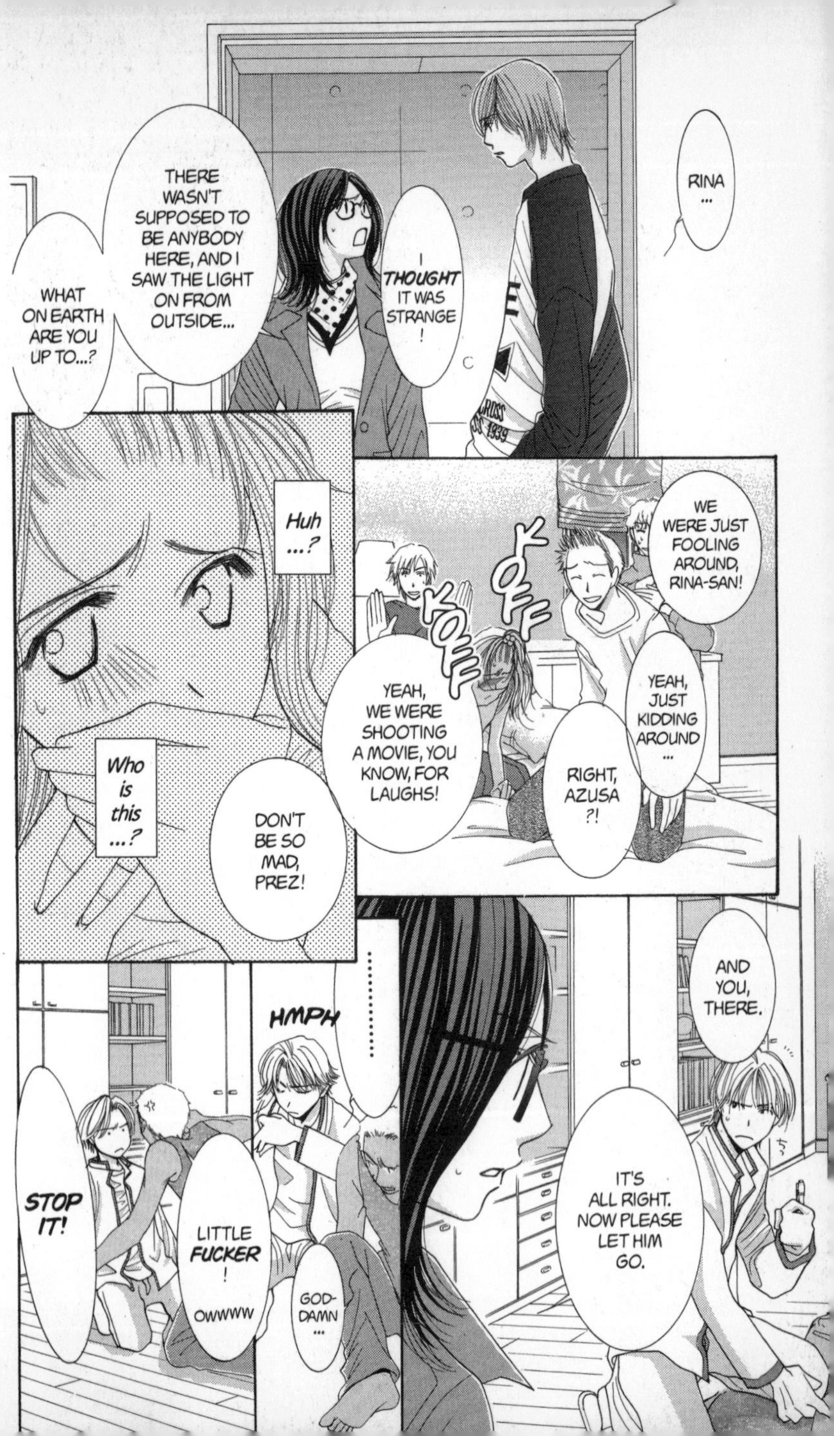
RINA ...
I THOUGHT IT WAS STRANGE!
THERE WASN'T SUPPOSED TO BE ANYBODY HERE, AND I SAW THE LIGHT ON FROM OUTSIDE...
WHAT ON EARTH ARE YOU UP TO...?
WE WERE JUST FOOLING AROUND, RINA-SAN!
KOFF
KOFF
YEAH, JUST KIDDING AROUND ...
RIGHT, AZUSA?!
YEAH, WE WERE SHOOTING A MOVIE, YOU KNOW, FOR LAUGHS!
DON'T BE SO MAD, PREZ!
Huh ...?
Who is this ...?
AND YOU, THERE.
IT'S ALL RIGHT. NOW PLEASE LET HIM GO.
......
HMPH
LITTLE FUCKER!
OWWWW
GOD-DAMN ...
STOP IT!

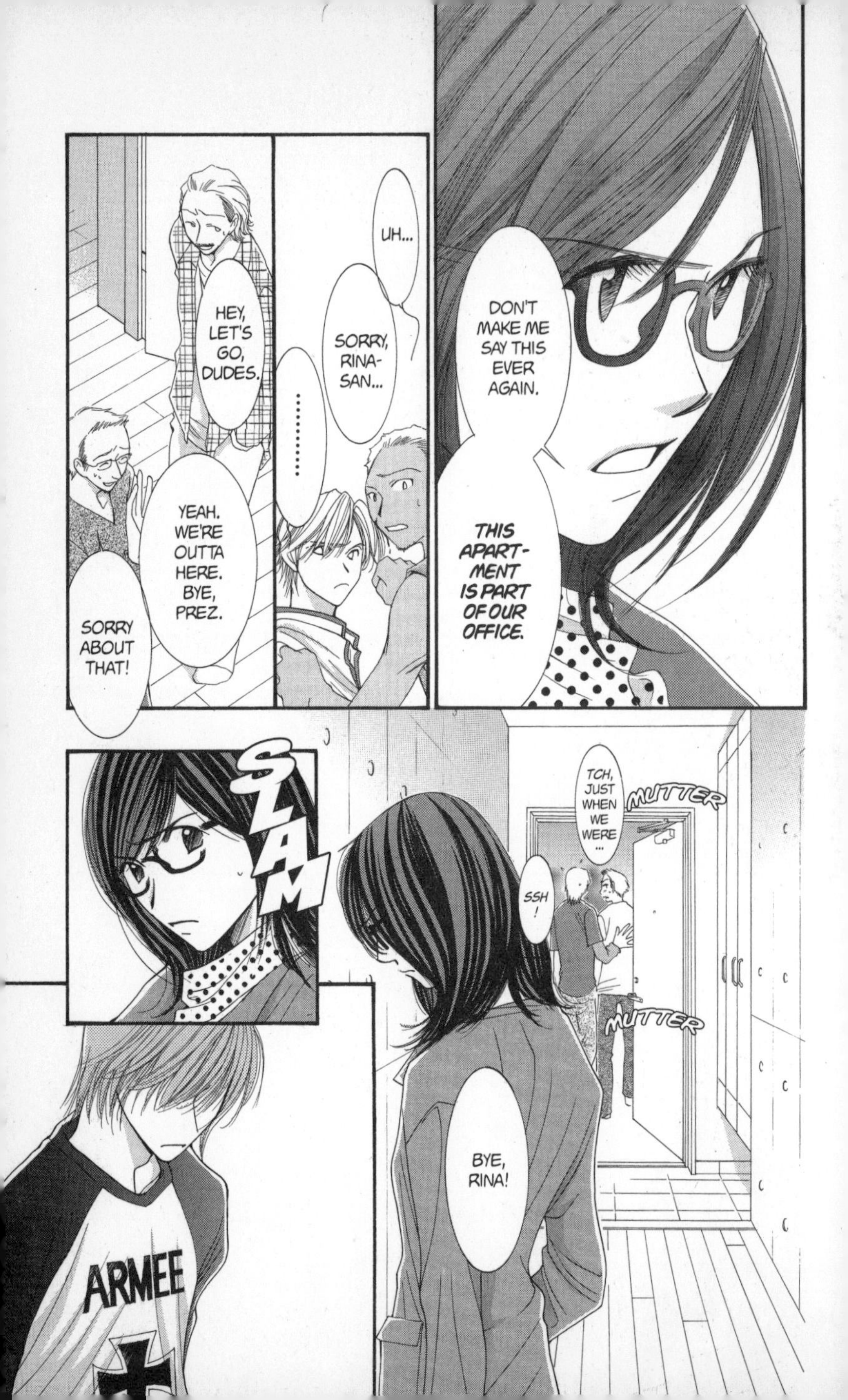
DON'T MAKE ME SAY THIS EVER AGAIN.
THIS APARTMENT IS PART OF OUR OFFICE.
UH...
SORRY, RINA-SAN...
......
HEY, LET'S GO, DUDES.
YEAH. WE'RE OUTTA HERE. BYE, PREZ.
SORRY ABOUT THAT!
TCH, JUST WHEN WE WERE...
MUTTER
SSH!
MUTTER
BYE, RINA!
SLAM
ARMEE

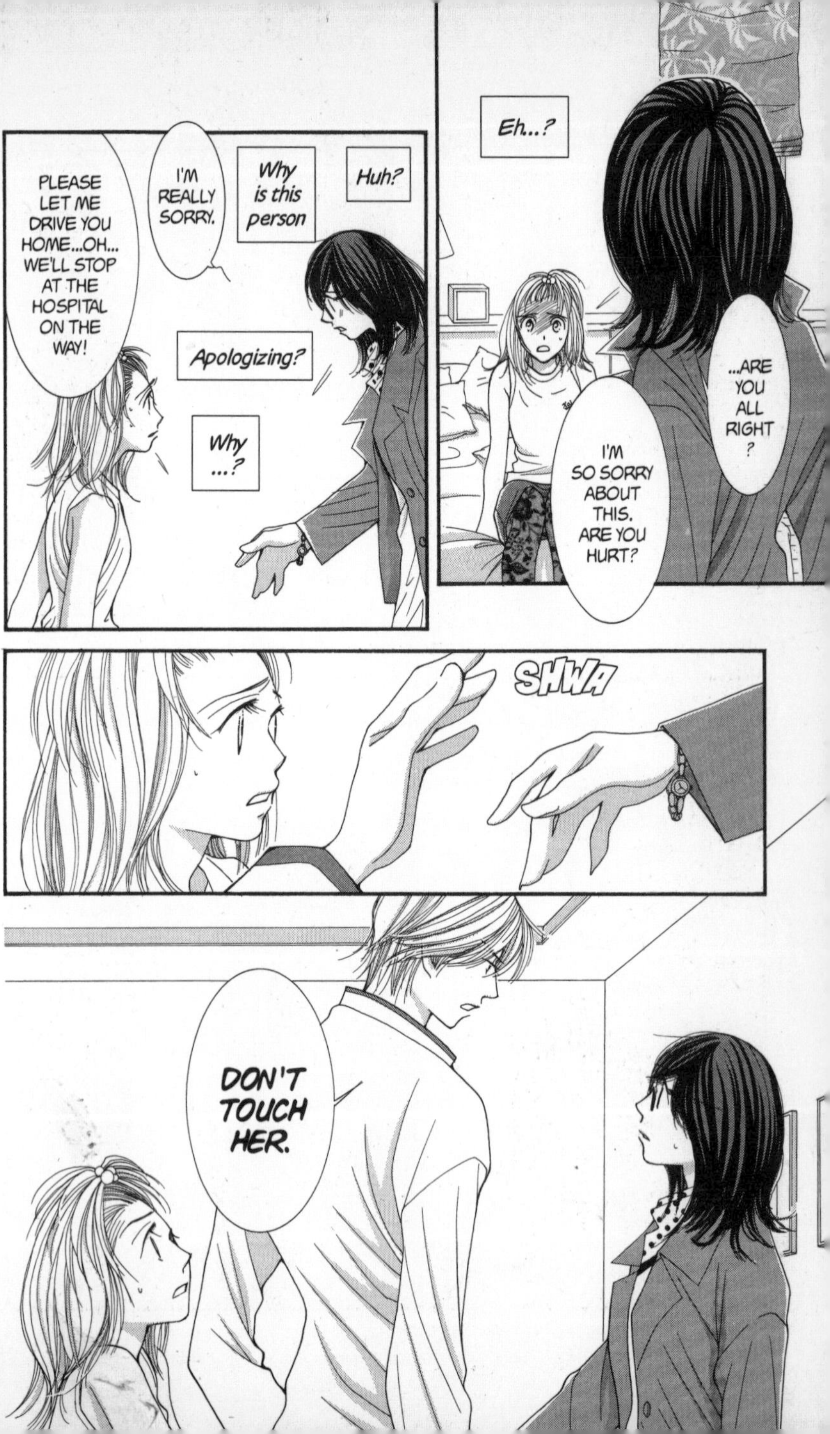
...ARE YOU ALL RIGHT?
Eh...?
I'M SO SORRY ABOUT THIS. ARE YOU HURT?
Huh?
Why is this person
I'M REALLY SORRY.
PLEASE LET ME DRIVE YOU HOME...OH... WE'LL STOP AT THE HOSPITAL ON THE WAY!
Apologizing?
Why ...?
SHWA
DON'T TOUCH HER.

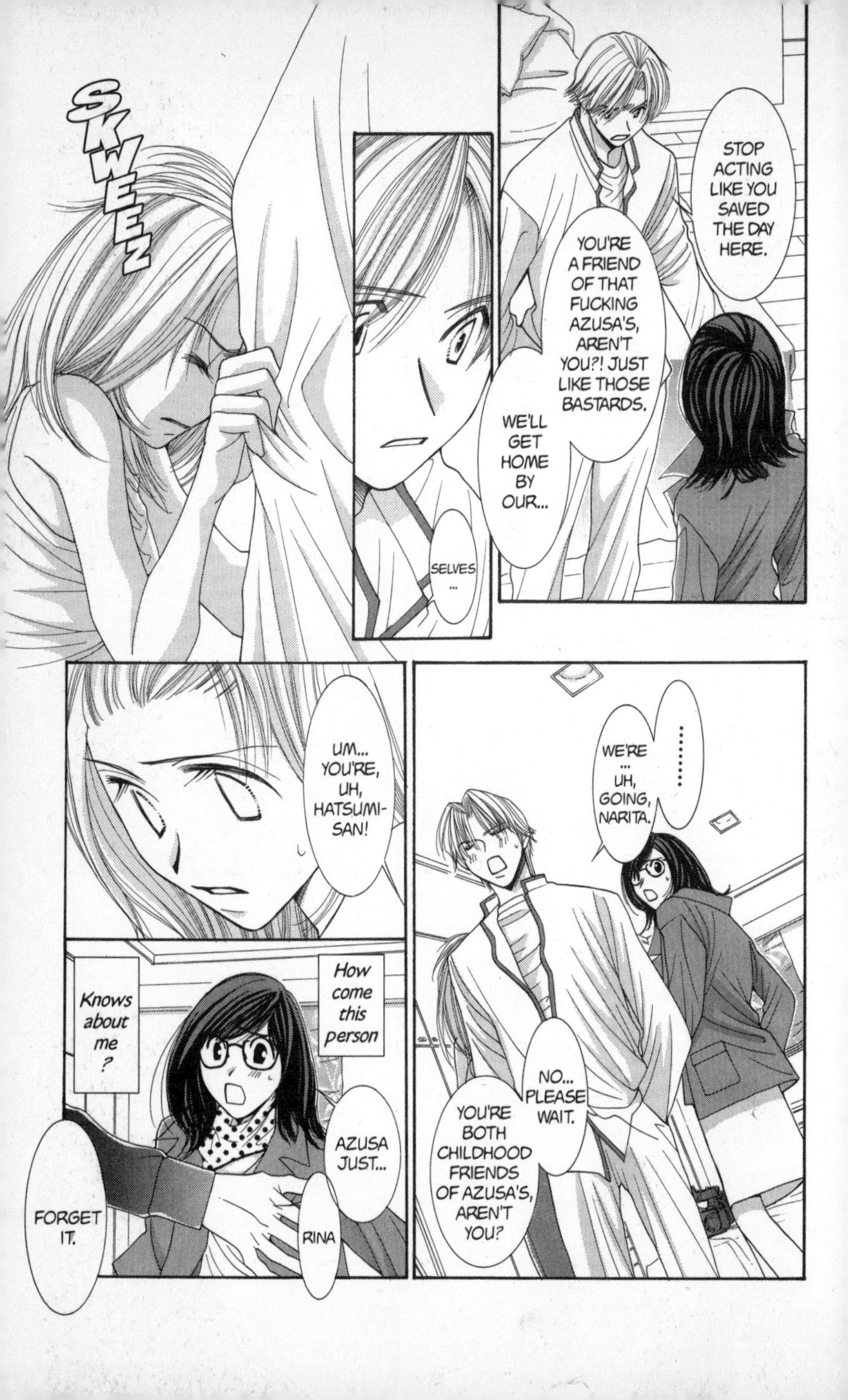
STOP ACTING LIKE YOU SAVED THE DAY HERE.
YOU'RE A FRIEND OF THAT FUCKING AZUSA'S, AREN'T YOU?! JUST LIKE THOSE BASTARDS.
WE'LL GET HOME BY OUR...
SELVES ...
SKWEEZ
......
WE'RE ... UH, GOING, NARITA.
NO... PLEASE WAIT.
YOU'RE BOTH CHILDHOOD FRIENDS OF AZUSA'S, AREN'T YOU?
UM... YOU'RE, UH, HATSUMI-SAN!
How come this person
Knows about me ?
AZUSA JUST...
RINA
FORGET IT.

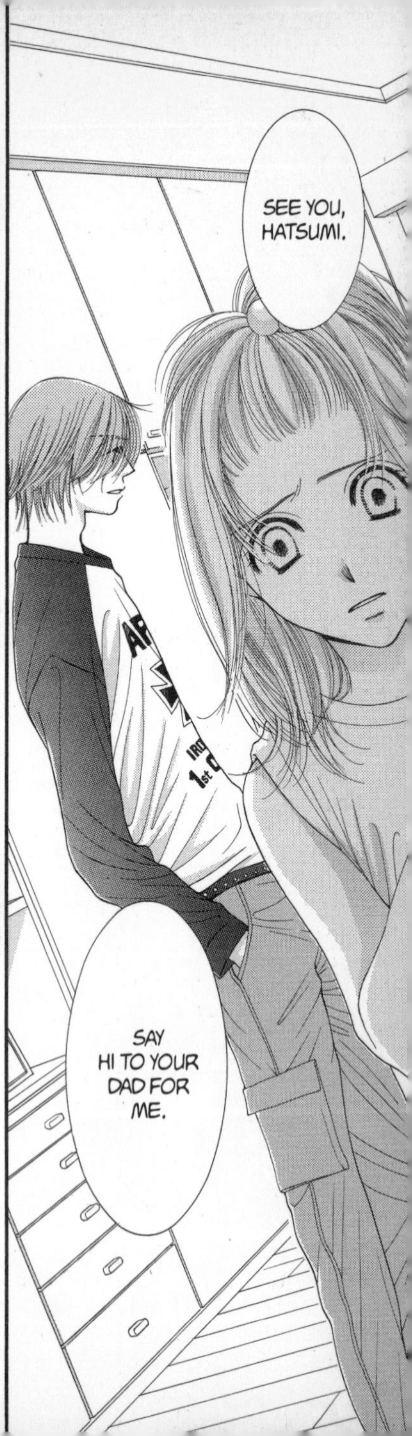
SEE YOU, HATSUMI.
SAY HI TO YOUR DAD FOR ME.

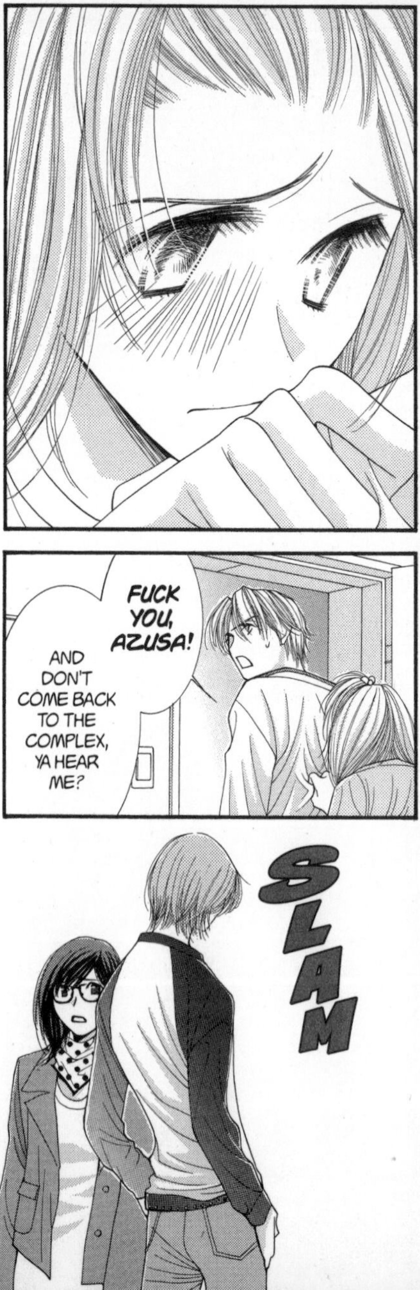
FUCK YOU, AZUSA!
AND DON'T COME BACK TO THE COMPLEX, YA HEAR ME?
SLAM

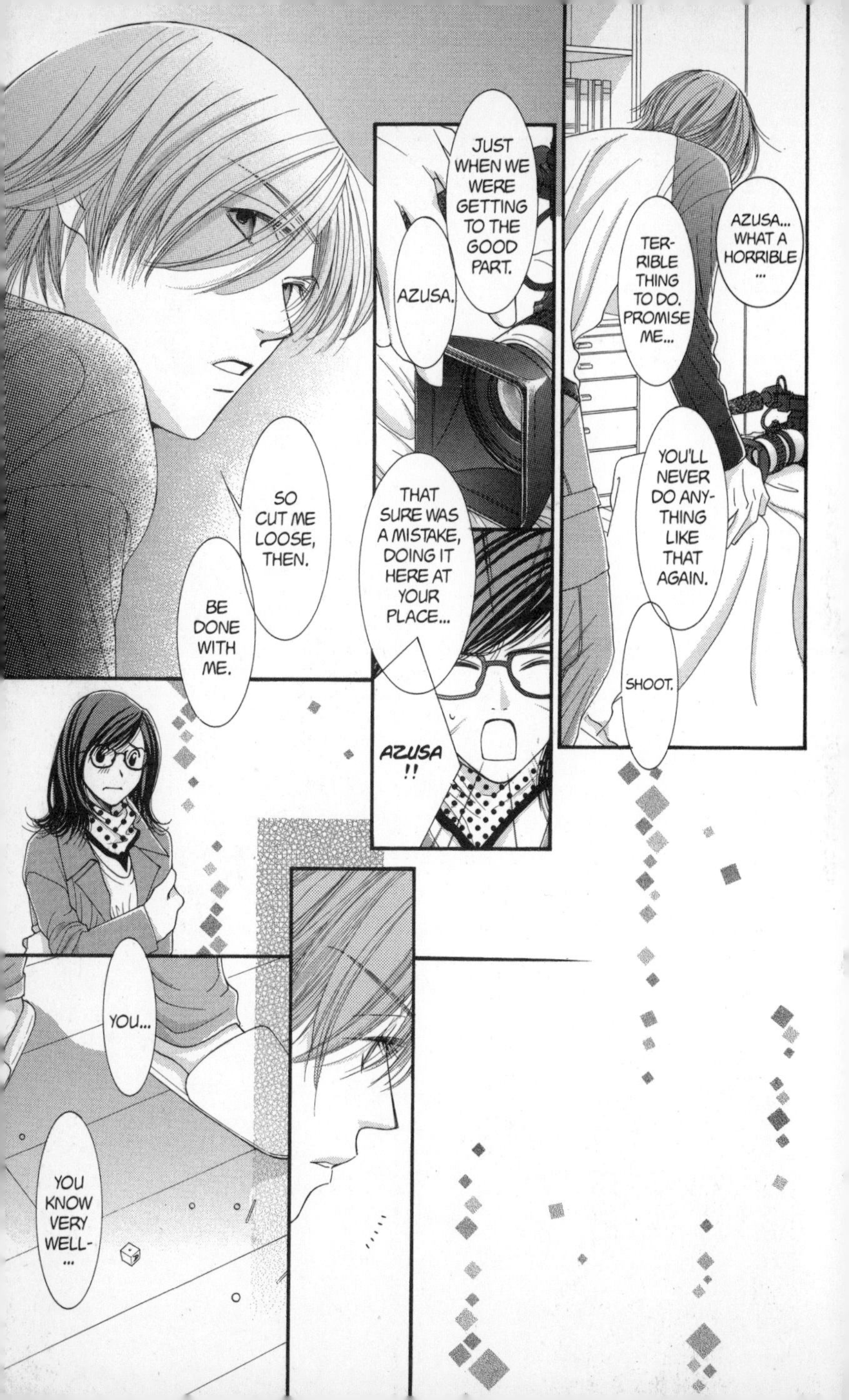
AZUSA... WHAT A HORRIBLE ...
TER-RIBLE THING TO DO. PROMISE ME...
YOU'LL NEVER DO ANY-THING LIKE THAT AGAIN.
SHOOT.
JUST WHEN WE WERE GETTING TO THE GOOD PART.
AZUSA.
THAT SURE WAS A MISTAKE, DOING IT HERE AT YOUR PLACE...
AZUSA !!
SO CUT ME LOOSE, THEN.
BE DONE WITH ME.
YOU...
YOU KNOW VERY WELL-...

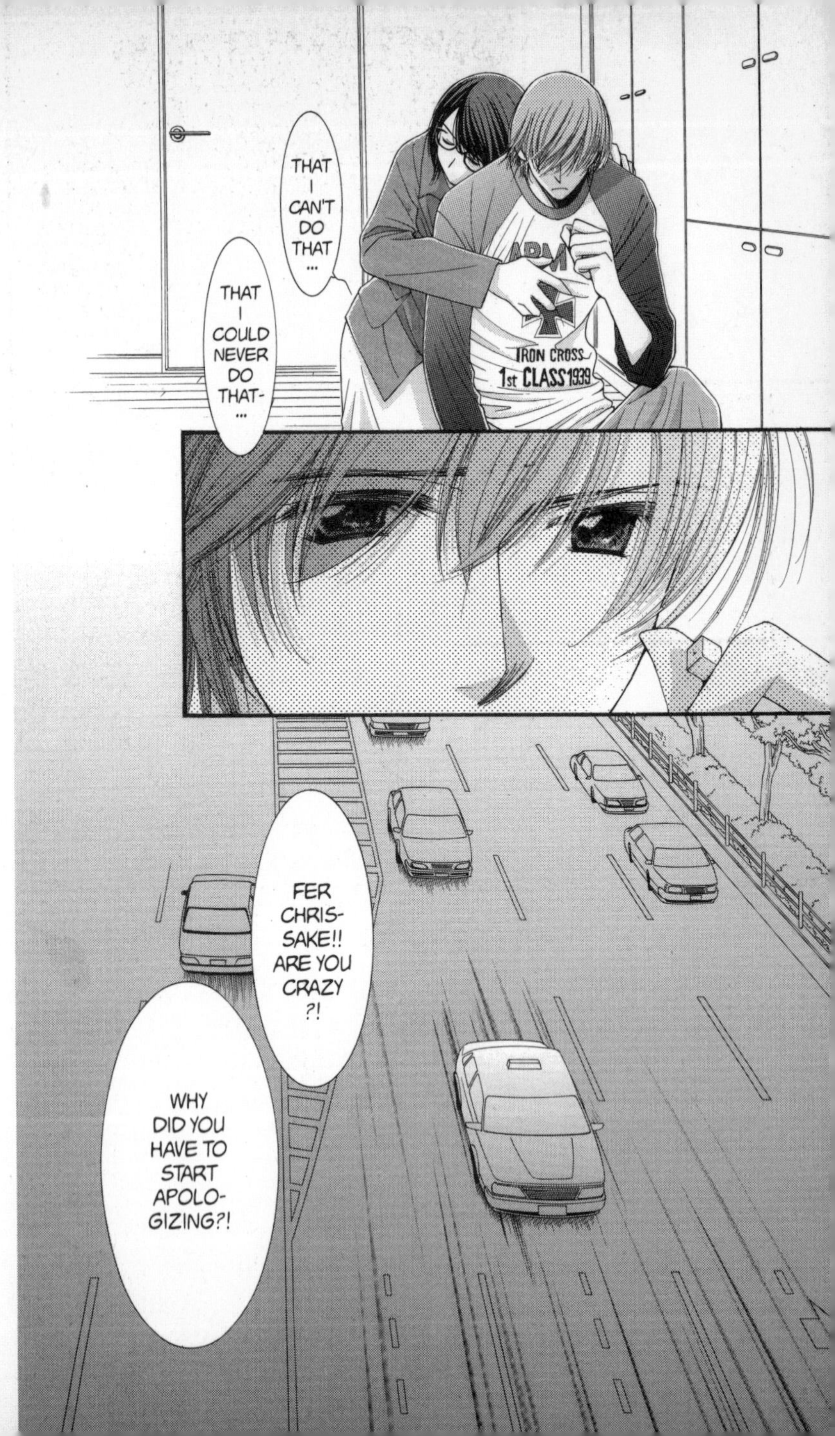
THAT I CAN'T DO THAT...
THAT I COULD NEVER DO THAT-...
IRON CROSS 1st CLASS 1939
FER CHRIS-SAKE!! ARE YOU CRAZY?!
WHY DID YOU HAVE TO START APOLO-GIZING?!

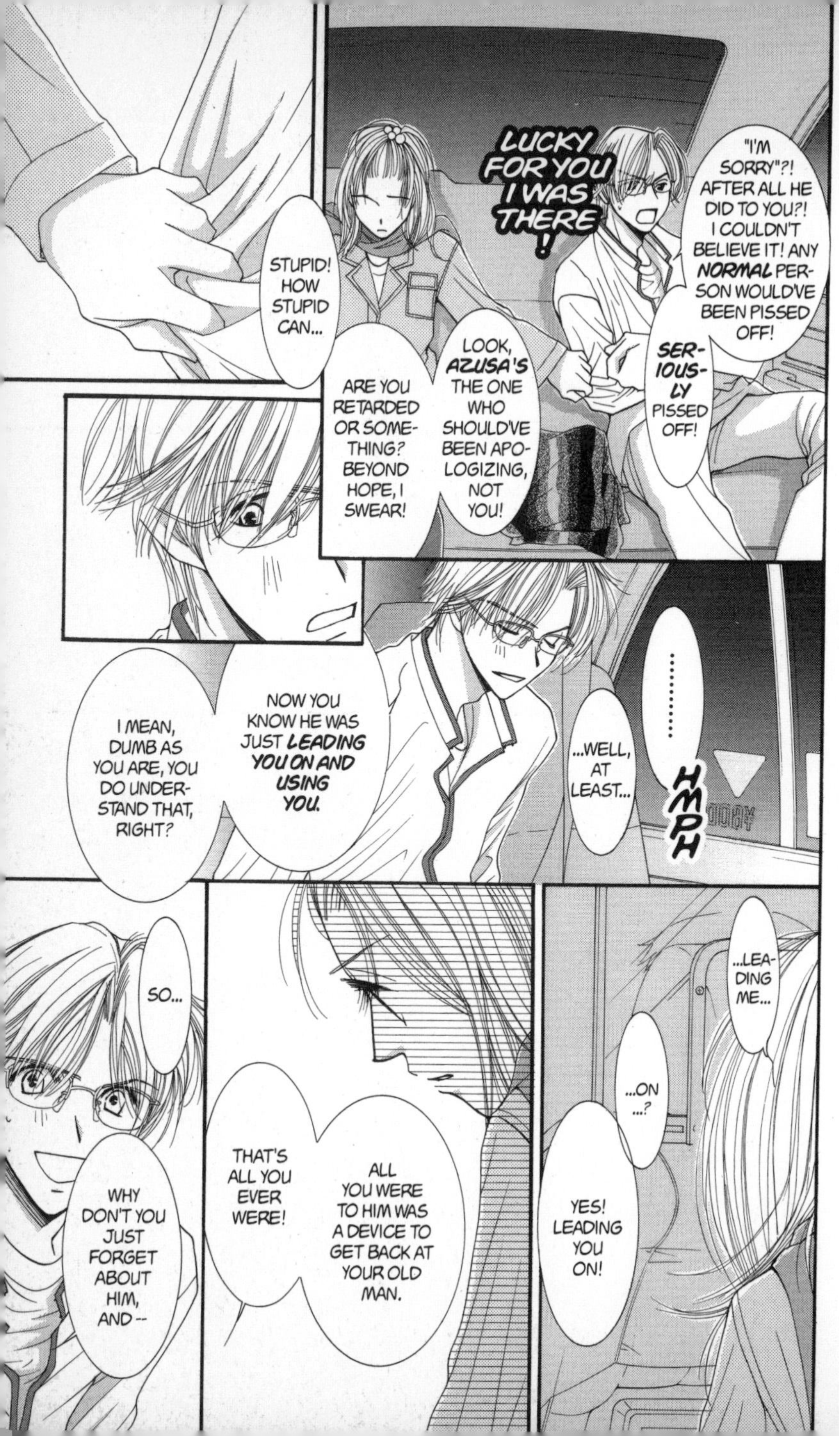

"I'M SORRY"?! AFTER ALL HE DID TO YOU?! I COULDN'T BELIEVE IT! ANY NORMAL PERSON WOULD'VE BEEN PISSED OFF!
SERIOUSLY PISSED OFF!
LUCKY FOR YOU I WAS THERE!
LOOK, AZUSA'S THE ONE WHO SHOULD'VE BEEN APOLOGIZING, NOT YOU!
STUPID! HOW STUPID CAN...
ARE YOU RETARDED OR SOMETHING? BEYOND HOPE, I SWEAR!
....
HMPH
...WELL, AT LEAST...
NOW YOU KNOW HE WAS JUST LEADING YOU ON AND USING YOU.
I MEAN, DUMB AS YOU ARE, YOU DO UNDERSTAND THAT, RIGHT?
...LEADING ME...
...ON ...?
YES! LEADING YOU ON!
ALL YOU WERE TO HIM WAS A DEVICE TO GET BACK AT YOUR OLD MAN.
THAT'S ALL YOU EVER WERE!
SO...
WHY DON'T YOU JUST FORGET ABOUT HIM, AND --

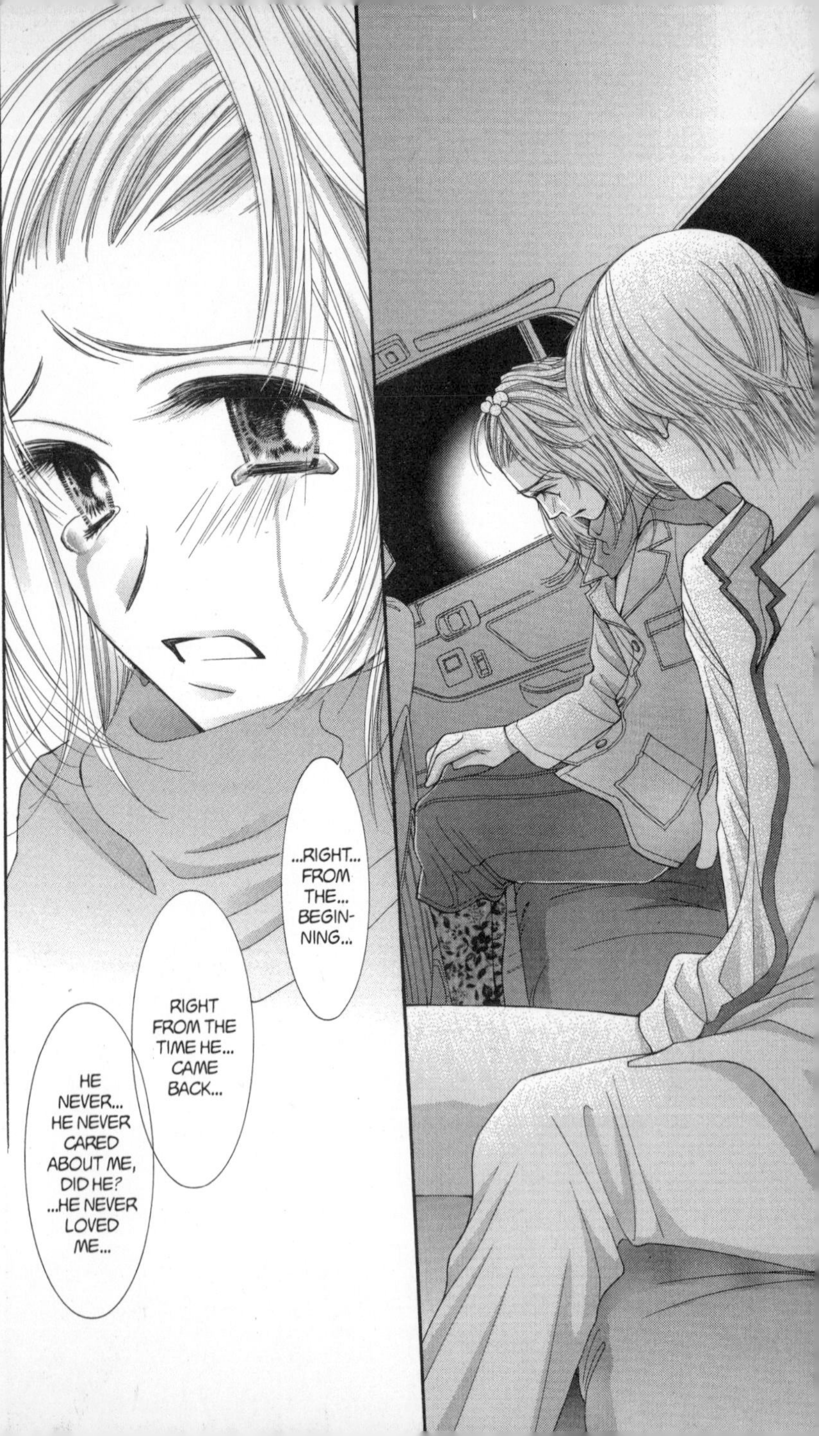
...RIGHT... FROM THE... BEGIN- NING...
RIGHT FROM THE TIME HE... CAME BACK...
HE NEVER... HE NEVER CARED ABOUT ME, DID HE? ...HE NEVER LOVED ME...

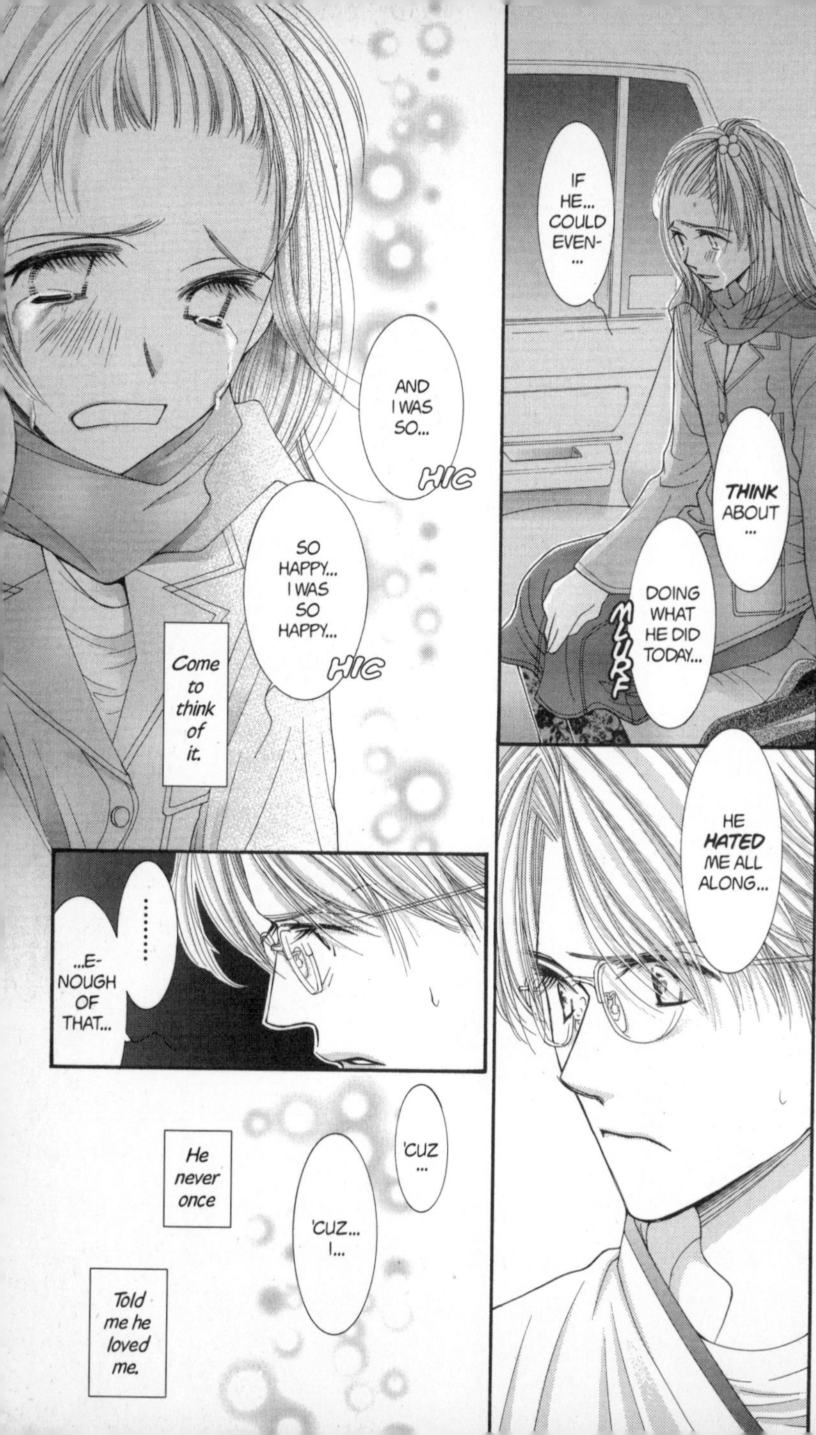
IF HE... COULD EVEN-...
THINK ABOUT...
DOING WHAT HE DID TODAY...
AND I WAS SO...
HIC
SO HAPPY... I WAS SO HAPPY...
HIC
Come to think of it.
HE HATED ME ALL ALONG...
....
...E-NOUGH OF THAT...
'CUZ...
'CUZ... I...
He never once
Told me he loved me.

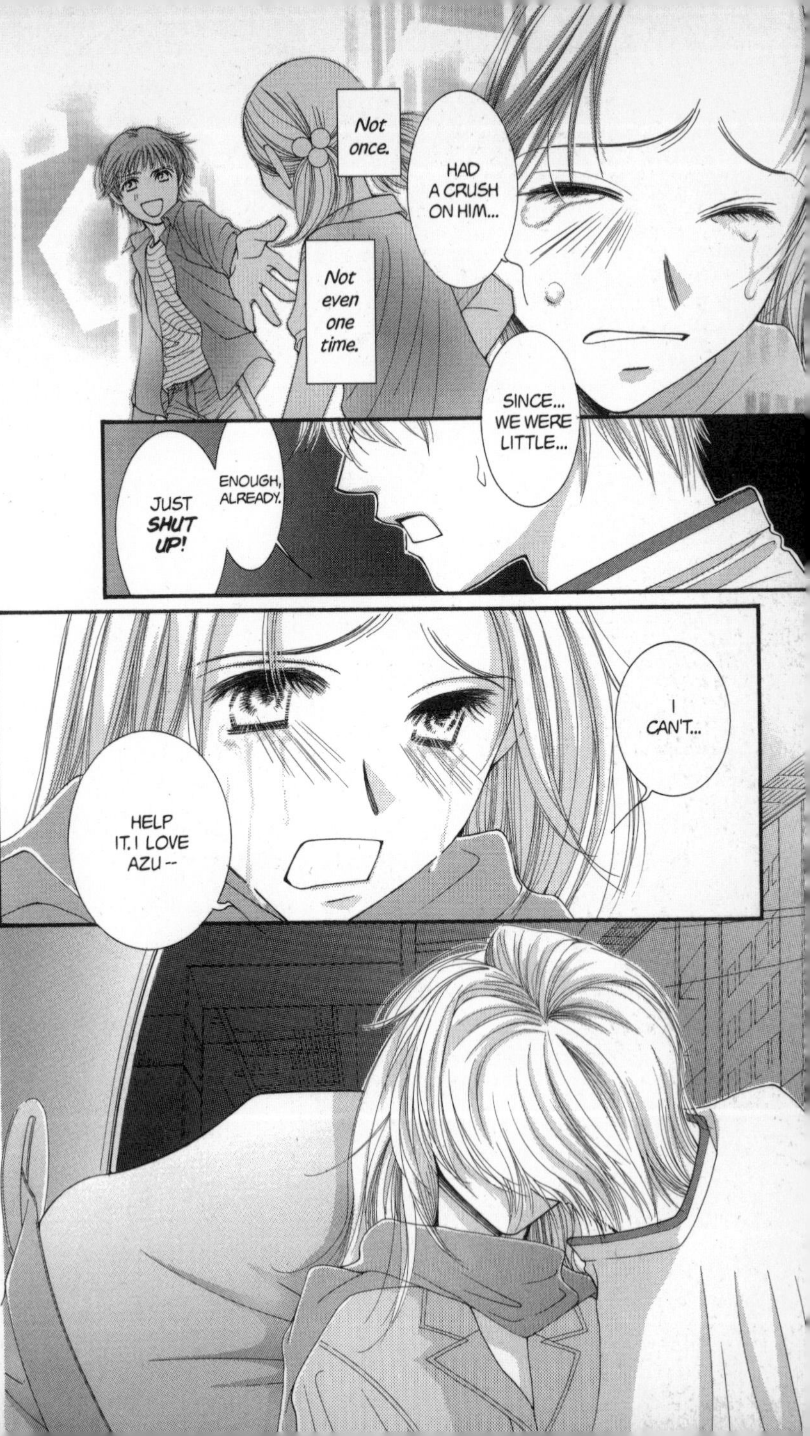

HAD A CRUSH ON HIM...
Not once.
Not even one time.
SINCE... WE WERE LITTLE...
ENOUGH, ALREADY.
JUST **SHUT UP!**
I CAN'T...
HELP IT. I LOVE AZU --

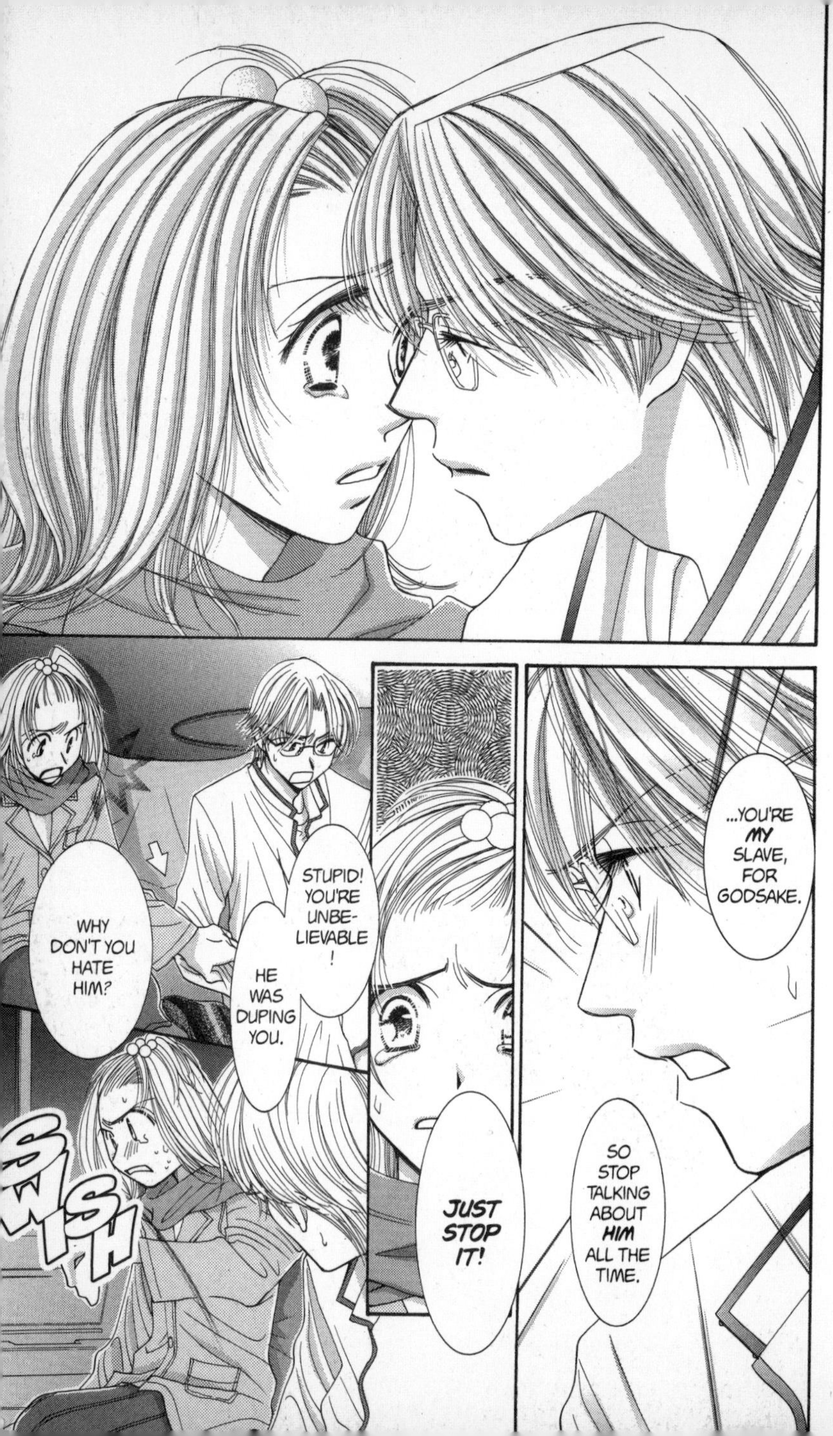
...YOU'RE MY SLAVE, FOR GODSAKE.
SO STOP TALKING ABOUT HIM ALL THE TIME.
JUST STOP IT!
STUPID! YOU'RE UNBE-LIEVABLE!
HE WAS DUPING YOU.
WHY DON'T YOU HATE HIM?
SWISH

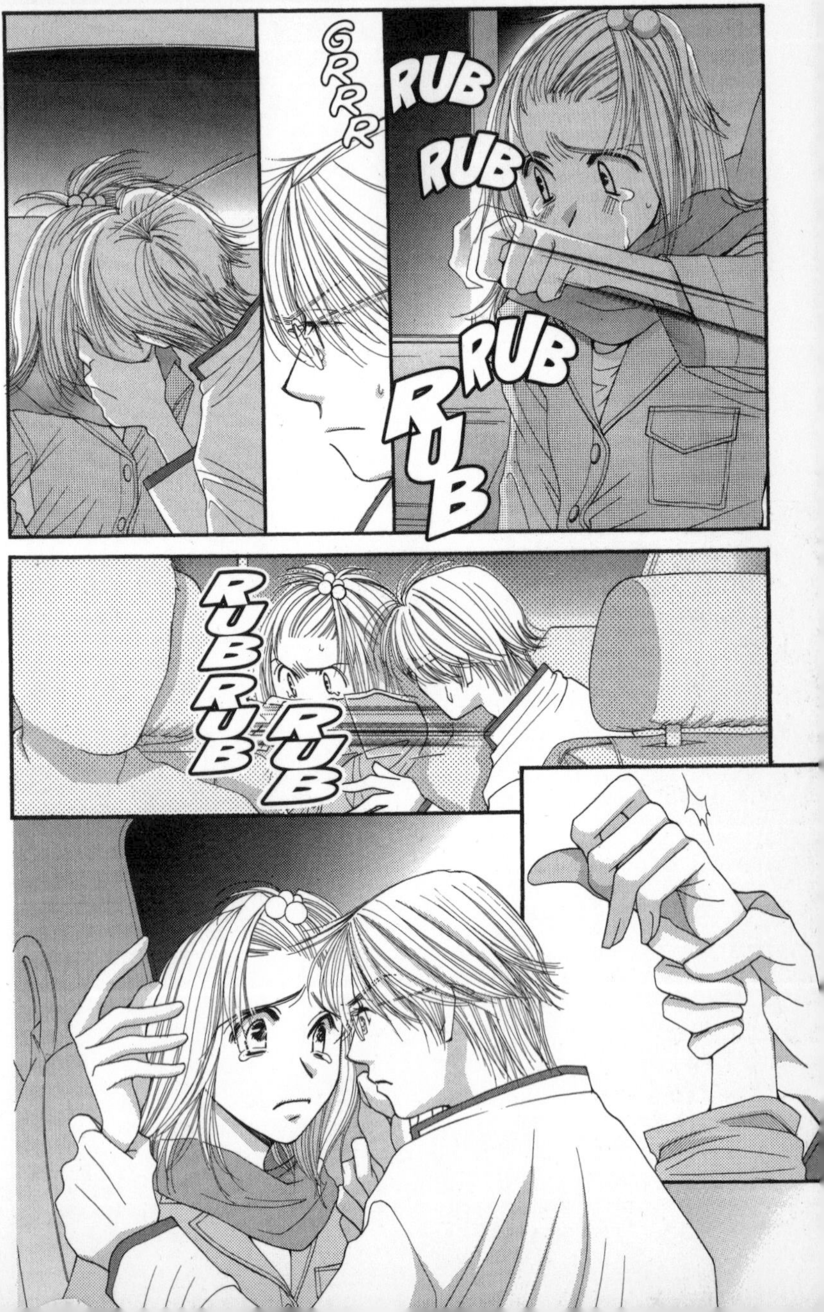

RUB
RUB
RUB
RUB
GRRR
RUB RUB
RUBRUB

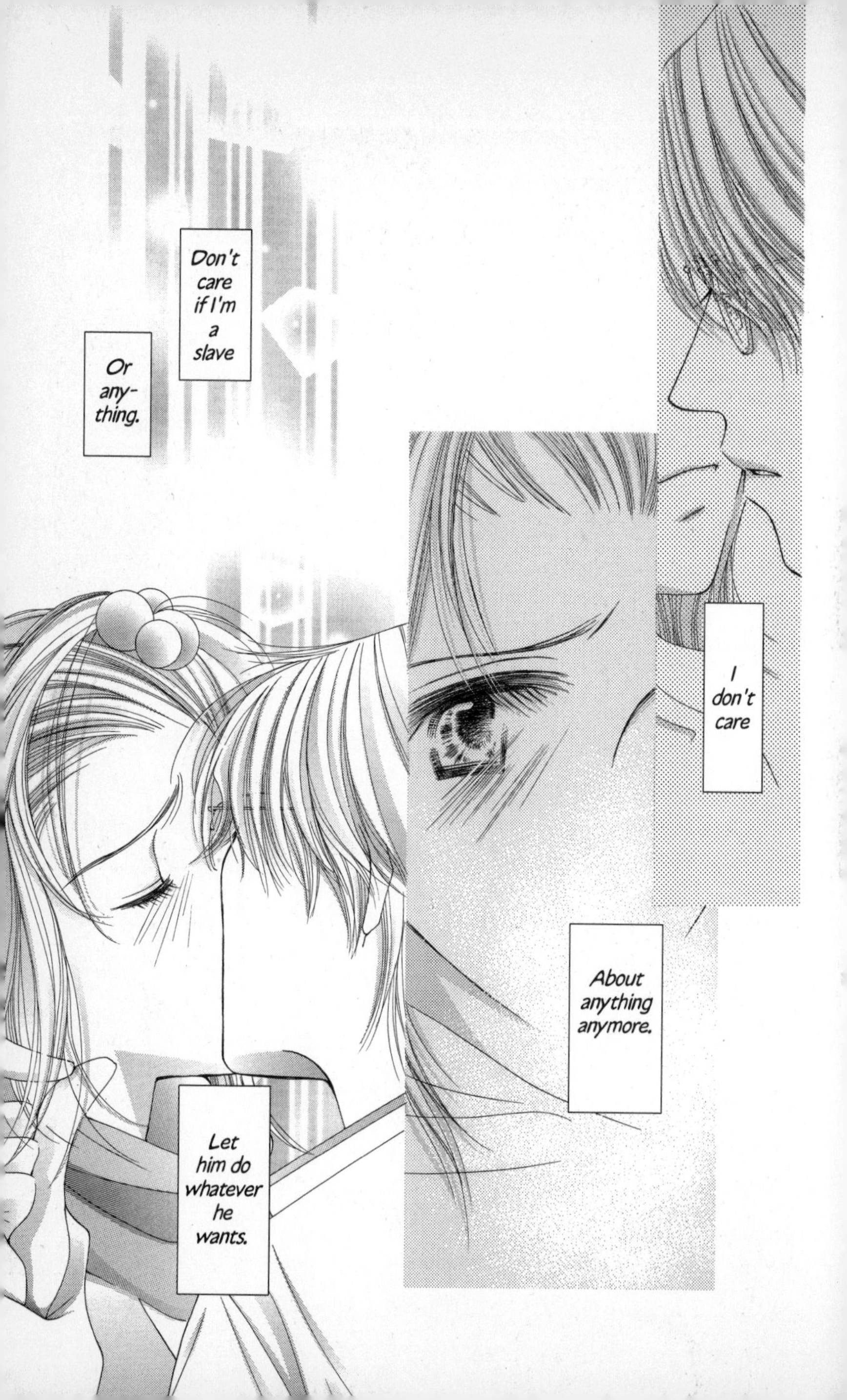
I don't care
About anything anymore.
Don't care if I'm a slave
Or anything.
Let him do whatever he wants.

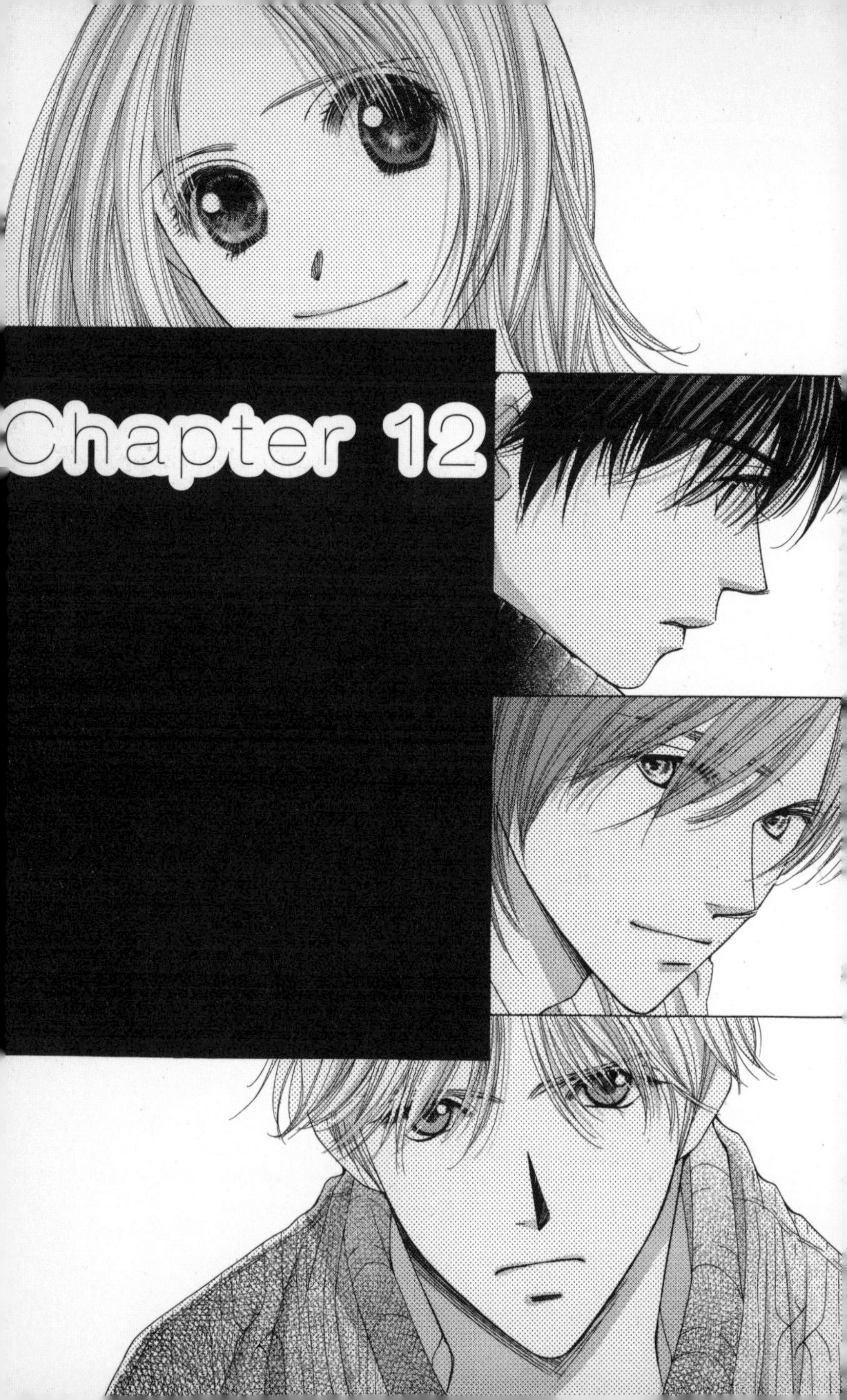
Chapter 12

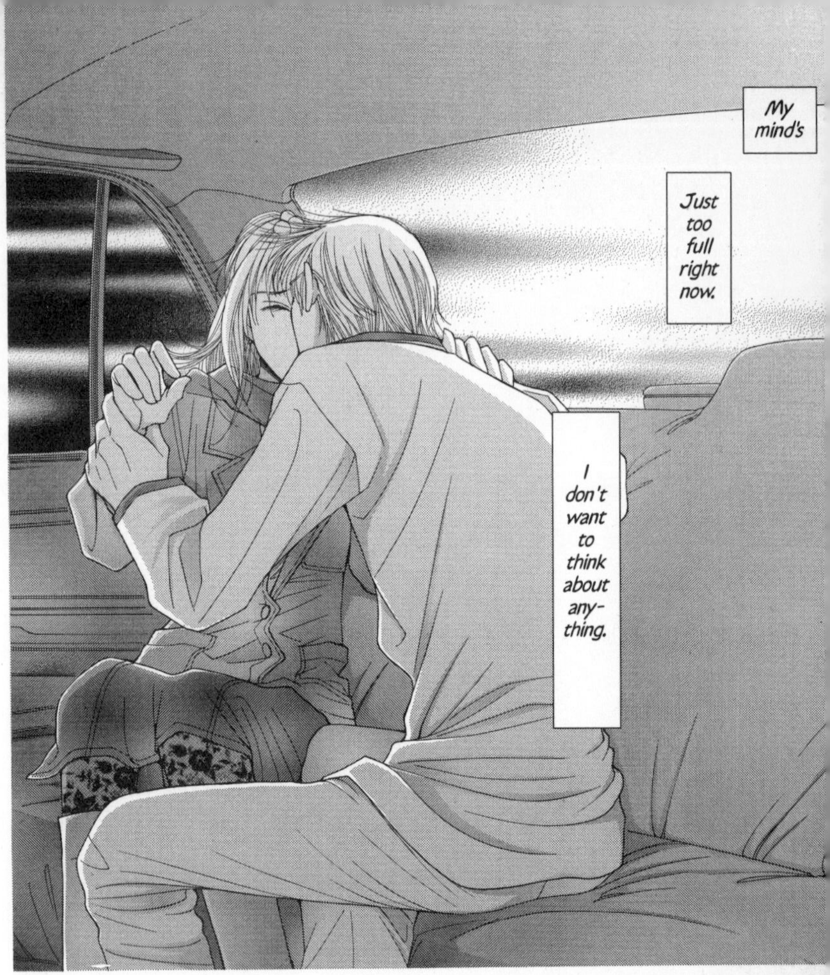
My mind's
Just too full right now.
I don't want to think about any-thing.

hot gimmick

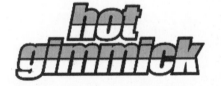

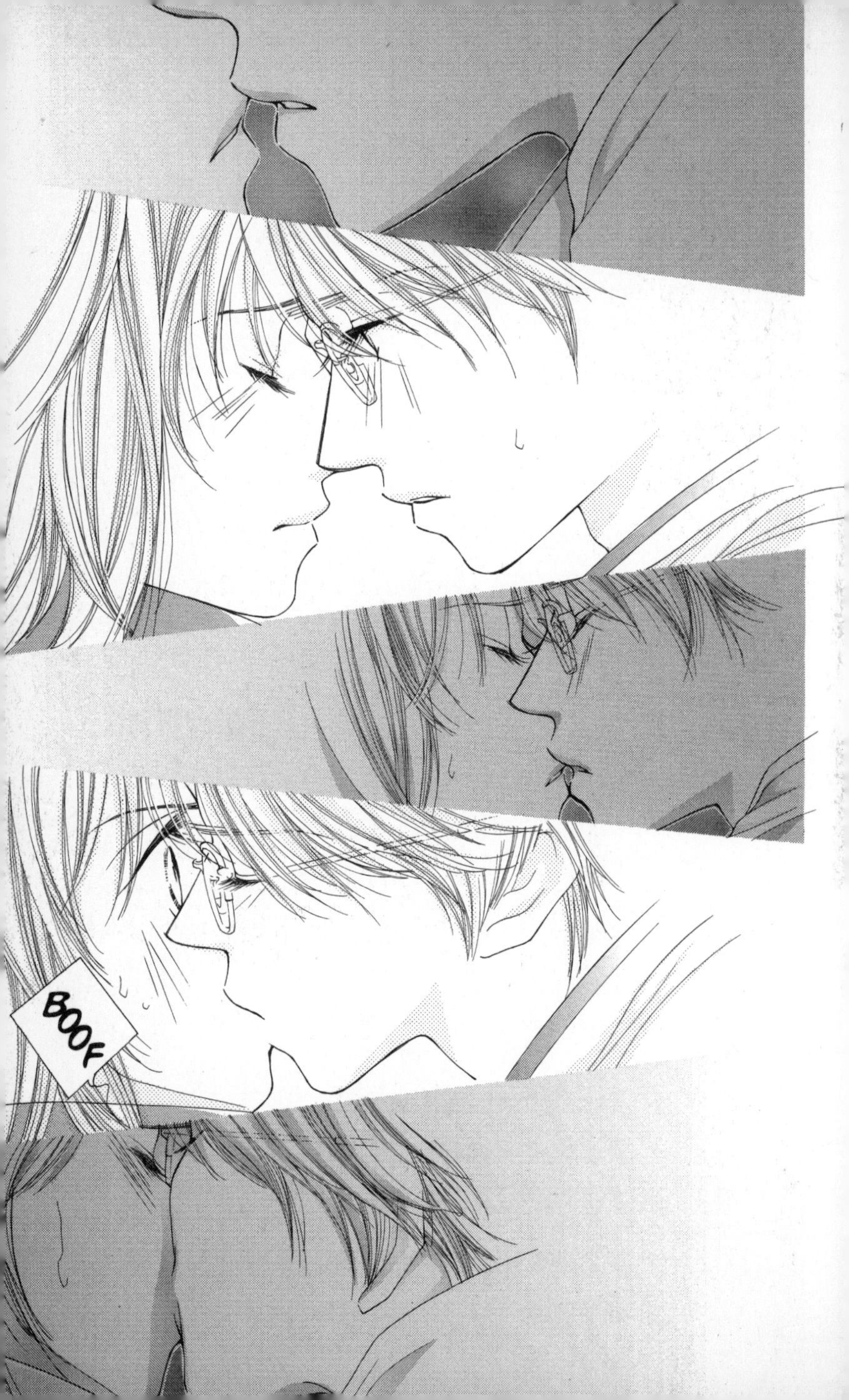
BOOF

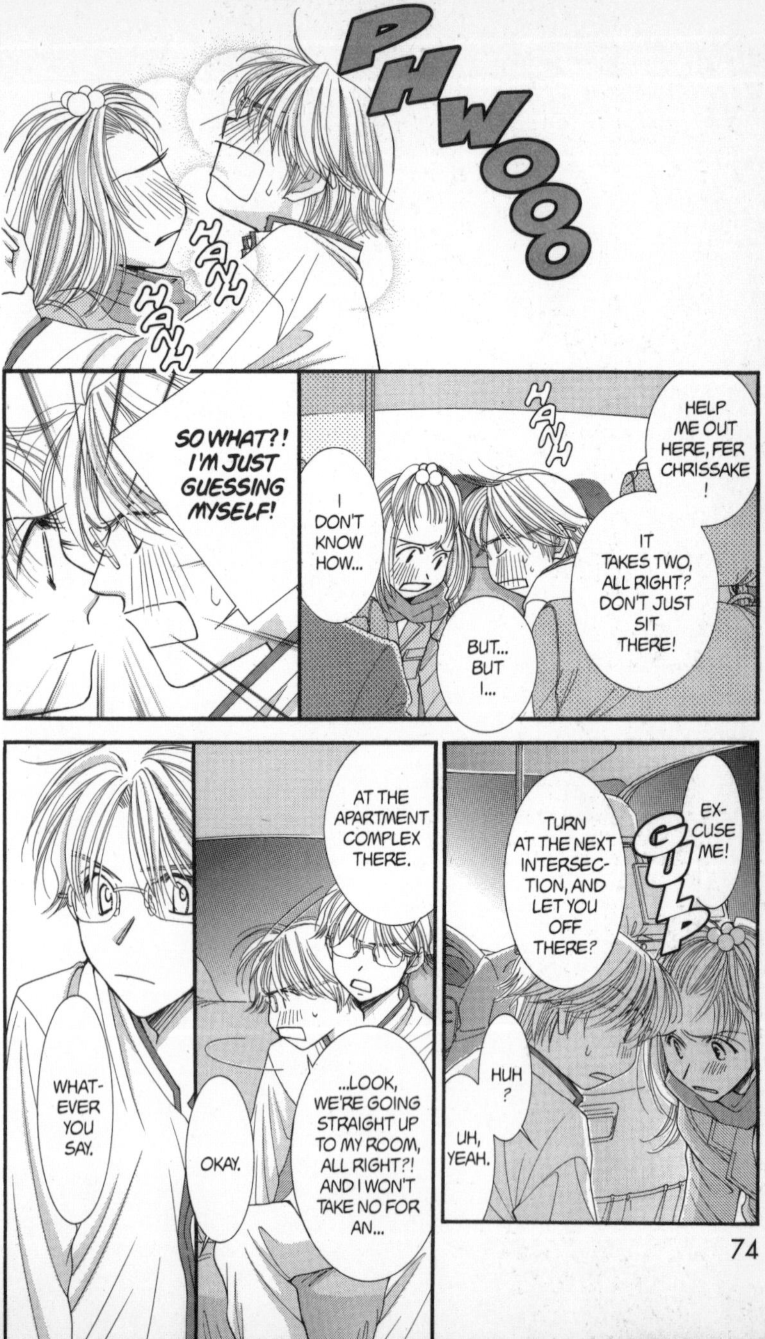
PHWOOO
HANH
HANH
HANH
HELP ME OUT HERE, FER CHRISSAKE!
I DON'T KNOW HOW...
IT TAKES TWO, ALL RIGHT? DON'T JUST SIT THERE!
BUT... BUT I...
SO WHAT?! I'M JUST GUESSING MYSELF!
EX-CUSE ME!
GULP
TURN AT THE NEXT INTERSEC-TION, AND LET YOU OFF THERE?
HUH?
UH, YEAH.
AT THE APARTMENT COMPLEX THERE.
...LOOK, WE'RE GOING STRAIGHT UP TO MY ROOM, ALL RIGHT?! AND I WON'T TAKE NO FOR AN...
OKAY.
WHAT-EVER YOU SAY.

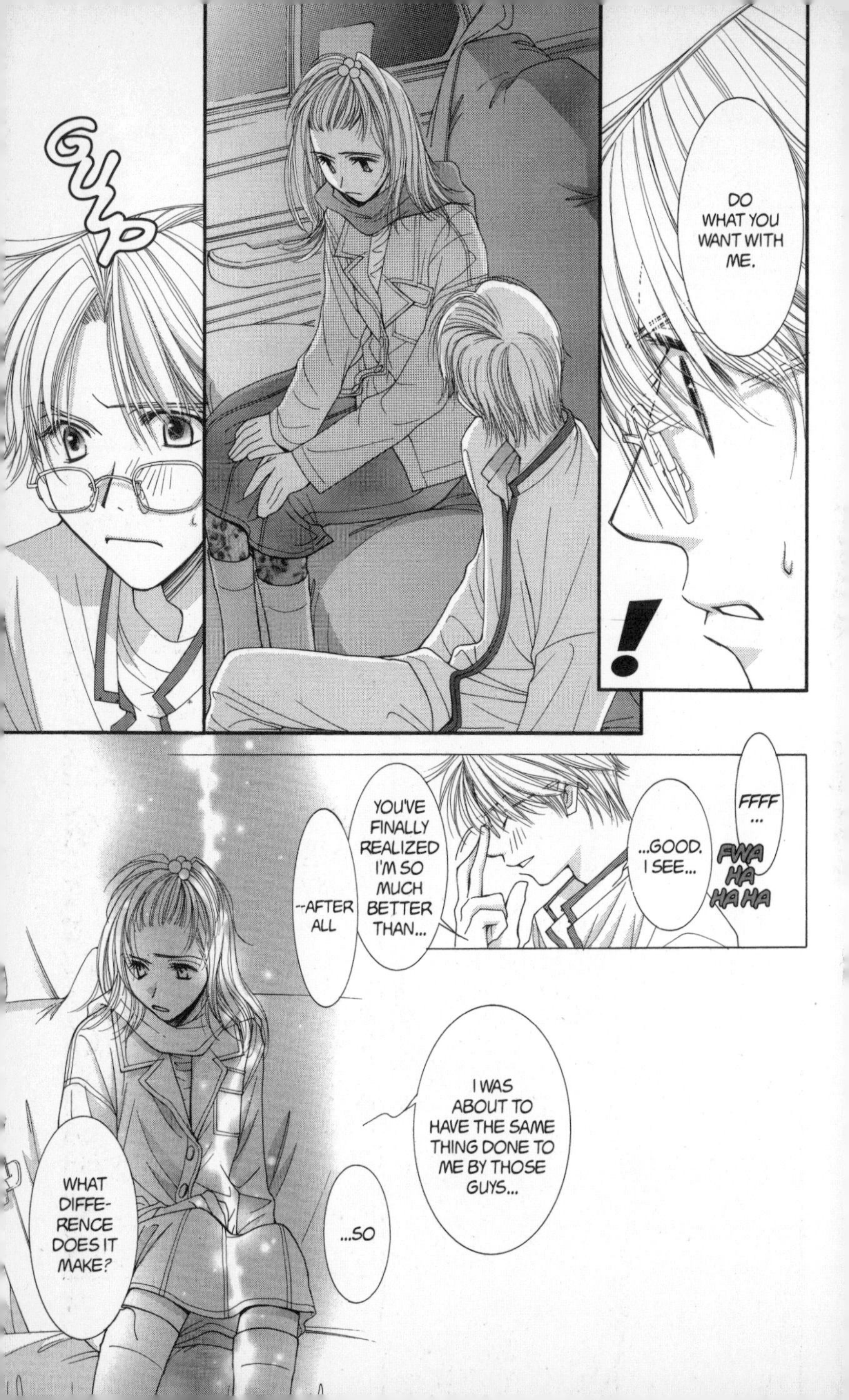
DO WHAT YOU WANT WITH ME.
!
GULP
FFFF...
FWA HA HA HA
...GOOD. I SEE...
YOU'VE FINALLY REALIZED I'M SO MUCH BETTER THAN...
--AFTER ALL
I WAS ABOUT TO HAVE THE SAME THING DONE TO ME BY THOSE GUYS...
...SO
WHAT DIFFE-RENCE DOES IT MAKE?

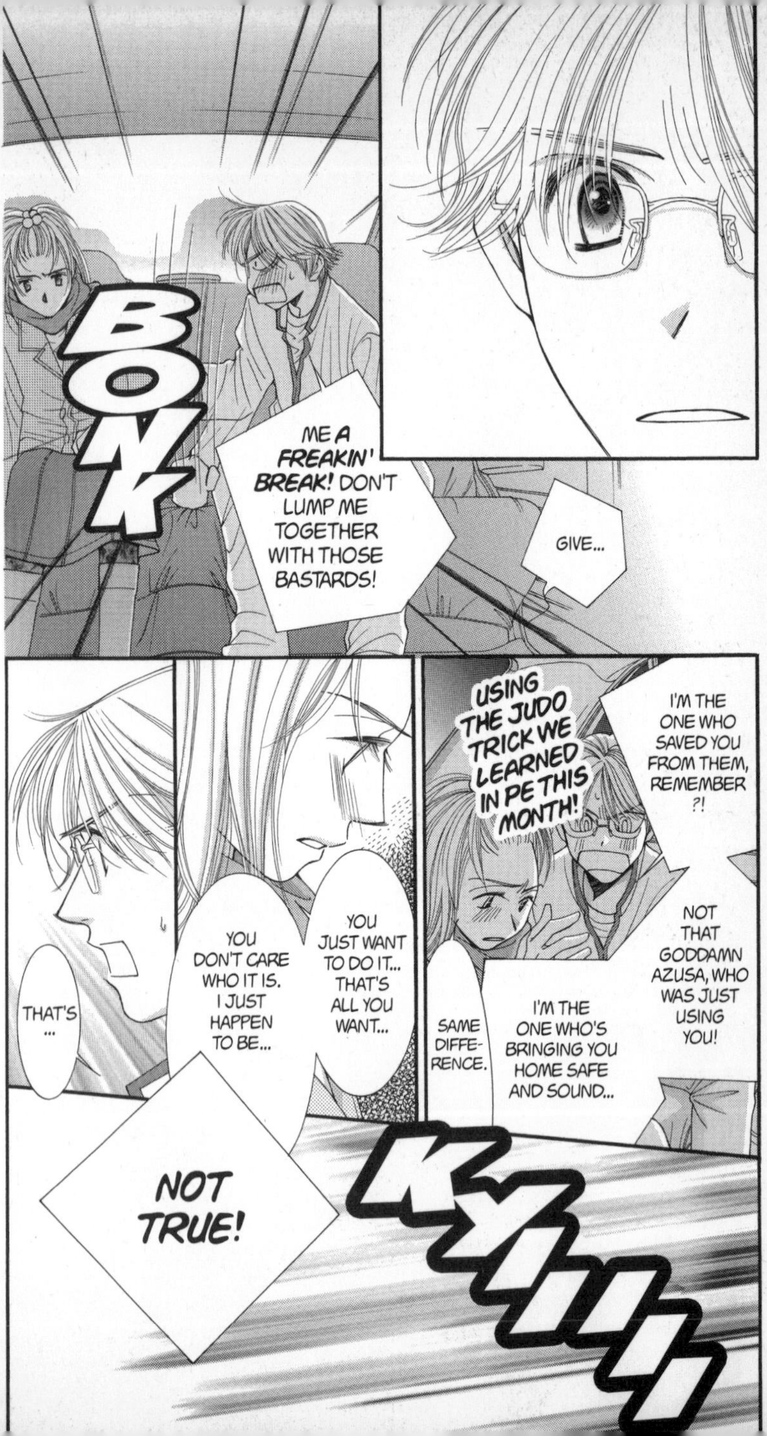
GIVE...
ME A FREAKIN' BREAK! DON'T LUMP ME TOGETHER WITH THOSE BASTARDS!
BONK
I'M THE ONE WHO SAVED YOU FROM THEM, REMEMBER ?!
USING THE JUDO TRICK WE LEARNED IN PE THIS MONTH!
NOT THAT GODDAMN AZUSA, WHO WAS JUST USING YOU!
I'M THE ONE WHO'S BRINGING YOU HOME SAFE AND SOUND...
SAME DIFFE- RENCE.
YOU JUST WANT TO DO IT... THAT'S ALL YOU WANT...
YOU DON'T CARE WHO IT IS. I JUST HAPPEN TO BE...
THAT'S ...
NOT TRUE!
KYIIII

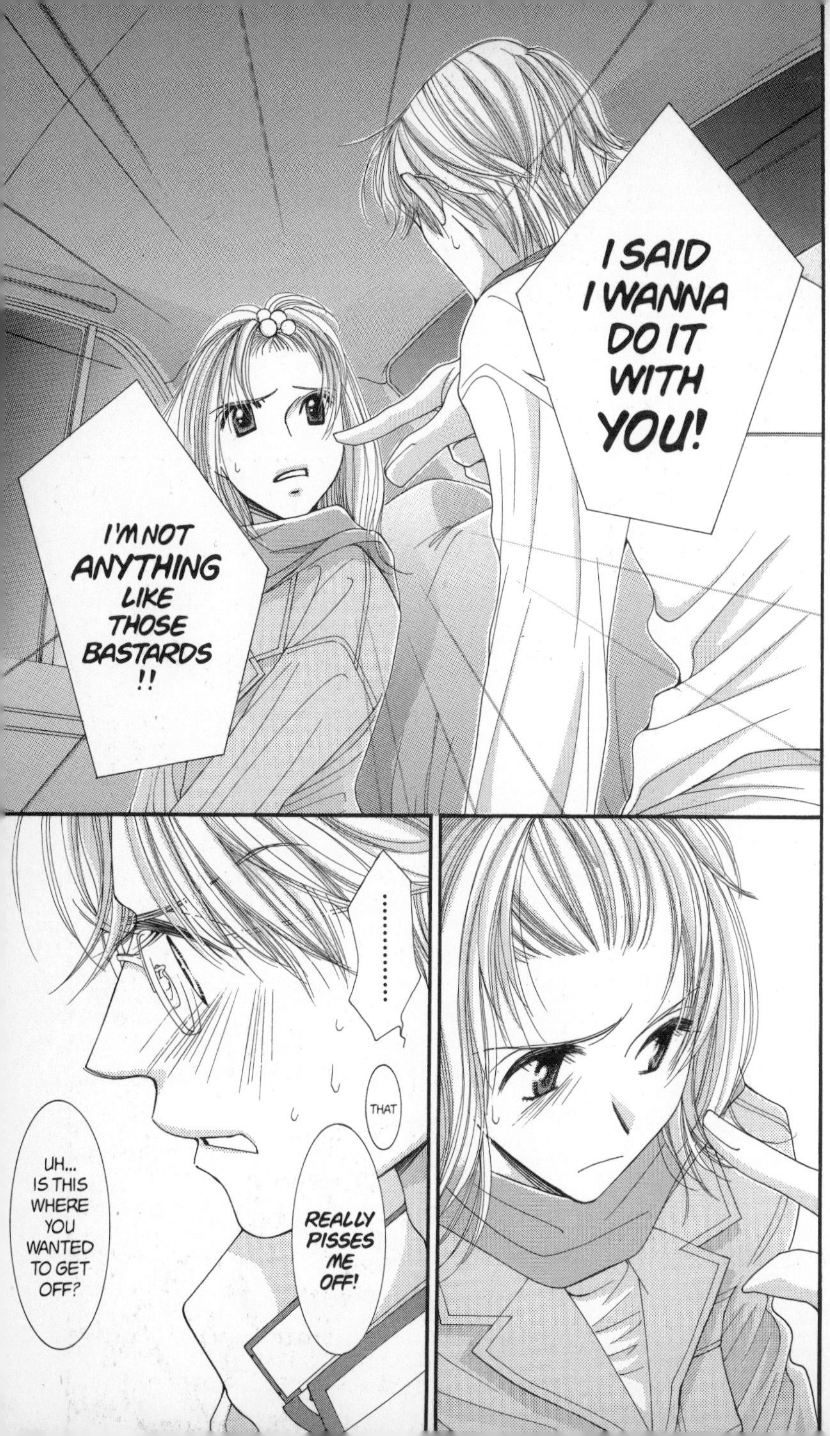
I SAID I WANNA DO IT WITH YOU!
I'M NOT ANYTHING LIKE THOSE BASTARDS!!
......
THAT
REALLY PISSES ME OFF!
UH... IS THIS WHERE YOU WANTED TO GET OFF?

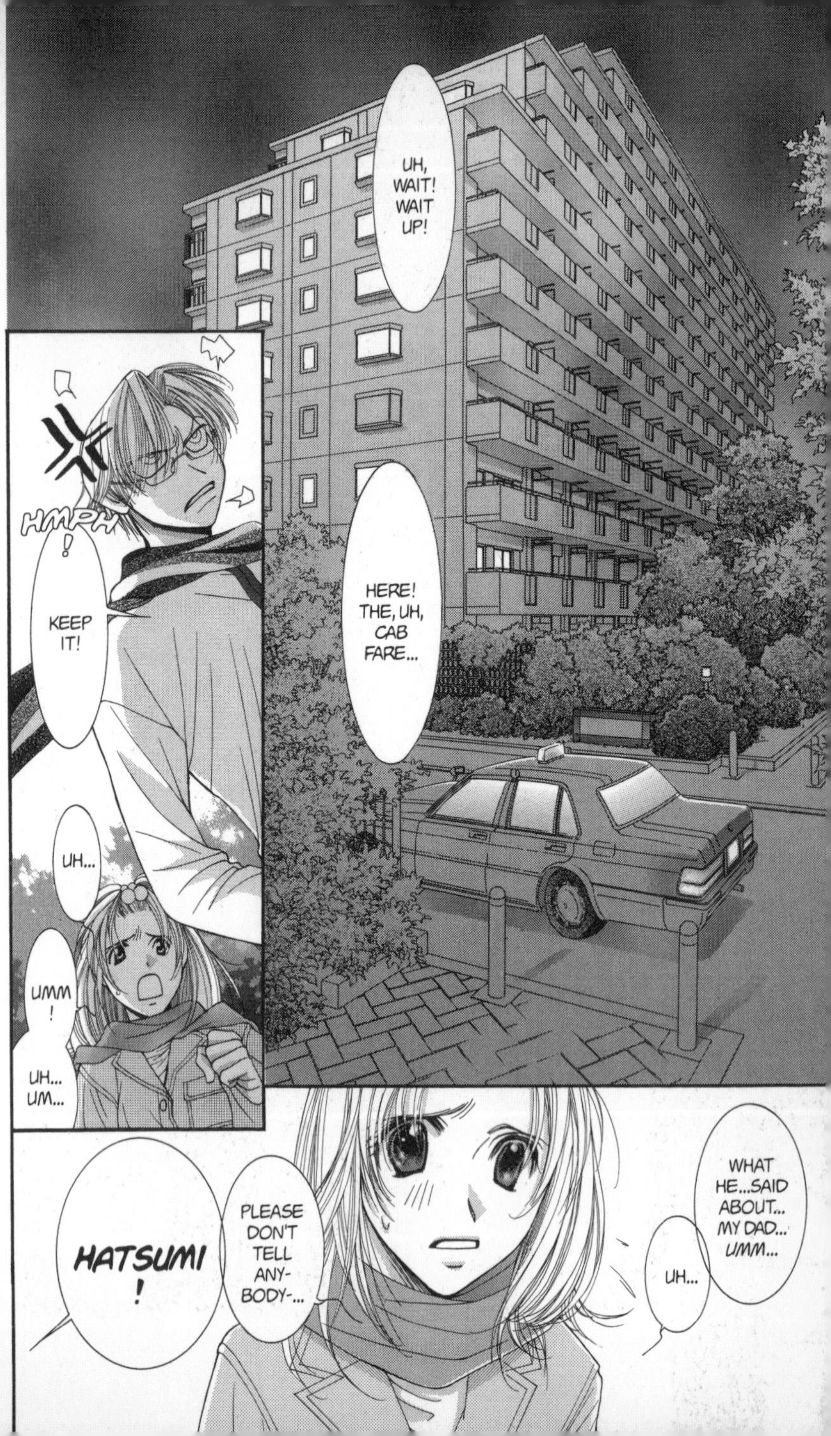
UH, WAIT! WAIT UP!
HERE! THE, UH, CAB FARE...
HMPH!
KEEP IT!
UH...
UMM!
UH... UM...
WHAT HE...SAID ABOUT... MY DAD... UMM...
UH...
PLEASE DON'T TELL ANY-BODY-...
HATSUMI!

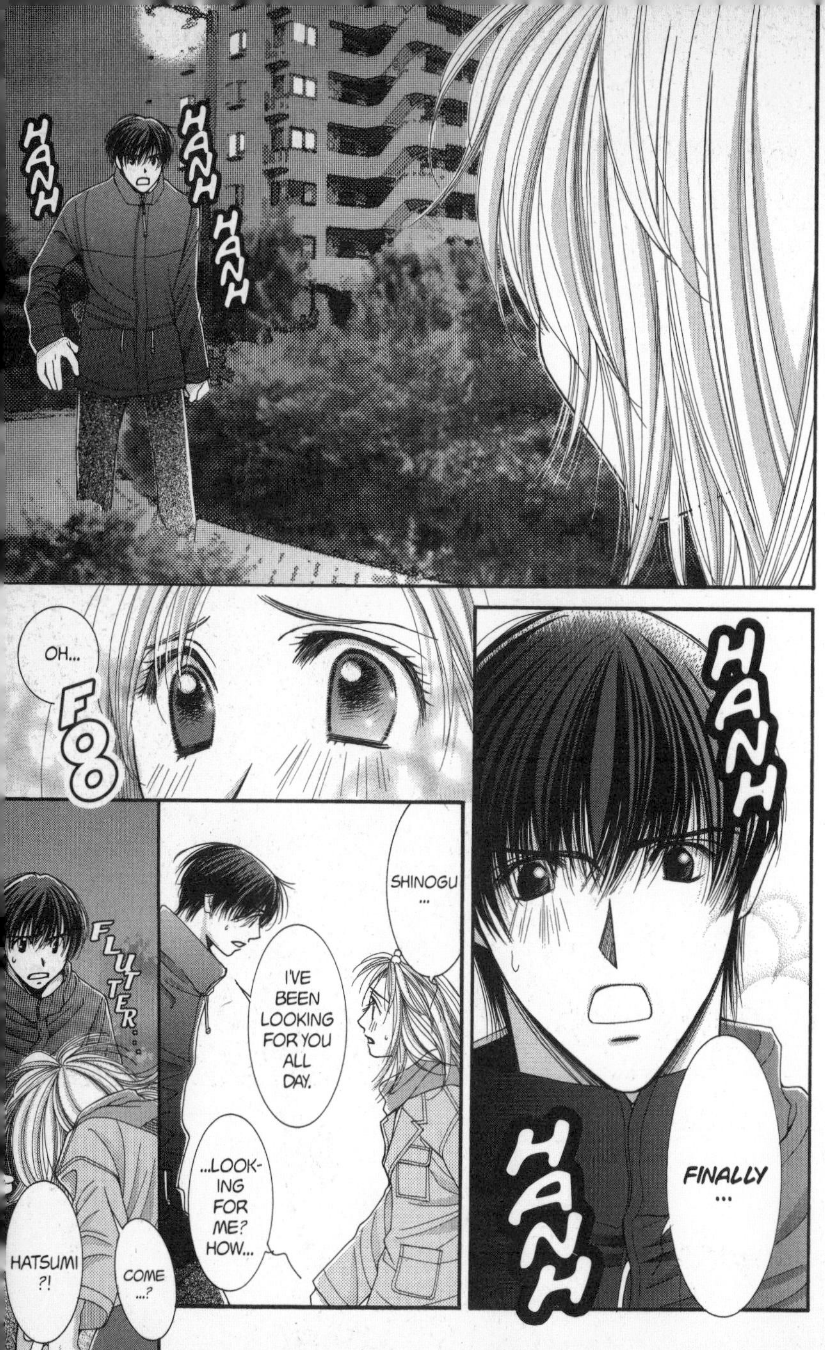
HANH HANH
HANH HANH
HANH HANH
FINALLY...
HANH HANH
OH...
SHINOGU...
I'VE BEEN LOOKING FOR YOU ALL DAY.
...LOOKING FOR ME? HOW...
COME...?
FLUTTER...
HATSUMI?!

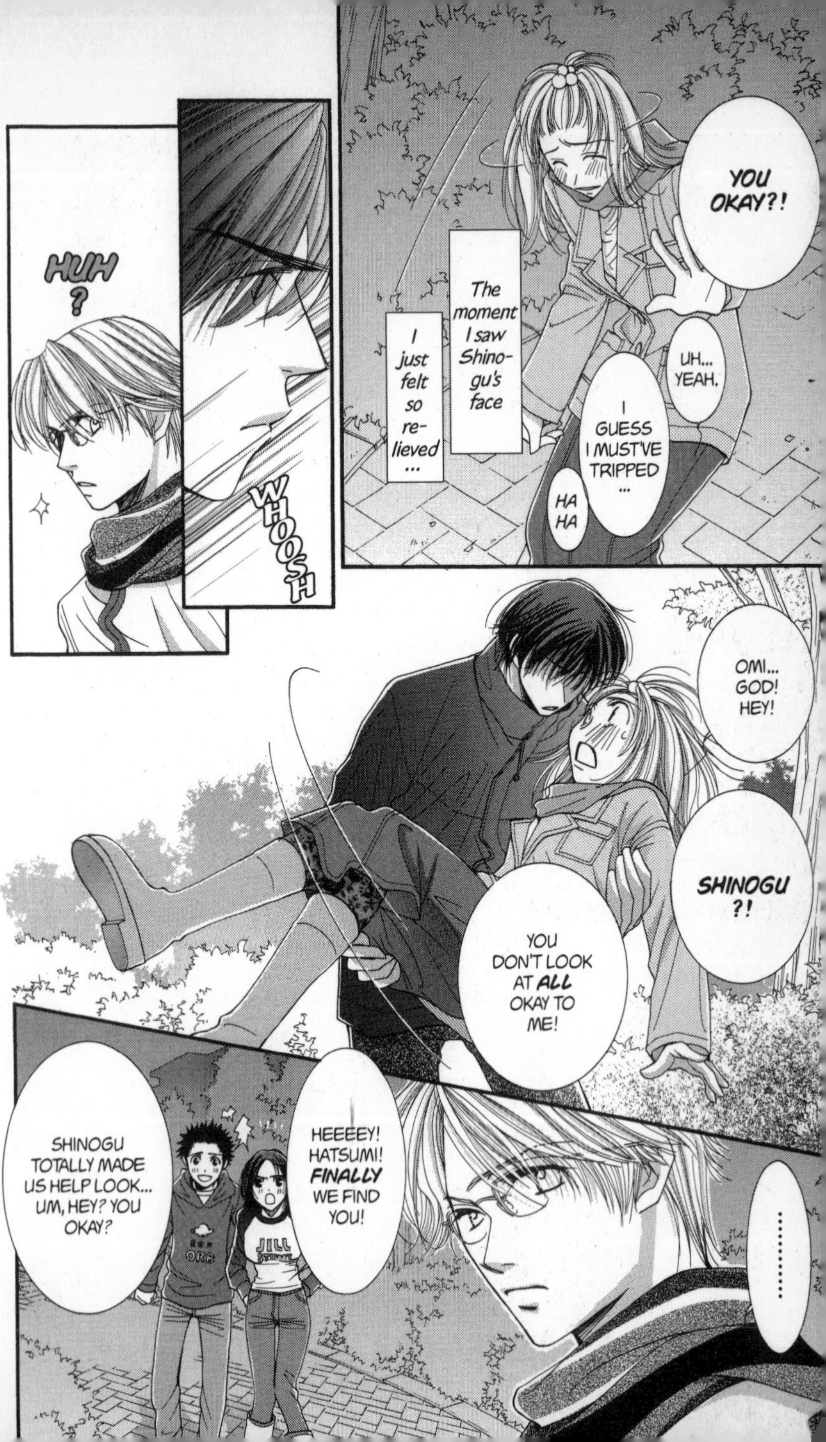
YOU OKAY?!
UH... YEAH.
I GUESS I MUST'VE TRIPPED ...
HA HA
The moment I saw Shinogu's face
I just felt so relieved ...
WHOOSH
HUH ?
OMI... GOD! HEY!
SHINOGU ?!
YOU DON'T LOOK AT ALL OKAY TO ME!
......
HEEEEY! HATSUMI! FINALLY WE FIND YOU!
SHINOGU TOTALLY MADE US HELP LOOK... UM, HEY? YOU OKAY?

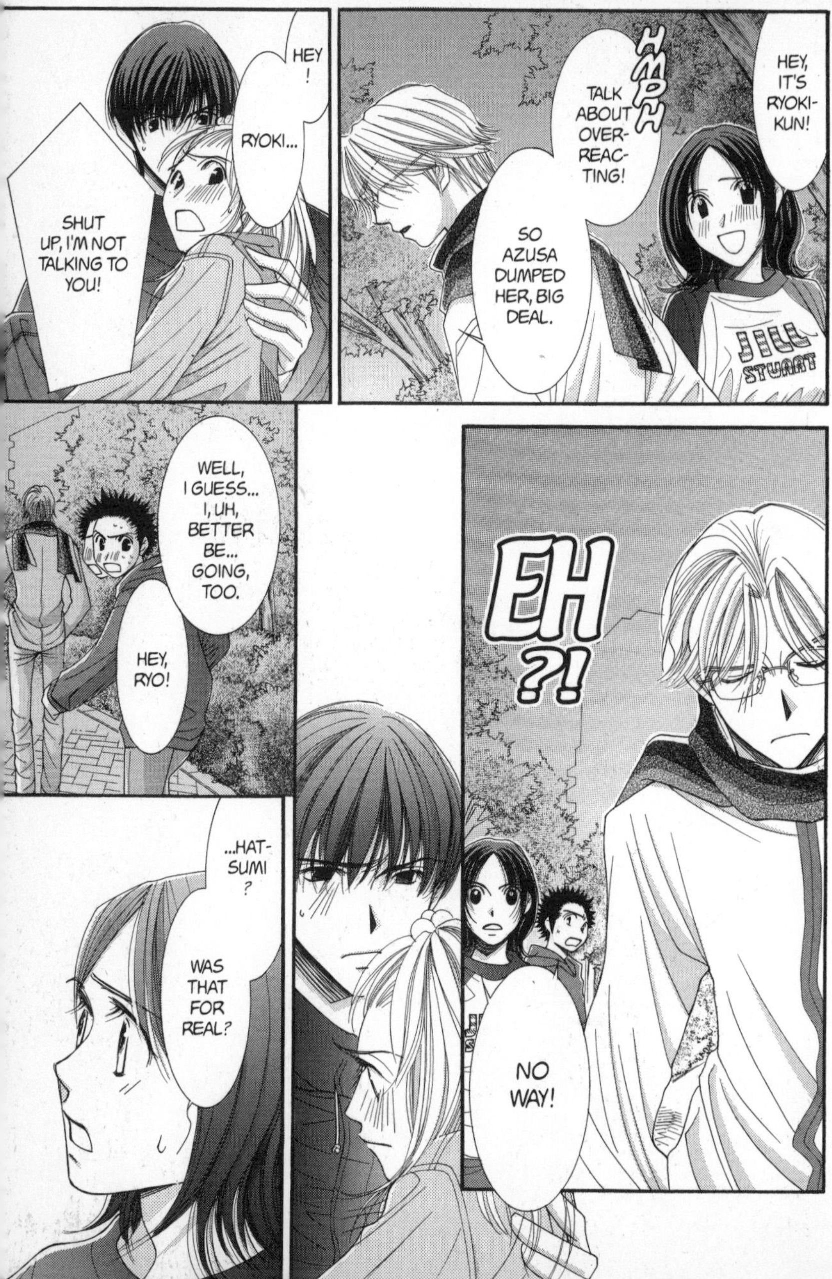
HEY, IT'S RYOKI-KUN!
JILL STUART
HMPH
TALK ABOUT OVER-REACTING!
SO AZUSA DUMPED HER, BIG DEAL.
HEY!
RYOKI...
SHUT UP, I'M NOT TALKING TO YOU!
EH?!
NO WAY!
WELL, I GUESS... I, UH, BETTER BE... GOING, TOO.
HEY, RYO!
...HAT-SUMI?
WAS THAT FOR REAL?

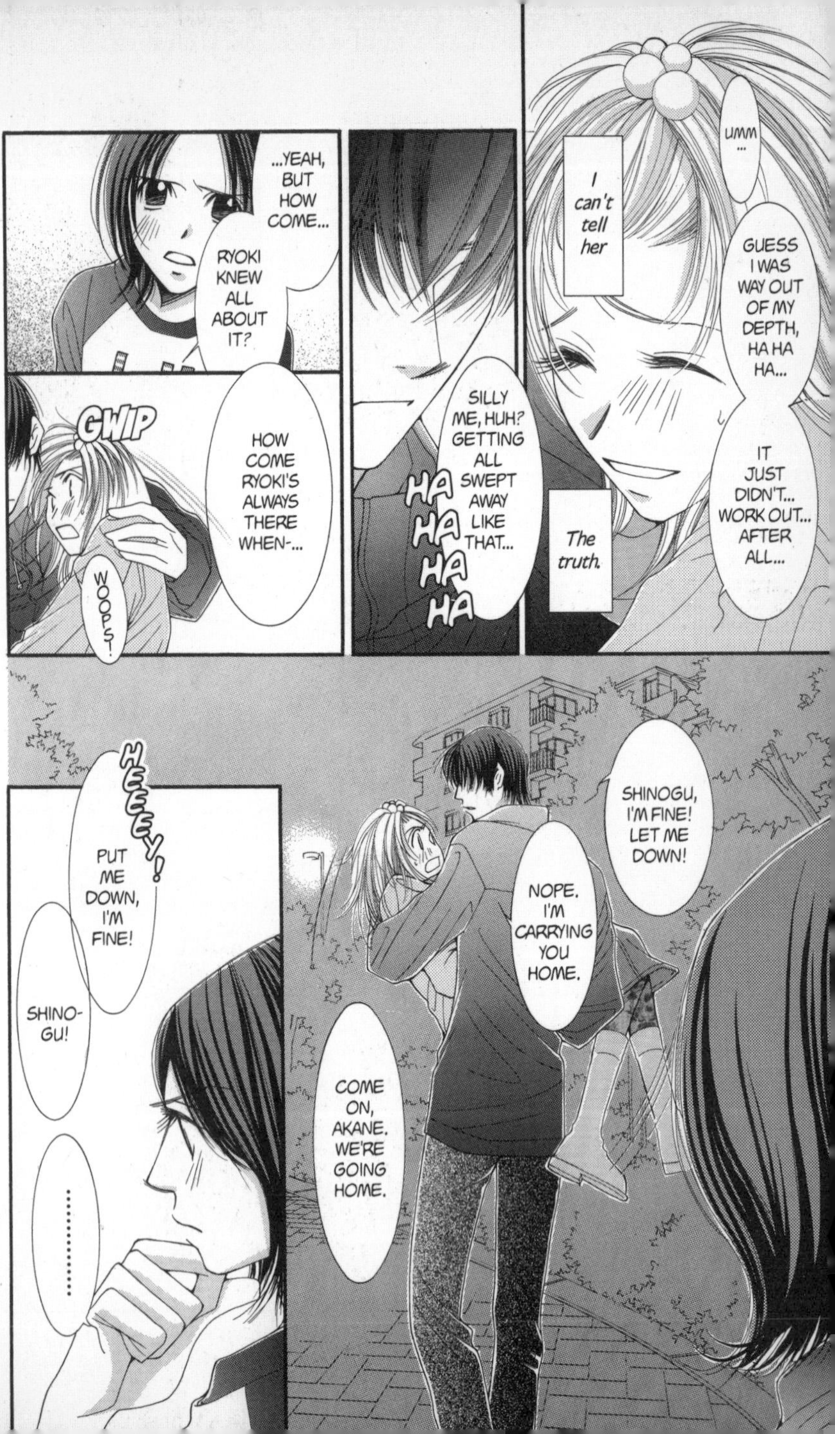
UMM...
GUESS I WAS WAY OUT OF MY DEPTH, HA HA HA...
I can't tell her
IT JUST DIDN'T... WORK OUT... AFTER ALL...
The truth.
SILLY ME, HUH? GETTING ALL SWEPT AWAY LIKE THAT...
HA HA HA HA
...YEAH, BUT HOW COME...
RYOKI KNEW ALL ABOUT IT?
GWIP
HOW COME RYOKI'S ALWAYS THERE WHEN-...
WOOPS!
SHINOGU, I'M FINE! LET ME DOWN!
NOPE. I'M CARRYING YOU HOME.
HEEEY!
PUT ME DOWN, I'M FINE!
COME ON, AKANE. WE'RE GOING HOME.
SHINO-GU!
....

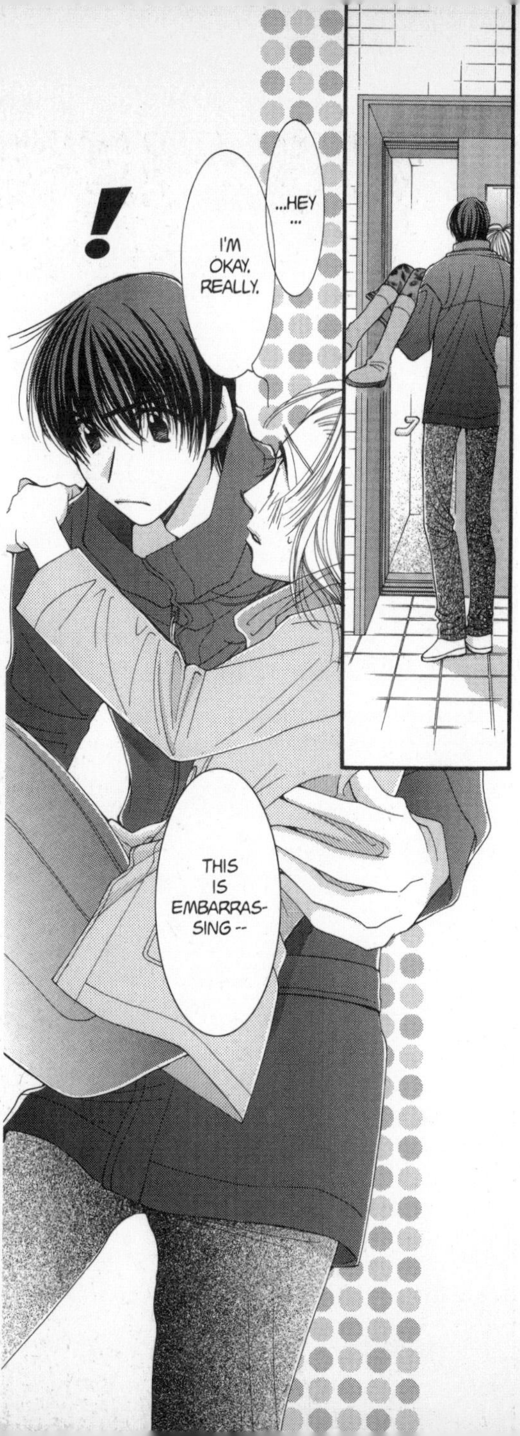
...HEY ...
I'M OKAY. REALLY.
!
THIS IS EMBARRAS-SING --

hotgimmick

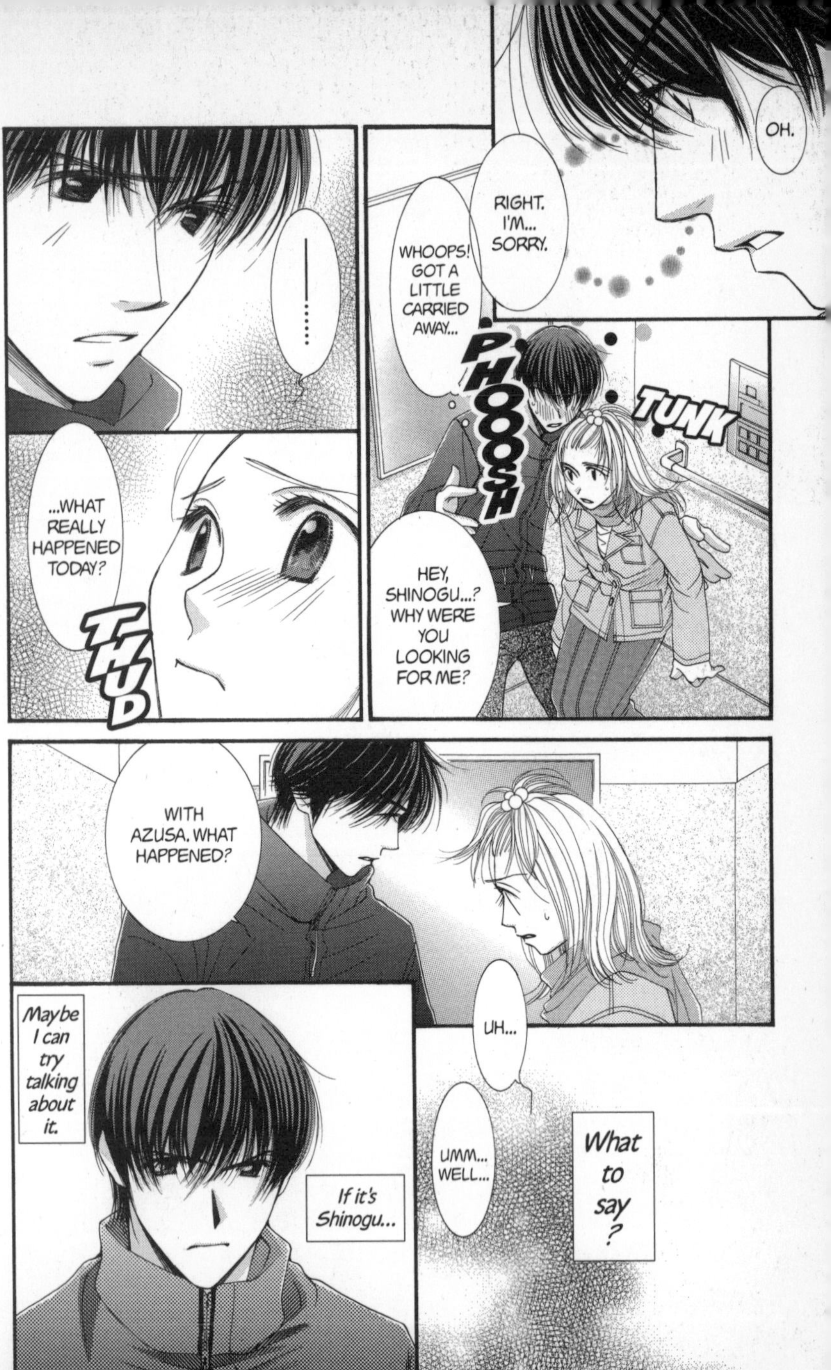
OH.
RIGHT. I'M... SORRY.
WHOOPS! GOT A LITTLE CARRIED AWAY...
PHOOOSH
TUNK
HEY, SHINOGU...? WHY WERE YOU LOOKING FOR ME?
......
...WHAT REALLY HAPPENED TODAY?
THUD
WITH AZUSA. WHAT HAPPENED?
UH...
What to say?
UMM... WELL...
Maybe I can try talking about it.
If it's Shinogu...

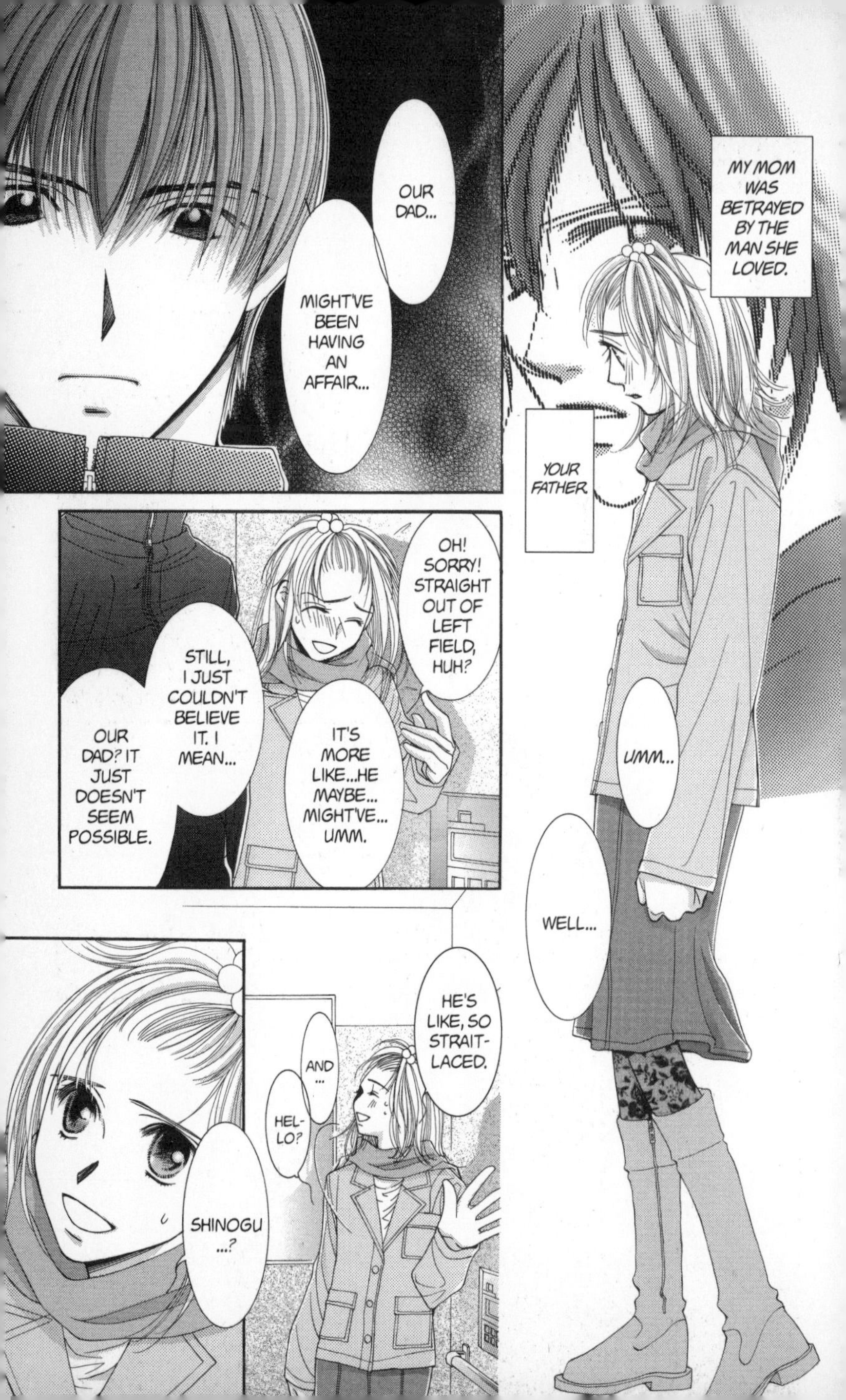
MY MOM WAS BETRAYED BY THE MAN SHE LOVED.
YOUR FATHER.
UMM...
WELL...
OUR DAD...
MIGHT'VE BEEN HAVING AN AFFAIR...
OH! SORRY! STRAIGHT OUT OF LEFT FIELD, HUH?
IT'S MORE LIKE...HE MAYBE... MIGHT'VE... UMM.
STILL, I JUST COULDN'T BELIEVE IT. I MEAN...
OUR DAD? IT JUST DOESN'T SEEM POSSIBLE.
HE'S LIKE, SO STRAIT-LACED.
AND ...
HEL-LO?
SHINOGU ...?

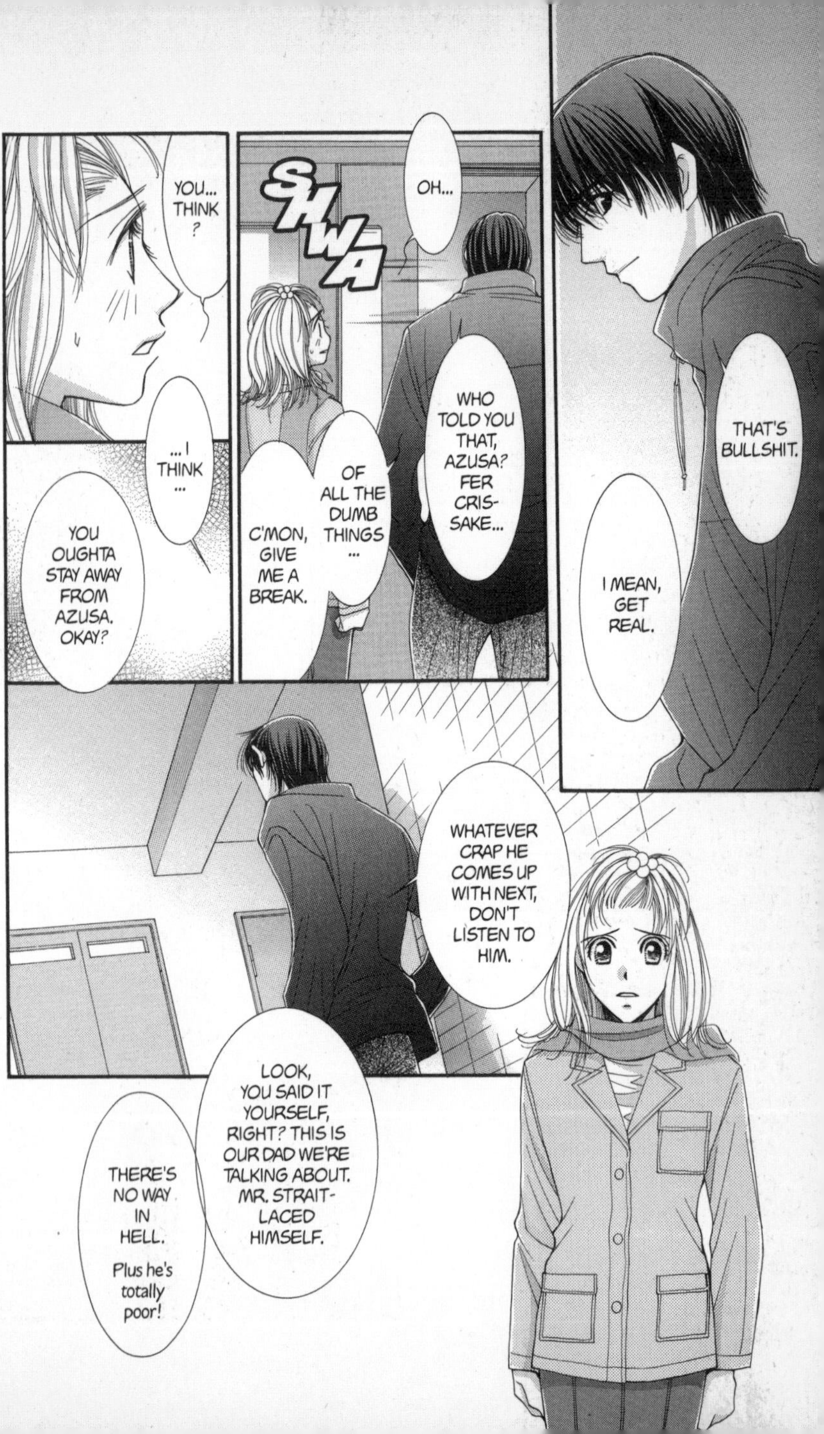
THAT'S BULLSHIT.
I MEAN, GET REAL.
OH...
SHWA
WHO TOLD YOU THAT, AZUSA? FER CRIS-SAKE...
OF ALL THE DUMB THINGS...
C'MON, GIVE ME A BREAK.
YOU... THINK?
...I THINK...
YOU OUGHTA STAY AWAY FROM AZUSA. OKAY?
WHATEVER CRAP HE COMES UP WITH NEXT, DON'T LISTEN TO HIM.
LOOK, YOU SAID IT YOURSELF, RIGHT? THIS IS OUR DAD WE'RE TALKING ABOUT. MR. STRAIT-LACED HIMSELF.
THERE'S NO WAY IN HELL.
Plus he's totally poor!

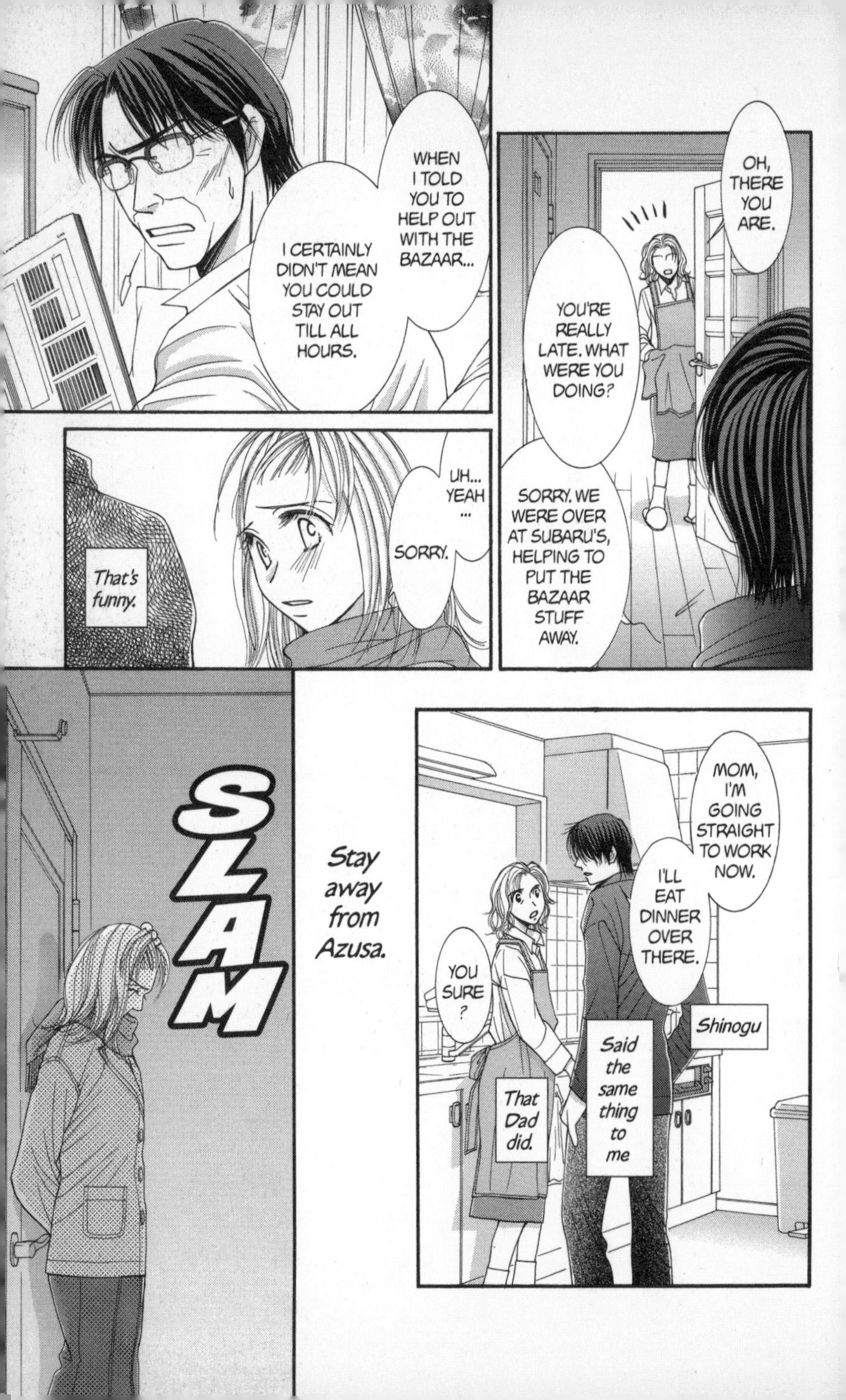
OH, THERE YOU ARE.
YOU'RE REALLY LATE. WHAT WERE YOU DOING?
SORRY. WE WERE OVER AT SUBARU'S, HELPING TO PUT THE BAZAAR STUFF AWAY.
WHEN I TOLD YOU TO HELP OUT WITH THE BAZAAR...
I CERTAINLY DIDN'T MEAN YOU COULD STAY OUT TILL ALL HOURS.
UH... YEAH ...
SORRY.
That's funny.
MOM, I'M GOING STRAIGHT TO WORK NOW.
I'LL EAT DINNER OVER THERE.
YOU SURE?
Shinogu
Said the same thing to me
That Dad did.
Stay away from Azusa.
SLAM

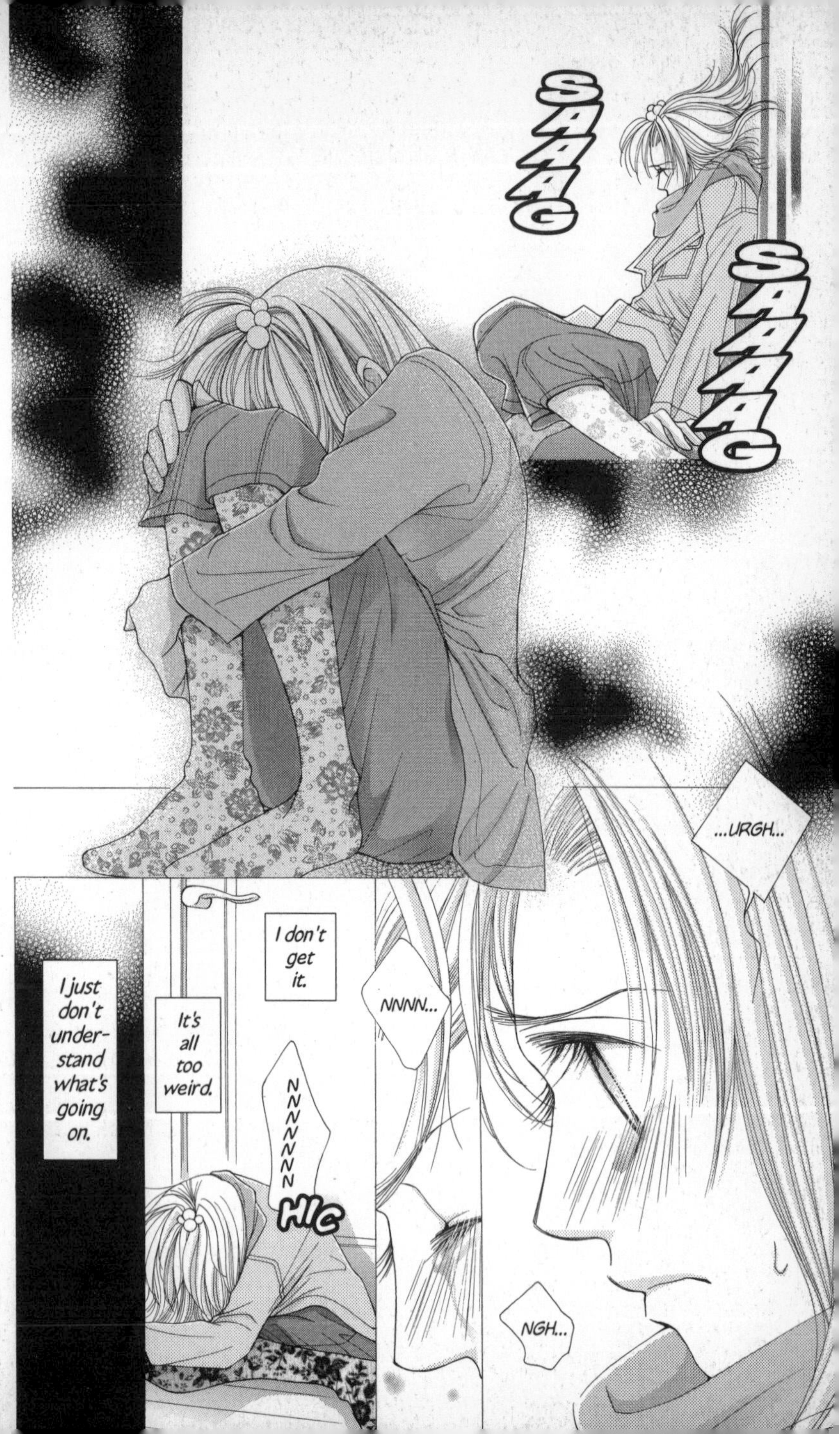
SAAAAG
SAAAG
...URGH...
NNNN...
NGH...
I don't get it.
It's all too weird.
NNNNNNNN
HIC
I just don't under-stand what's going on.

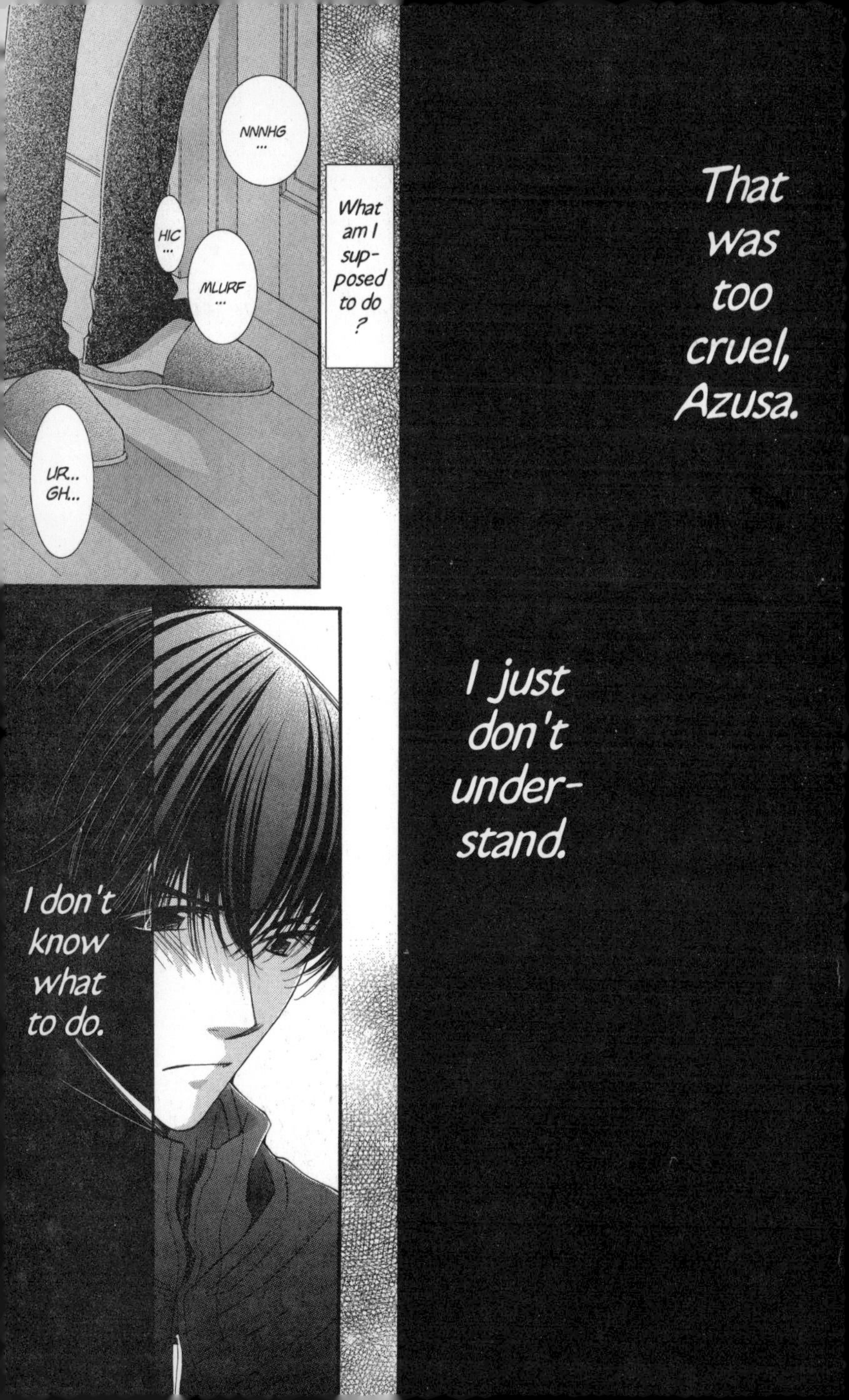
That was too cruel, Azusa.
I just don't understand.
What am I sup-posed to do?
NNNHG...
HIC...
MLURF...
UR... GH...
I don't know what to do.

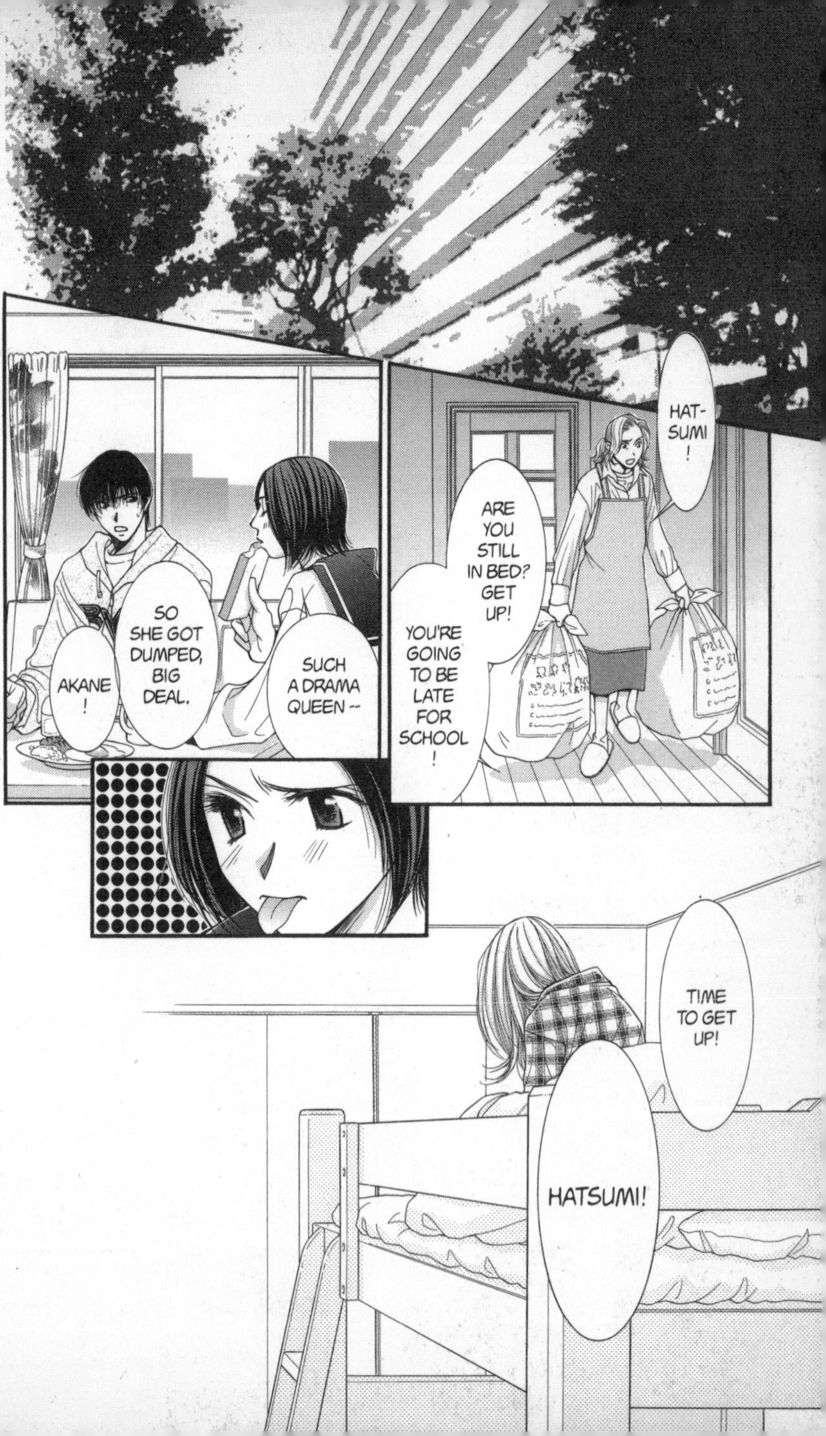
HAT-SUMI!
ARE YOU STILL IN BED? GET UP!
YOU'RE GOING TO BE LATE FOR SCHOOL!
SUCH A DRAMA QUEEN --
SO SHE GOT DUMPED, BIG DEAL.
AKANE!
TIME TO GET UP!
HATSUMI!

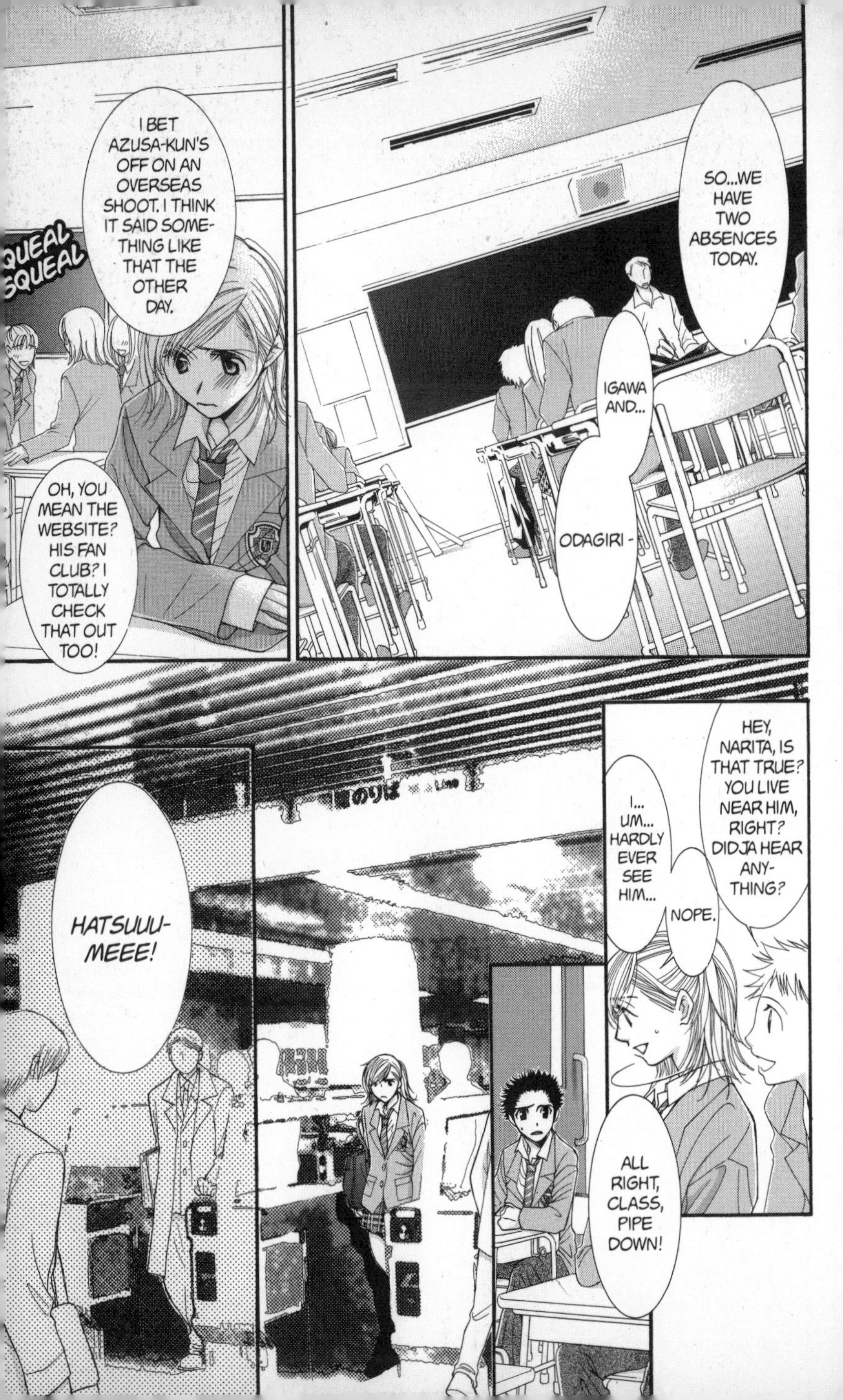
SO...WE HAVE TWO ABSENCES TODAY.
IGAWA AND...
ODAGIRI -
I BET AZUSA-KUN'S OFF ON AN OVERSEAS SHOOT. I THINK IT SAID SOME-THING LIKE THAT THE OTHER DAY.
SQUEAL SQUEAL
OH, YOU MEAN THE WEBSITE? HIS FAN CLUB? I TOTALLY CHECK THAT OUT TOO!
HEY, NARITA, IS THAT TRUE? YOU LIVE NEAR HIM, RIGHT? DIDJA HEAR ANY-THING?
NOPE.
I... UM... HARDLY EVER SEE HIM...
ALL RIGHT, CLASS, PIPE DOWN!
HATSUUU-MEEE!

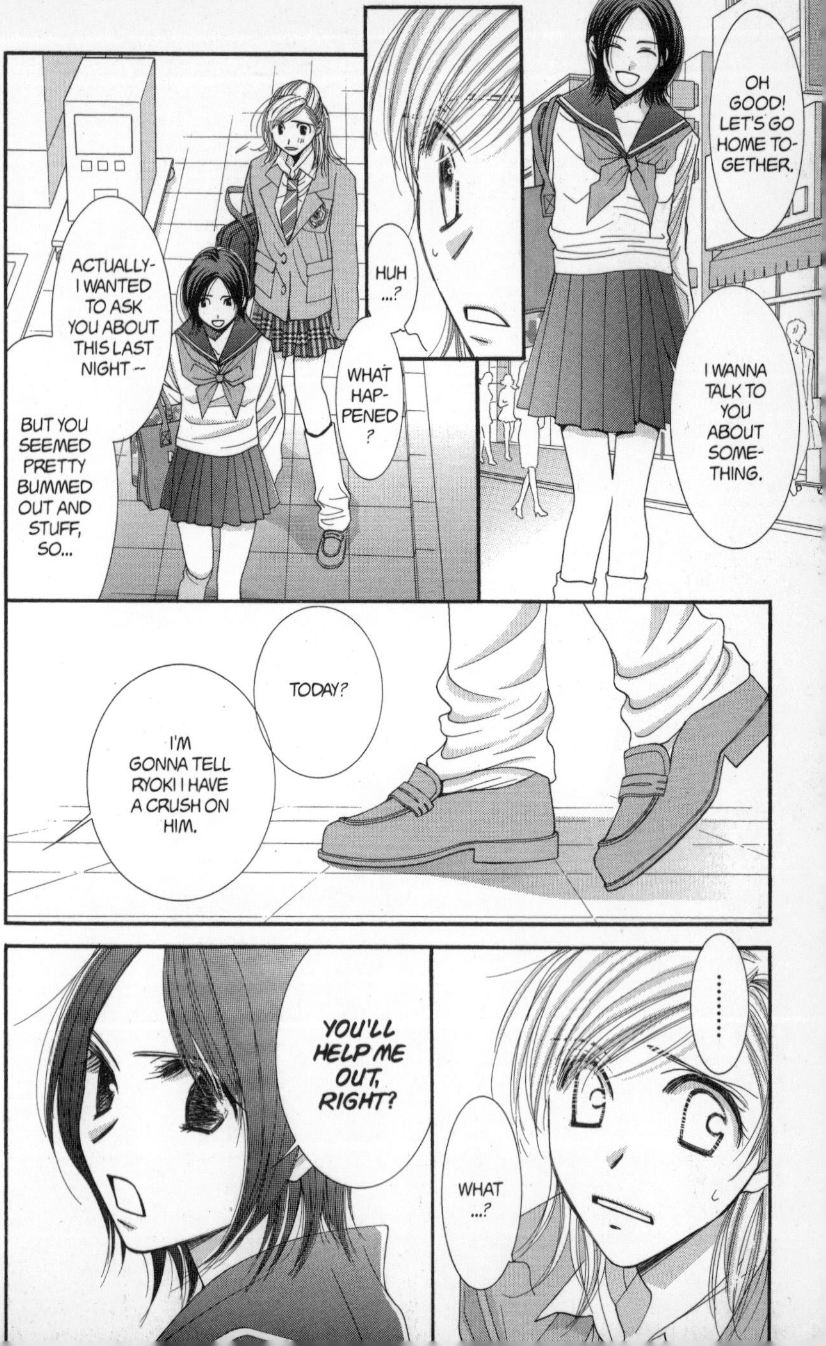
OH GOOD! LET'S GO HOME TOGETHER.
I WANNA TALK TO YOU ABOUT SOMETHING.
HUH ...?
WHAT HAPPENED ?
ACTUALLY- I WANTED TO ASK YOU ABOUT THIS LAST NIGHT --
BUT YOU SEEMED PRETTY BUMMED OUT AND STUFF, SO...
TODAY?
I'M GONNA TELL RYOKI I HAVE A CRUSH ON HIM.
......
WHAT ...?
YOU'LL HELP ME OUT, RIGHT?

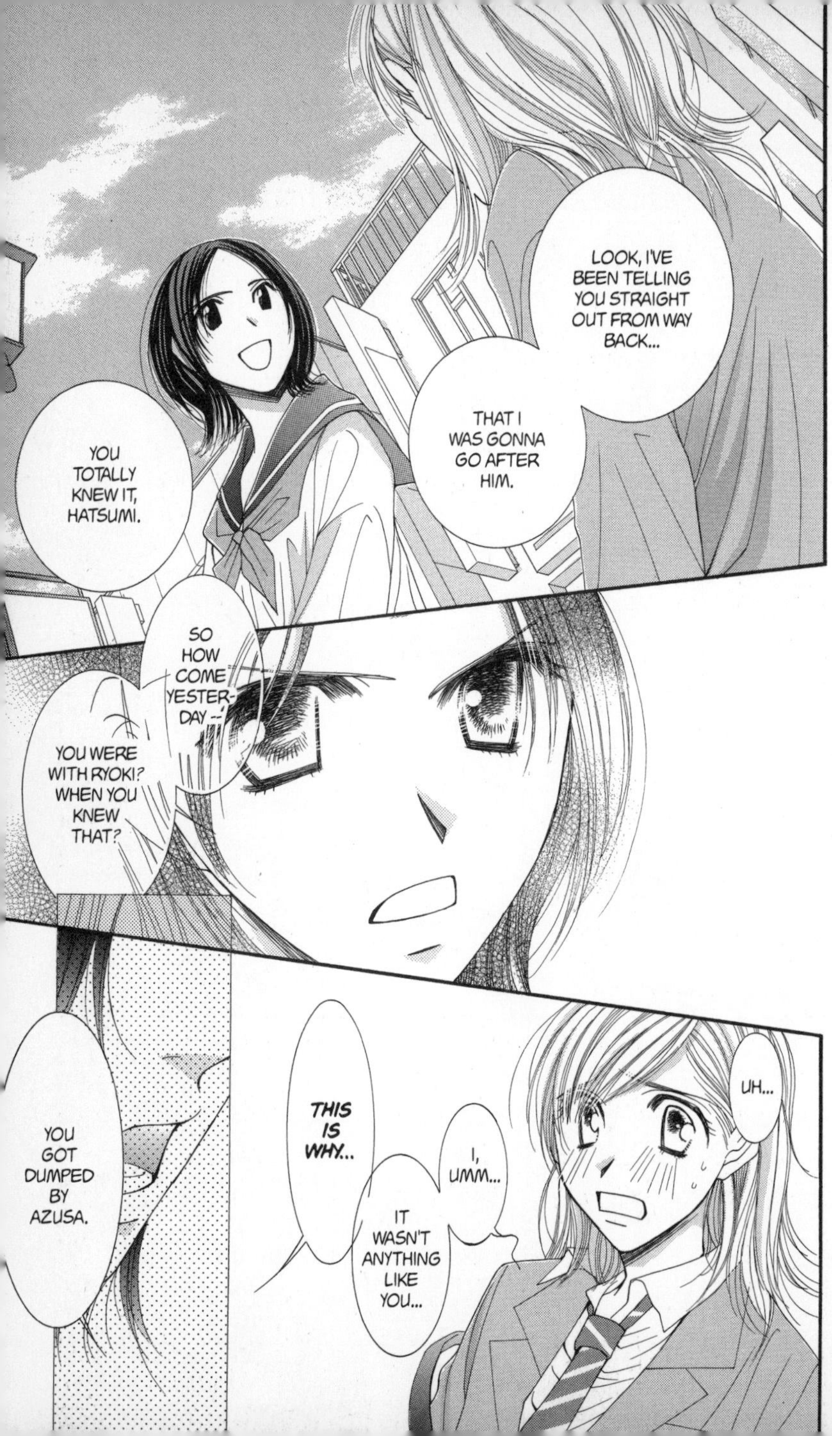
LOOK, I'VE BEEN TELLING YOU STRAIGHT OUT FROM WAY BACK...
THAT I WAS GONNA GO AFTER HIM.
YOU TOTALLY KNEW IT, HATSUMI.
SO HOW COME YESTER-DAY --
YOU WERE WITH RYOKI? WHEN YOU KNEW THAT?
UH...
I, UMM...
IT WASN'T ANYTHING LIKE YOU...
THIS IS WHY...
YOU GOT DUMPED BY AZUSA.

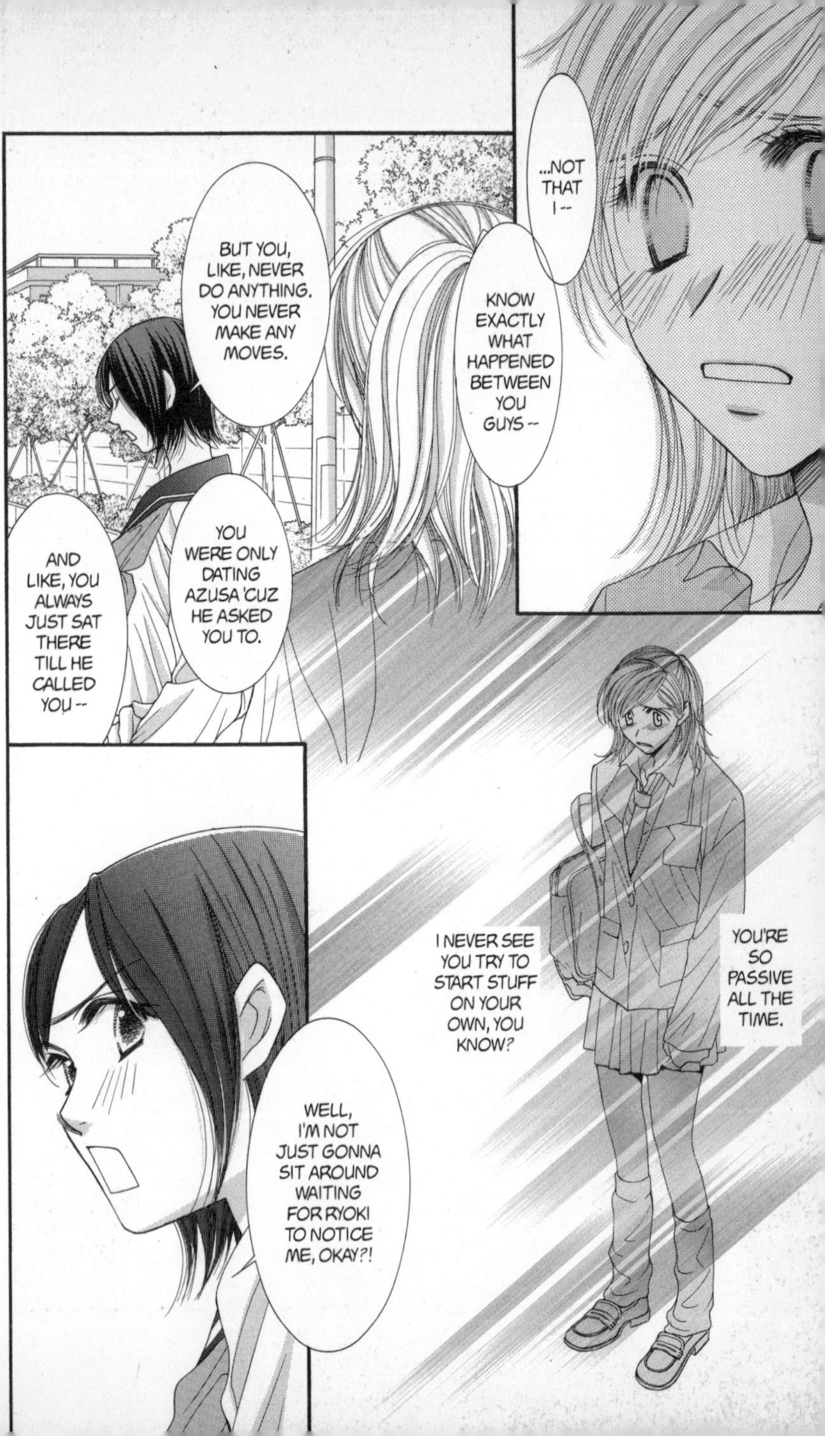
...NOT THAT I --
KNOW EXACTLY WHAT HAPPENED BETWEEN YOU GUYS --
BUT YOU, LIKE, NEVER DO ANYTHING. YOU NEVER MAKE ANY MOVES.
YOU WERE ONLY DATING AZUSA 'CUZ HE ASKED YOU TO.
AND LIKE, YOU ALWAYS JUST SAT THERE TILL HE CALLED YOU --
YOU'RE SO PASSIVE ALL THE TIME.
I NEVER SEE YOU TRY TO START STUFF ON YOUR OWN, YOU KNOW?
WELL, I'M NOT JUST GONNA SIT AROUND WAITING FOR RYOKI TO NOTICE ME, OKAY?!

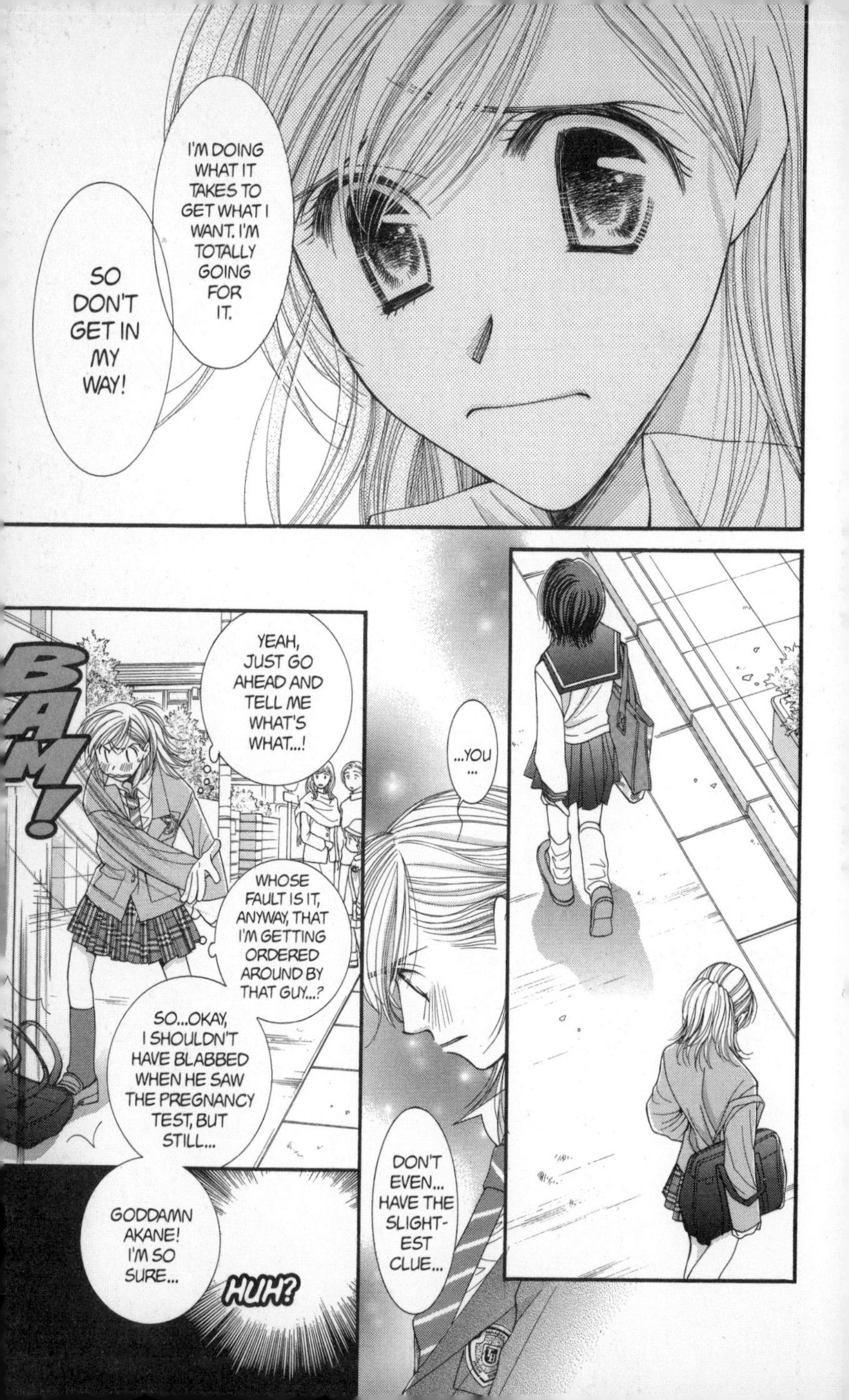
I'M DOING WHAT IT TAKES TO GET WHAT I WANT. I'M TOTALLY GOING FOR IT.
SO DON'T GET IN MY WAY!
...YOU ...
DON'T EVEN... HAVE THE SLIGHT-EST CLUE...
YEAH, JUST GO AHEAD AND TELL ME WHAT'S WHAT...!
BAM!
WHOSE FAULT IS IT, ANYWAY, THAT I'M GETTING ORDERED AROUND BY THAT GUY...?
SO...OKAY, I SHOULDN'T HAVE BLABBED WHEN HE SAW THE PREGNANCY TEST, BUT STILL...
GODDAMN AKANE! I'M SO SURE...
HUH?

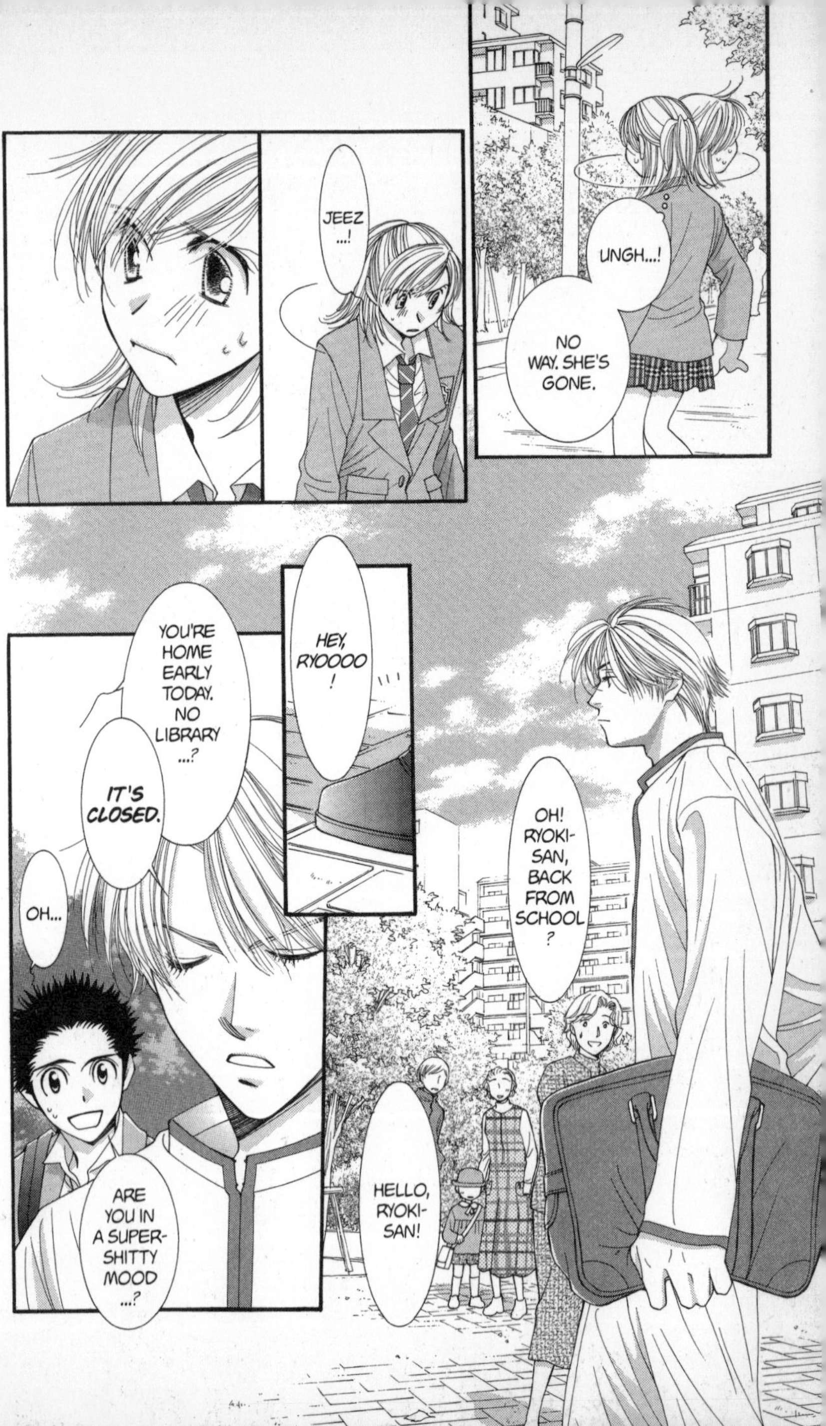
UNGH...!
NO WAY. SHE'S GONE.
JEEZ ...!
OH! RYOKI-SAN, BACK FROM SCHOOL ?
HELLO, RYOKI-SAN!
HEY, RYOOOO !
YOU'RE HOME EARLY TODAY. NO LIBRARY ...?
IT'S CLOSED.
OH...
ARE YOU IN A SUPER-SHITTY MOOD ...?

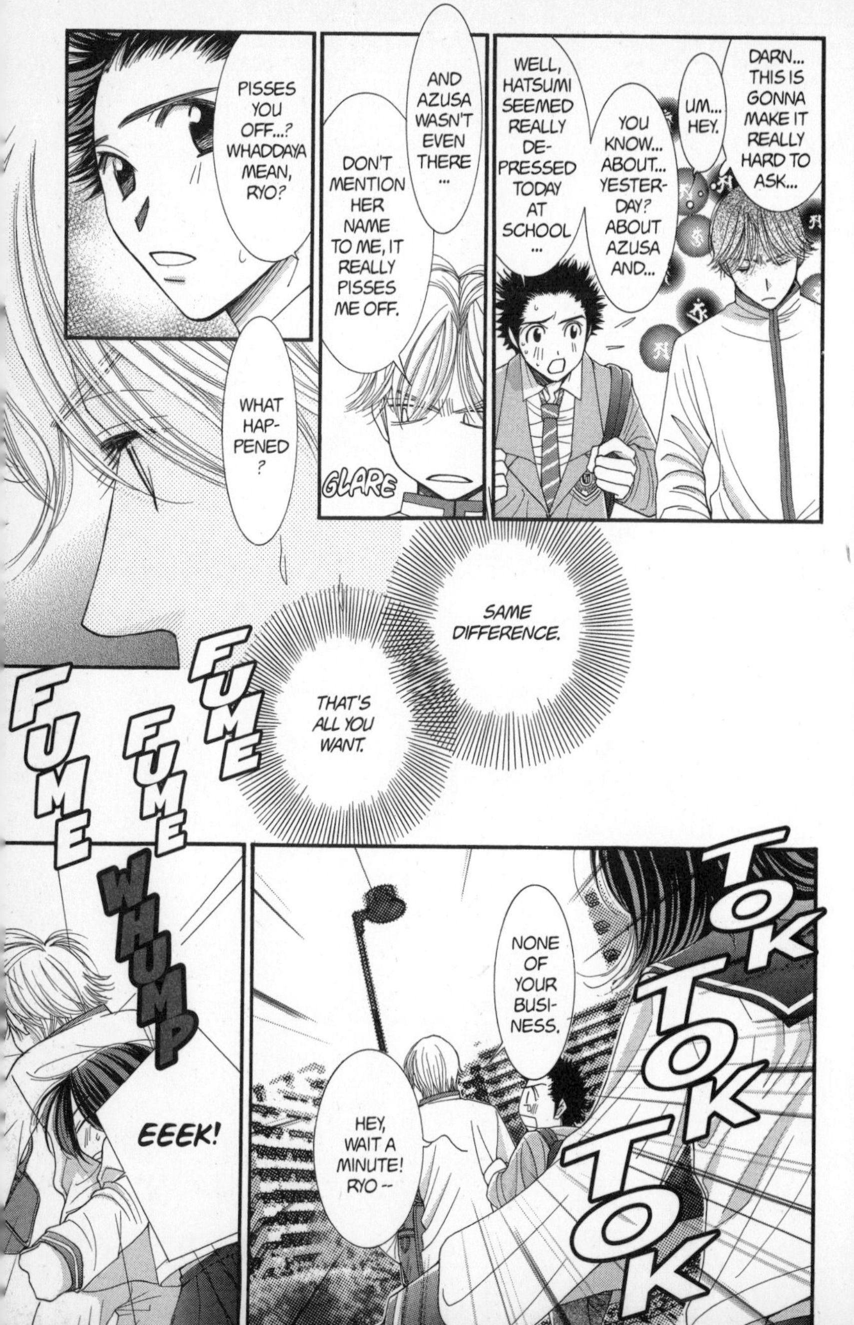

DARN... THIS IS GONNA MAKE IT REALLY HARD TO ASK...
UM... HEY.
YOU KNOW... ABOUT... YESTERDAY? ABOUT AZUSA AND...
WELL, HATSUMI SEEMED REALLY DE-PRESSED TODAY AT SCHOOL...
AND AZUSA WASN'T EVEN THERE...
DON'T MENTION HER NAME TO ME, IT REALLY PISSES ME OFF.
GLARE
PISSES YOU OFF...? WHADDAYA MEAN, RYO?
WHAT HAP-PENED?
SAME DIFFERENCE.
THAT'S ALL YOU WANT.
FUME
FUME
FUME
TOK TOK TOK
NONE OF YOUR BUSI-NESS.
HEY, WAIT A MINUTE! RYO --
WHUMP
EEEK!

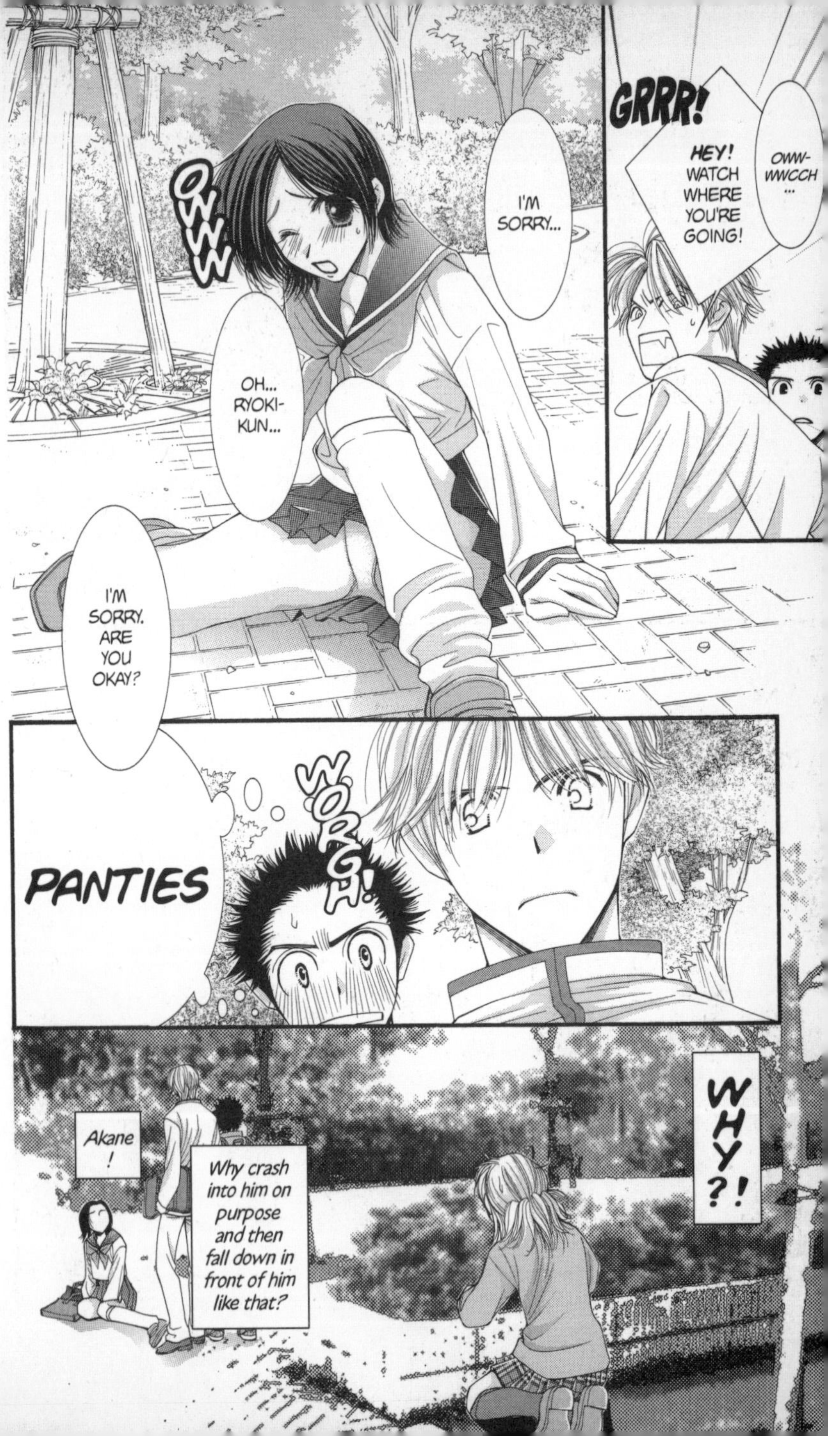
OWW-WWCCH...
GRRR!
HEY! WATCH WHERE YOU'RE GOING!
I'M SORRY...
OWWW
OH... RYOKI-KUN...
I'M SORRY. ARE YOU OKAY?
WORGH!
PANTIES
WHY?!
Why crash into him on purpose and then fall down in front of him like that?
Akane!

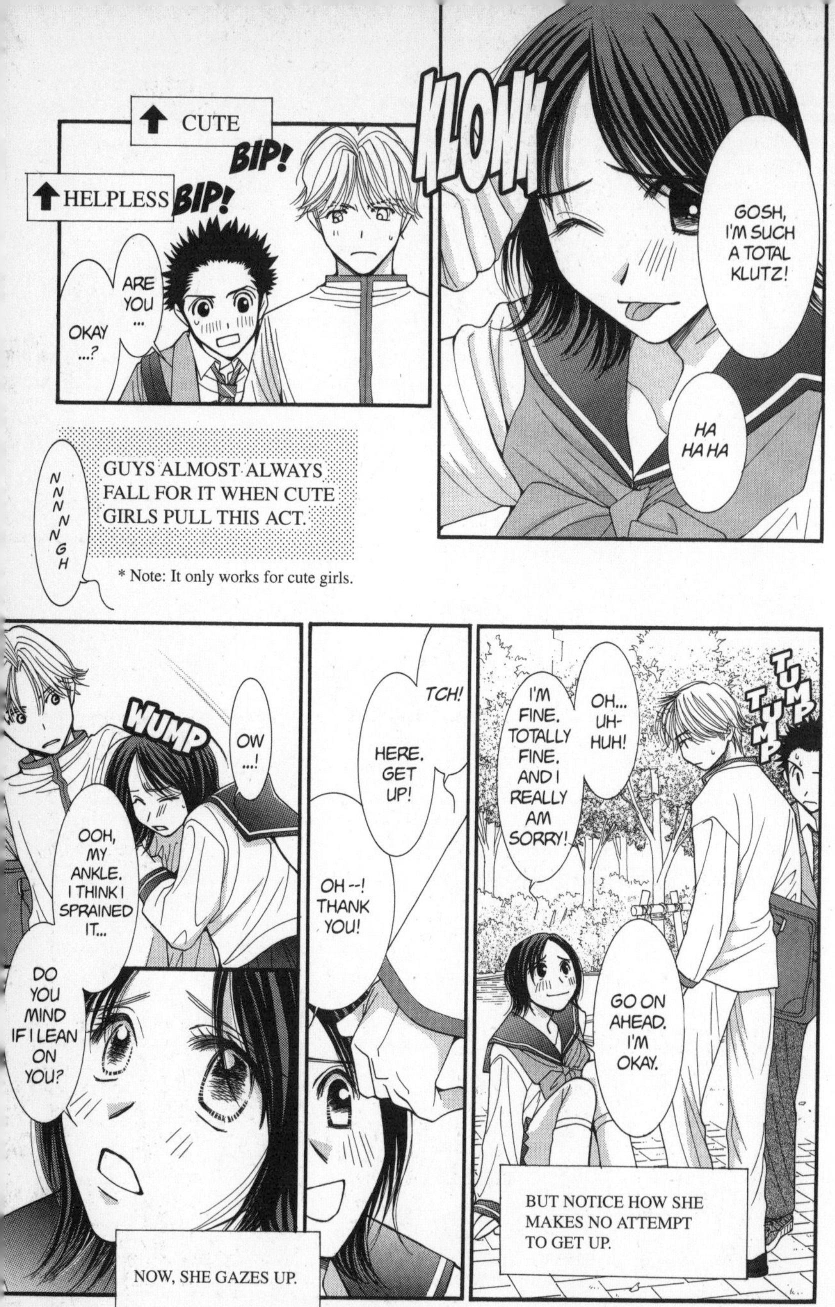
KLONK
GOSH, I'M SUCH A TOTAL KLUTZ!
HA HA HA
BIP!
CUTE
BIP!
HELPLESS
ARE YOU ...
OKAY ...?
GUYS ALMOST ALWAYS FALL FOR IT WHEN CUTE GIRLS PULL THIS ACT.
NNNNNGH
* Note: It only works for cute girls.
TUMP TUMP
OH... UH-HUH!
I'M FINE. TOTALLY FINE. AND I REALLY AM SORRY!
GO ON AHEAD. I'M OKAY.
BUT NOTICE HOW SHE MAKES NO ATTEMPT TO GET UP.
TCH!
HERE. GET UP!
OH --! THANK YOU!
OW ...!
WUMP
OOH, MY ANKLE. I THINK I SPRAINED IT...
DO YOU MIND IF I LEAN ON YOU?
NOW, SHE GAZES UP.

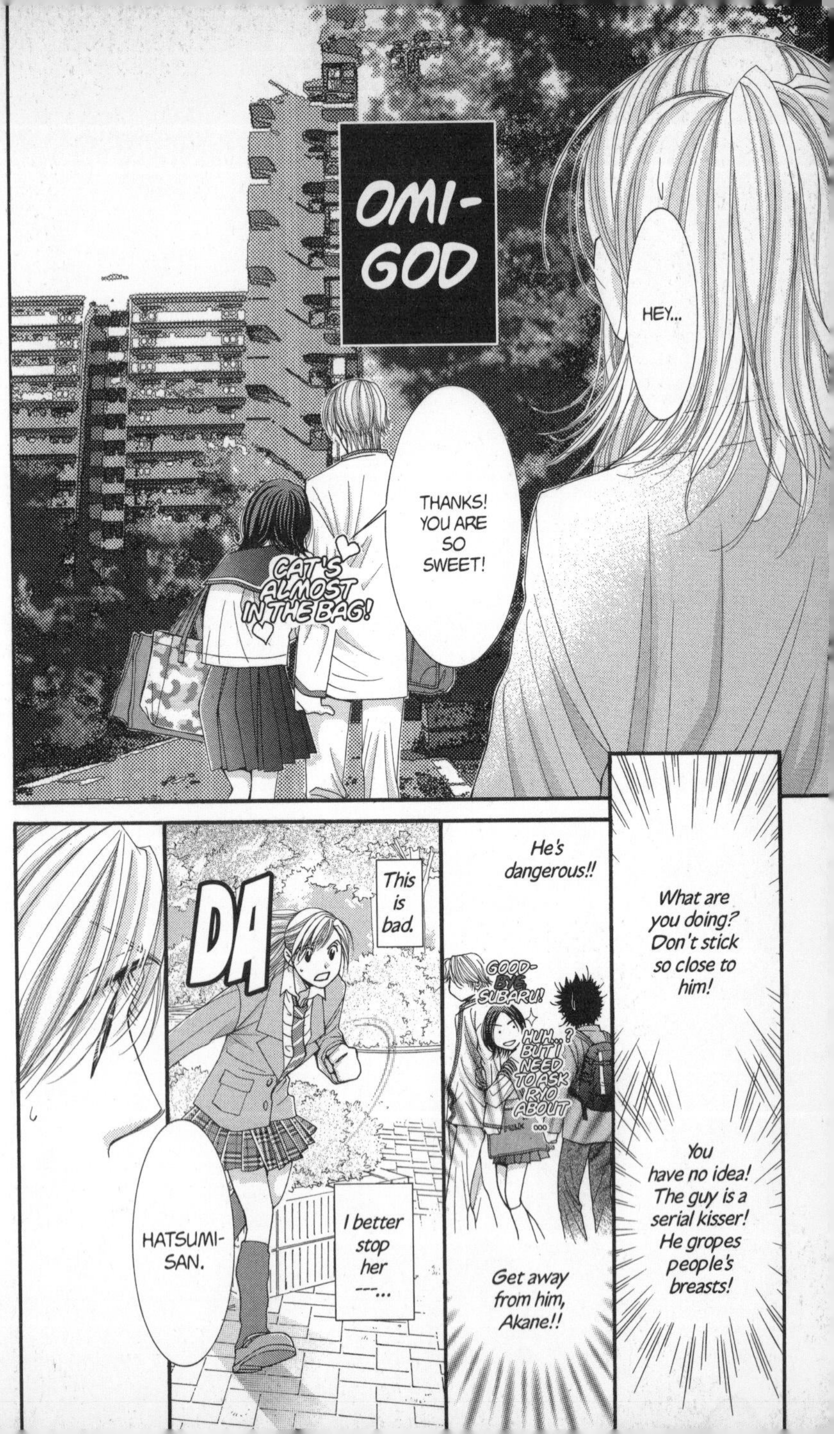

HEY...
OMI-GOD
THANKS! YOU ARE SO SWEET!
CAT'S ALMOST IN THE BAG!
What are you doing? Don't stick so close to him!
You have no idea! The guy is a serial kisser! He gropes people's breasts!
He's dangerous!!
GOOD-BYE SUBARU!
HUH...? BUT I NEED TO ASK RYO ABOUT...
Get away from him, Akane!!
This is bad.
DA
I better stop her---...
HATSUMI-SAN.

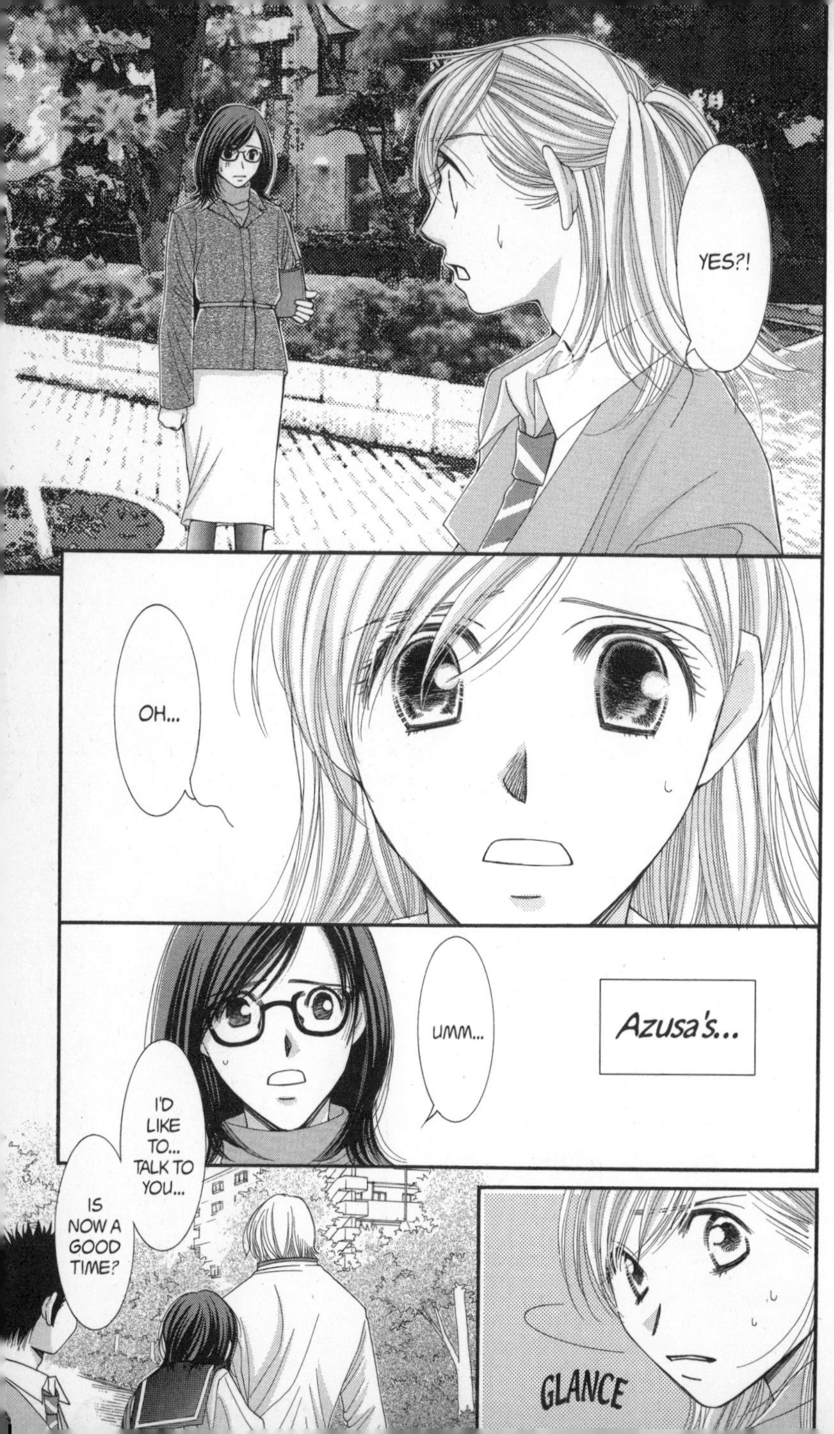
YES?!
OH...
Azusa's...
UMM...
I'D LIKE TO... TALK TO YOU...
GLANCE
IS NOW A GOOD TIME?

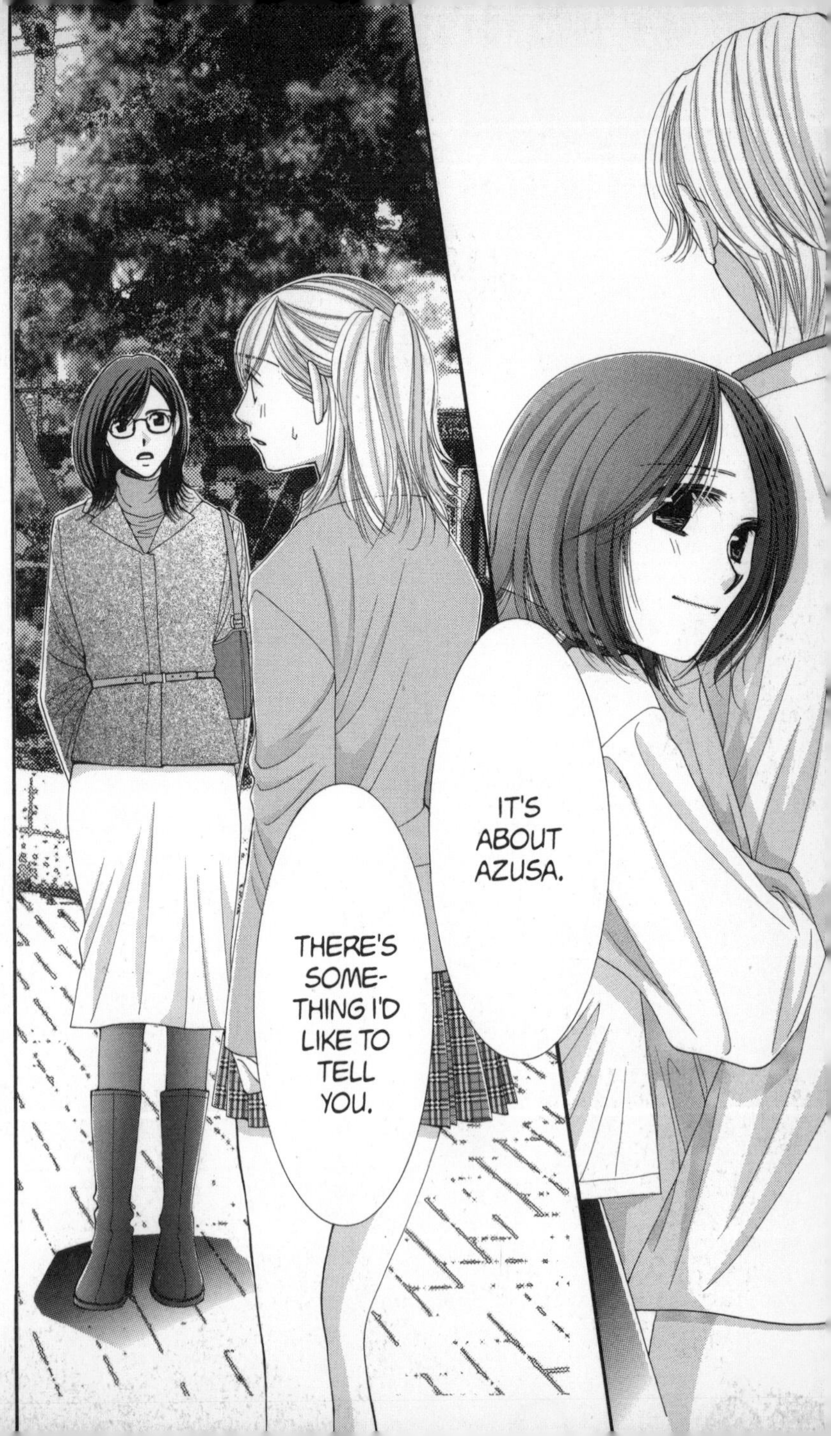
IT'S ABOUT AZUSA.
THERE'S SOME-THING I'D LIKE TO TELL YOU.

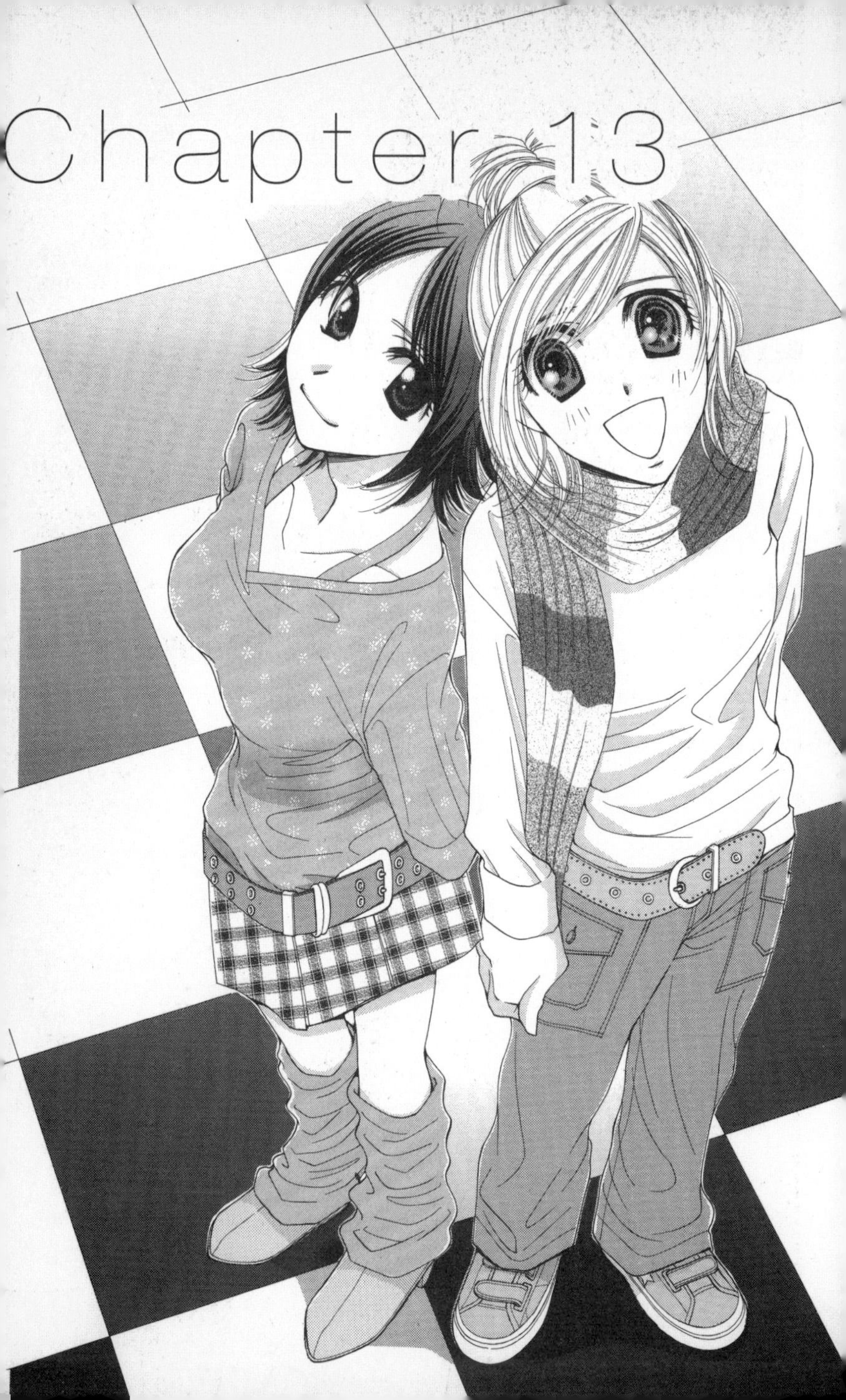
Chapter 13

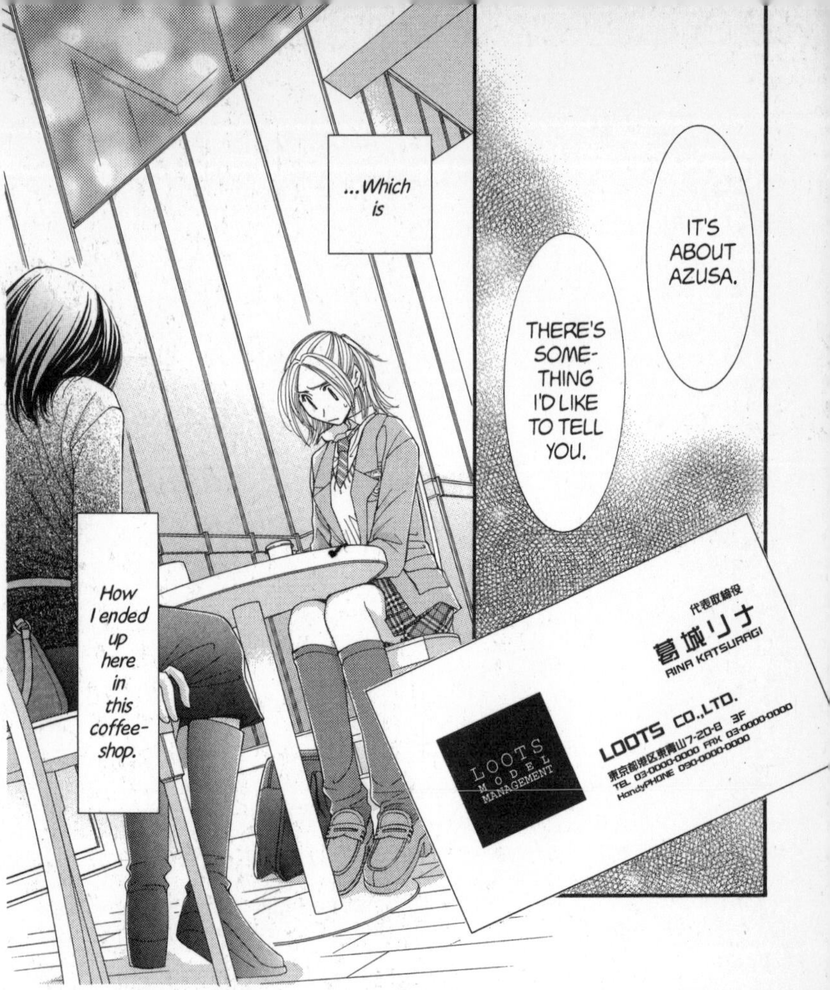
IT'S ABOUT AZUSA.
THERE'S SOME-THING I'D LIKE TO TELL YOU.
...Which is
How I ended up here in this coffee-shop.
代表取締役
葛城リナ
RINA KATSURAGI
LOOTS MODEL MANAGEMENT
LOOTS CO.,LTD.
東京都港区東青山7-20-8 3F
TEL 03-0000-0000 FAX 03-0000-0000
HandyPHONE 090-0000-0000

hot gimmick

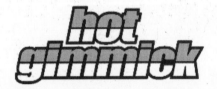

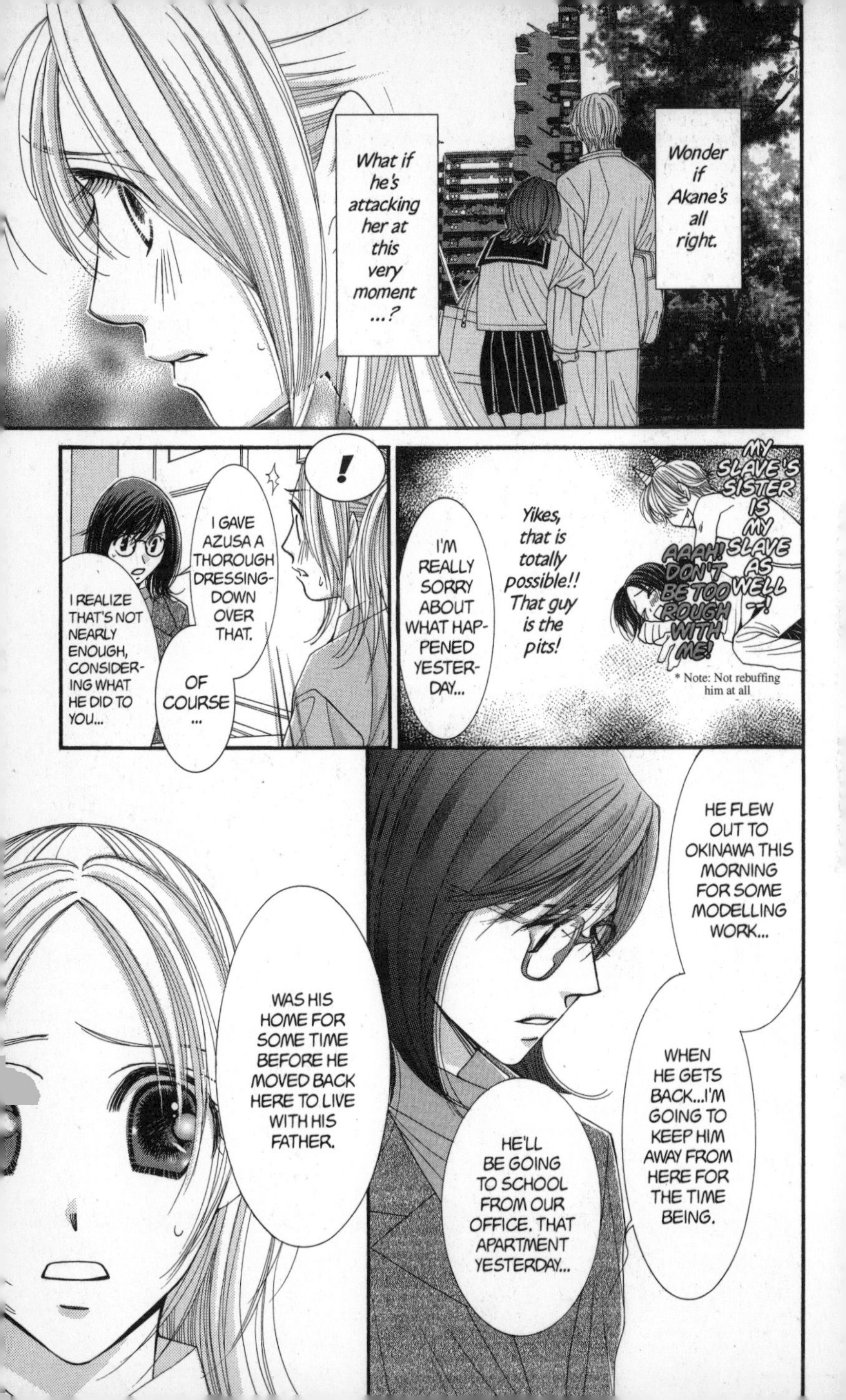
Wonder if Akane's all right.
What if he's attacking her at this very moment ...?
MY SLAVE'S SISTER IS MY SLAVE AS WELL--!
AAAH! DON'T BE TOO ROUGH WITH ME!
* Note: Not rebuffing him at all
Yikes, that is totally possible!! That guy is the pits!
I'M REALLY SORRY ABOUT WHAT HAPPENED YESTERDAY...
!
I GAVE AZUSA A THOROUGH DRESSING-DOWN OVER THAT.
OF COURSE ...
I REALIZE THAT'S NOT NEARLY ENOUGH, CONSIDERING WHAT HE DID TO YOU...
HE FLEW OUT TO OKINAWA THIS MORNING FOR SOME MODELLING WORK...
WHEN HE GETS BACK...I'M GOING TO KEEP HIM AWAY FROM HERE FOR THE TIME BEING.
HE'LL BE GOING TO SCHOOL FROM OUR OFFICE. THAT APARTMENT YESTERDAY...
WAS HIS HOME FOR SOME TIME BEFORE HE MOVED BACK HERE TO LIVE WITH HIS FATHER.

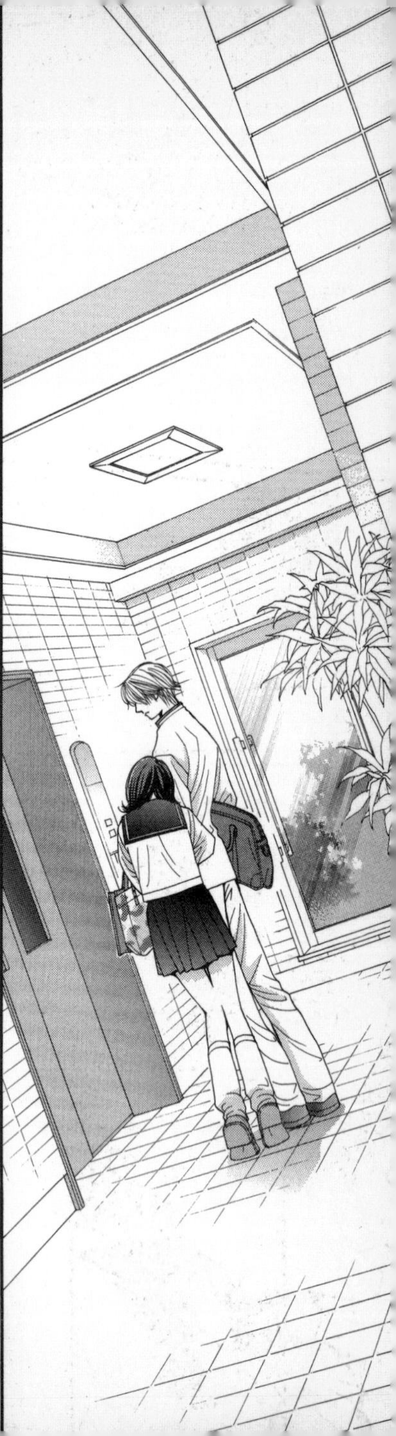
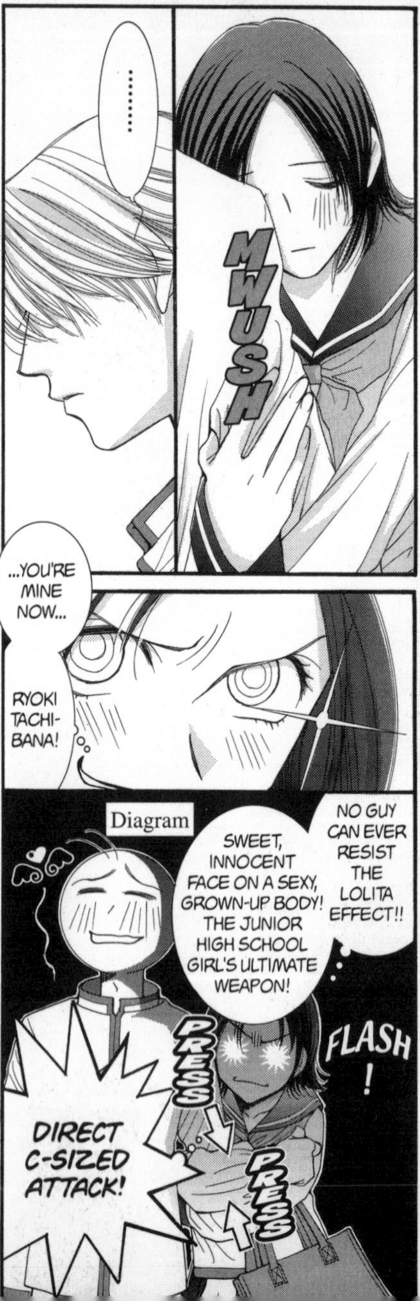
MWUSH
......
...YOU'RE MINE NOW...
RYOKI TACHIBANA!
Diagram
NO GUY CAN EVER RESIST THE LOLITA EFFECT!!
SWEET, INNOCENT FACE ON A SEXY, GROWN-UP BODY! THE JUNIOR HIGH SCHOOL GIRL'S ULTIMATE WEAPON!
FLASH !
PRESS
PRESS
DIRECT C-SIZED ATTACK!

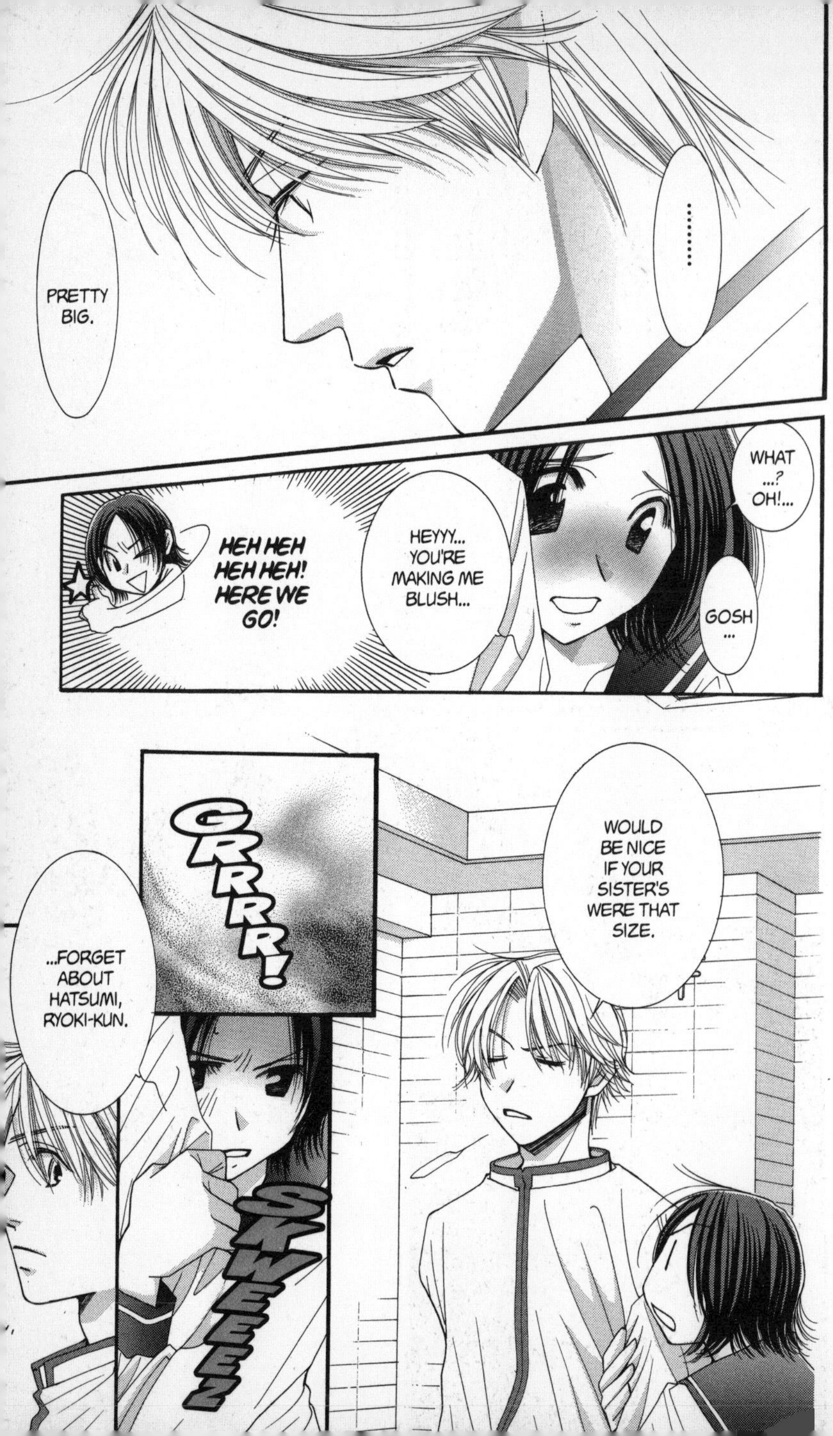
......
PRETTY BIG.
WHAT ...? OH!...
GOSH ...
HEYYY... YOU'RE MAKING ME BLUSH...
HEH HEH HEH HEH! HERE WE GO!
WOULD BE NICE IF YOUR SISTER'S WERE THAT SIZE.
GRRRR!
...FORGET ABOUT HATSUMI, RYOKI-KUN.
SKWEEEZ

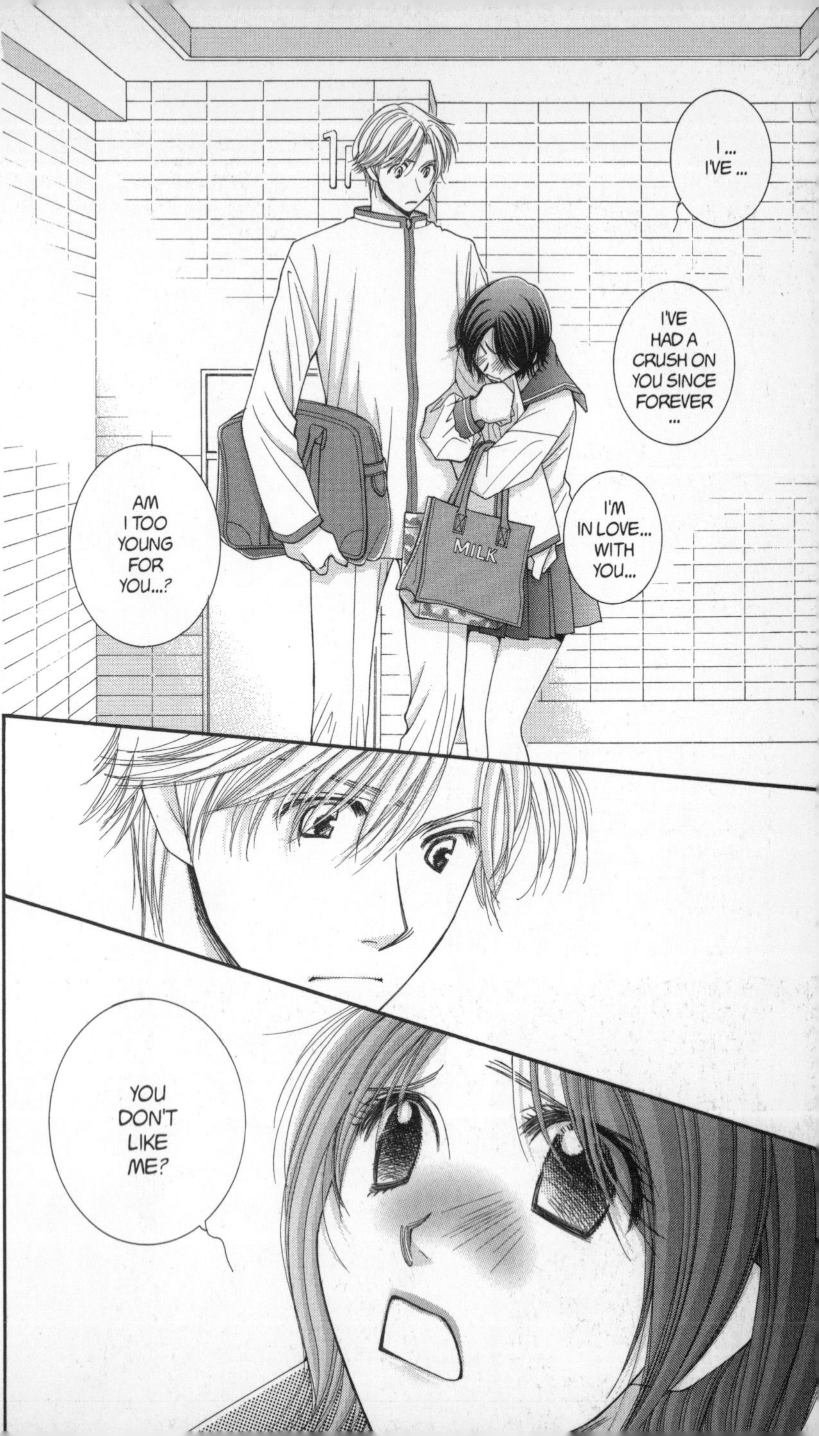
I... I'VE...
I'VE HAD A CRUSH ON YOU SINCE FOREVER ...
I'M IN LOVE... WITH YOU...
AM I TOO YOUNG FOR YOU...?
YOU DON'T LIKE ME?

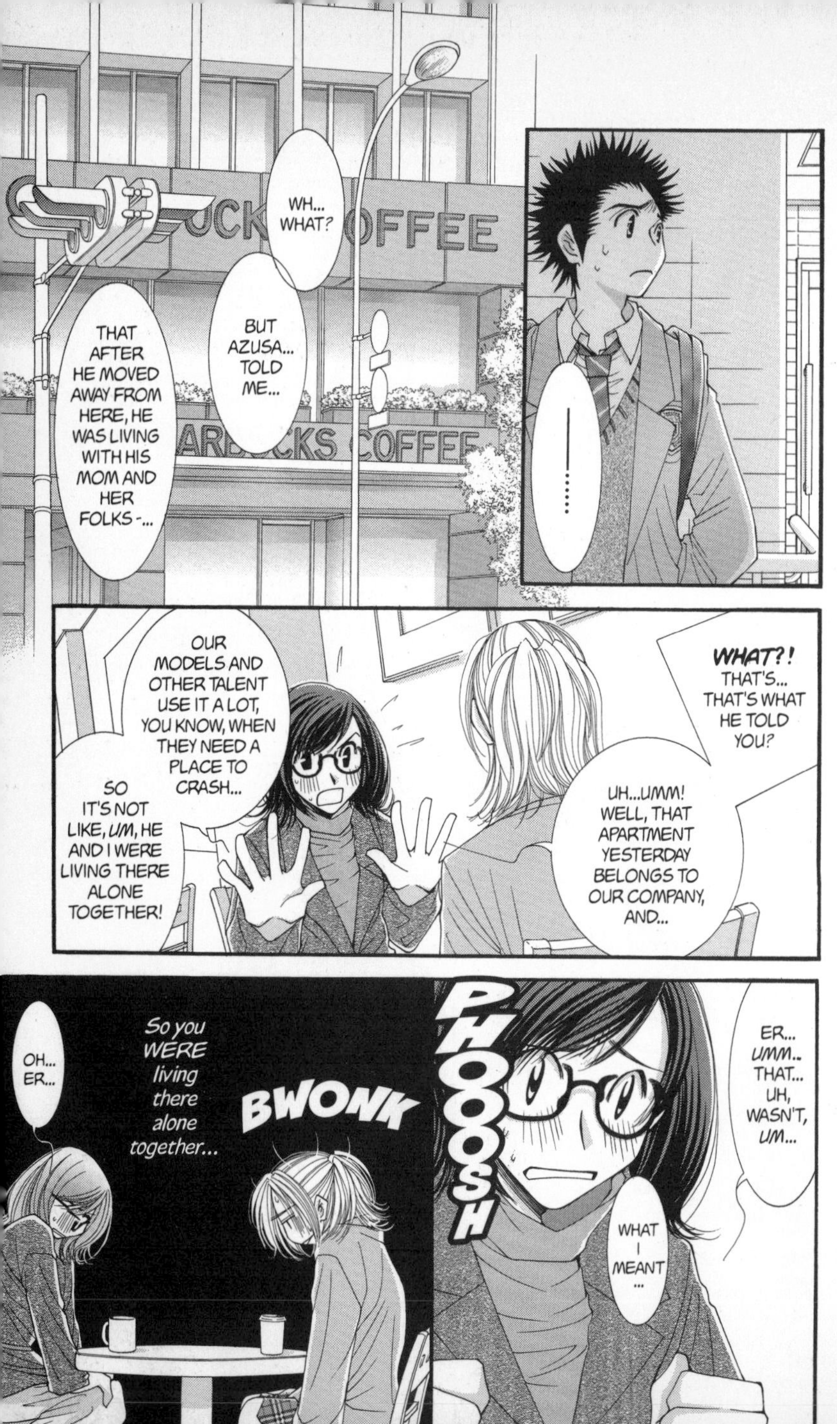
—......
WH... WHAT?
BUT AZUSA... TOLD ME...
THAT AFTER HE MOVED AWAY FROM HERE, HE WAS LIVING WITH HIS MOM AND HER FOLKS -...
WHAT?! THAT'S... THAT'S WHAT HE TOLD YOU?
UH...UMM! WELL, THAT APARTMENT YESTERDAY BELONGS TO OUR COMPANY, AND...
OUR MODELS AND OTHER TALENT USE IT A LOT, YOU KNOW, WHEN THEY NEED A PLACE TO CRASH...
SO IT'S NOT LIKE, UM, HE AND I WERE LIVING THERE ALONE TOGETHER!
ER... UMM.. THAT... UH, WASN'T, UM...
PHOOOOSH
WHAT I MEANT ...
So you WERE living there alone together...
OH... ER...
BWONK

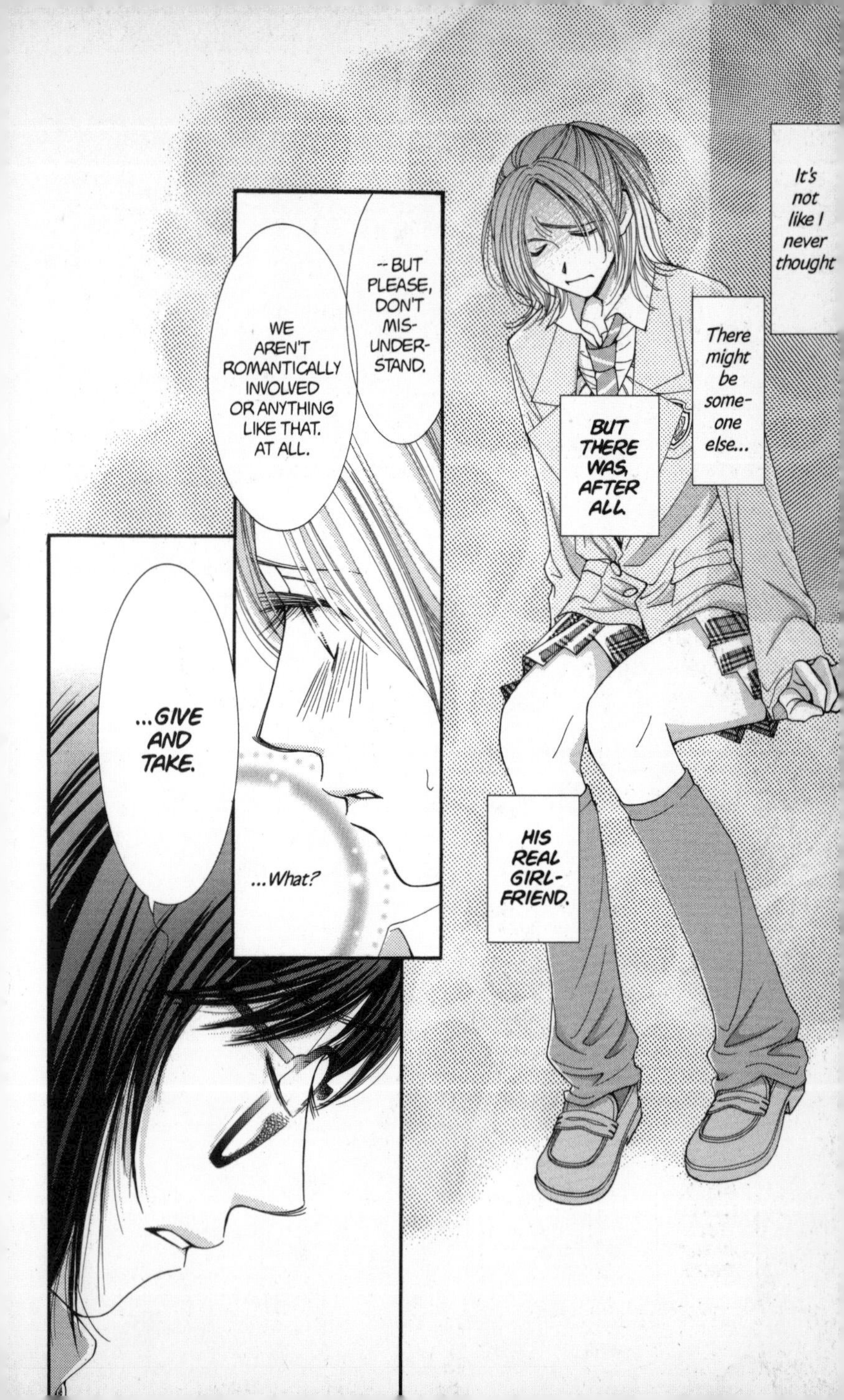
It's not like I never thought
There might be some-one else...
BUT THERE WAS, AFTER ALL.
HIS REAL GIRL-FRIEND.
--BUT PLEASE, DON'T MIS-UNDER-STAND.
WE AREN'T ROMANTICALLY INVOLVED OR ANYTHING LIKE THAT. AT ALL.
...What?
...GIVE AND TAKE.

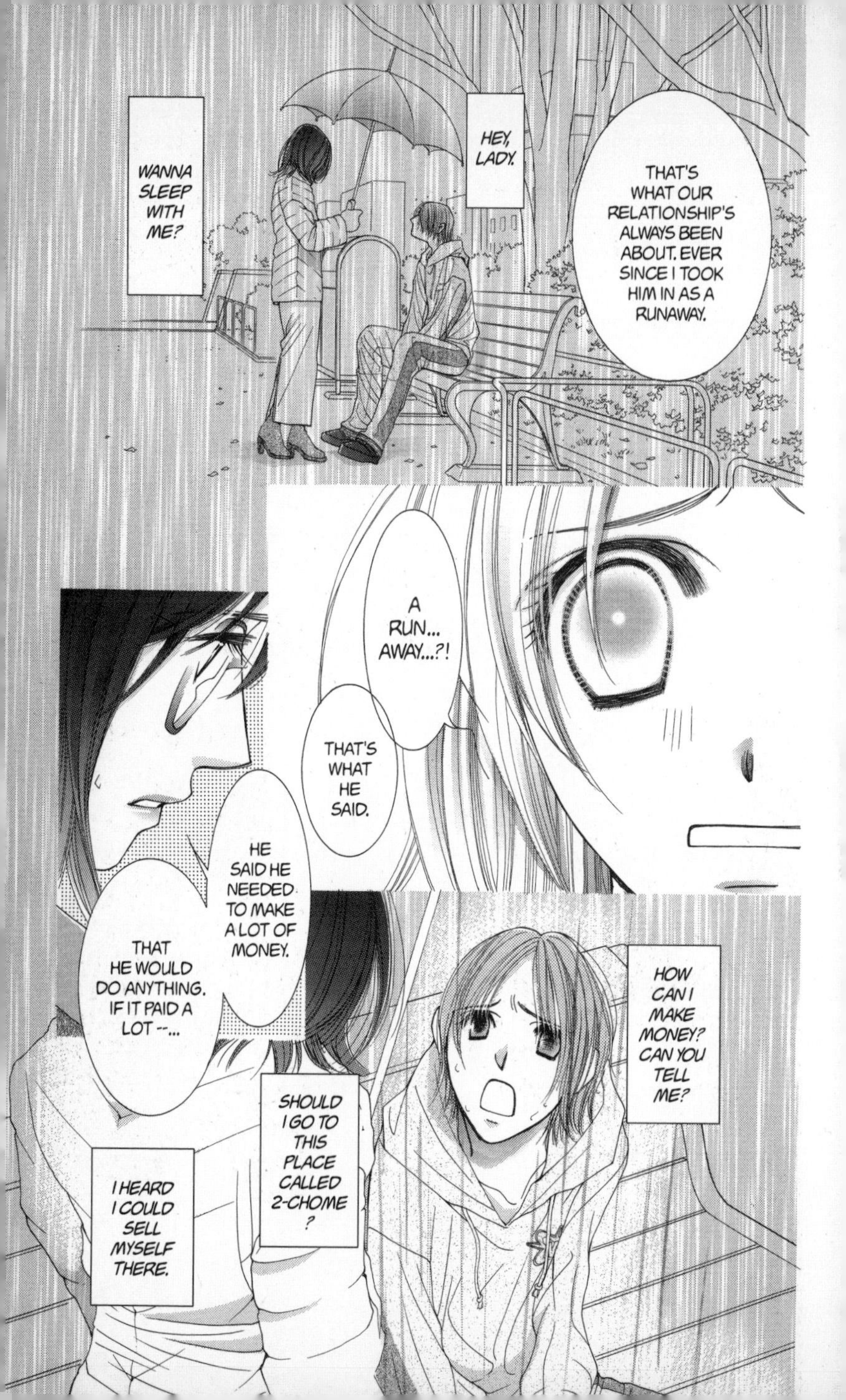
THAT'S WHAT OUR RELATIONSHIP'S ALWAYS BEEN ABOUT. EVER SINCE I TOOK HIM IN AS A RUNAWAY.
HEY, LADY.
WANNA SLEEP WITH ME?
A RUN... AWAY...?!
THAT'S WHAT HE SAID.
HE SAID HE NEEDED TO MAKE A LOT OF MONEY.
THAT HE WOULD DO ANYTHING. IF IT PAID A LOT --...
HOW CAN I MAKE MONEY? CAN YOU TELL ME?
SHOULD I GO TO THIS PLACE CALLED 2-CHOME?
I HEARD I COULD SELL MYSELF THERE.

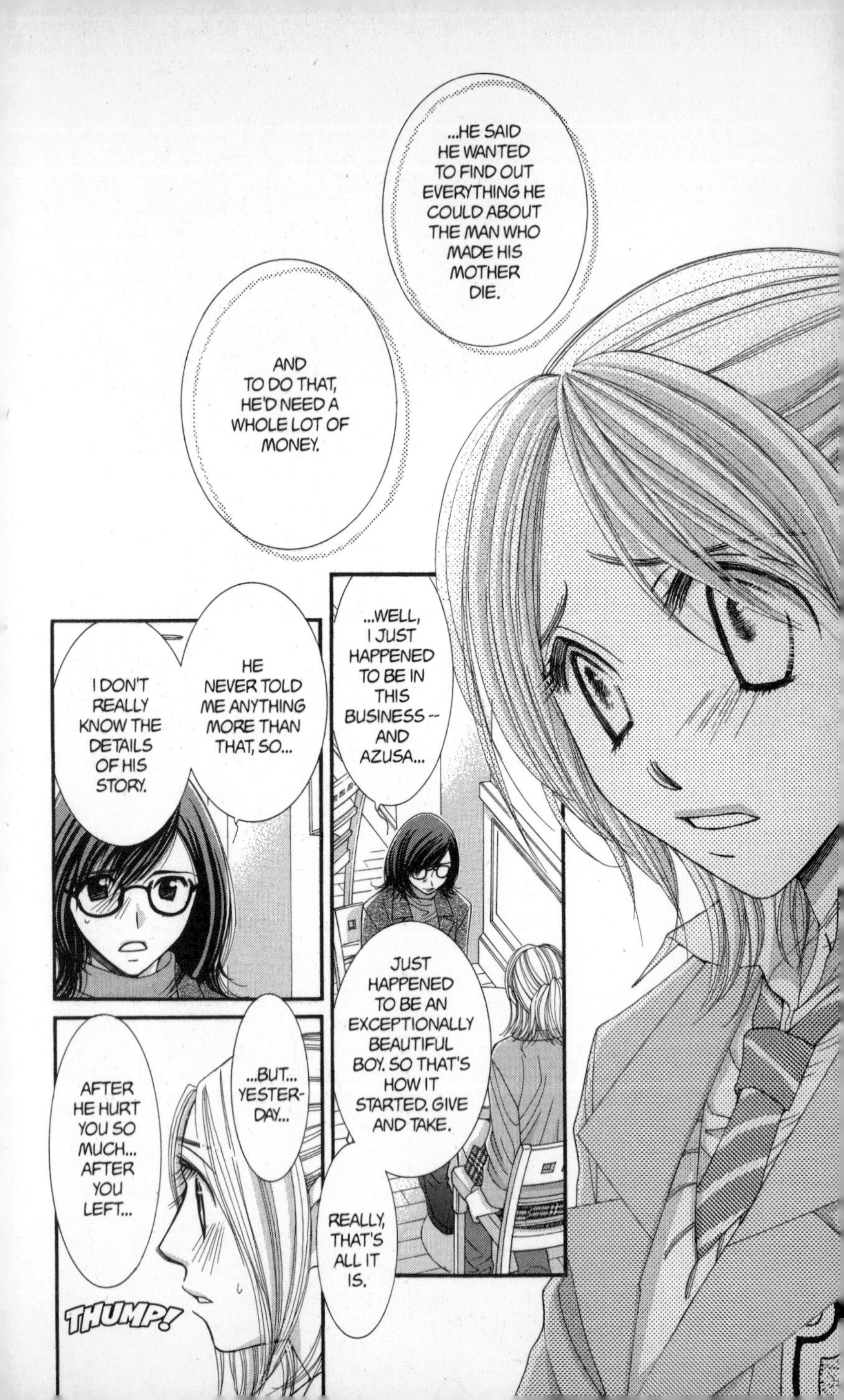
...HE SAID HE WANTED TO FIND OUT EVERYTHING HE COULD ABOUT THE MAN WHO MADE HIS MOTHER DIE.
AND TO DO THAT, HE'D NEED A WHOLE LOT OF MONEY.
...WELL, I JUST HAPPENED TO BE IN THIS BUSINESS -- AND AZUSA...
JUST HAPPENED TO BE AN EXCEPTIONALLY BEAUTIFUL BOY. SO THAT'S HOW IT STARTED. GIVE AND TAKE.
REALLY, THAT'S ALL IT IS.
HE NEVER TOLD ME ANYTHING MORE THAN THAT, SO...
I DON'T REALLY KNOW THE DETAILS OF HIS STORY.
...BUT... YESTER-DAY...
AFTER HE HURT YOU SO MUCH... AFTER YOU LEFT...
THUMP!

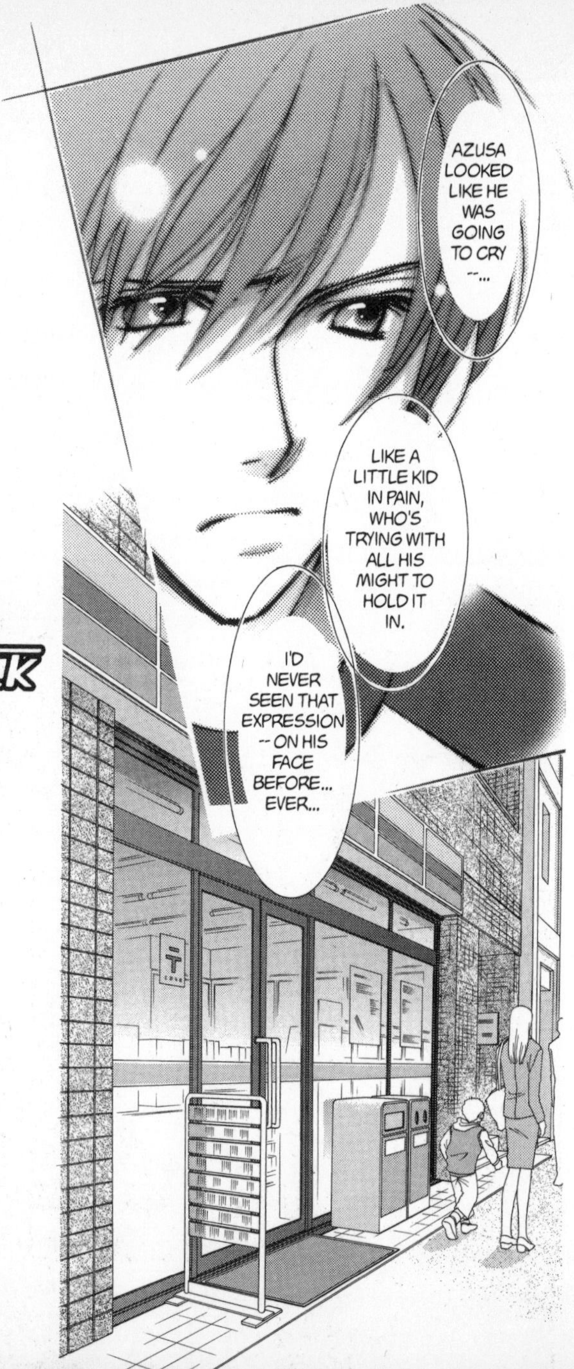
AZUSA LOOKED LIKE HE WAS GOING TO CRY --...
LIKE A LITTLE KID IN PAIN, WHO'S TRYING WITH ALL HIS MIGHT TO HOLD IT IN.
I'D NEVER SEEN THAT EXPRESSION -- ON HIS FACE BEFORE... EVER...

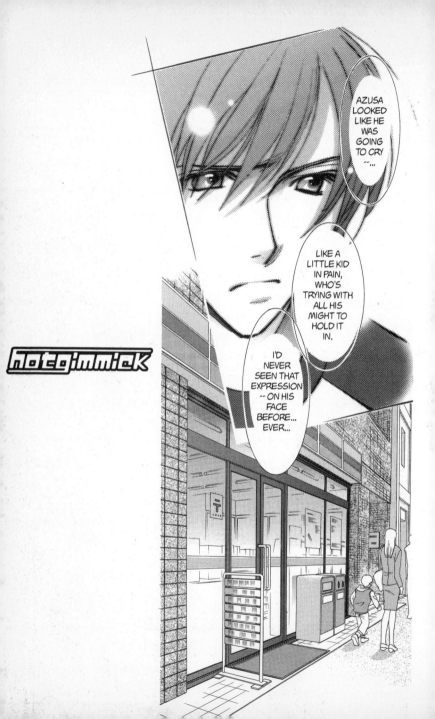

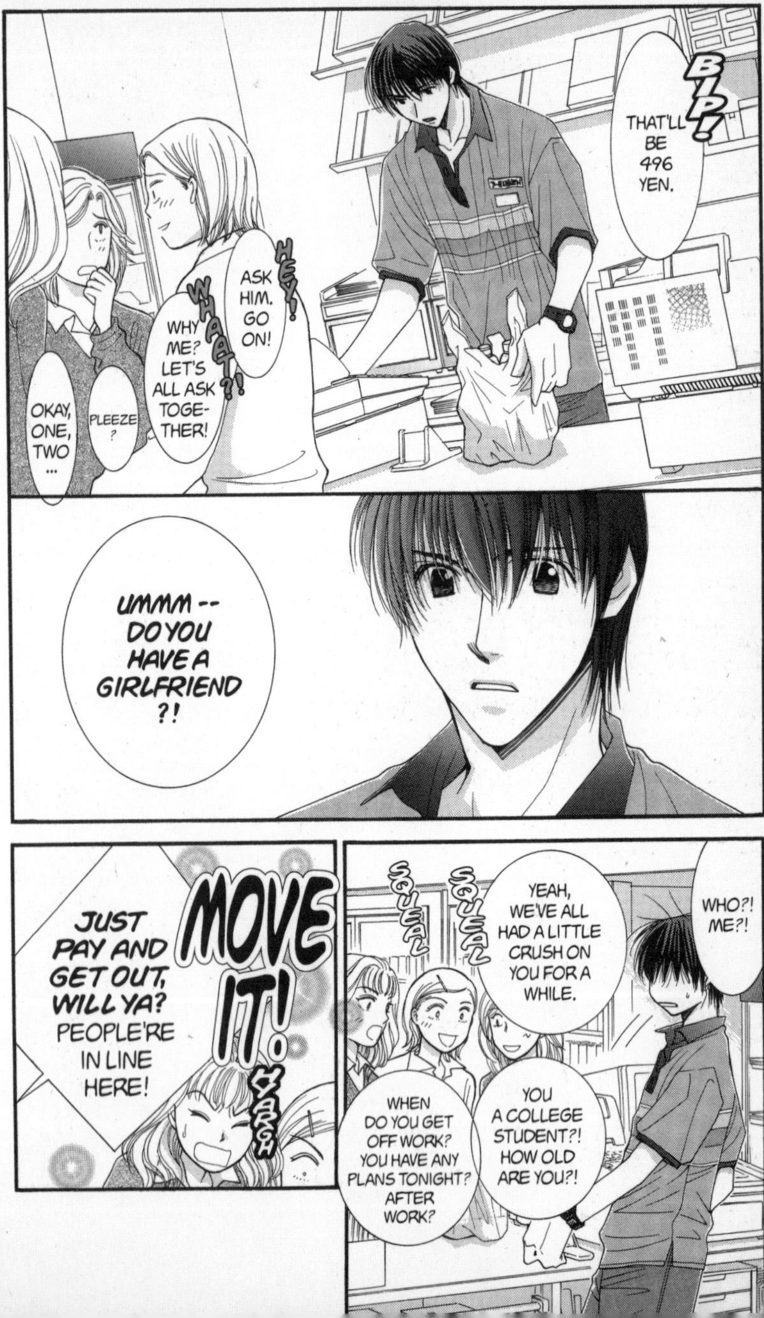
BIP!
THAT'LL BE 496 YEN.
HEY!
ASK HIM. GO ON!
WHAAT?!
WHY ME? LET'S ALL ASK TOGE-THER!
PLEEZE?
OKAY, ONE, TWO...
UMMM -- DO YOU HAVE A GIRLFRIEND?!
WHO?! ME?!
SQUEAL
SQUEAL
YEAH, WE'VE ALL HAD A LITTLE CRUSH ON YOU FOR A WHILE.
YOU A COLLEGE STUDENT?! HOW OLD ARE YOU?!
WHEN DO YOU GET OFF WORK? YOU HAVE ANY PLANS TONIGHT? AFTER WORK?
MOVE IT!
JUST PAY AND GET OUT, WILL YA? PEOPLE'RE IN LINE HERE!
HYARGH

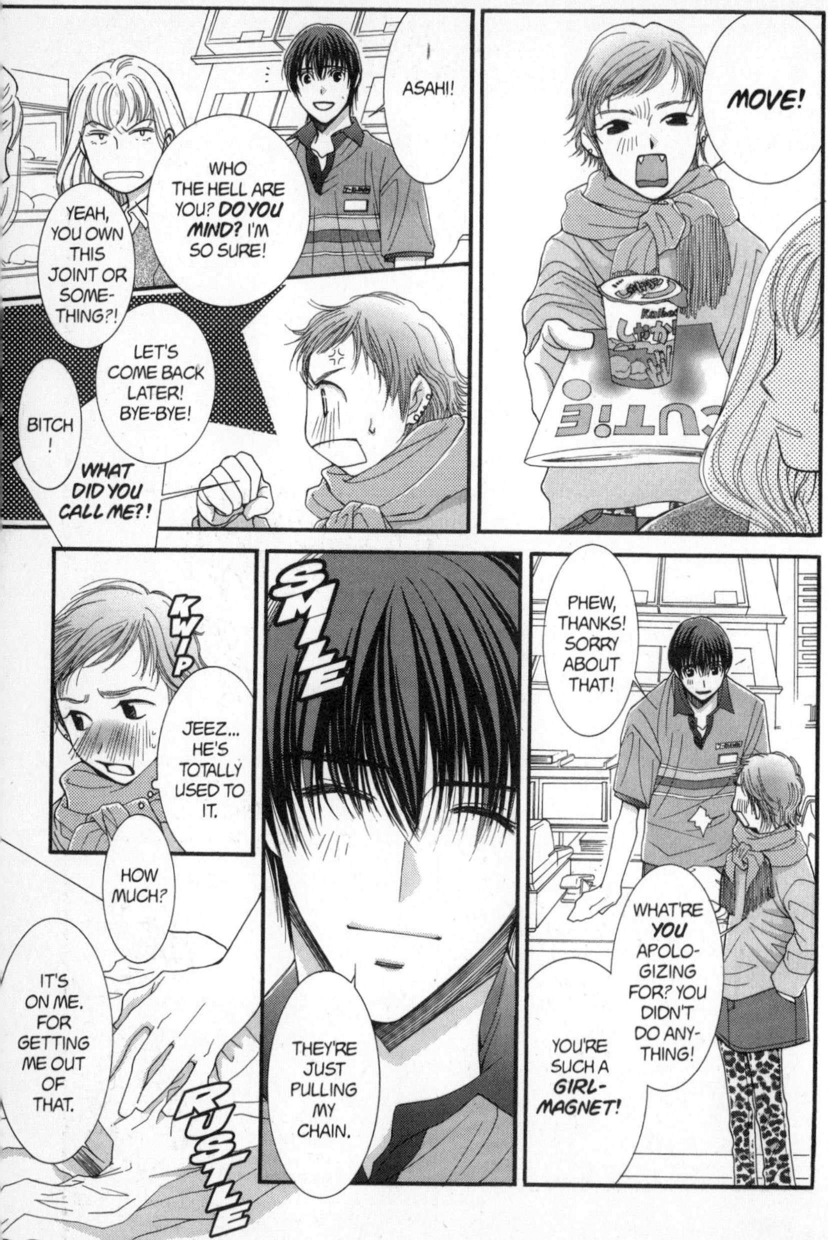
MOVE!
I
ASAHI!
WHO THE HELL ARE YOU? DO YOU MIND? I'M SO SURE!
YEAH, YOU OWN THIS JOINT OR SOME-THING?!
LET'S COME BACK LATER! BYE-BYE!
BITCH!
WHAT DID YOU CALL ME?!
PHEW, THANKS! SORRY ABOUT THAT!
WHAT'RE YOU APOLO-GIZING FOR? YOU DIDN'T DO ANY-THING!
YOU'RE SUCH A GIRL-MAGNET!
SMILE
THEY'RE JUST PULLING MY CHAIN.
KWIP
JEEZ... HE'S TOTALLY USED TO IT.
HOW MUCH?
IT'S ON ME. FOR GETTING ME OUT OF THAT.
RUSTLE

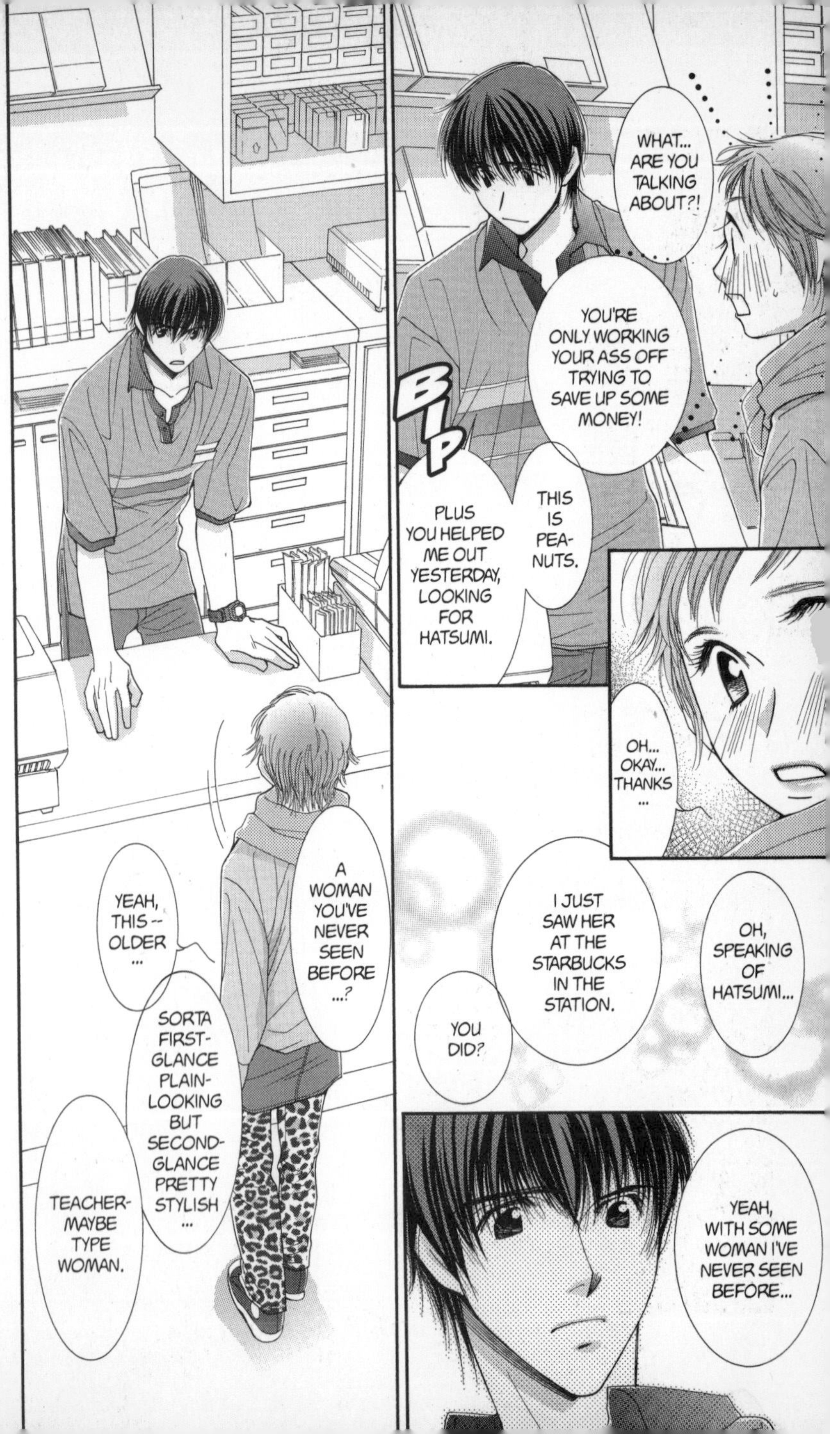
WHAT... ARE YOU TALKING ABOUT?!
YOU'RE ONLY WORKING YOUR ASS OFF TRYING TO SAVE UP SOME MONEY!
BIP
THIS IS PEA-NUTS.
PLUS YOU HELPED ME OUT YESTERDAY, LOOKING FOR HATSUMI.
OH... OKAY... THANKS ...
OH, SPEAKING OF HATSUMI...
I JUST SAW HER AT THE STARBUCKS IN THE STATION.
YOU DID?
YEAH, WITH SOME WOMAN I'VE NEVER SEEN BEFORE...
A WOMAN YOU'VE NEVER SEEN BEFORE ...?
YEAH, THIS -- OLDER ...
SORTA FIRST-GLANCE PLAIN-LOOKING BUT SECOND-GLANCE PRETTY STYLISH ...
TEACHER-MAYBE TYPE WOMAN.

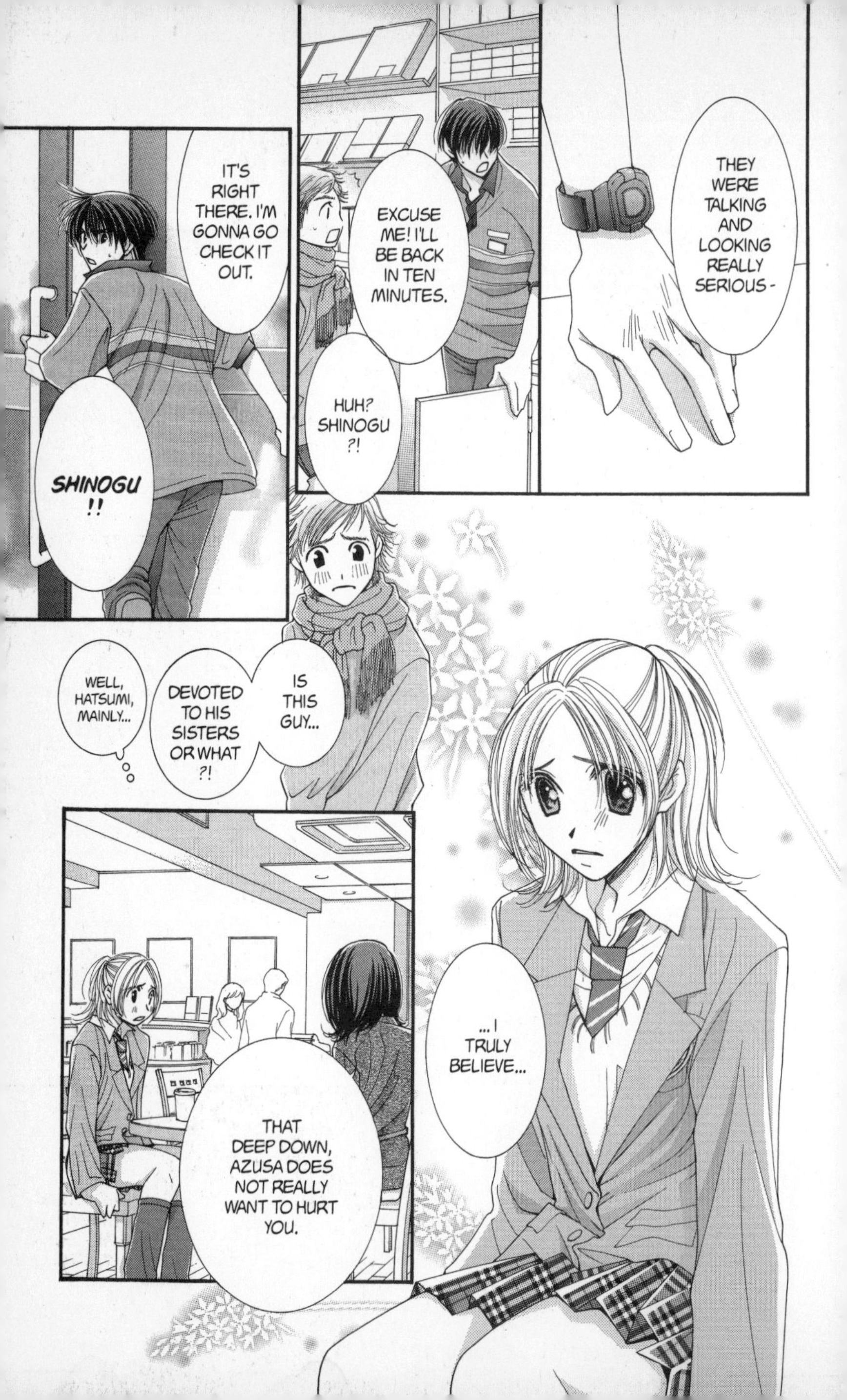
THEY WERE TALKING AND LOOKING REALLY SERIOUS -
EXCUSE ME! I'LL BE BACK IN TEN MINUTES.
HUH? SHINOGU ?!
IT'S RIGHT THERE. I'M GONNA GO CHECK IT OUT.
SHINOGU !!
IS THIS GUY...
DEVOTED TO HIS SISTERS OR WHAT ?!
WELL, HATSUMI, MAINLY...
...I TRULY BELIEVE...
THAT DEEP DOWN, AZUSA DOES NOT REALLY WANT TO HURT YOU.

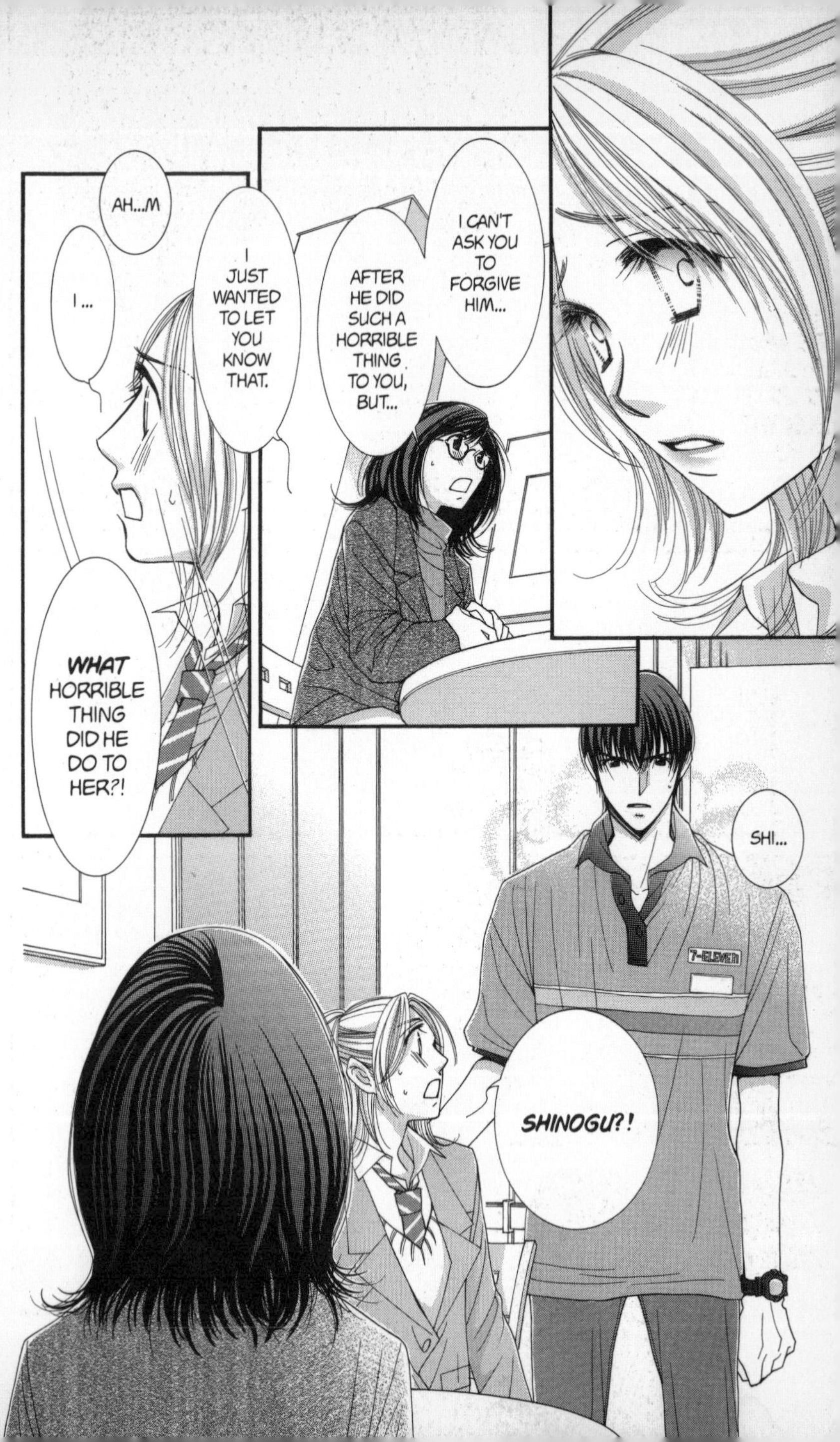
I CAN'T ASK YOU TO FORGIVE HIM...
AFTER HE DID SUCH A HORRIBLE THING TO YOU, BUT...
I JUST WANTED TO LET YOU KNOW THAT.
AH...M
I...
WHAT HORRIBLE THING DID HE DO TO HER?!
SHI...
7-ELEVEN
SHINOGU?!

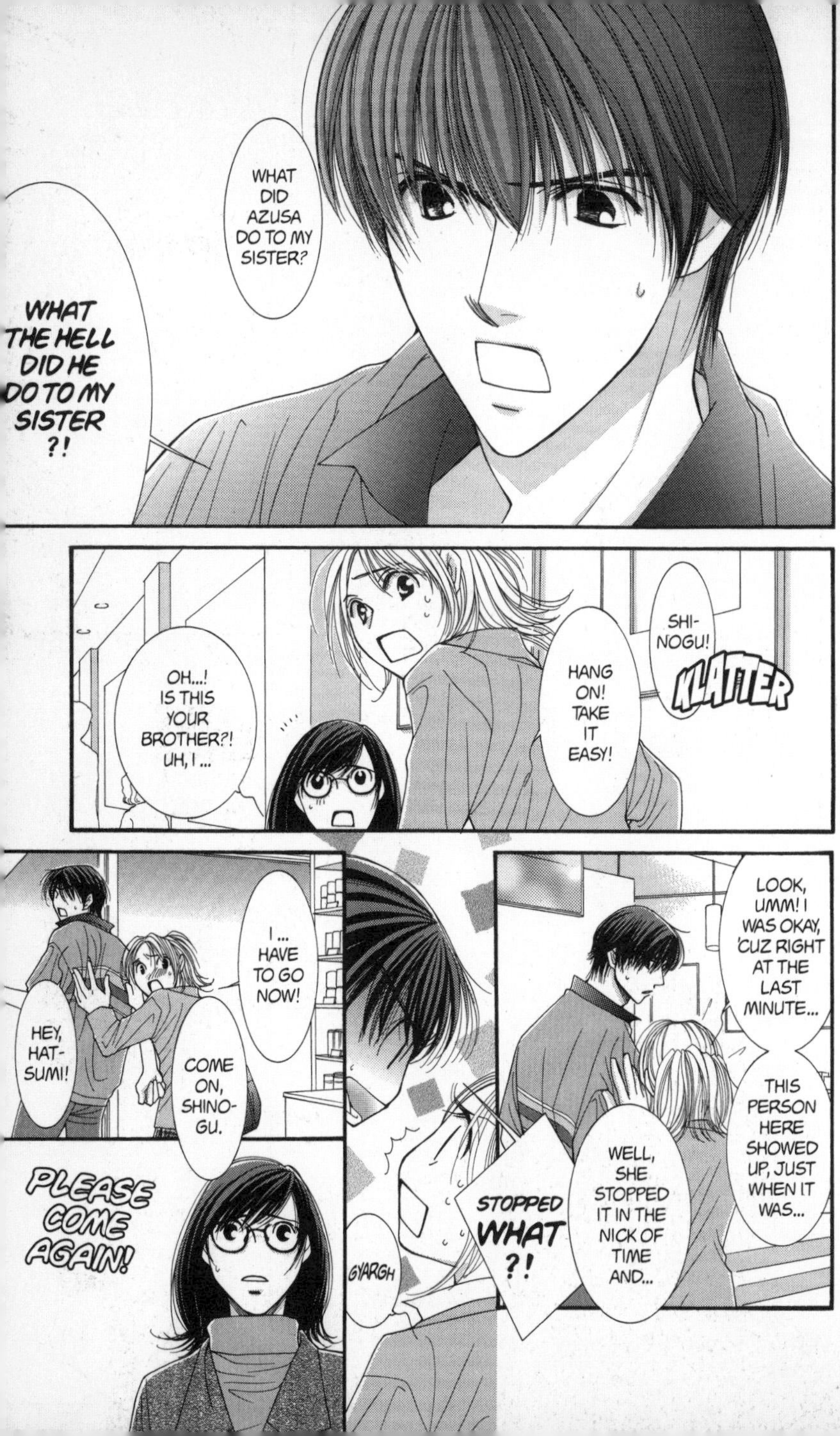
WHAT DID AZUSA DO TO MY SISTER?
WHAT THE HELL DID HE DO TO MY SISTER?!
KLATTER
SHI-NOGU!
HANG ON! TAKE IT EASY!
OH...! IS THIS YOUR BROTHER?! UH, I ...
LOOK, UMM! I WAS OKAY, 'CUZ RIGHT AT THE LAST MINUTE...
THIS PERSON HERE SHOWED UP, JUST WHEN IT WAS...
WELL, SHE STOPPED IT IN THE NICK OF TIME AND...
STOPPED WHAT?!
GYARGH
I ... HAVE TO GO NOW!
COME ON, SHINO-GU.
HEY, HAT-SUMI!
PLEASE COME AGAIN!

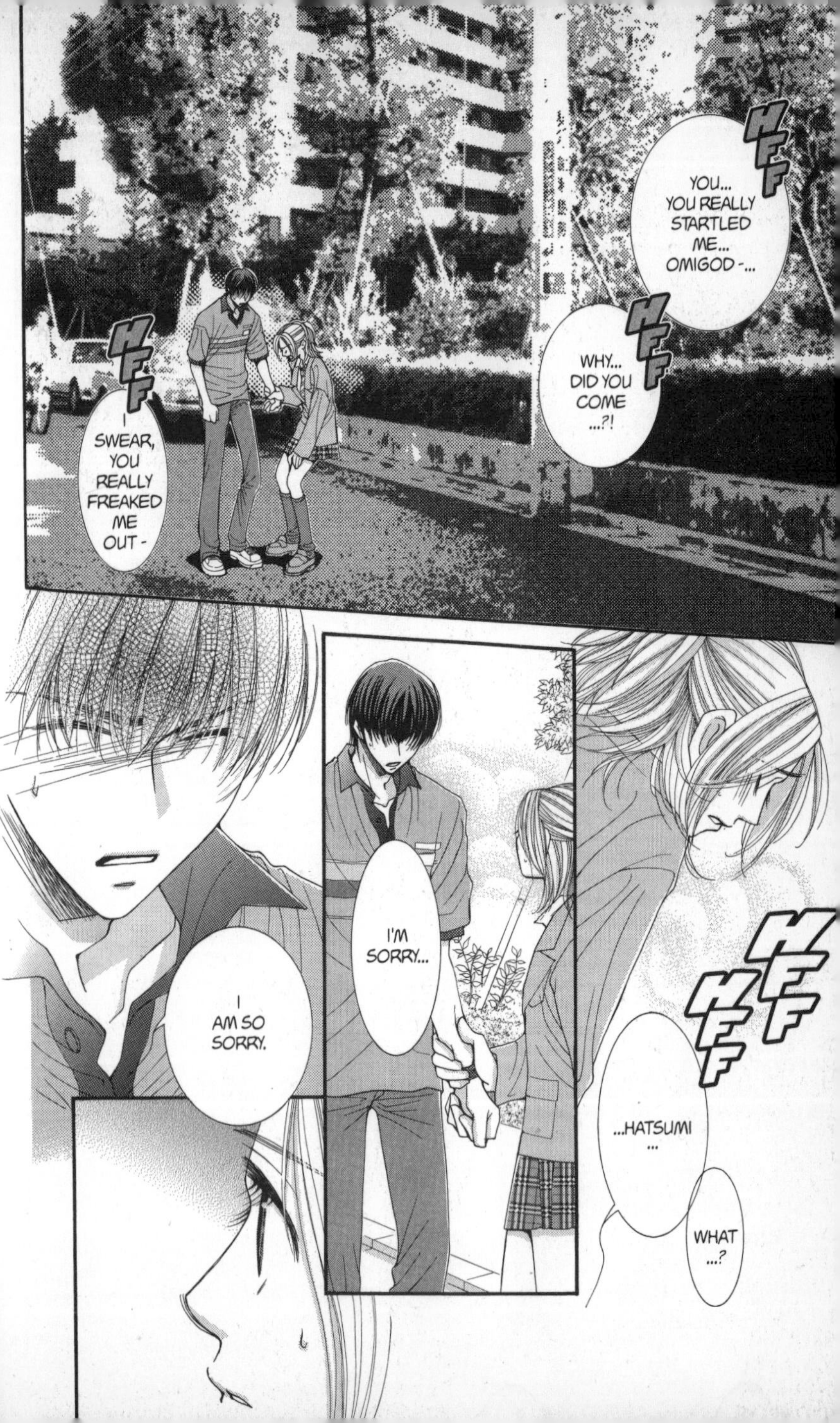
HFF
YOU... YOU REALLY STARTLED ME... OMIGOD -...
HFF
WHY... DID YOU COME ...?!
HFF
I SWEAR, YOU REALLY FREAKED ME OUT -
HFF
HFF
...HATSUMI ...
WHAT ...?
I'M SORRY...
I AM SO SORRY.

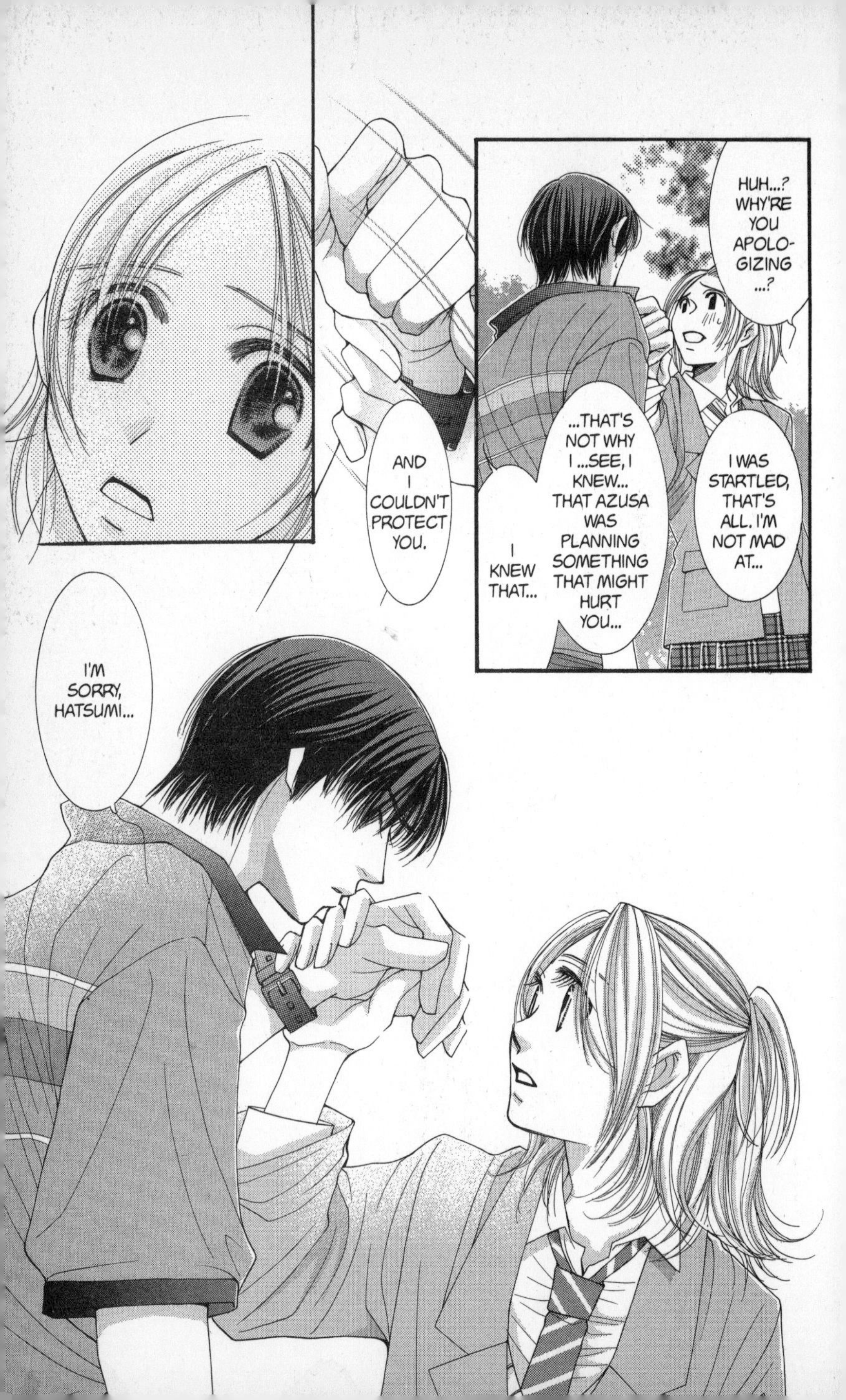
HUH...? WHY'RE YOU APOLOGIZING ...?
I WAS STARTLED, THAT'S ALL. I'M NOT MAD AT...
...THAT'S NOT WHY I ...SEE, I KNEW... THAT AZUSA WAS PLANNING SOMETHING THAT MIGHT HURT YOU...
I KNEW THAT...
AND I COULDN'T PROTECT YOU.
I'M SORRY, HATSUMI...

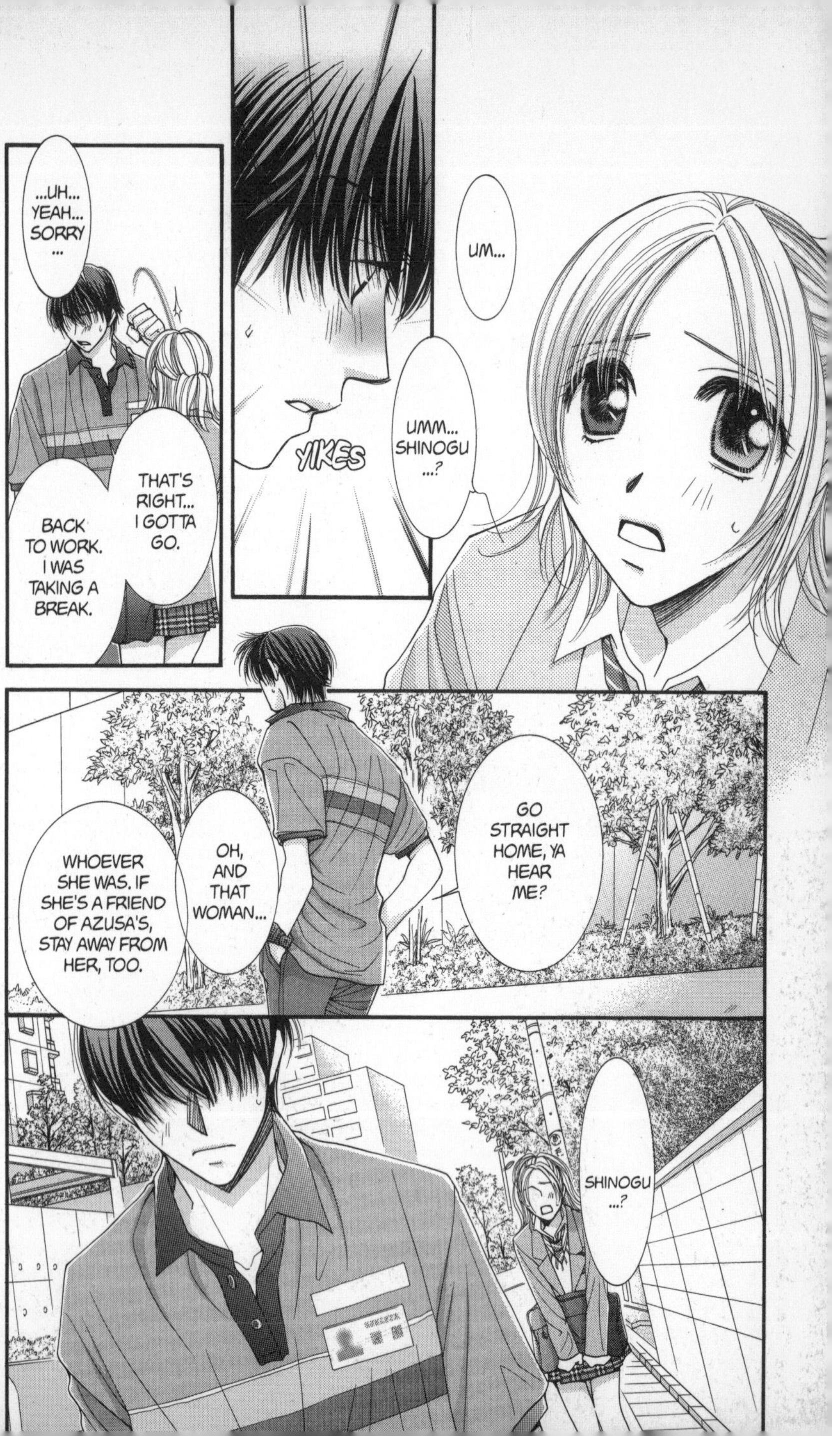
UM...
UMM... SHINOGU ...?
YIKES
...UH... YEAH... SORRY ...
THAT'S RIGHT... I GOTTA GO.
BACK TO WORK. I WAS TAKING A BREAK.
GO STRAIGHT HOME, YA HEAR ME?
OH, AND THAT WOMAN...
WHOEVER SHE WAS. IF SHE'S A FRIEND OF AZUSA'S, STAY AWAY FROM HER, TOO.
SHINOGU ...?
...

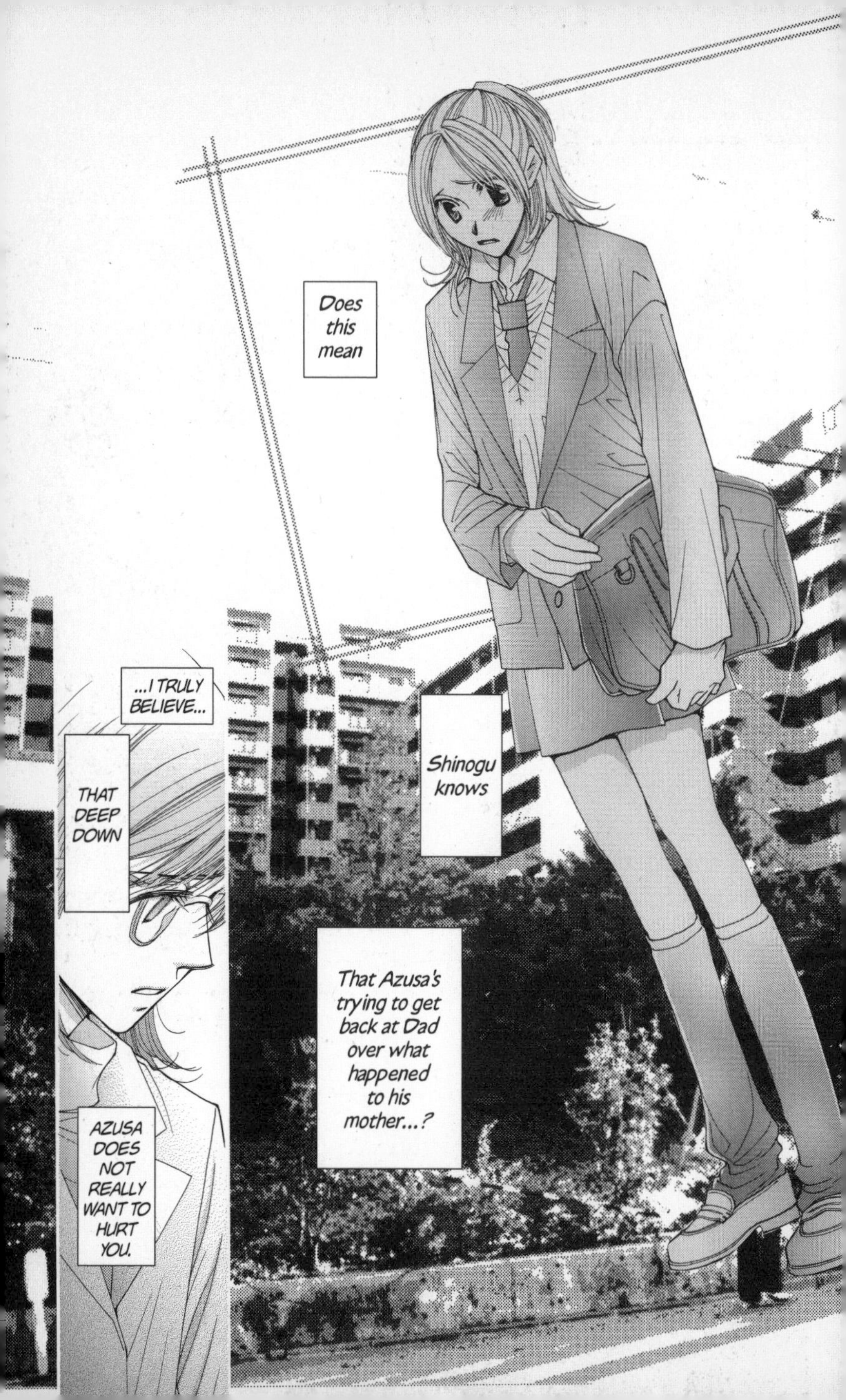
Does this mean
Shinogu knows
That Azusa's trying to get back at Dad over what happened to his mother...?
...I TRULY BELIEVE...
THAT DEEP DOWN
AZUSA DOES NOT REALLY WANT TO HURT YOU.

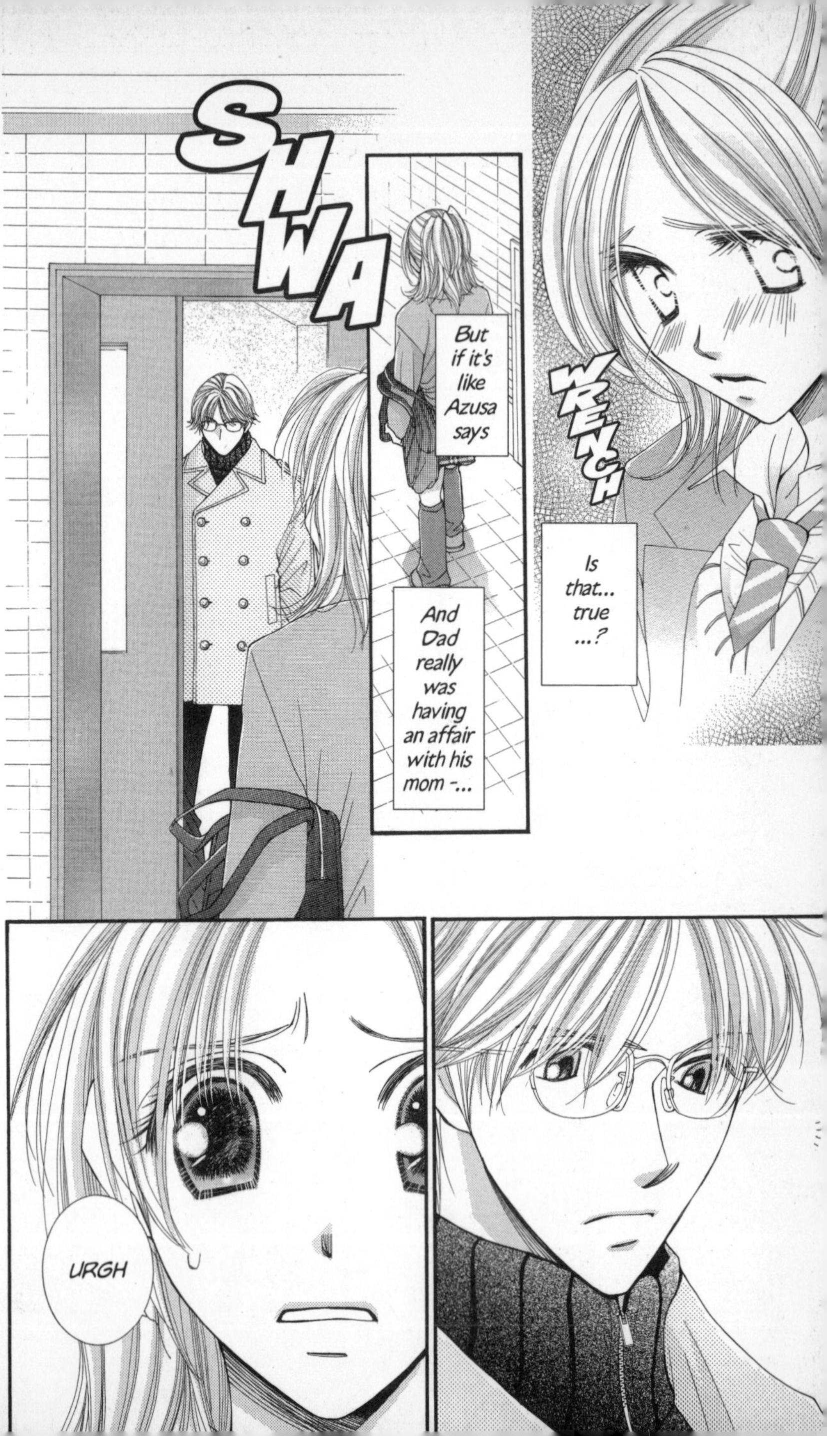

Is that... true ...?
WRENCH
But if it's like Azusa says
And Dad really was having an affair with his mom -...
SHWA
URGH

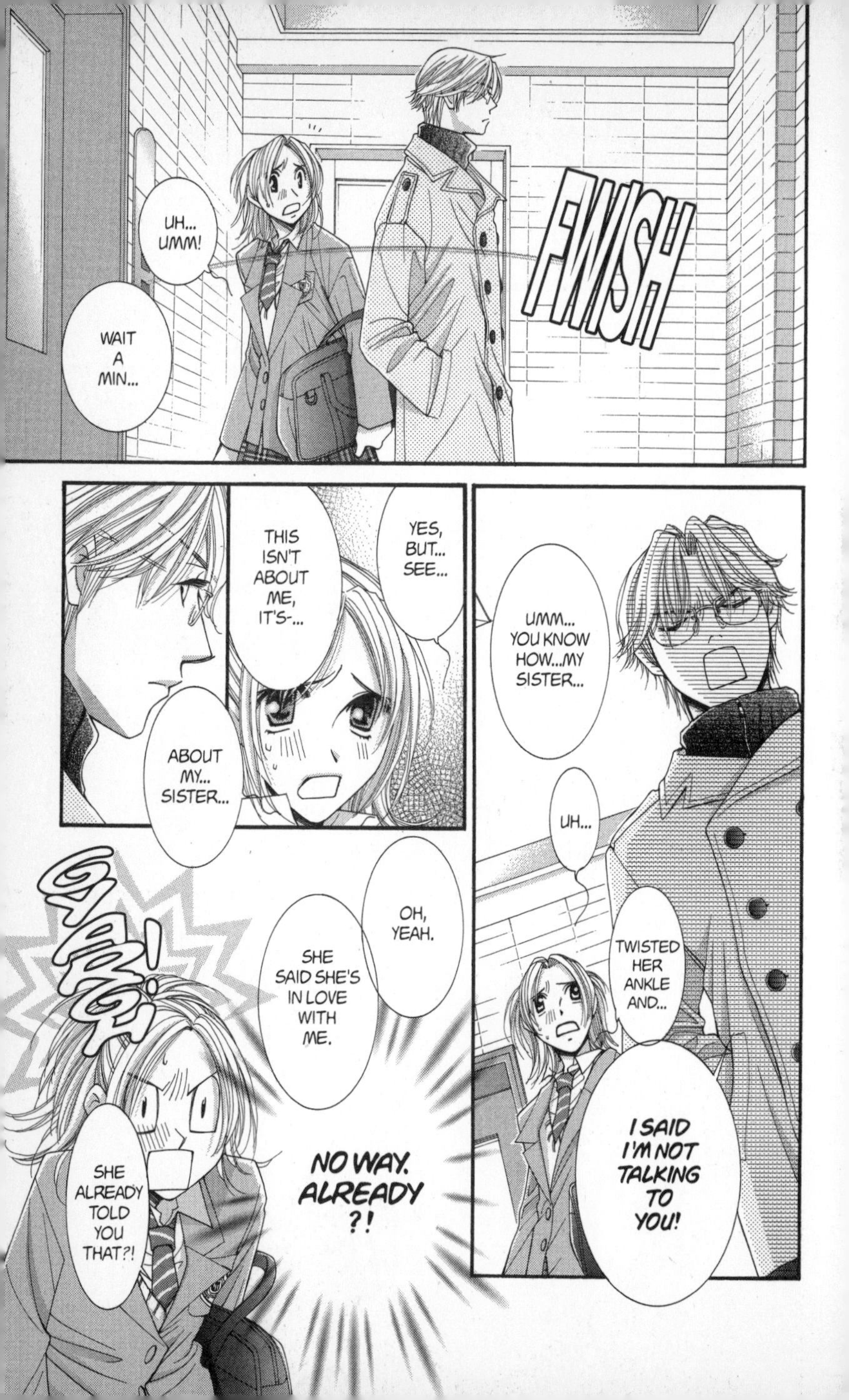
FWISH
UH... UMM!
WAIT A MIN...
UMM... YOU KNOW HOW...MY SISTER...
UH...
TWISTED HER ANKLE AND...
I SAID I'M NOT TALKING TO YOU!
YES, BUT... SEE...
THIS ISN'T ABOUT ME, IT'S-...
ABOUT MY... SISTER...
OH, YEAH.
SHE SAID SHE'S IN LOVE WITH ME.
NO WAY. ALREADY?!
GAWK!
SHE ALREADY TOLD YOU THAT?!

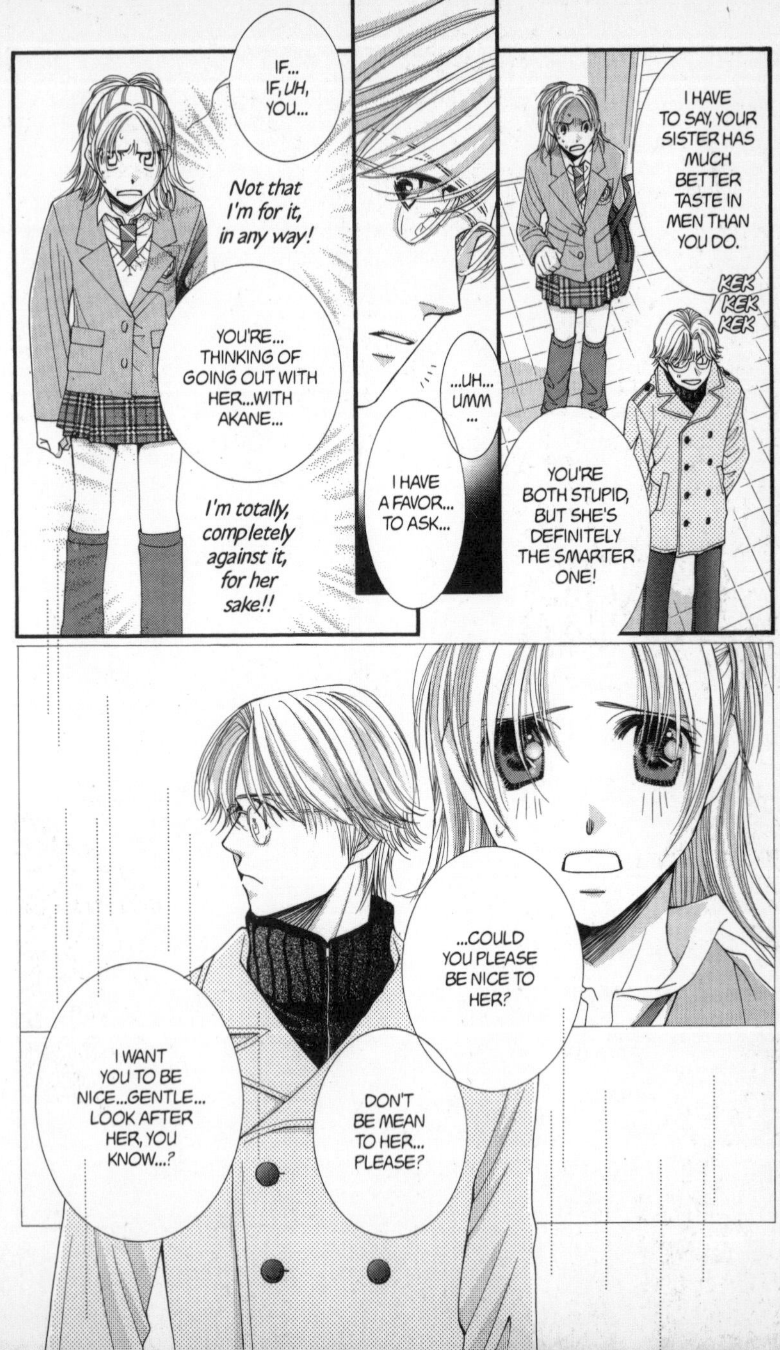
I HAVE TO SAY, YOUR SISTER HAS MUCH BETTER TASTE IN MEN THAN YOU DO.
KEK KEK KEK
YOU'RE BOTH STUPID, BUT SHE'S DEFINITELY THE SMARTER ONE!
...UH... UMM...
I HAVE A FAVOR... TO ASK...
IF... IF, UH, YOU...
Not that I'm for it, in any way!
YOU'RE... THINKING OF GOING OUT WITH HER...WITH AKANE...
I'm totally, completely against it, for her sake!!
...COULD YOU PLEASE BE NICE TO HER?
DON'T BE MEAN TO HER... PLEASE?
I WANT YOU TO BE NICE...GENTLE... LOOK AFTER HER, YOU KNOW...?

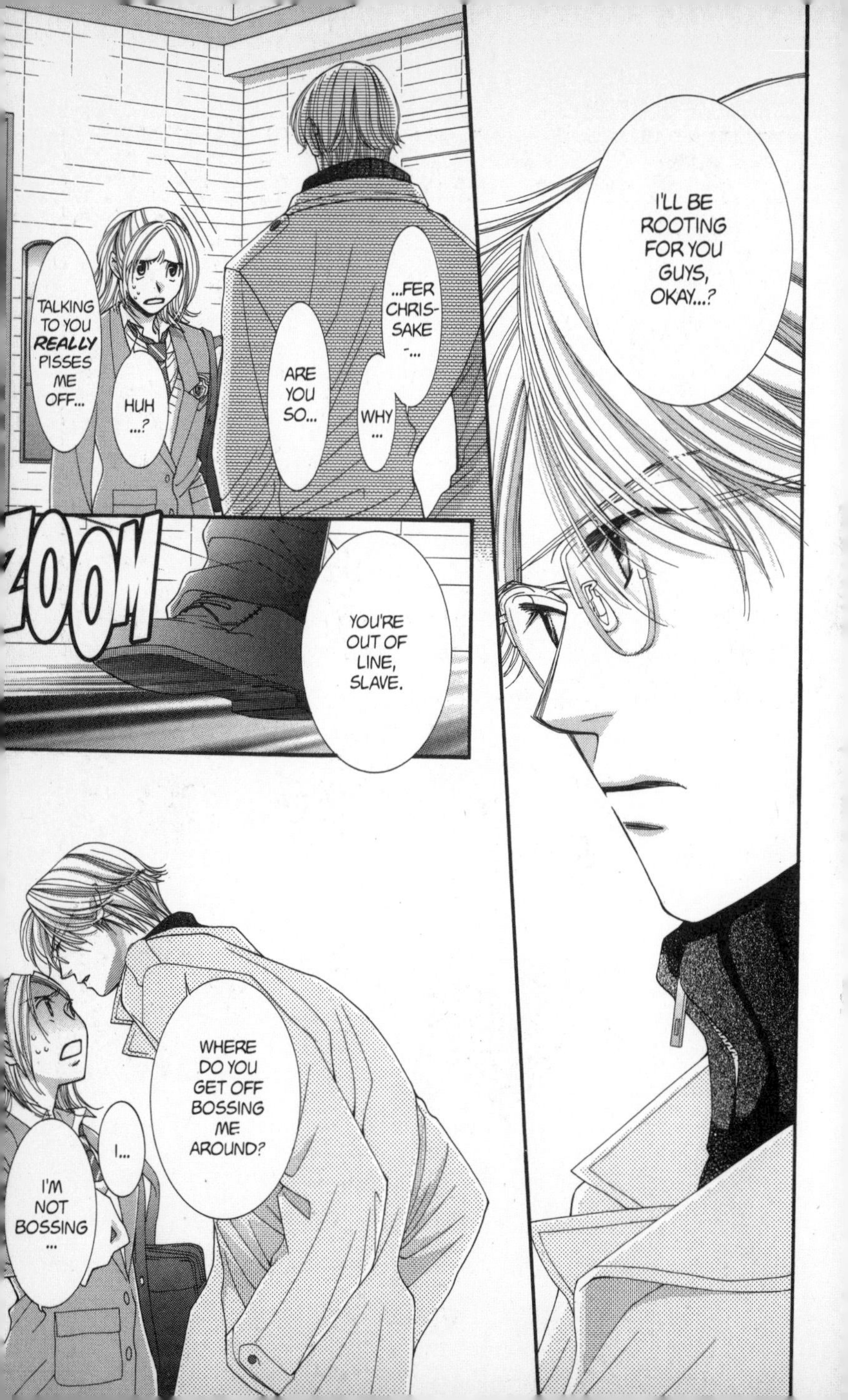
I'LL BE ROOTING FOR YOU GUYS, OKAY...?
...FER CHRIS-SAKE-...
WHY...
ARE YOU SO...
HUH...?
TALKING TO YOU **REALLY** PISSES ME OFF...
ZOOM
YOU'RE OUT OF LINE, SLAVE.
WHERE DO YOU GET OFF BOSSING ME AROUND?
I...
I'M NOT BOSSING...

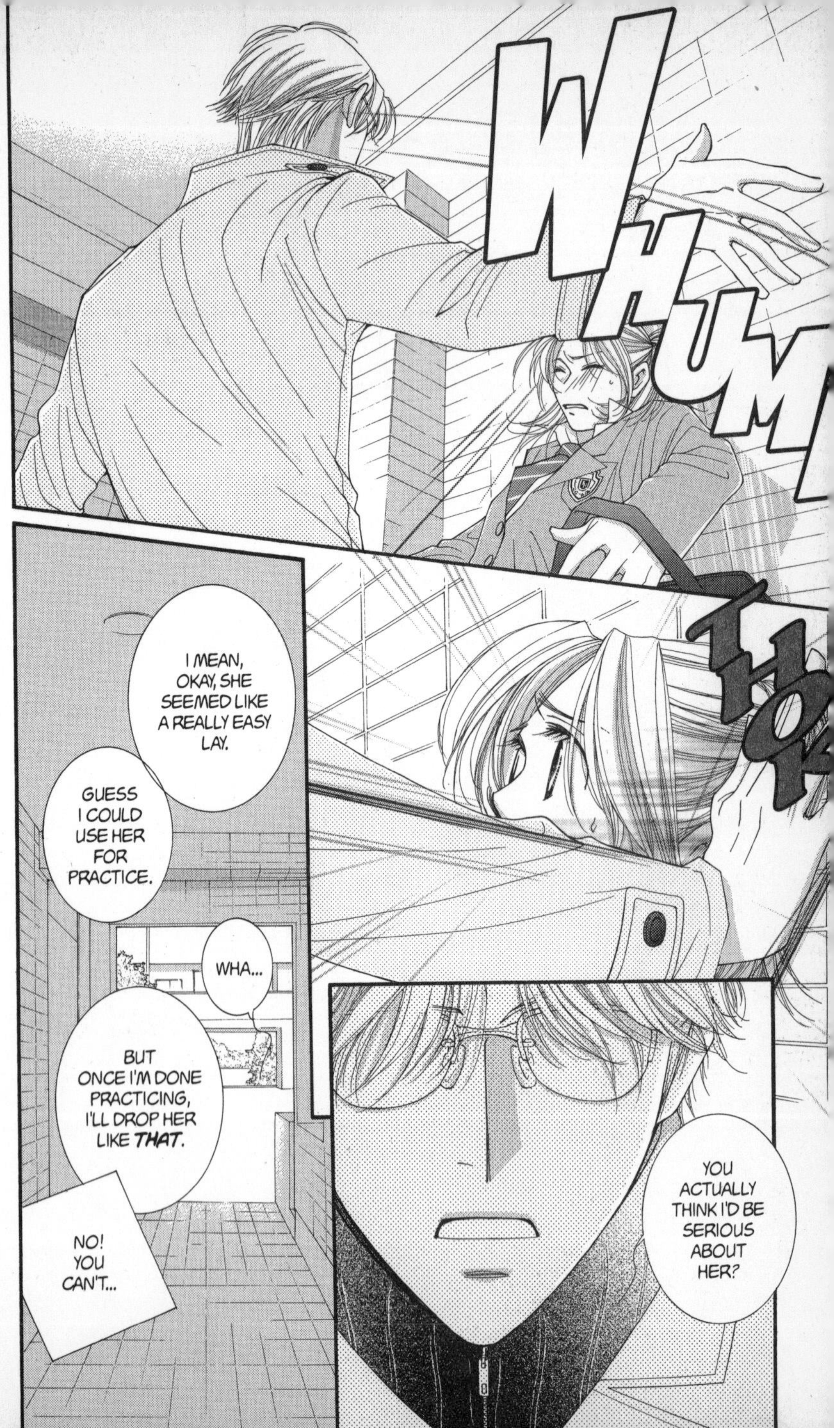

WHUM
THOK
YOU ACTUALLY THINK I'D BE SERIOUS ABOUT HER?
I MEAN, OKAY, SHE SEEMED LIKE A REALLY EASY LAY.
GUESS I COULD USE HER FOR PRACTICE.
WHA...
BUT ONCE I'M DONE PRACTICING, I'LL DROP HER LIKE *THAT*.
NO! YOU CAN'T...

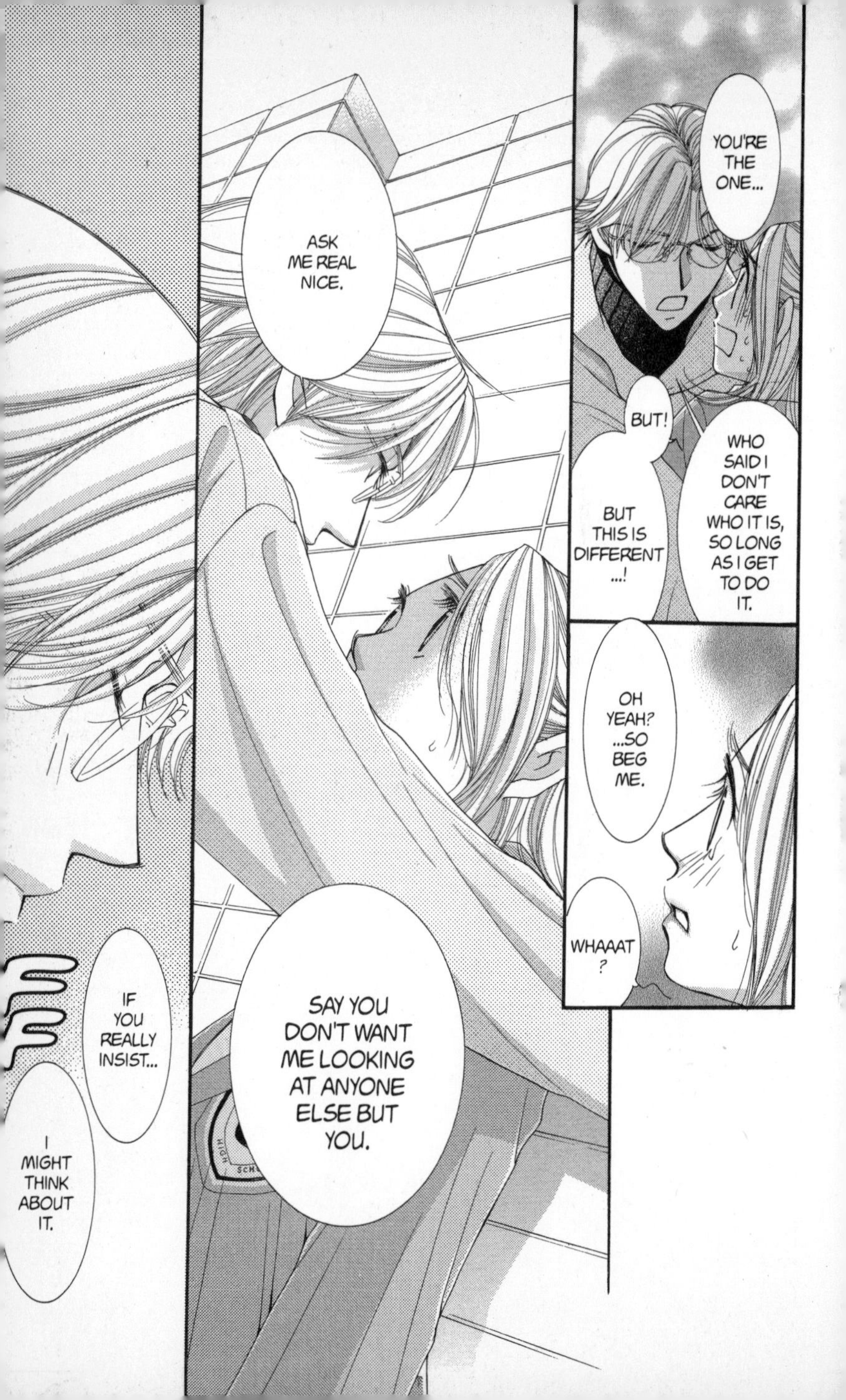
YOU'RE THE ONE...
WHO SAID I DON'T CARE WHO IT IS, SO LONG AS I GET TO DO IT.
BUT!
BUT THIS IS DIFFERENT...!
OH YEAH? ...SO BEG ME.
WHAAAT?
ASK ME REAL NICE.
SAY YOU DON'T WANT ME LOOKING AT ANYONE ELSE BUT YOU.
IF YOU REALLY INSIST...
I MIGHT THINK ABOUT IT.

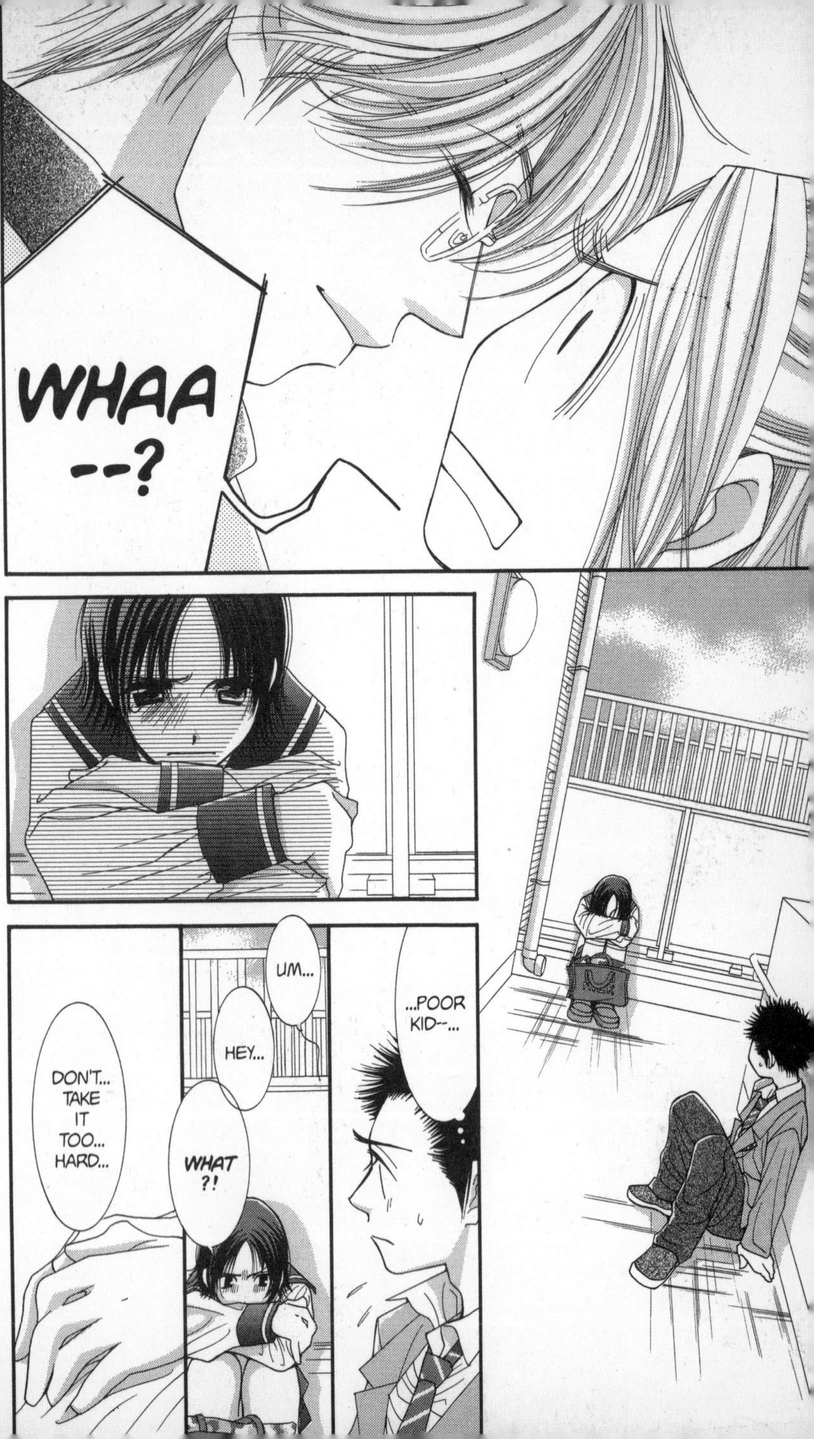
WHAA--?
...POOR KID--...
UM...
HEY...
WHAT?!
DON'T... TAKE IT TOO... HARD...

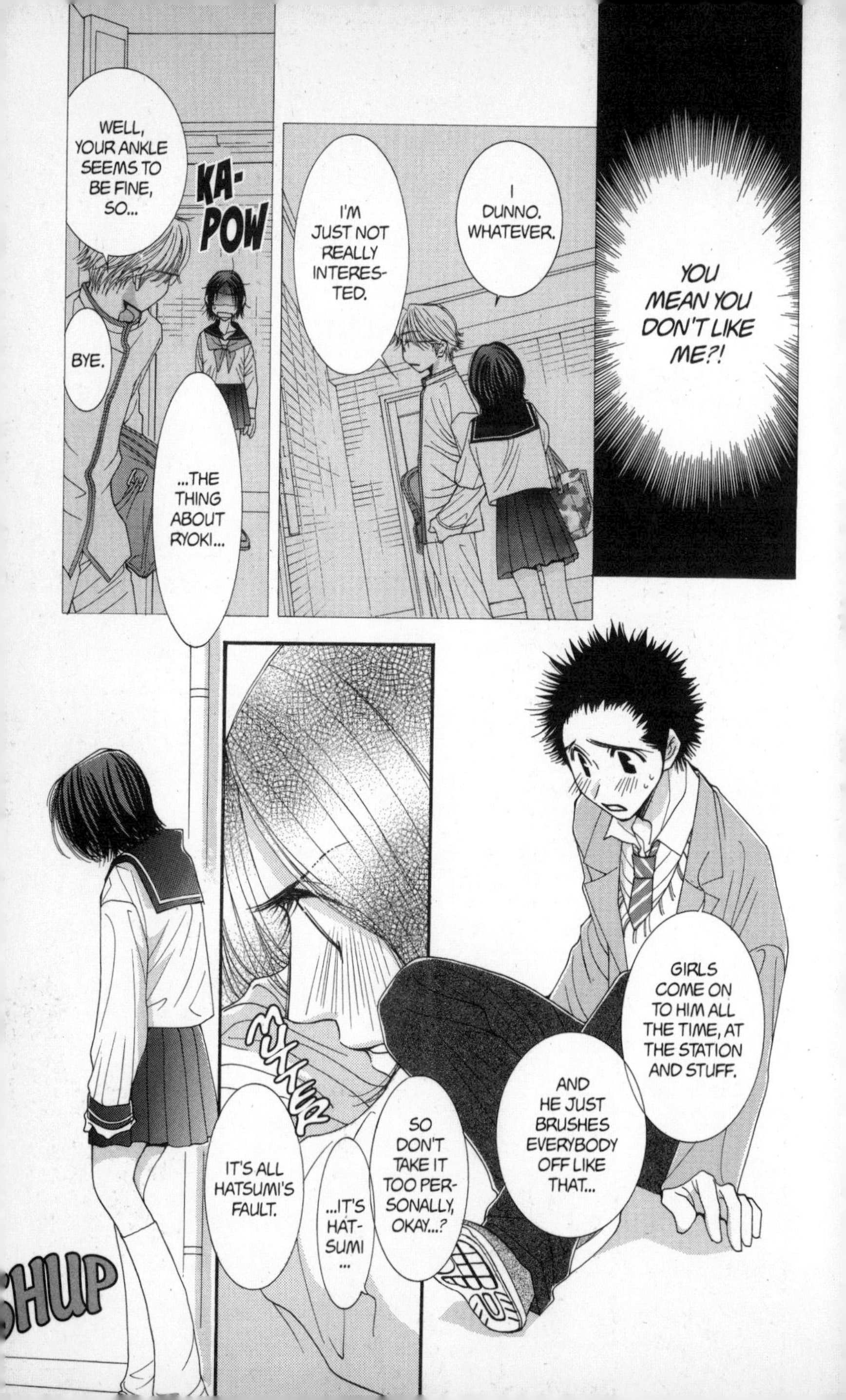
YOU MEAN YOU DON'T LIKE ME?!
I DUNNO. WHATEVER.
I'M JUST NOT REALLY INTERES-TED.
WELL, YOUR ANKLE SEEMS TO BE FINE, SO...
KA-POW
BYE.
...THE THING ABOUT RYOKI...
GIRLS COME ON TO HIM ALL THE TIME, AT THE STATION AND STUFF.
AND HE JUST BRUSHES EVERYBODY OFF LIKE THAT...
SO DON'T TAKE IT TOO PER-SONALLY, OKAY...?
...IT'S HAT-SUMI...
IT'S ALL HATSUMI'S FAULT.
SHUP

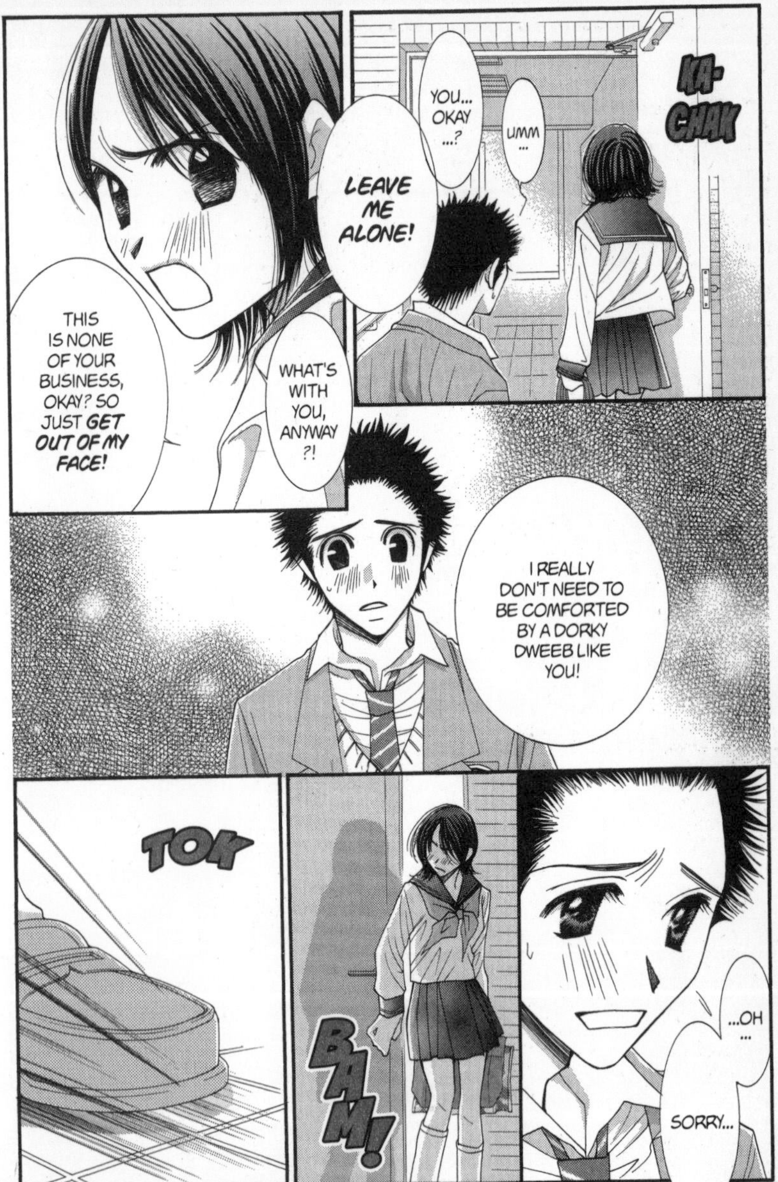
KA-CHAK
UMM ...
YOU... OKAY ...?
LEAVE ME ALONE!
WHAT'S WITH YOU, ANYWAY ?!
THIS IS NONE OF YOUR BUSINESS, OKAY? SO JUST GET OUT OF MY FACE!
I REALLY DON'T NEED TO BE COMFORTED BY A DORKY DWEEB LIKE YOU!
...OH ...
SORRY...
BAM!
TOK

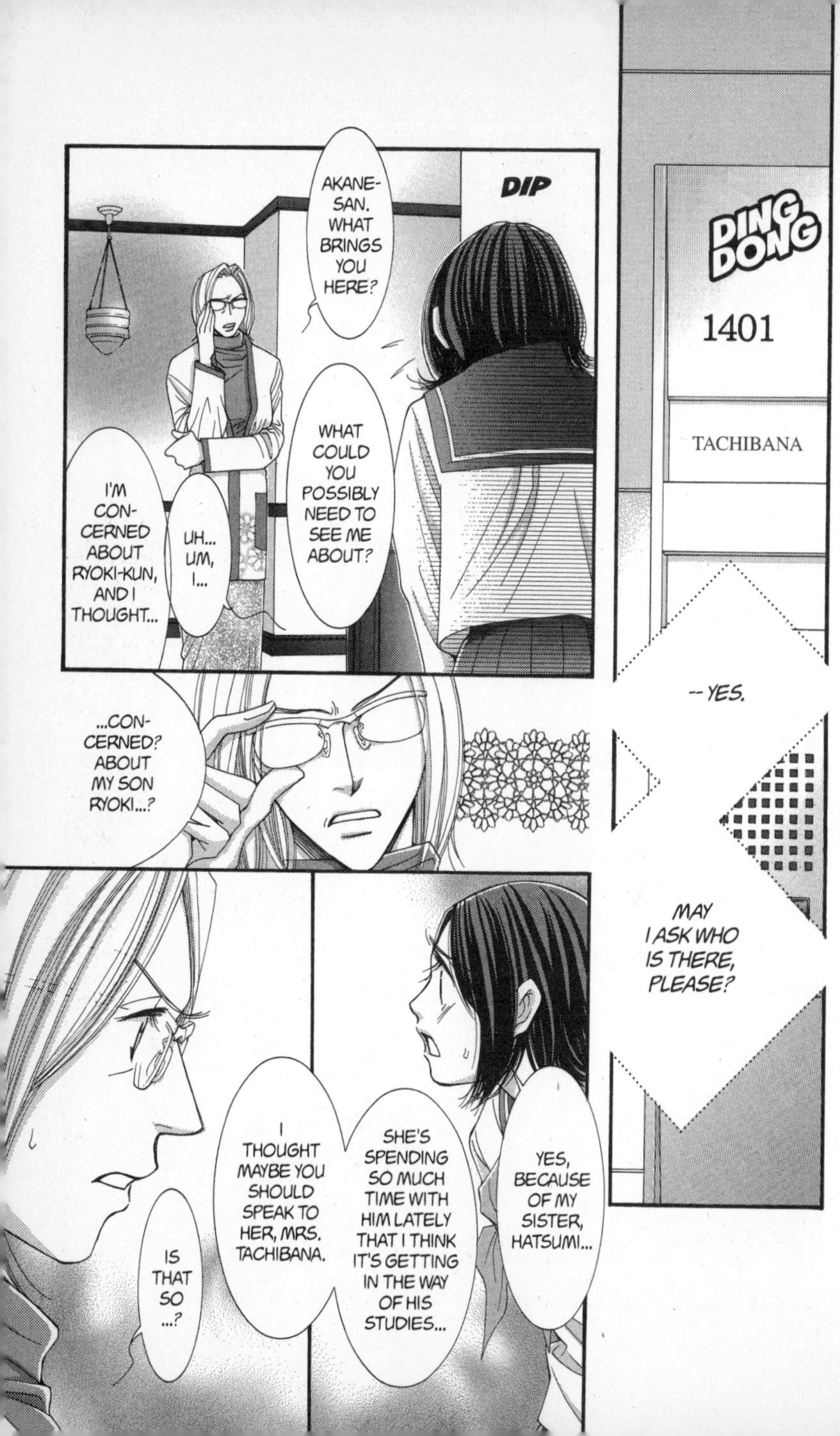
DING DONG
1401
TACHIBANA
--YES.
MAY I ASK WHO IS THERE, PLEASE?
DIP
AKANE-SAN. WHAT BRINGS YOU HERE?
WHAT COULD YOU POSSIBLY NEED TO SEE ME ABOUT?
UH... UM, I...
I'M CONCERNED ABOUT RYOKI-KUN, AND I THOUGHT...
...CONCERNED? ABOUT MY SON RYOKI...?
YES, BECAUSE OF MY SISTER, HATSUMI...
SHE'S SPENDING SO MUCH TIME WITH HIM LATELY THAT I THINK IT'S GETTING IN THE WAY OF HIS STUDIES...
I THOUGHT MAYBE YOU SHOULD SPEAK TO HER, MRS. TACHIBANA.
IS THAT SO ...?

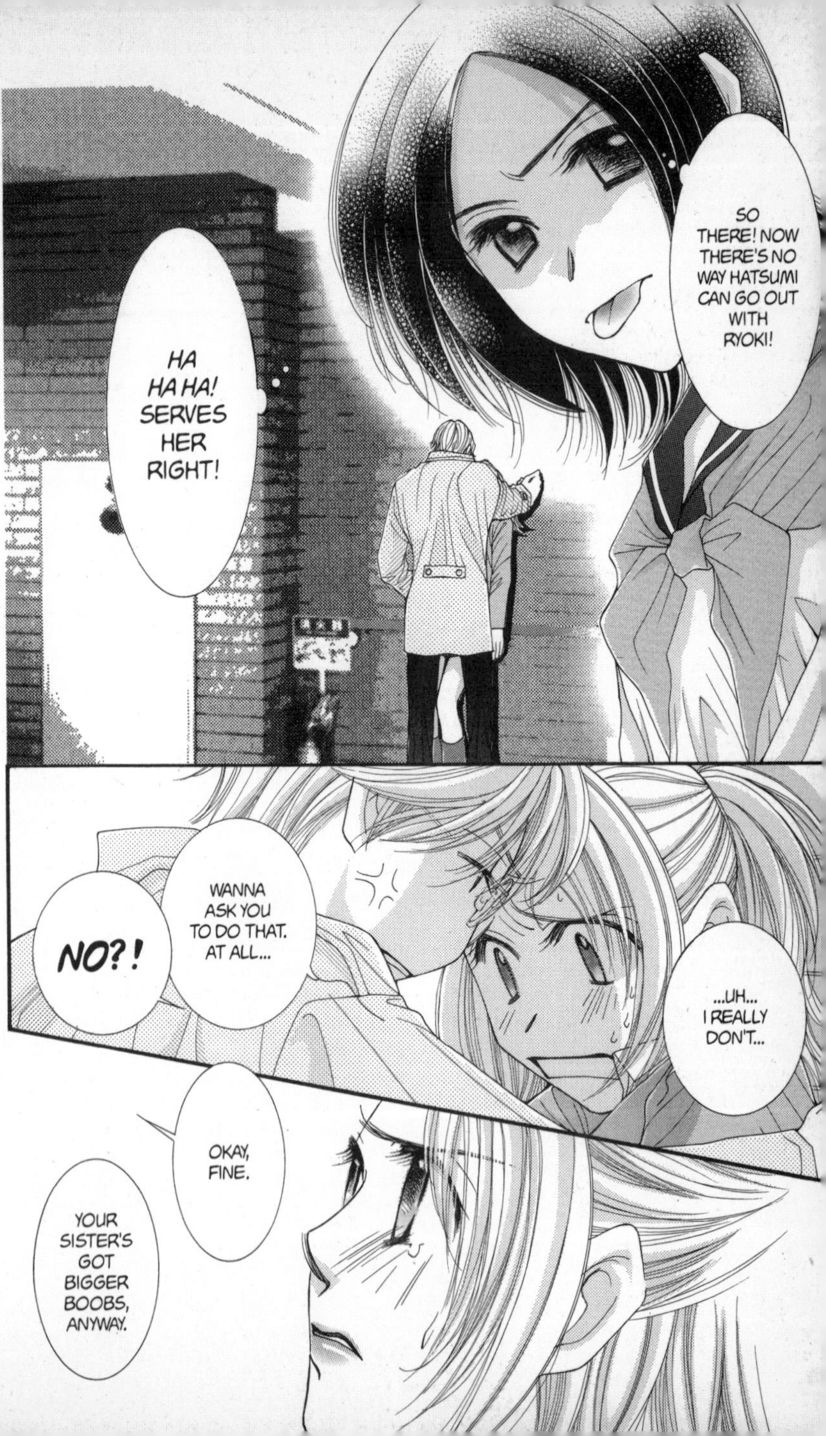
SO THERE! NOW THERE'S NO WAY HATSUMI CAN GO OUT WITH RYOKI!
HA HA HA! SERVES HER RIGHT!
...UH... I REALLY DON'T...
WANNA ASK YOU TO DO THAT. AT ALL...
NO?!
OKAY, FINE.
YOUR SISTER'S GOT BIGGER BOOBS, ANYWAY.

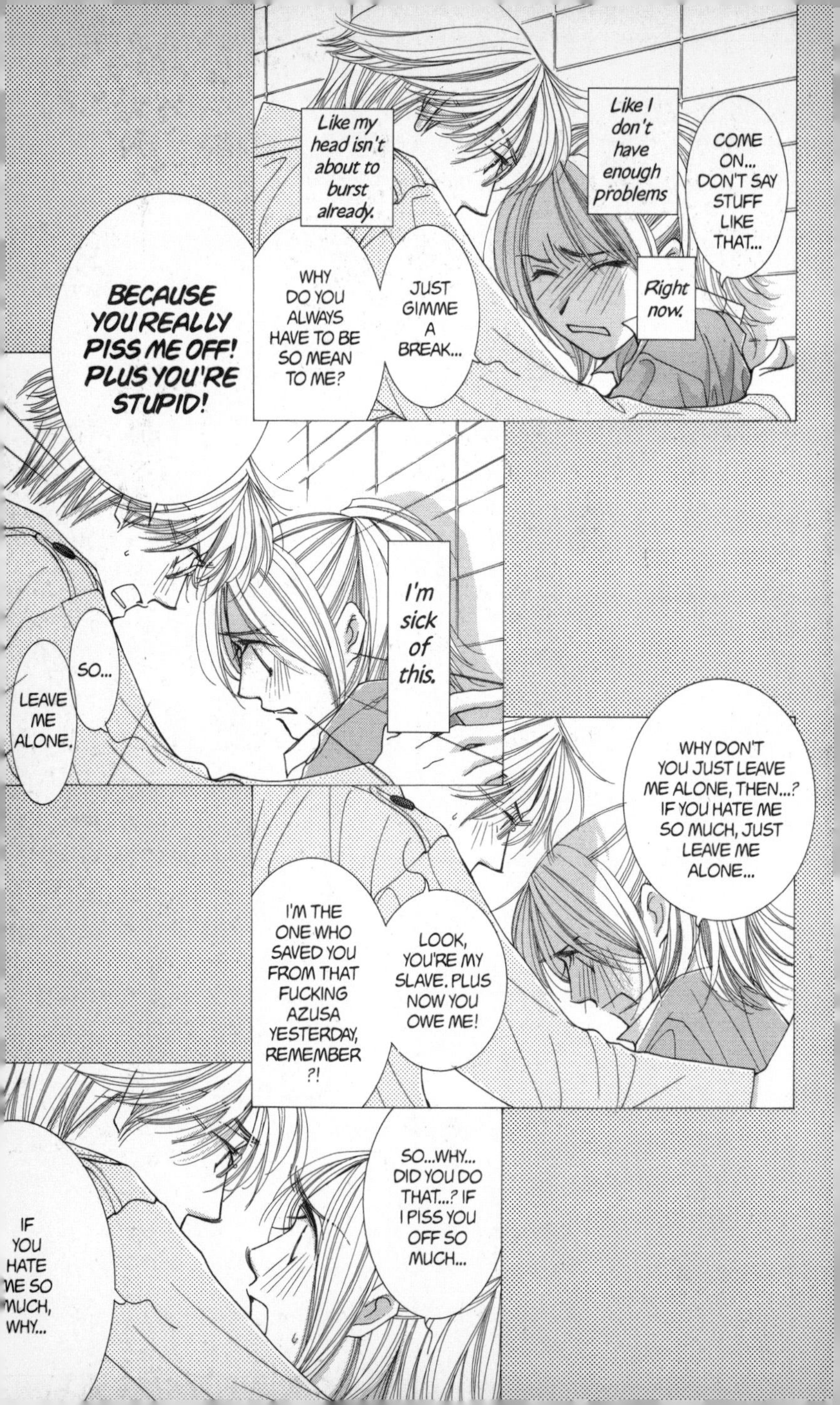
Like I don't have enough problems
COME ON... DON'T SAY STUFF LIKE THAT...
Right now.
Like my head isn't about to burst already.
JUST GIMME A BREAK...
WHY DO YOU ALWAYS HAVE TO BE SO MEAN TO ME?
BECAUSE YOU REALLY PISS ME OFF! PLUS YOU'RE STUPID!
I'm sick of this.
SO...
LEAVE ME ALONE.
WHY DON'T YOU JUST LEAVE ME ALONE, THEN...? IF YOU HATE ME SO MUCH, JUST LEAVE ME ALONE...
LOOK, YOU'RE MY SLAVE. PLUS NOW YOU OWE ME!
I'M THE ONE WHO SAVED YOU FROM THAT FUCKING AZUSA YESTERDAY, REMEMBER?!
SO...WHY... DID YOU DO THAT...? IF I PISS YOU OFF SO MUCH...
IF YOU HATE ME SO MUCH, WHY...

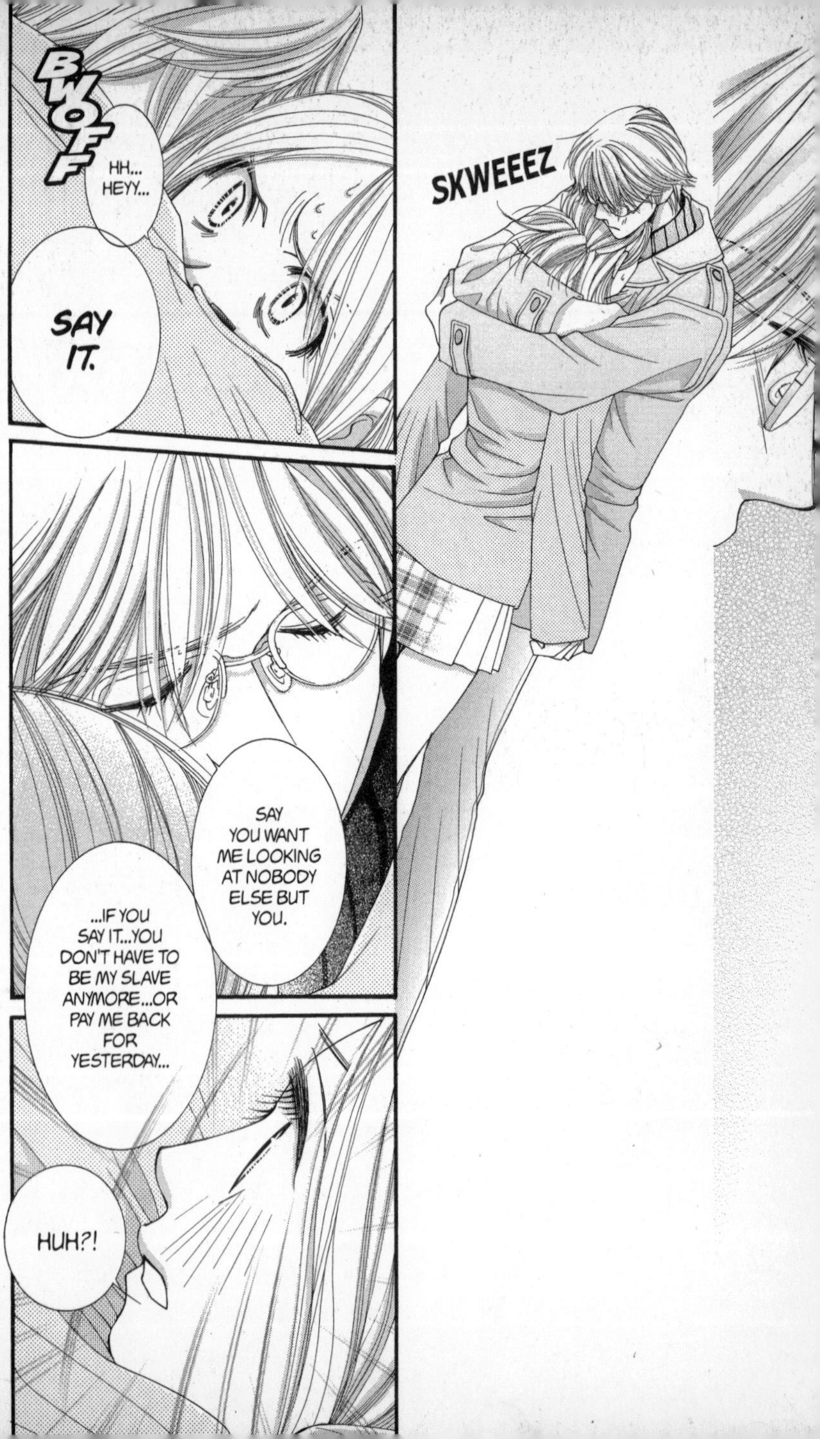
SKWEEEZ
BWOFF
HH... HEYY...
SAY IT.
SAY YOU WANT ME LOOKING AT NOBODY ELSE BUT YOU.
...IF YOU SAY IT...YOU DON'T HAVE TO BE MY SLAVE ANYMORE...OR PAY ME BACK FOR YESTERDAY...
HUH?!

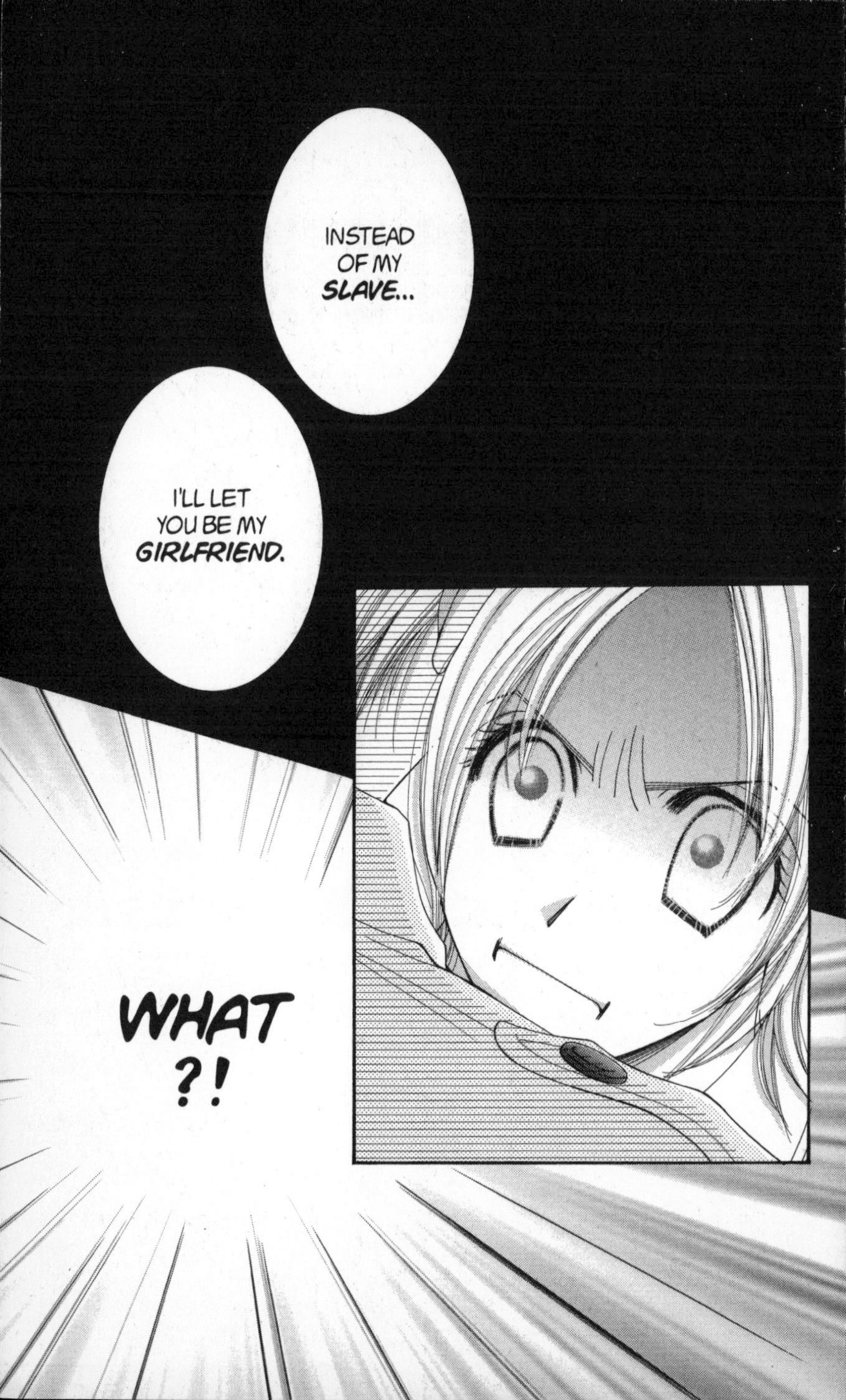
INSTEAD OF MY SLAVE...
I'LL LET YOU BE MY GIRLFRIEND.
WHAT ?!

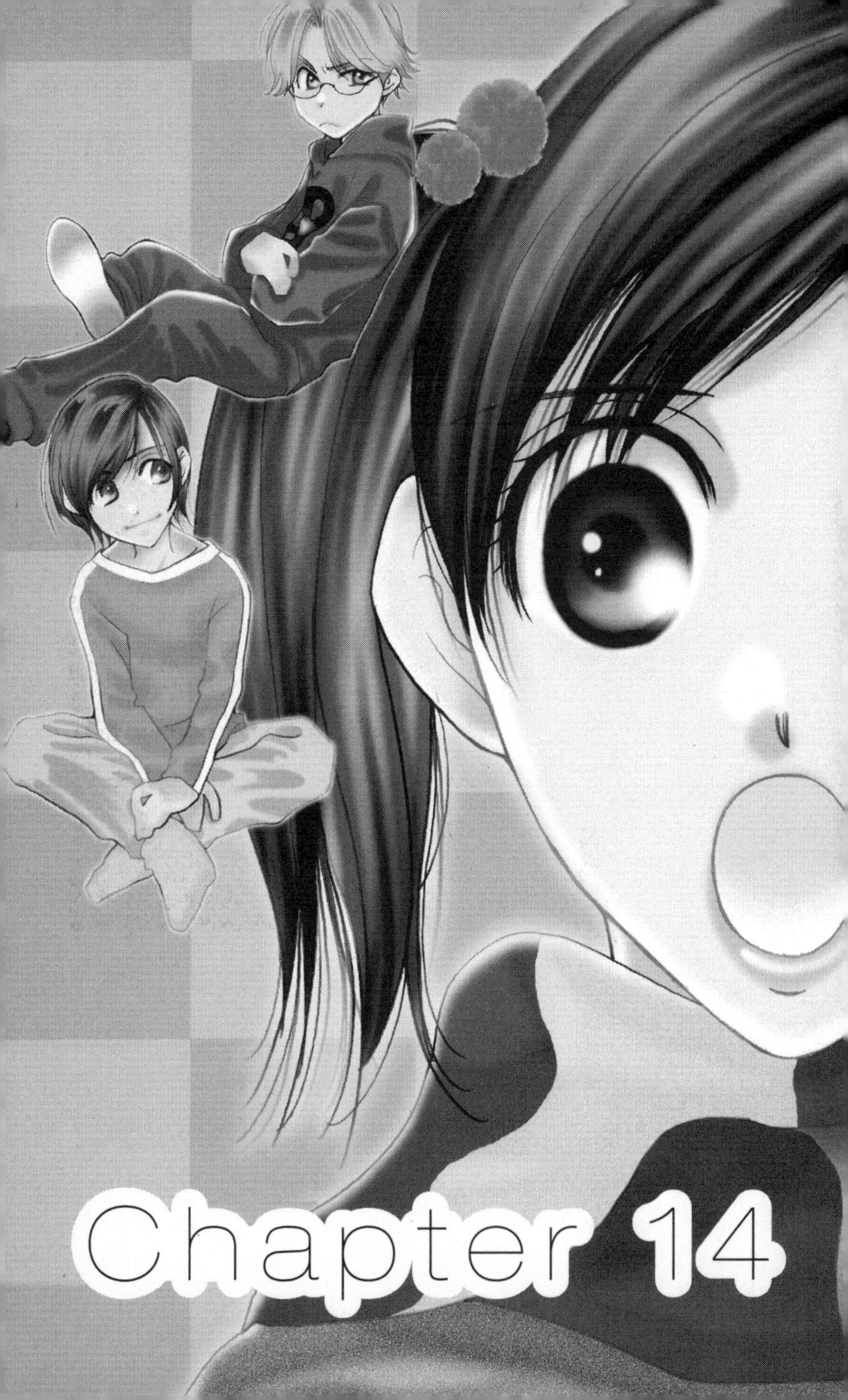
Chapter 14

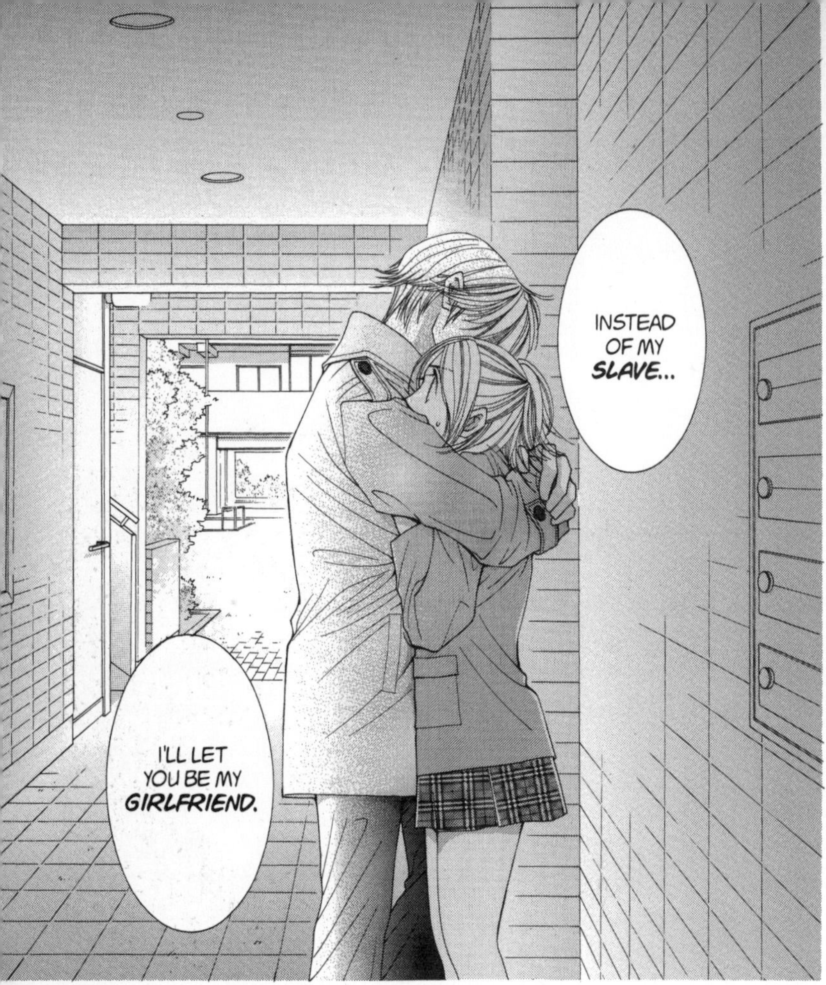
INSTEAD OF MY SLAVE...
I'LL LET YOU BE MY GIRLFRIEND.

hot gimmick

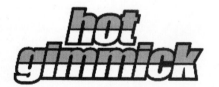

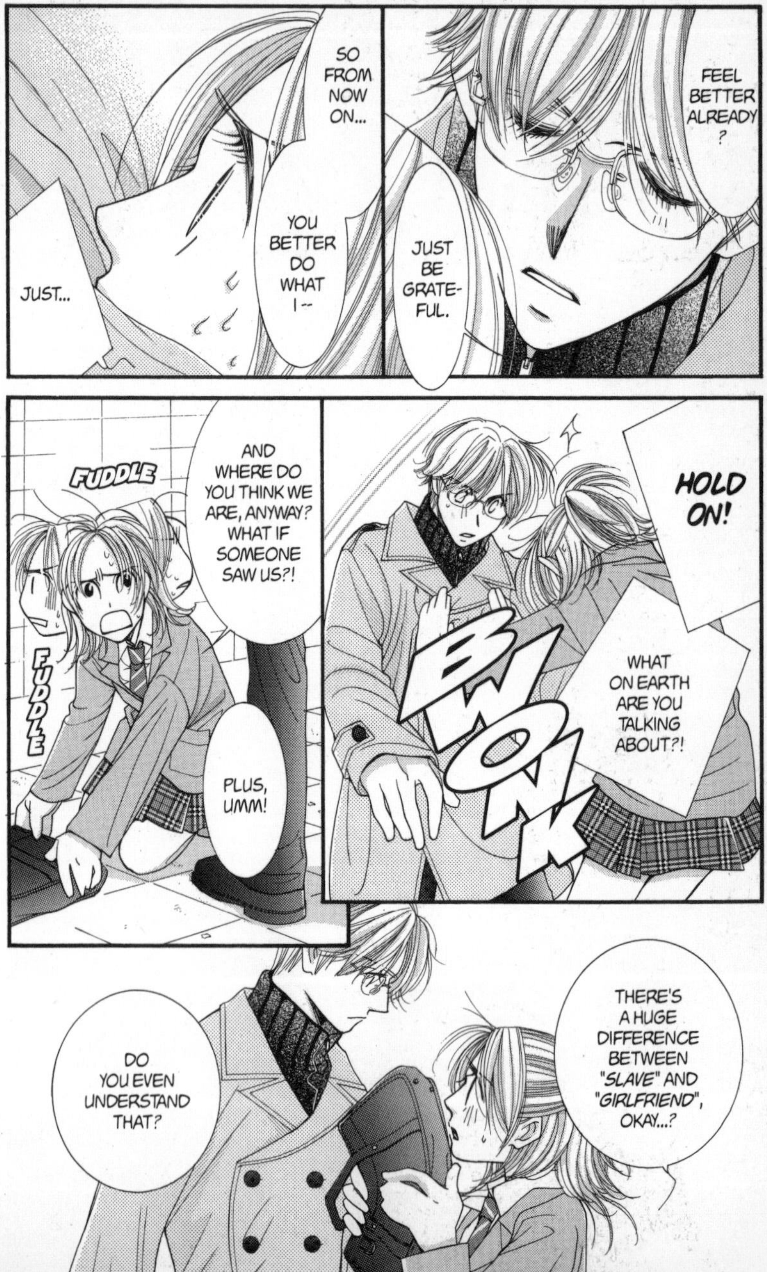
FEEL BETTER ALREADY?
JUST BE GRATEFUL.
SO FROM NOW ON...
YOU BETTER DO WHAT I --
JUST...
HOLD ON!
BWONK
WHAT ON EARTH ARE YOU TALKING ABOUT?!
AND WHERE DO YOU THINK WE ARE, ANYWAY? WHAT IF SOMEONE SAW US?!
FUDDLE
FUDDLE
PLUS, UMM!
THERE'S A HUGE DIFFERENCE BETWEEN "SLAVE" AND "GIRLFRIEND", OKAY...?
DO YOU EVEN UNDERSTAND THAT?

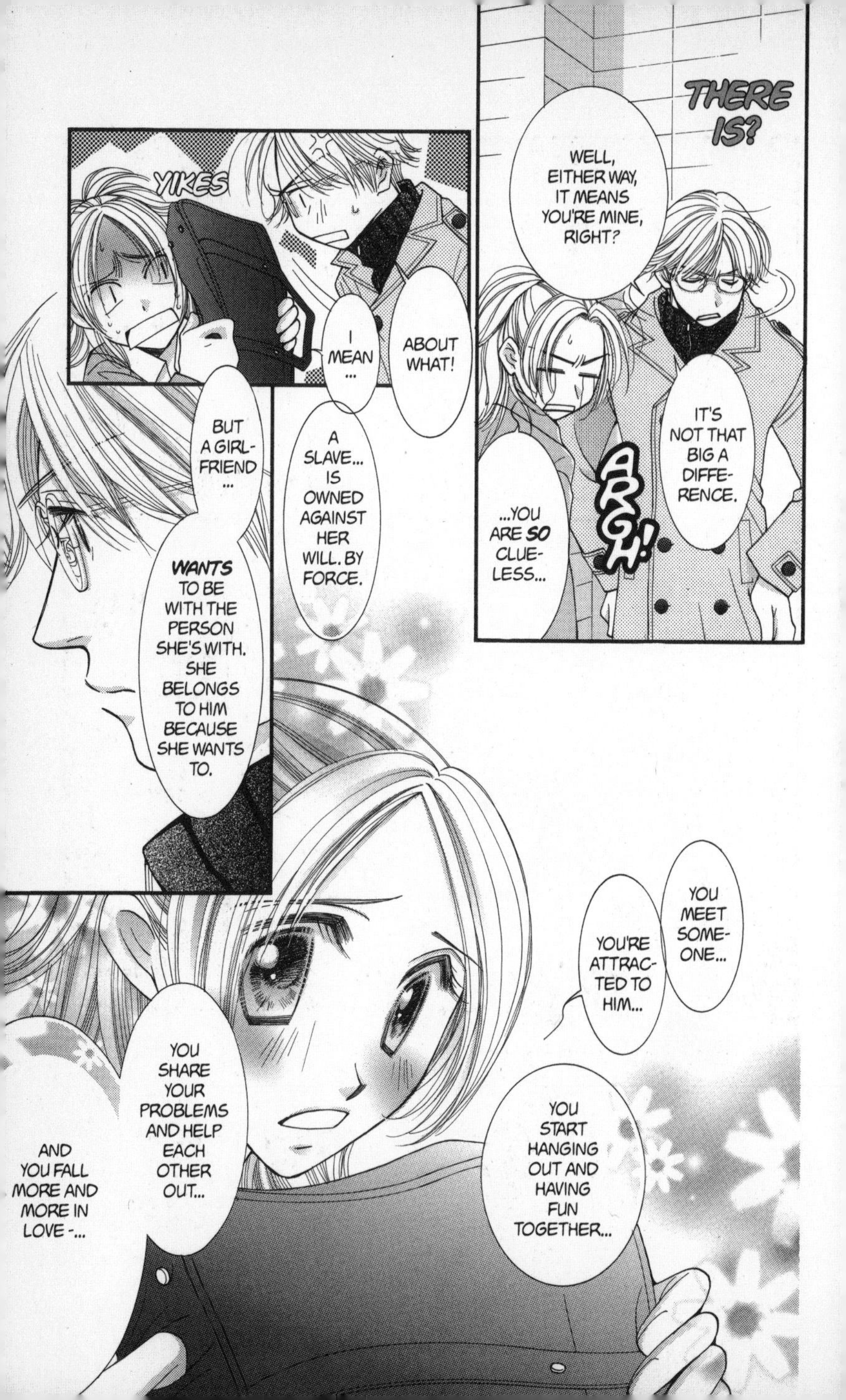
THERE IS?
WELL, EITHER WAY, IT MEANS YOU'RE MINE, RIGHT?
IT'S NOT THAT BIG A DIFFERENCE.
ARGH!
...YOU ARE SO CLUELESS...
YIKES
ABOUT WHAT!
I MEAN ...
A SLAVE... IS OWNED AGAINST HER WILL. BY FORCE.
BUT A GIRLFRIEND ...
WANTS TO BE WITH THE PERSON SHE'S WITH. SHE BELONGS TO HIM BECAUSE SHE WANTS TO.
YOU MEET SOME-ONE...
YOU'RE ATTRAC-TED TO HIM...
YOU START HANGING OUT AND HAVING FUN TOGETHER...
YOU SHARE YOUR PROBLEMS AND HELP EACH OTHER OUT...
AND YOU FALL MORE AND MORE IN LOVE -...

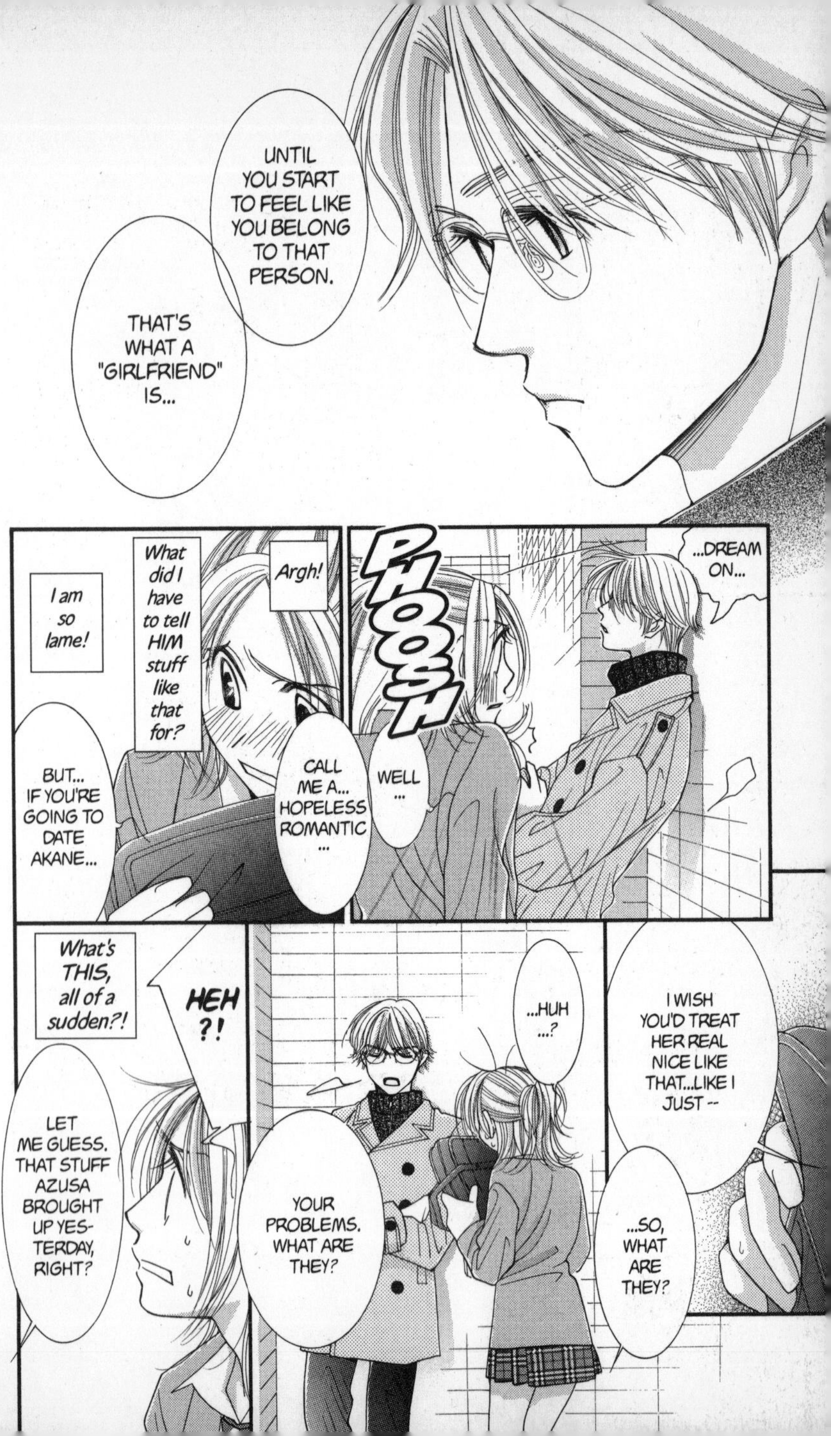
UNTIL YOU START TO FEEL LIKE YOU BELONG TO THAT PERSON.
THAT'S WHAT A "GIRLFRIEND" IS...
...DREAM ON...
PHOOSH
WELL ...
CALL ME A... HOPELESS ROMANTIC ...
Argh!
What did I have to tell HIM stuff like that for?
I am so lame!
BUT... IF YOU'RE GOING TO DATE AKANE...
I WISH YOU'D TREAT HER REAL NICE LIKE THAT...LIKE I JUST --
...SO, WHAT ARE THEY?
...HUH ...?
YOUR PROBLEMS. WHAT ARE THEY?
HEH ?!
What's THIS, all of a sudden?!
LET ME GUESS. THAT STUFF AZUSA BROUGHT UP YESTERDAY, RIGHT?

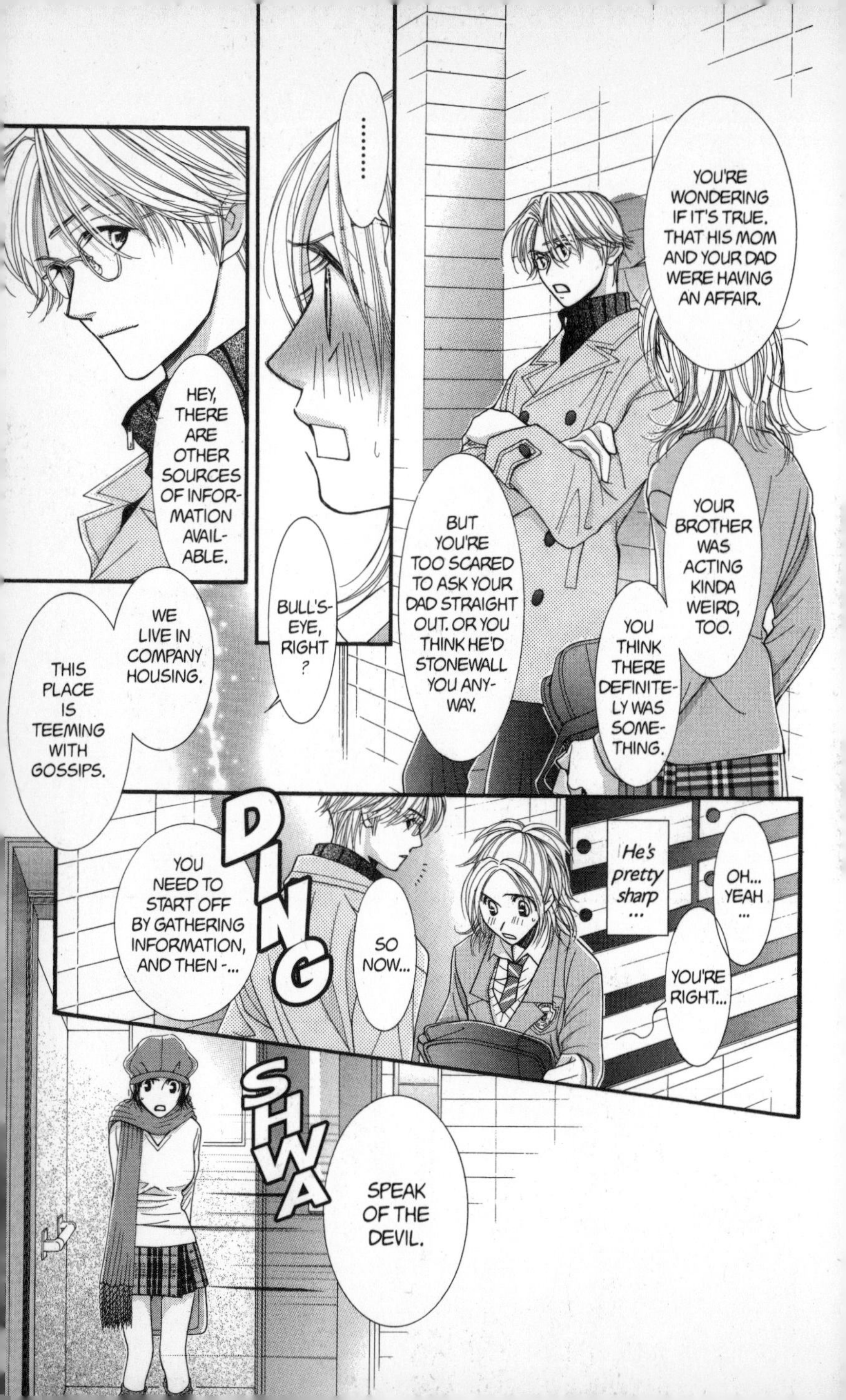

YOU'RE WONDERING IF IT'S TRUE. THAT HIS MOM AND YOUR DAD WERE HAVING AN AFFAIR.
YOUR BROTHER WAS ACTING KINDA WEIRD, TOO.
YOU THINK THERE DEFINITE-LY WAS SOME-THING.
BUT YOU'RE TOO SCARED TO ASK YOUR DAD STRAIGHT OUT. OR YOU THINK HE'D STONEWALL YOU ANY-WAY.
......
BULL'S-EYE, RIGHT?
HEY, THERE ARE OTHER SOURCES OF INFOR-MATION AVAIL-ABLE.
WE LIVE IN COMPANY HOUSING.
THIS PLACE IS TEEMING WITH GOSSIPS.
He's pretty sharp...
OH... YEAH...
YOU'RE RIGHT...
SO NOW...
YOU NEED TO START OFF BY GATHERING INFORMATION, AND THEN -...
DING
SHWA
SPEAK OF THE DEVIL.

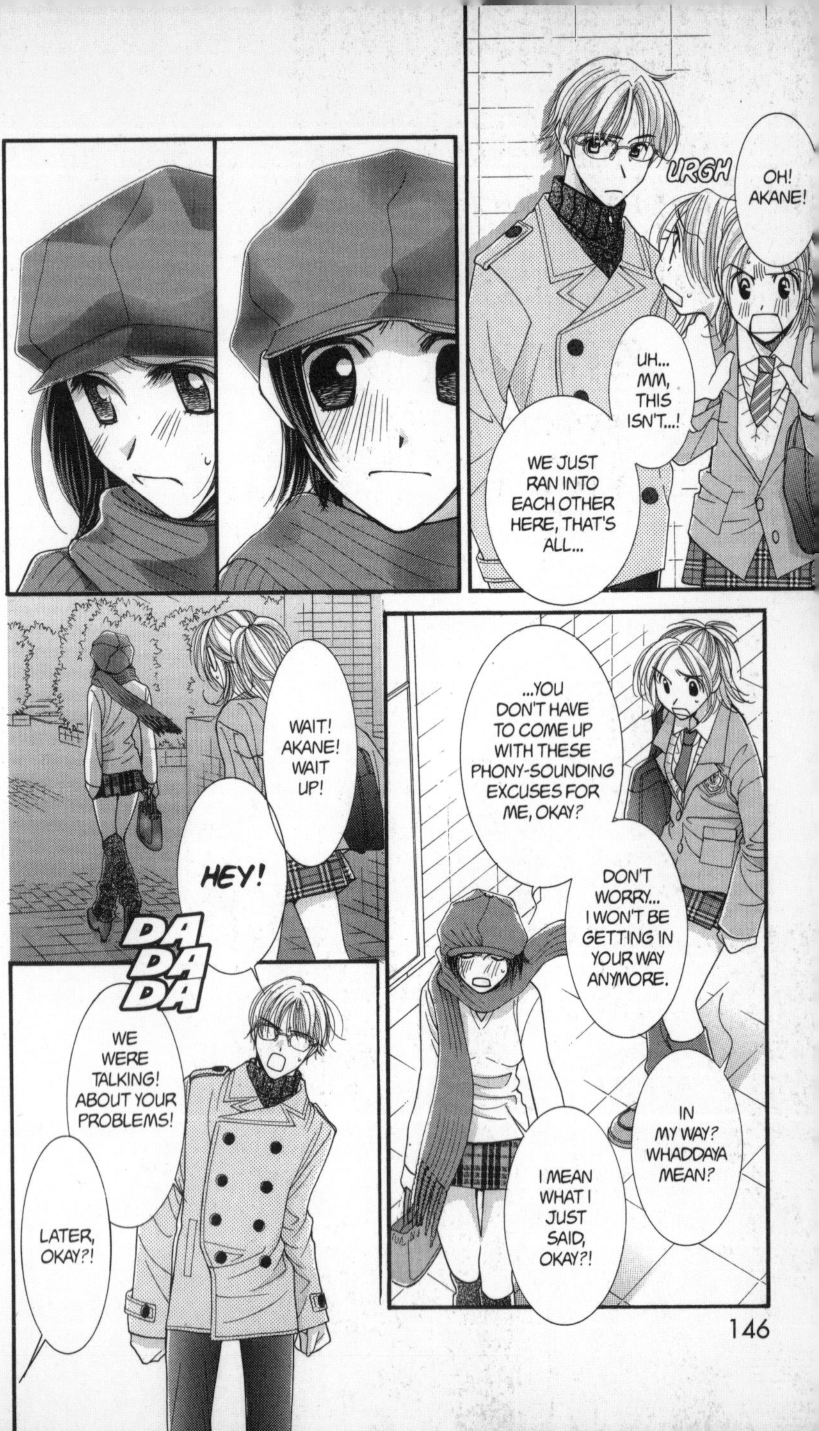
OH! AKANE!
URGH
UH... MM, THIS ISN'T...!
WE JUST RAN INTO EACH OTHER HERE, THAT'S ALL...
...YOU DON'T HAVE TO COME UP WITH THESE PHONY-SOUNDING EXCUSES FOR ME, OKAY?
DON'T WORRY... I WON'T BE GETTING IN YOUR WAY ANYMORE.
IN MY WAY? WHADDAYA MEAN?
I MEAN WHAT I JUST SAID, OKAY?!
WAIT! AKANE! WAIT UP!
HEY!
DA DA DA
WE WERE TALKING! ABOUT YOUR PROBLEMS!
LATER, OKAY?!

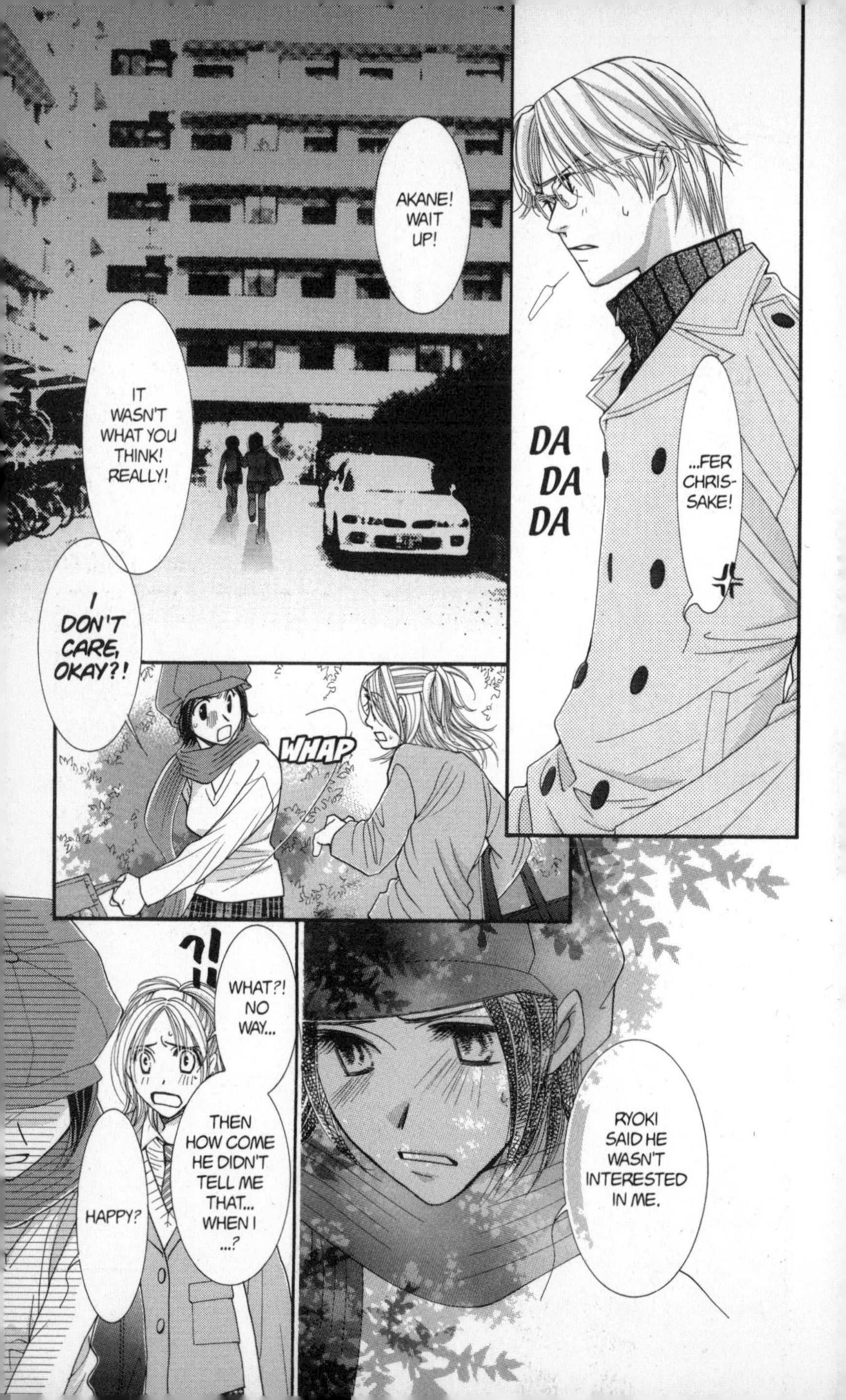
DA DA DA
...FER CHRIS-SAKE!
AKANE! WAIT UP!
IT WASN'T WHAT YOU THINK! REALLY!
I DON'T CARE, OKAY?!
WHAP
RYOKI SAID HE WASN'T INTERESTED IN ME.
?!
WHAT?! NO WAY...
THEN HOW COME HE DIDN'T TELL ME THAT... WHEN I ...?
HAPPY?

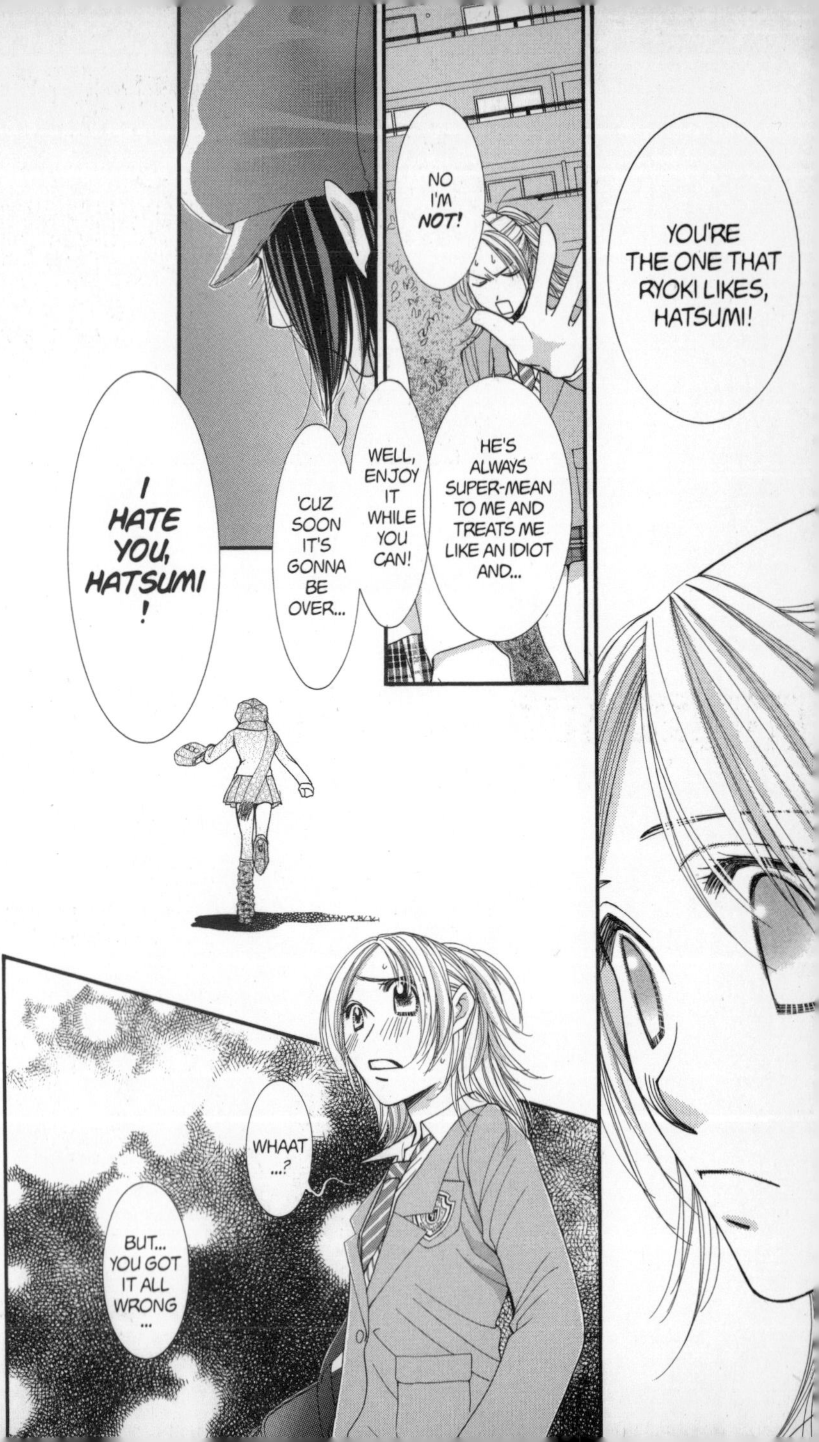
YOU'RE THE ONE THAT RYOKI LIKES, HATSUMI!
NO I'M **NOT**!
HE'S ALWAYS SUPER-MEAN TO ME AND TREATS ME LIKE AN IDIOT AND...
WELL, ENJOY IT WHILE YOU CAN!
'CUZ SOON IT'S GONNA BE OVER...
I HATE YOU, HATSUMI!
WHAAT ...?
BUT... YOU GOT IT ALL WRONG ...

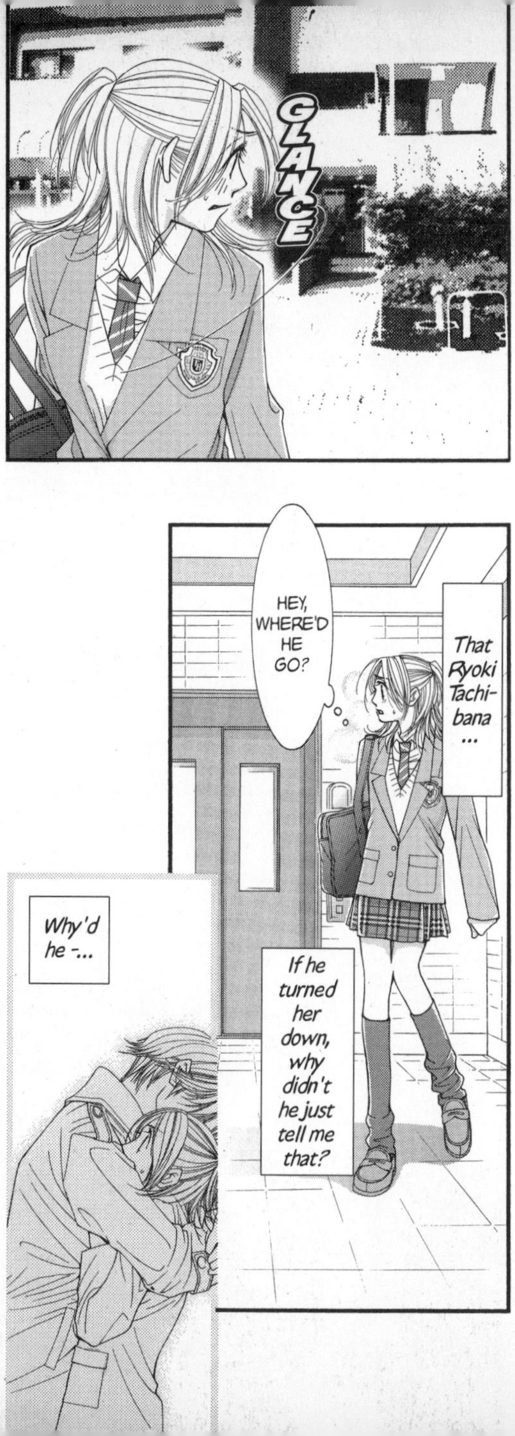
GLANCE
HEY, WHERE'D HE GO?
That Ryoki Tachibana...
If he turned her down, why didn't he just tell me that?
Why'd he -...

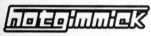

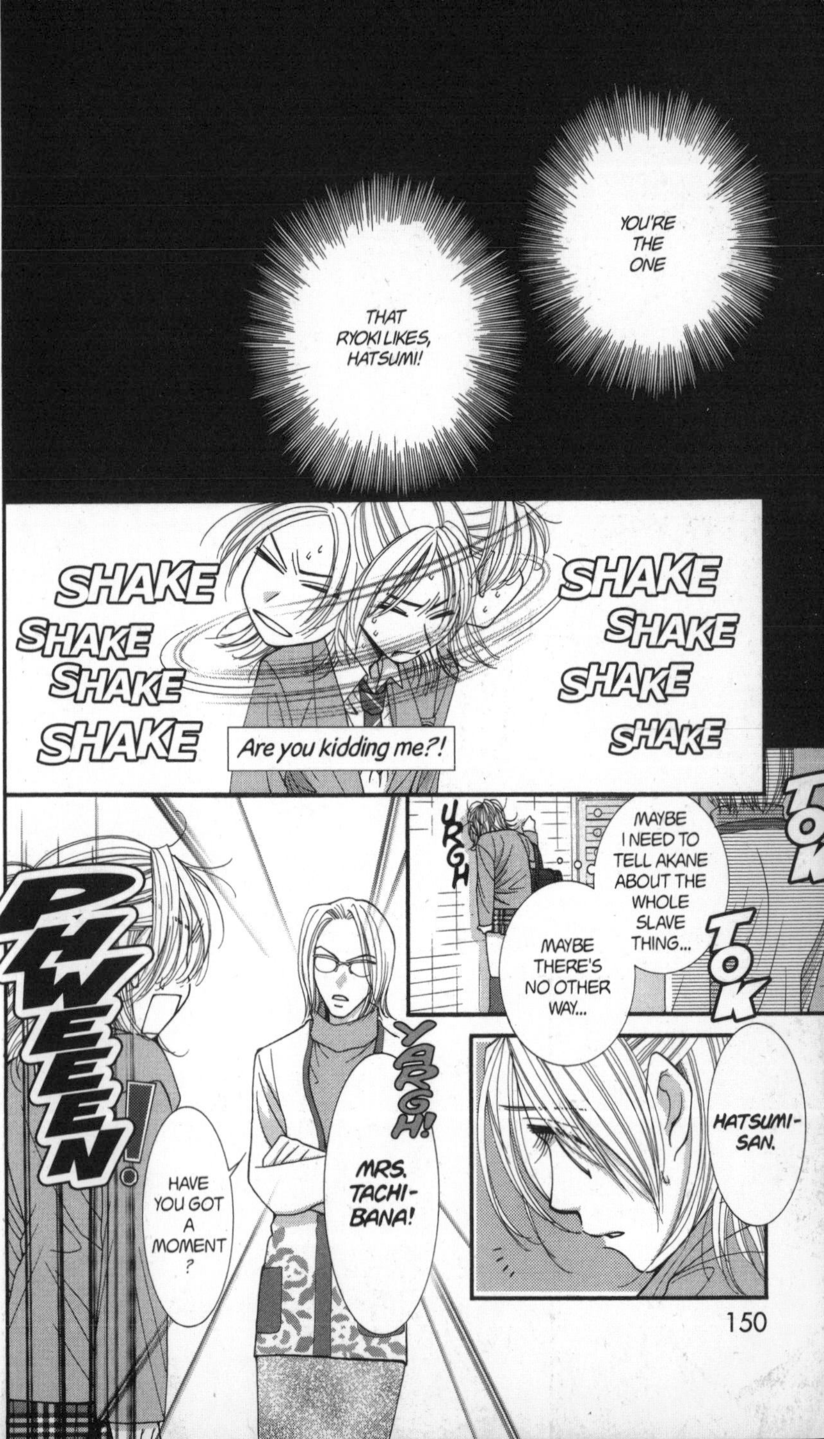
YOU'RE THE ONE
THAT RYOKI LIKES, HATSUMI!
SHAKE
SHAKE
SHAKE
SHAKE
Are you kidding me?!
SHAKE
SHAKE
SHAKE
SHAKE
TOK
TOK
URGH
MAYBE I NEED TO TELL AKANE ABOUT THE WHOLE SLAVE THING...
MAYBE THERE'S NO OTHER WAY...
HATSUMI-SAN.
YARGH!
MRS. TACHIBANA!
HAVE YOU GOT A MOMENT?
PWEEEN!

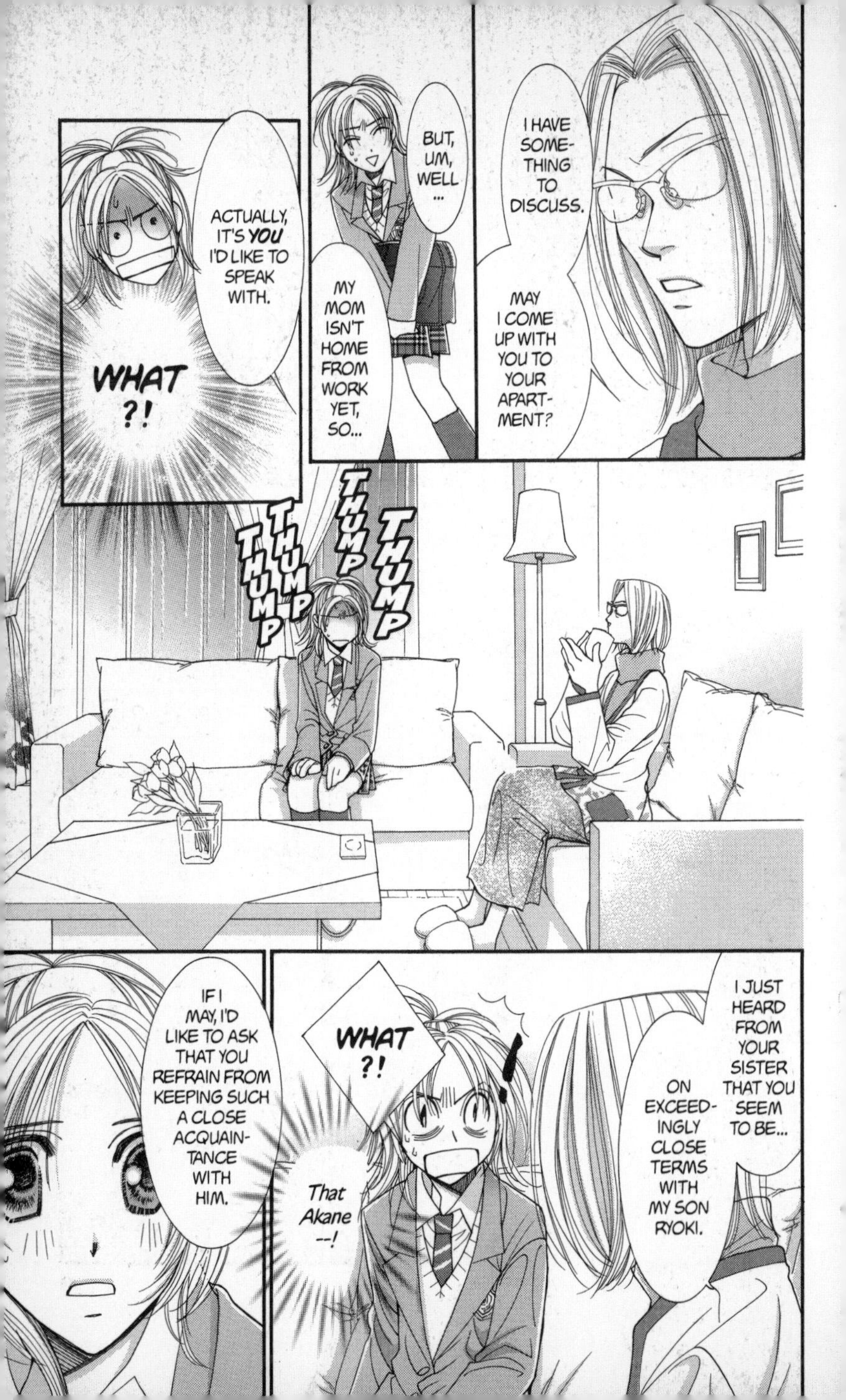
I HAVE SOMETHING TO DISCUSS.
MAY I COME UP WITH YOU TO YOUR APARTMENT?
BUT, UM, WELL...
MY MOM ISN'T HOME FROM WORK YET, SO...
ACTUALLY, IT'S ***YOU*** I'D LIKE TO SPEAK WITH.
WHAT?!
THUMP THUMP
THUMP THUMP
I JUST HEARD FROM YOUR SISTER THAT YOU SEEM TO BE...
ON EXCEEDINGLY CLOSE TERMS WITH MY SON RYOKI.
WHAT?!
That Akane--!
IF I MAY, I'D LIKE TO ASK THAT YOU REFRAIN FROM KEEPING SUCH A CLOSE ACQUAINTANCE WITH HIM.

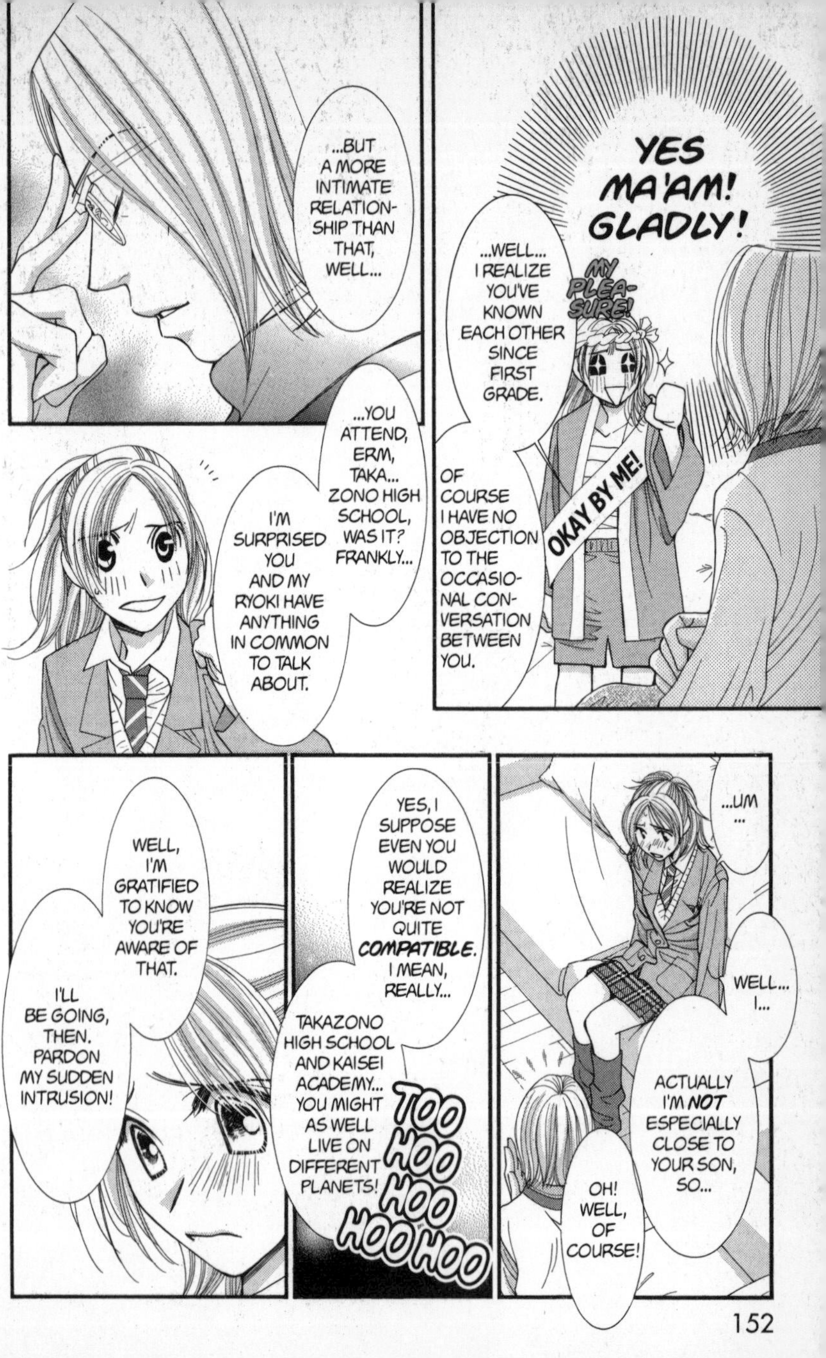
YES MA'AM! GLADLY!
...WELL... I REALIZE YOU'VE KNOWN EACH OTHER SINCE FIRST GRADE.
MY PLEA-SURE!
OKAY BY ME!
OF COURSE I HAVE NO OBJECTION TO THE OCCASIONAL CONVERSATION BETWEEN YOU.
...BUT A MORE INTIMATE RELATIONSHIP THAN THAT, WELL...
...YOU ATTEND, ERM, TAKA... ZONO HIGH SCHOOL, WAS IT? FRANKLY...
I'M SURPRISED YOU AND MY RYOKI HAVE ANYTHING IN COMMON TO TALK ABOUT.
...UM ...
WELL... I...
ACTUALLY I'M **NOT** ESPECIALLY CLOSE TO YOUR SON, SO...
OH! WELL, OF COURSE!
YES, I SUPPOSE EVEN YOU WOULD REALIZE YOU'RE NOT QUITE **COMPATIBLE**. I MEAN, REALLY...
TAKAZONO HIGH SCHOOL AND KAISEI ACADEMY... YOU MIGHT AS WELL LIVE ON DIFFERENT PLANETS!
TOO HOO HOO HOO HOO
WELL, I'M GRATIFIED TO KNOW YOU'RE AWARE OF THAT.
I'LL BE GOING, THEN. PARDON MY SUDDEN INTRUSION!

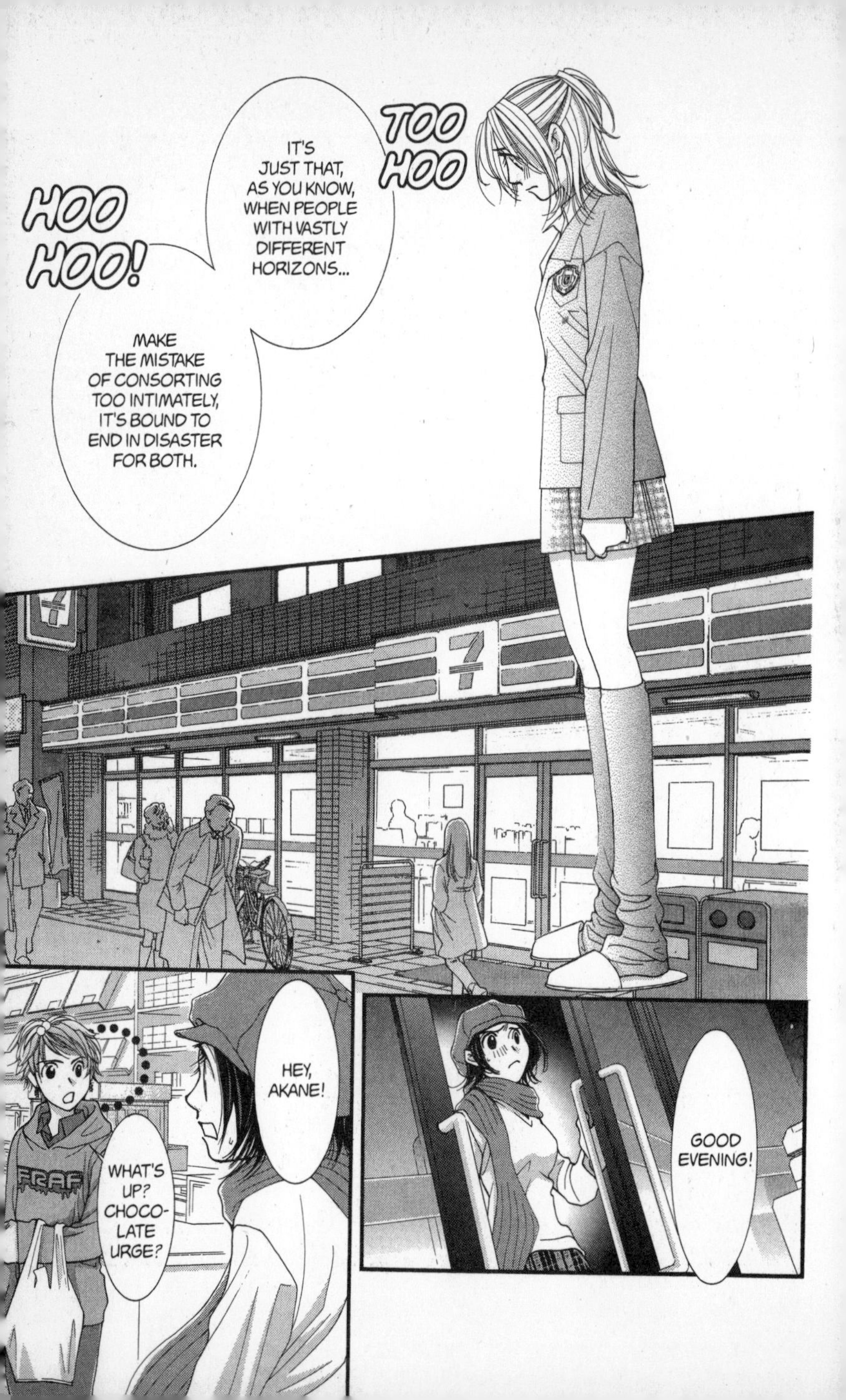
TOO HOO
IT'S JUST THAT, AS YOU KNOW, WHEN PEOPLE WITH VASTLY DIFFERENT HORIZONS...
HOO HOO!
MAKE THE MISTAKE OF CONSORTING TOO INTIMATELY, IT'S BOUND TO END IN DISASTER FOR BOTH.
GOOD EVENING!
HEY, AKANE!
WHAT'S UP? CHOCO-LATE URGE?

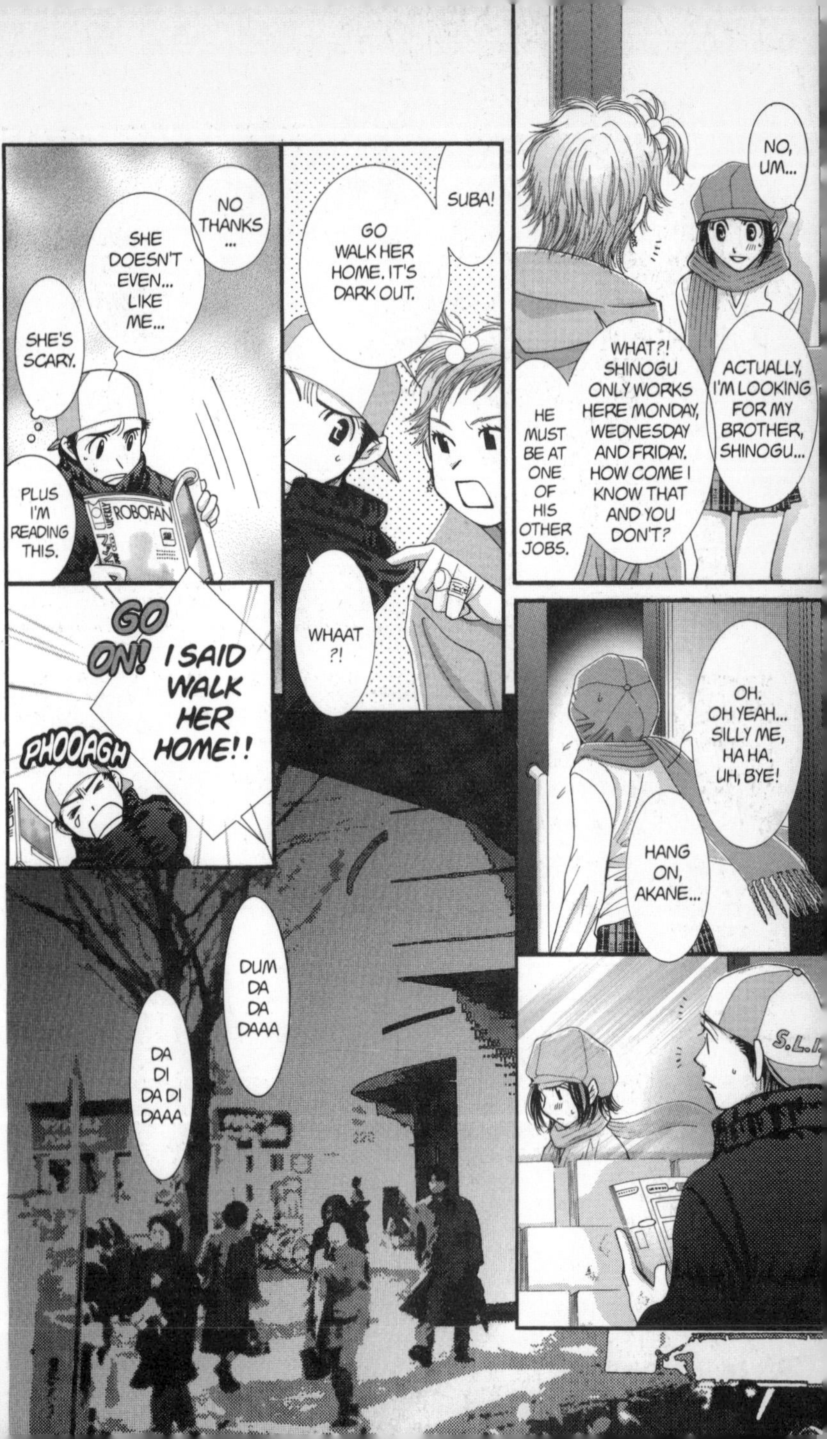
NO, UM...
ACTUALLY, I'M LOOKING FOR MY BROTHER, SHINOGU...
WHAT?! SHINOGU ONLY WORKS HERE MONDAY, WEDNESDAY AND FRIDAY. HOW COME I KNOW THAT AND YOU DON'T?
HE MUST BE AT ONE OF HIS OTHER JOBS.
SUBA!
GO WALK HER HOME. IT'S DARK OUT.
WHAAT ?!
NO THANKS ...
SHE DOESN'T EVEN... LIKE ME...
SHE'S SCARY.
ROBOFAN
PLUS I'M READING THIS.
OH. OH YEAH... SILLY ME, HA HA. UH, BYE!
HANG ON, AKANE...
GO ON!
I SAID WALK HER HOME!!
PHOOAGH
S.L.I.
DUM DA DA DAAA
DA DI DA DI DAAA

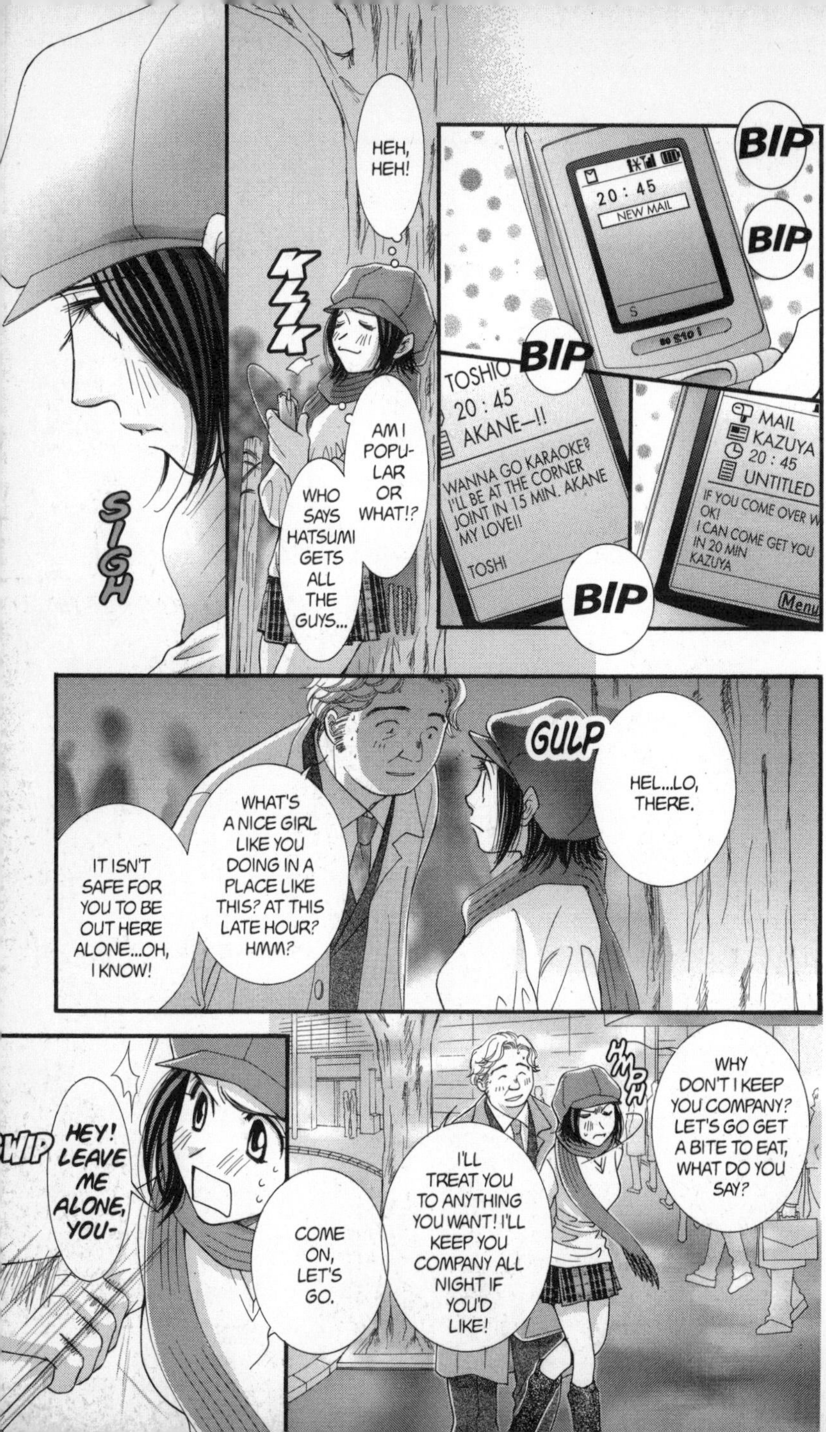

BIP
BIP
20 : 45
NEW MAIL
MAIL
KAZUYA
20 : 45
UNTITLED
IF YOU COME OVER W
OK!
I CAN COME GET YOU
IN 20 MIN
KAZUYA
Menu
BIP
TOSHIO
20 : 45
AKANE—!!
WANNA GO KARAOKE?
I'LL BE AT THE CORNER
JOINT IN 15 MIN. AKANE
MY LOVE!!
TOSHI
BIP
HEH, HEH!
KLIK
AM I POPULAR OR WHAT!?
WHO SAYS HATSUMI GETS ALL THE GUYS...
SIGH
GULP
HEL...LO, THERE.
WHAT'S A NICE GIRL LIKE YOU DOING IN A PLACE LIKE THIS? AT THIS LATE HOUR? HMM?
IT ISN'T SAFE FOR YOU TO BE OUT HERE ALONE...OH, I KNOW!
HMPH
WHY DON'T I KEEP YOU COMPANY? LET'S GO GET A BITE TO EAT, WHAT DO YOU SAY?
I'LL TREAT YOU TO ANYTHING YOU WANT! I'LL KEEP YOU COMPANY ALL NIGHT IF YOU'D LIKE!
COME ON, LET'S GO.
WIP
HEY! LEAVE ME ALONE, YOU-

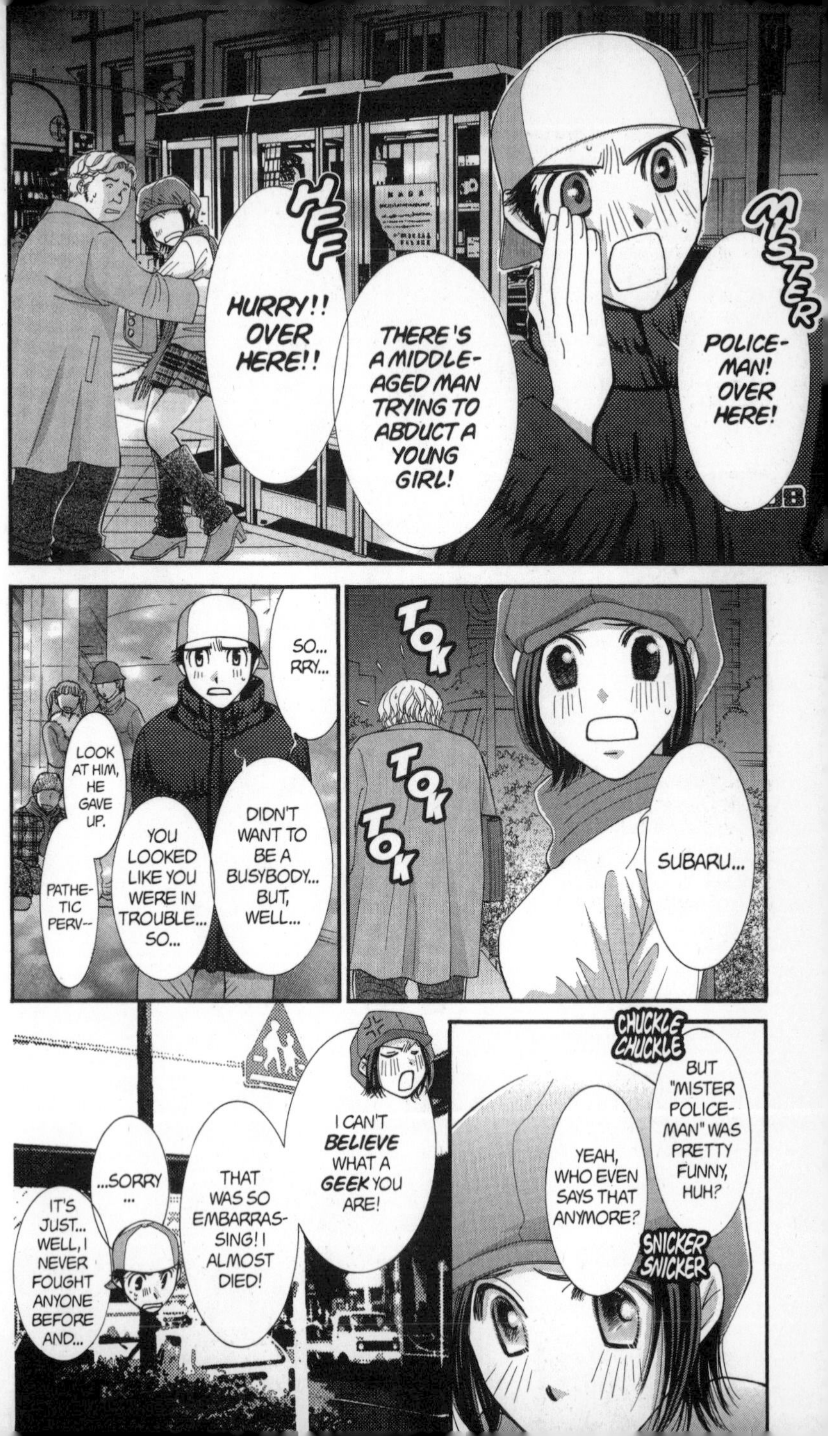
MISTER
POLICE-MAN! OVER HERE!
THERE'S A MIDDLE-AGED MAN TRYING TO ABDUCT A YOUNG GIRL!
HEF
HURRY!! OVER HERE!!
TOK
TOK
TOK
SUBARU...
SO... RRY...
DIDN'T WANT TO BE A BUSYBODY... BUT, WELL...
YOU LOOKED LIKE YOU WERE IN TROUBLE... SO...
LOOK AT HIM, HE GAVE UP.
PATHE-TIC PERV--
CHUCKLE CHUCKLE
BUT "MISTER POLICE-MAN" WAS PRETTY FUNNY, HUH?
YEAH, WHO EVEN SAYS THAT ANYMORE?
SNICKER SNICKER
I CAN'T **BELIEVE** WHAT A **GEEK** YOU ARE!
THAT WAS SO EMBARRAS-SING! I ALMOST DIED!
...SORRY ...
IT'S JUST... WELL, I NEVER FOUGHT ANYONE BEFORE AND...

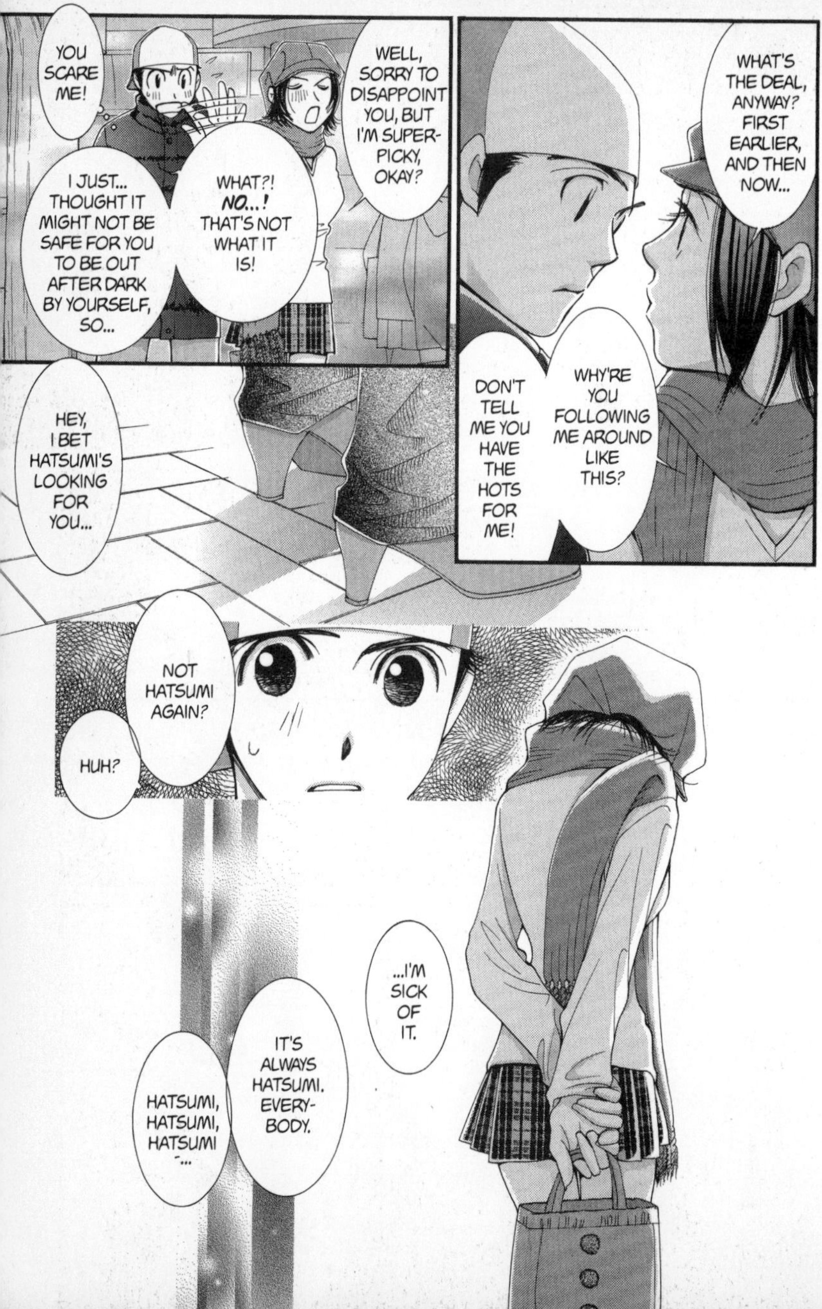
WHAT'S THE DEAL, ANYWAY? FIRST EARLIER, AND THEN NOW...
WHY'RE YOU FOLLOWING ME AROUND LIKE THIS?
DON'T TELL ME YOU HAVE THE HOTS FOR ME!
WHAT?! NO...! THAT'S NOT WHAT IT IS!
WELL, SORRY TO DISAPPOINT YOU, BUT I'M SUPER-PICKY, OKAY?
YOU SCARE ME!
I JUST... THOUGHT IT MIGHT NOT BE SAFE FOR YOU TO BE OUT AFTER DARK BY YOURSELF, SO...
HEY, I BET HATSUMI'S LOOKING FOR YOU...
NOT HATSUMI AGAIN?
HUH?
...I'M SICK OF IT.
IT'S ALWAYS HATSUMI. EVERY-BODY.
HATSUMI, HATSUMI, HATSUMI-...

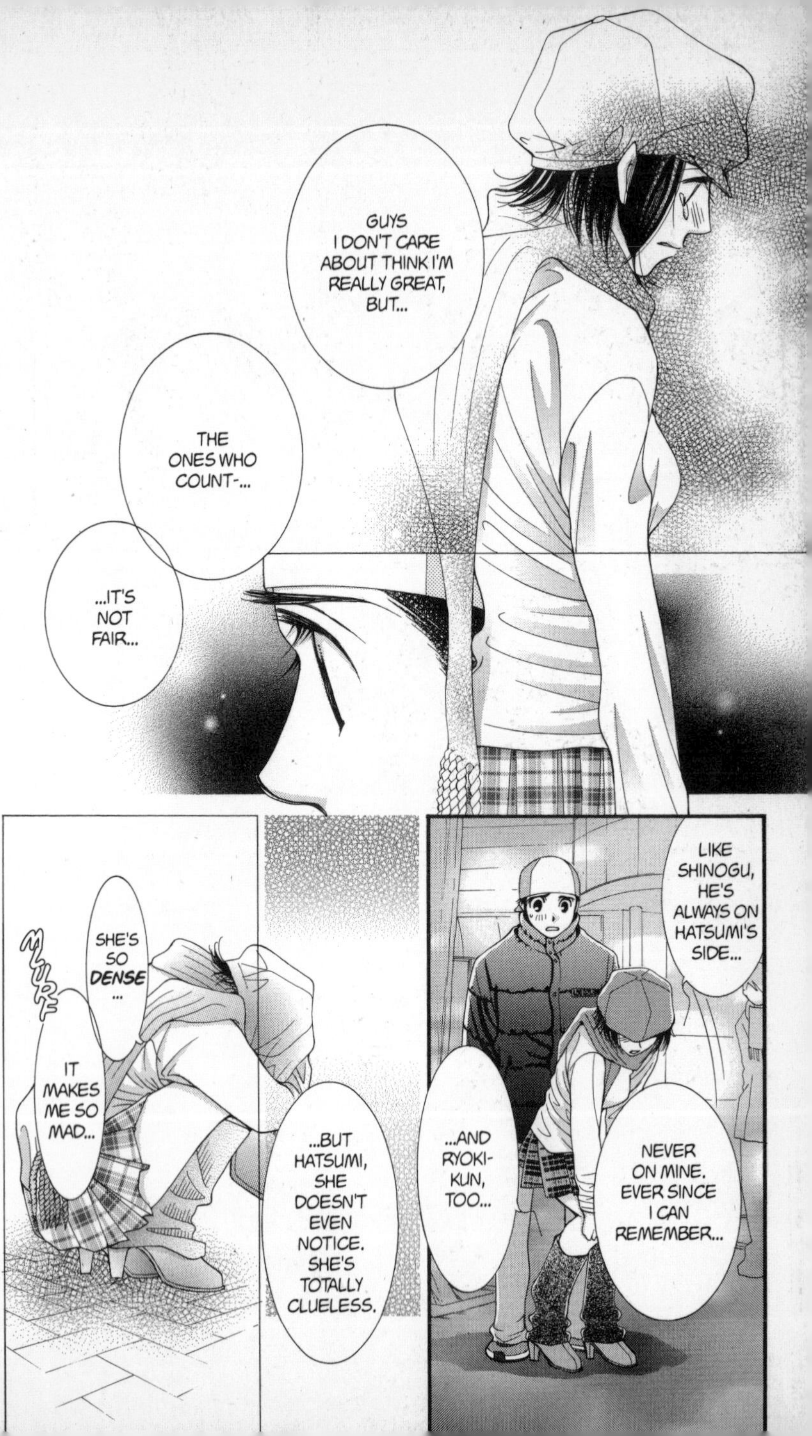
GUYS I DON'T CARE ABOUT THINK I'M REALLY GREAT, BUT...
THE ONES WHO COUNT-...
...IT'S NOT FAIR...
LIKE SHINOGU, HE'S ALWAYS ON HATSUMI'S SIDE...
NEVER ON MINE. EVER SINCE I CAN REMEMBER...
...AND RYOKI-KUN, TOO...
...BUT HATSUMI, SHE DOESN'T EVEN NOTICE. SHE'S TOTALLY CLUELESS.
SHE'S SO **DENSE**...
IT MAKES ME SO MAD...

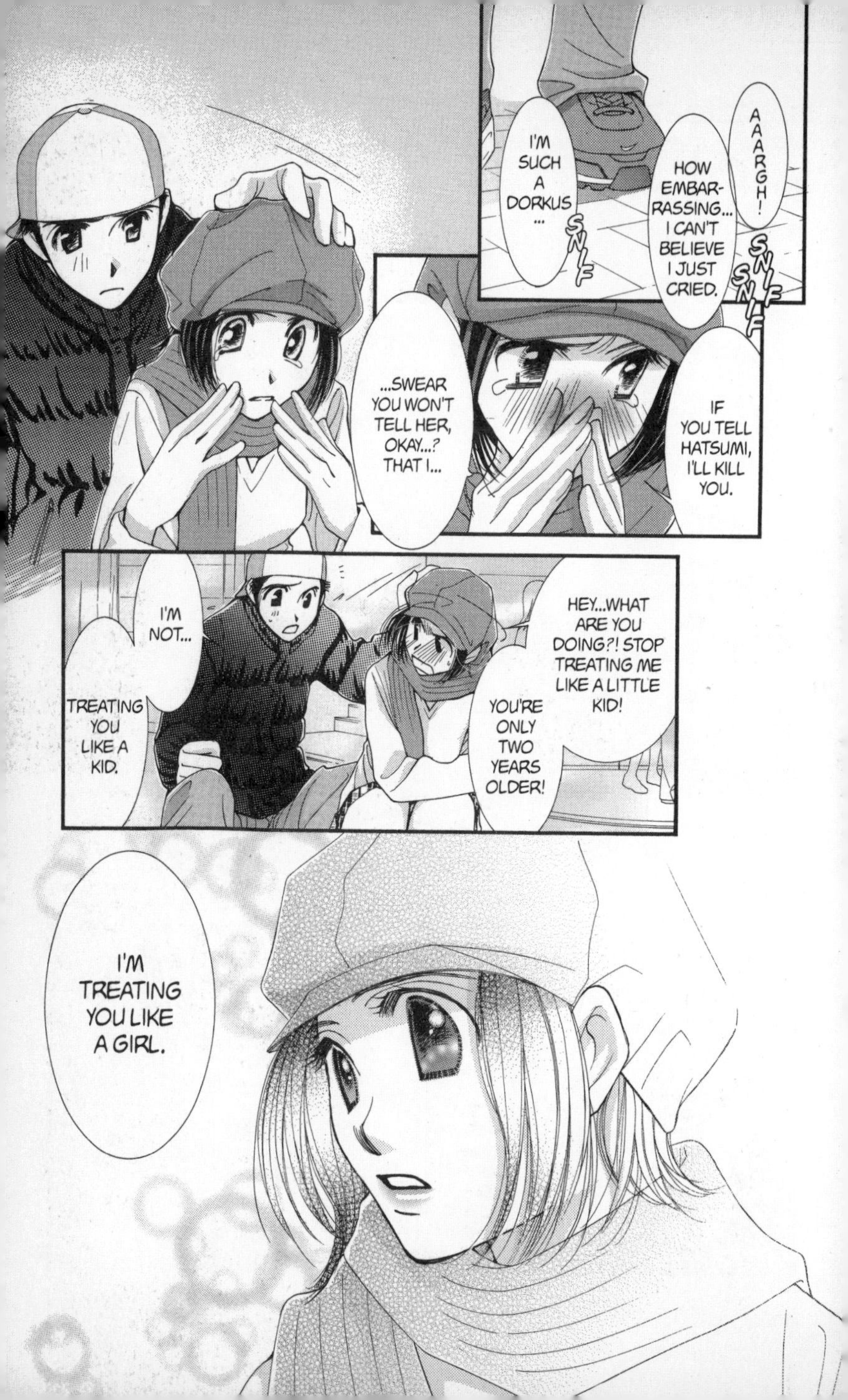
AAAARGH!
HOW EMBARRASSING... I CAN'T BELIEVE I JUST CRIED.
SNIF SNIF
I'M SUCH A DORKUS...
SNIF
IF YOU TELL HATSUMI, I'LL KILL YOU.
...SWEAR YOU WON'T TELL HER, OKAY...? THAT I...
HEY...WHAT ARE YOU DOING?! STOP TREATING ME LIKE A LITTLE KID!
YOU'RE ONLY TWO YEARS OLDER!
I'M NOT...
TREATING YOU LIKE A KID.
I'M TREATING YOU LIKE A GIRL.

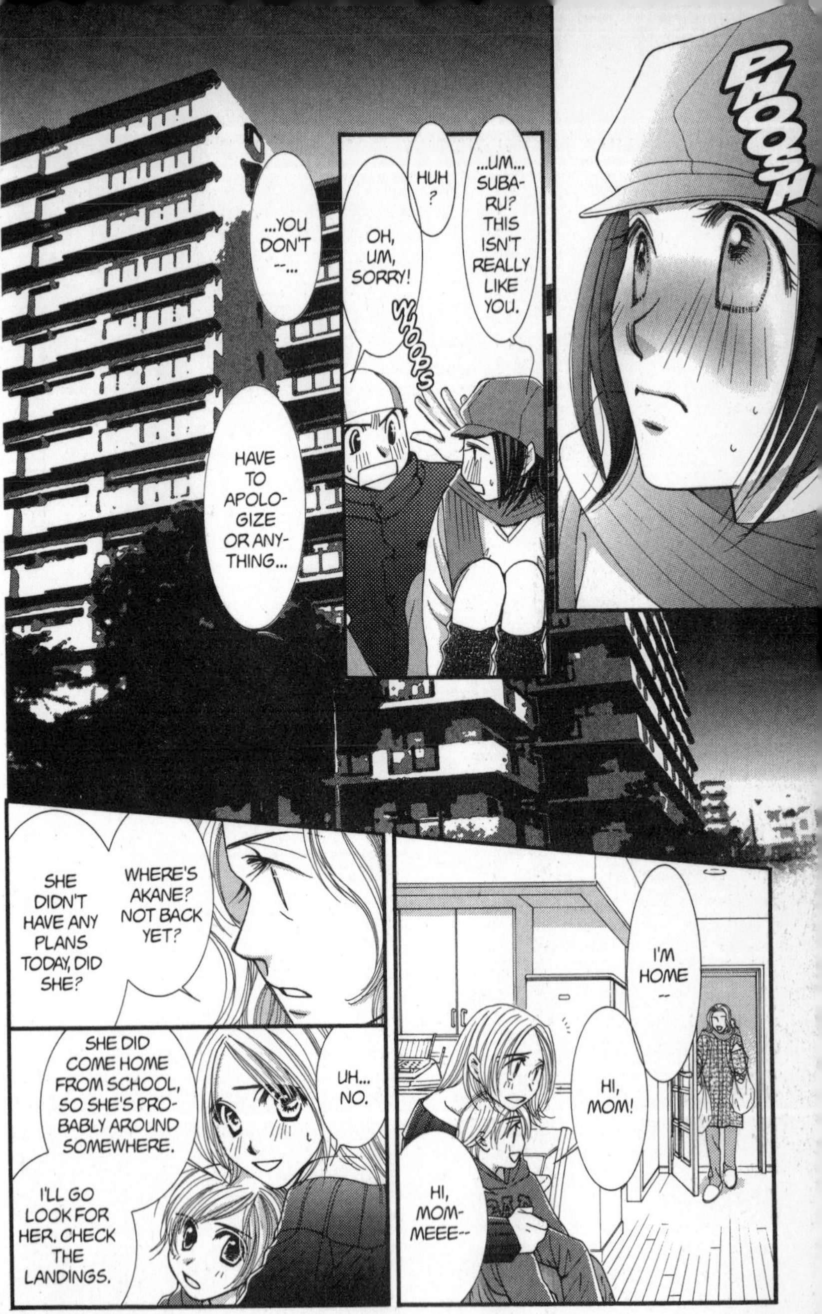
PHOOSH
...UM... SUBA-RU? THIS ISN'T REALLY LIKE YOU.
HUH?
OH, UM, SORRY!
WHOOPS
...YOU DON'T --...
HAVE TO APOLO-GIZE OR ANY-THING...
I'M HOME --
HI, MOM!
HI, MOM-MEEE--
WHERE'S AKANE? NOT BACK YET?
SHE DIDN'T HAVE ANY PLANS TODAY, DID SHE?
UH... NO.
SHE DID COME HOME FROM SCHOOL, SO SHE'S PRO-BABLY AROUND SOMEWHERE.
I'LL GO LOOK FOR HER. CHECK THE LANDINGS.

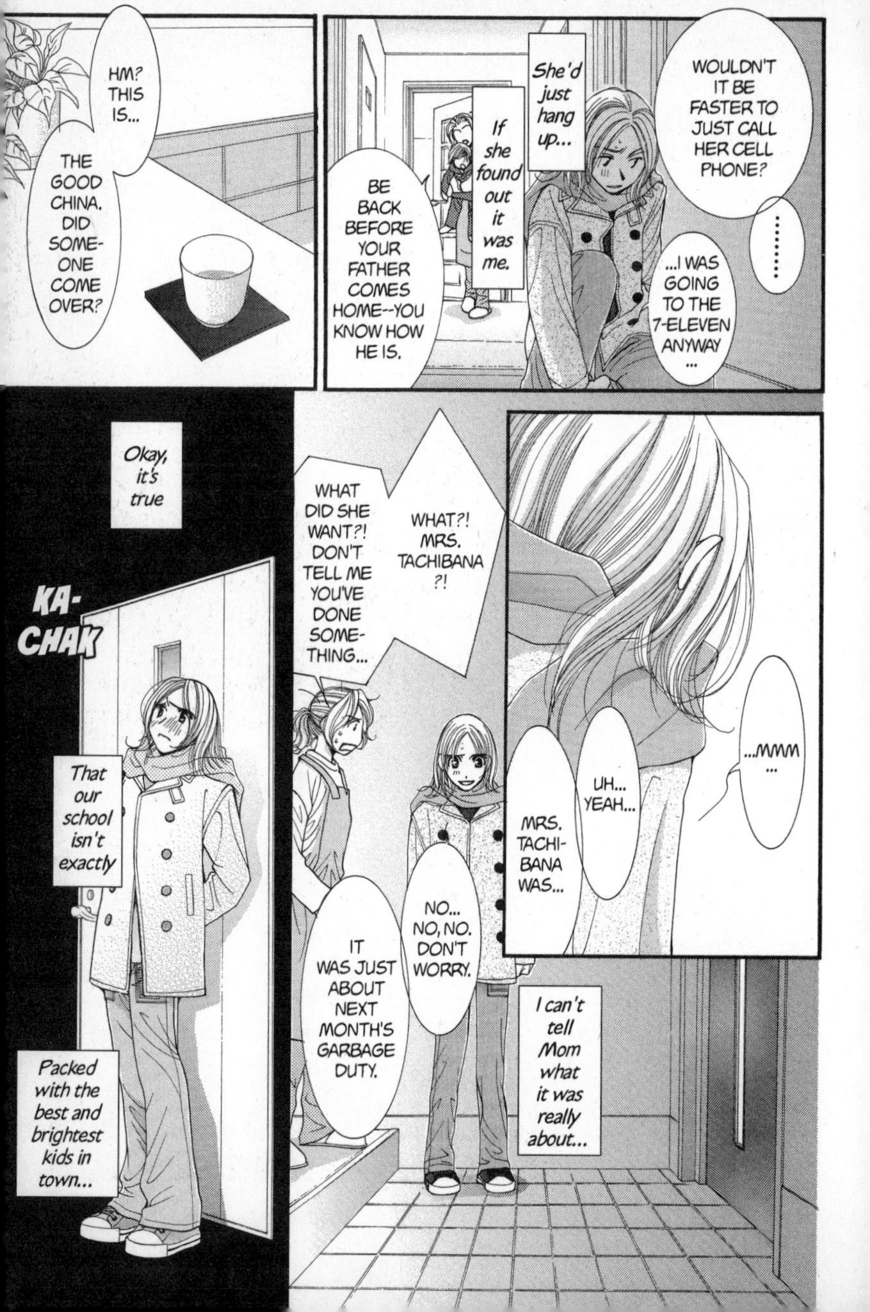
WOULDN'T IT BE FASTER TO JUST CALL HER CELL PHONE?
....
...I WAS GOING TO THE 7-ELEVEN ANYWAY ...
She'd just hang up...
If she found out it was me.
BE BACK BEFORE YOUR FATHER COMES HOME--YOU KNOW HOW HE IS.
HM? THIS IS...
THE GOOD CHINA. DID SOME-ONE COME OVER?
...MMM ...
UH... YEAH...
MRS. TACHI-BANA WAS...
WHAT?! MRS. TACHIBANA ?!
WHAT DID SHE WANT?! DON'T TELL ME YOU'VE DONE SOME-THING...
NO... NO, NO. DON'T WORRY.
IT WAS JUST ABOUT NEXT MONTH'S GARBAGE DUTY.
I can't tell Mom what it was really about...
Okay, it's true
KA-CHAK
That our school isn't exactly
Packed with the best and brightest kids in town...

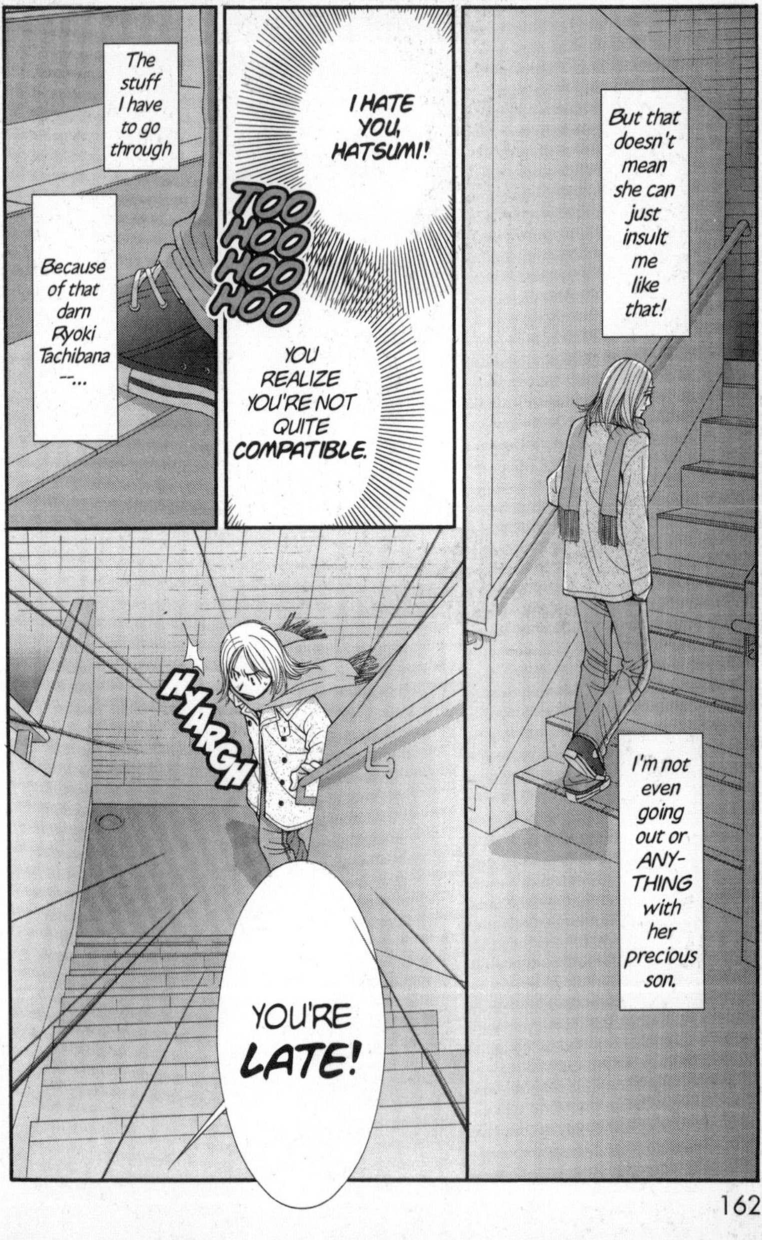
But that doesn't mean she can just insult me like that!
I'm not even going out or ANYTHING with her precious son.
I HATE YOU, HATSUMI!
TOO HOO HOO HOO
YOU REALIZE YOU'RE NOT QUITE COMPATIBLE.
The stuff I have to go through
Because of that darn Ryoki Tachibana--...
HYARGH
YOU'RE LATE!

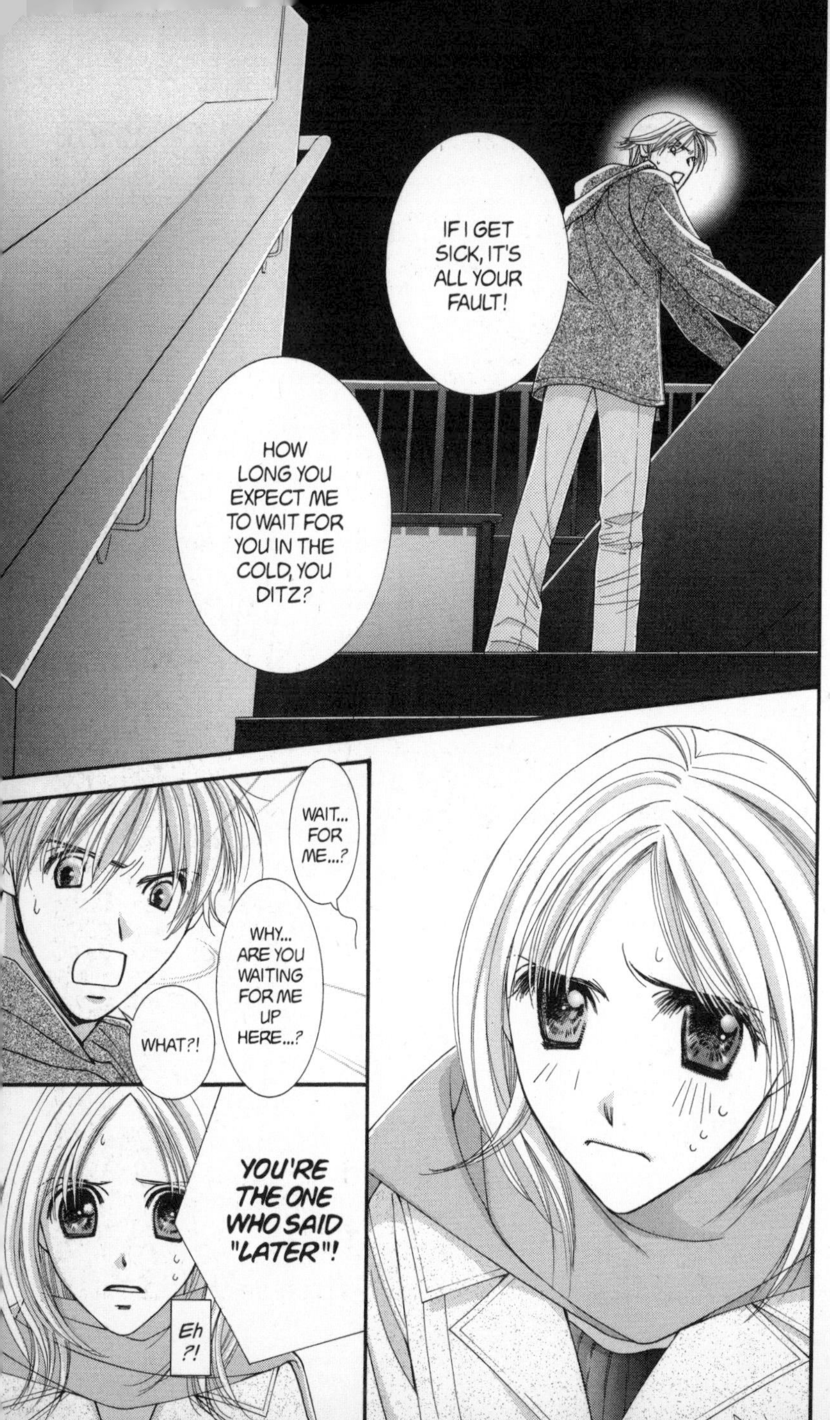
IF I GET SICK, IT'S ALL YOUR FAULT!
HOW LONG YOU EXPECT ME TO WAIT FOR YOU IN THE COLD, YOU DITZ?
WAIT... FOR ME...?
WHY... ARE YOU WAITING FOR ME UP HERE...?
WHAT?!
YOU'RE THE ONE WHO SAID "LATER"!
Eh ?!

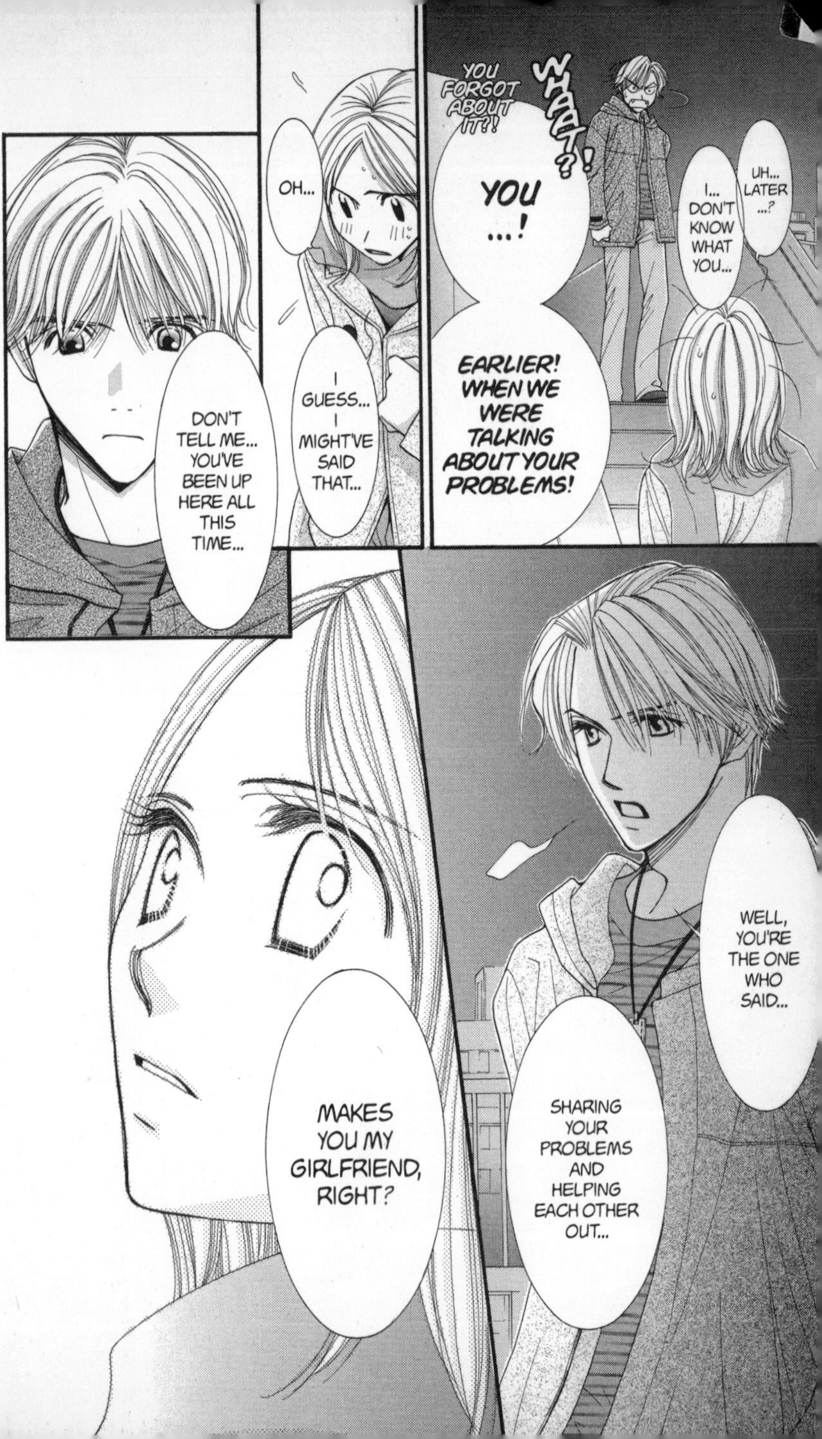
UH... LATER ...?
I... DON'T KNOW WHAT YOU...
WHAAT?!
YOU FORGOT ABOUT IT?!
YOU ...!
EARLIER! WHEN WE WERE TALKING ABOUT YOUR PROBLEMS!
OH...
I GUESS... I MIGHT'VE SAID THAT...
DON'T TELL ME... YOU'VE BEEN UP HERE ALL THIS TIME...
WELL, YOU'RE THE ONE WHO SAID...
SHARING YOUR PROBLEMS AND HELPING EACH OTHER OUT...
MAKES YOU MY GIRLFRIEND, RIGHT?

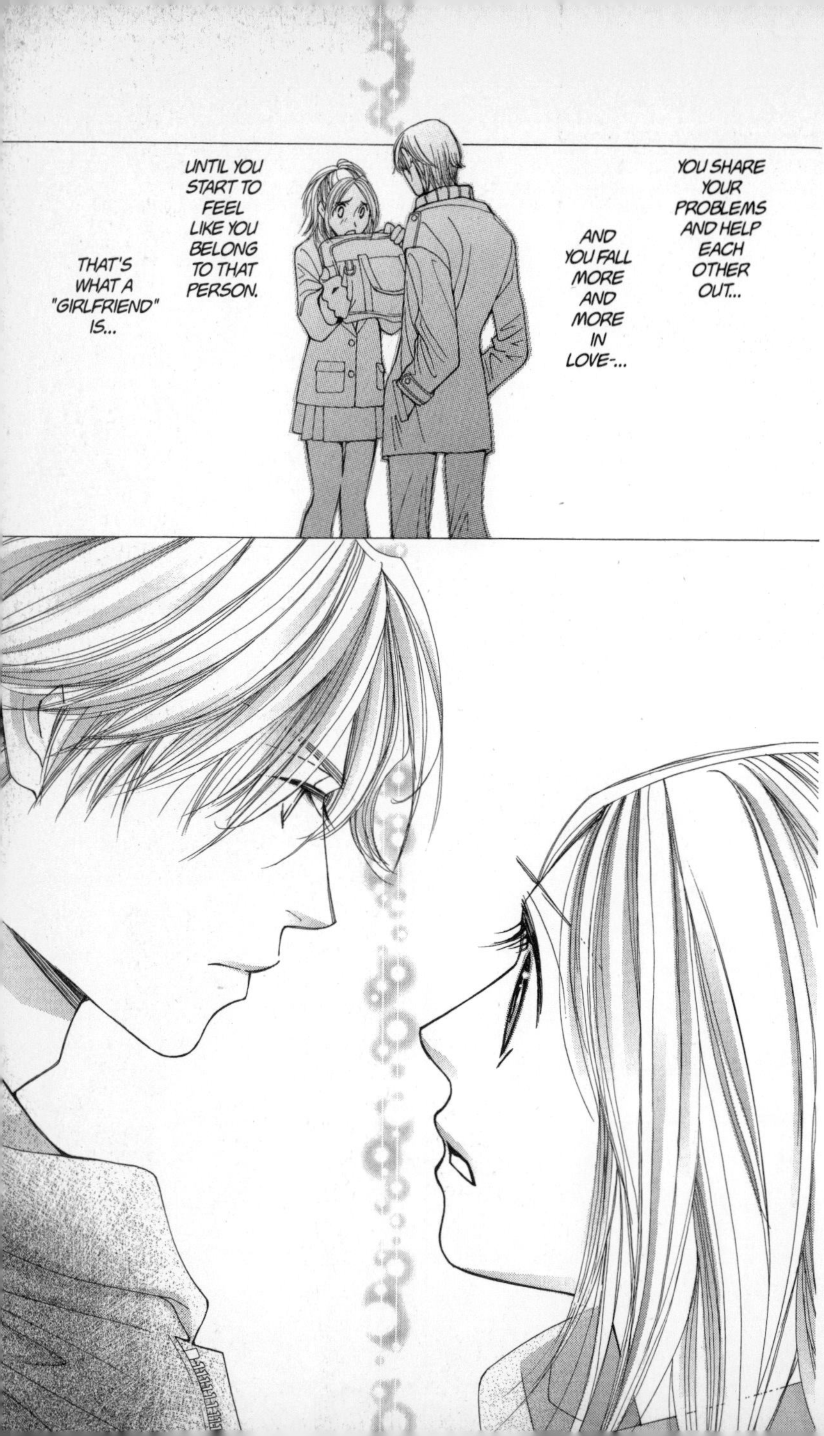
YOU SHARE YOUR PROBLEMS AND HELP EACH OTHER OUT...
AND YOU FALL MORE AND MORE IN LOVE-...
UNTIL YOU START TO FEEL LIKE YOU BELONG TO THAT PERSON.
THAT'S WHAT A "GIRLFRIEND" IS...

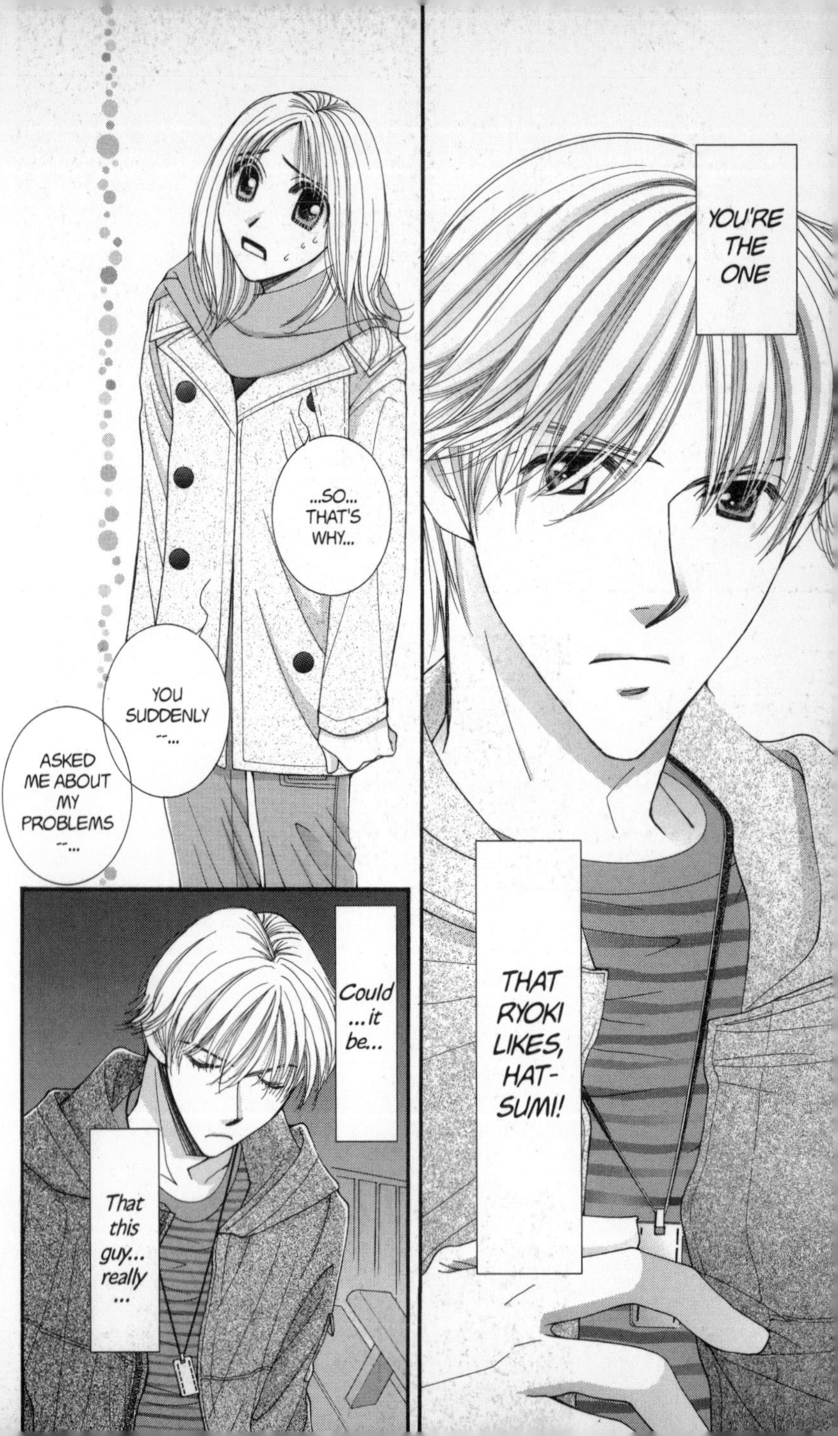
YOU'RE THE ONE
THAT RYOKI LIKES, HAT-SUMI!
...SO... THAT'S WHY...
YOU SUDDENLY --...
ASKED ME ABOUT MY PROBLEMS --...
Could ...it be...
That this guy... really ...

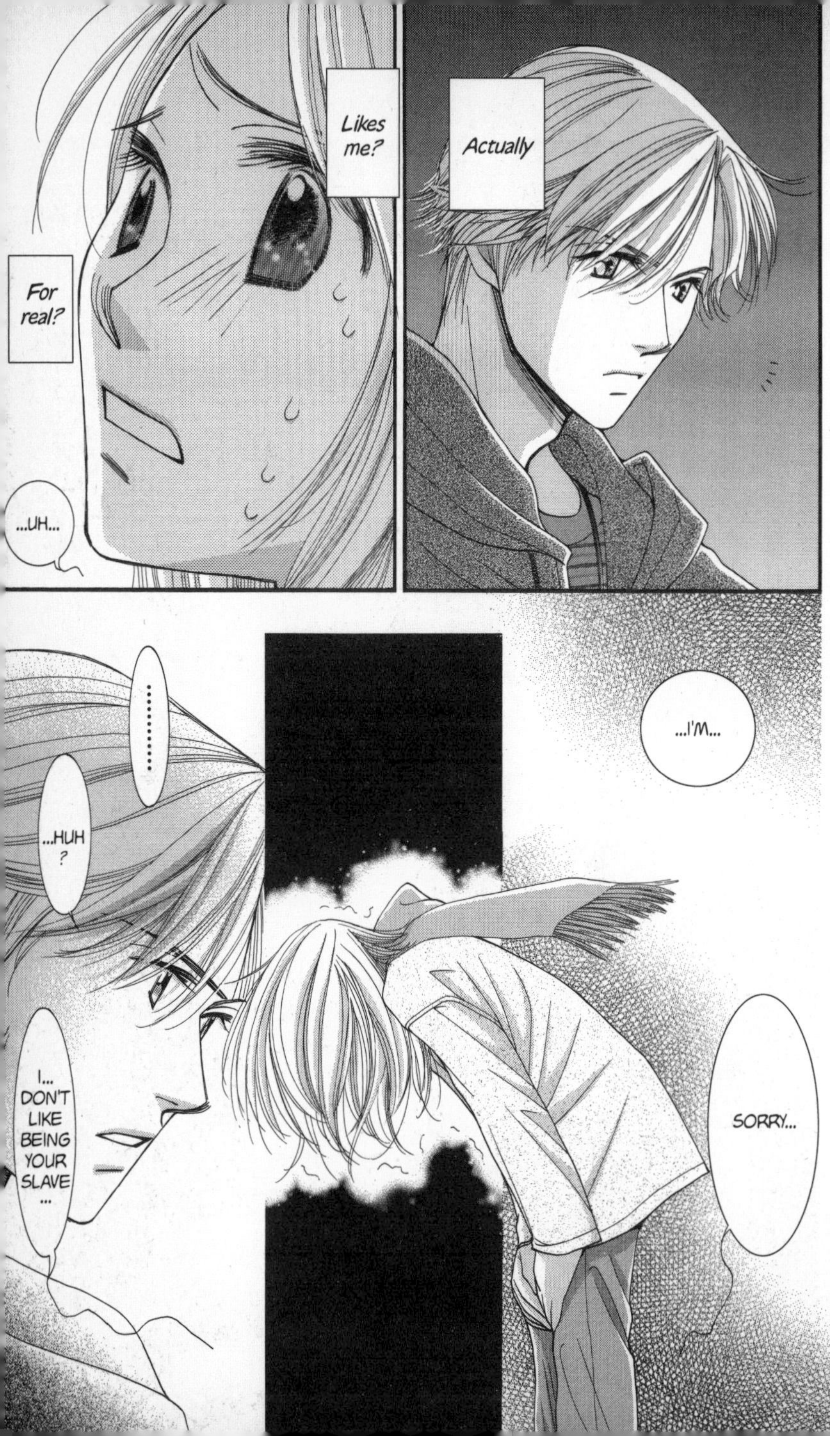

Actually
Likes me?
For real?
...UH...
...I'M...
SORRY...
I... DON'T LIKE BEING YOUR SLAVE ...
....
...HUH ?

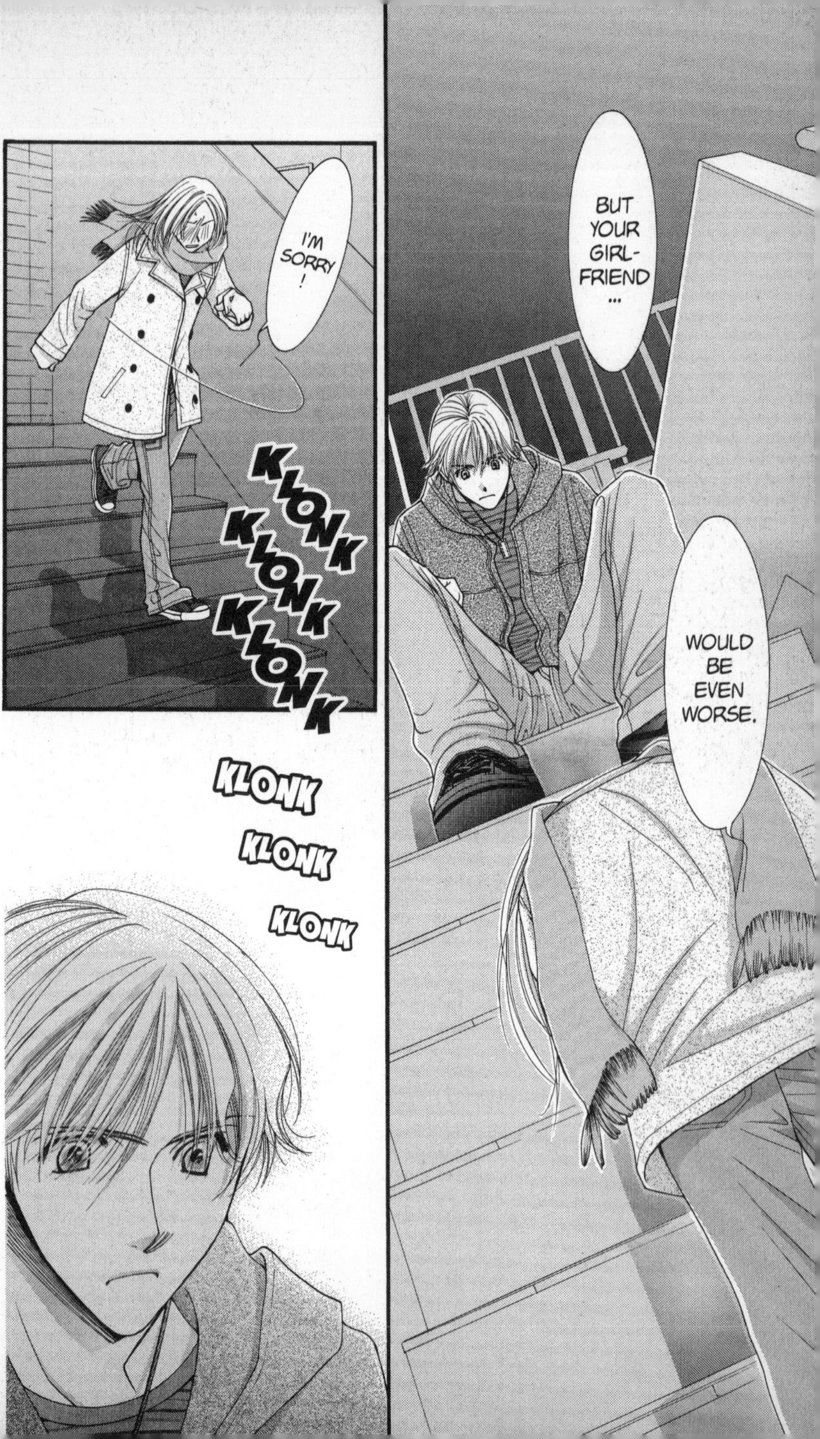
BUT YOUR GIRL-FRIEND ...
WOULD BE EVEN WORSE.
I'M SORRY!
KLONK
KLONK
KLONK
KLONK
KLONK
KLONK

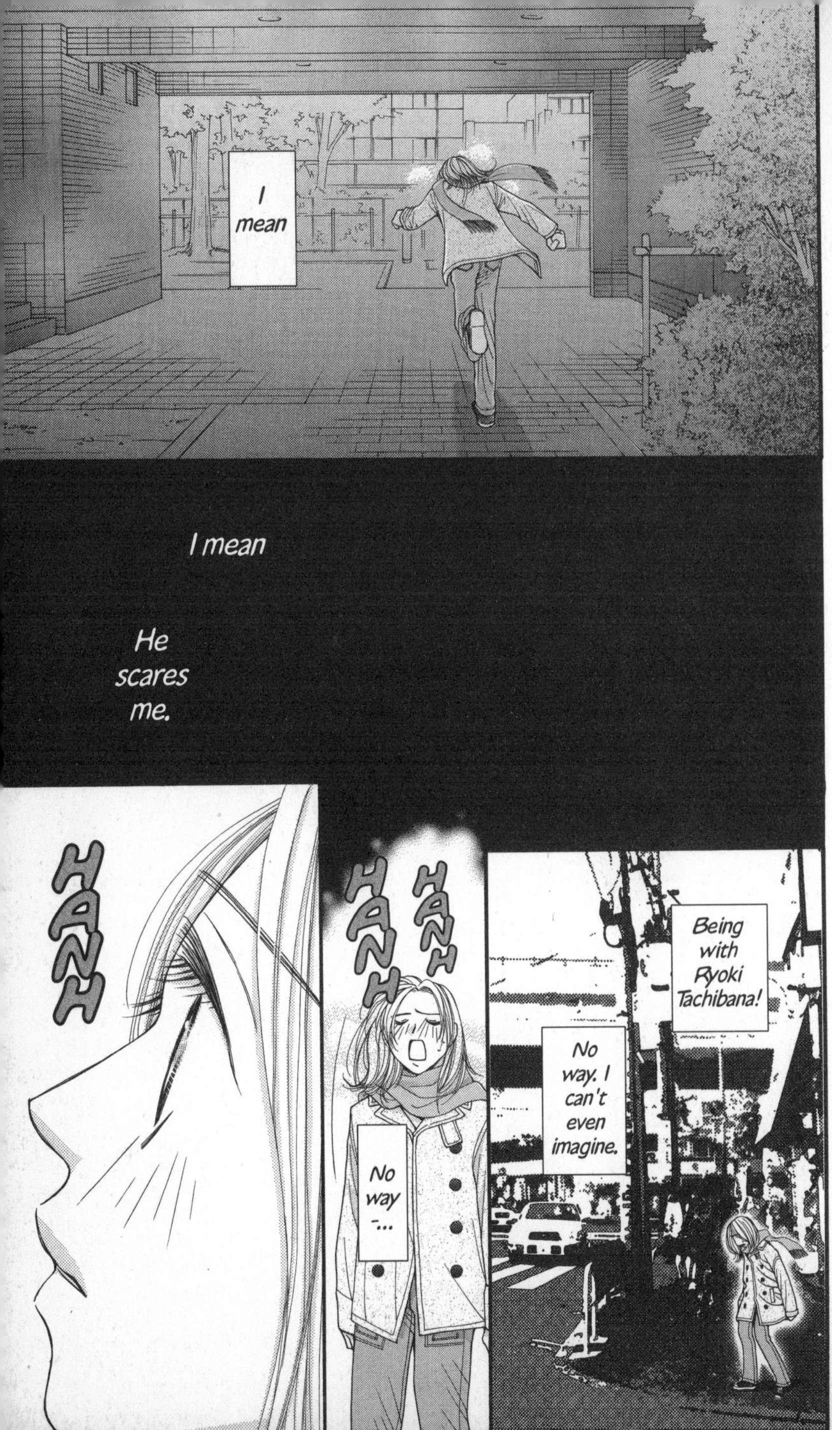
I mean
I mean
He scares me.
Being with Ryoki Tachibana!
No way. I can't even imagine.
HANH
HANH
No way -...
HANH

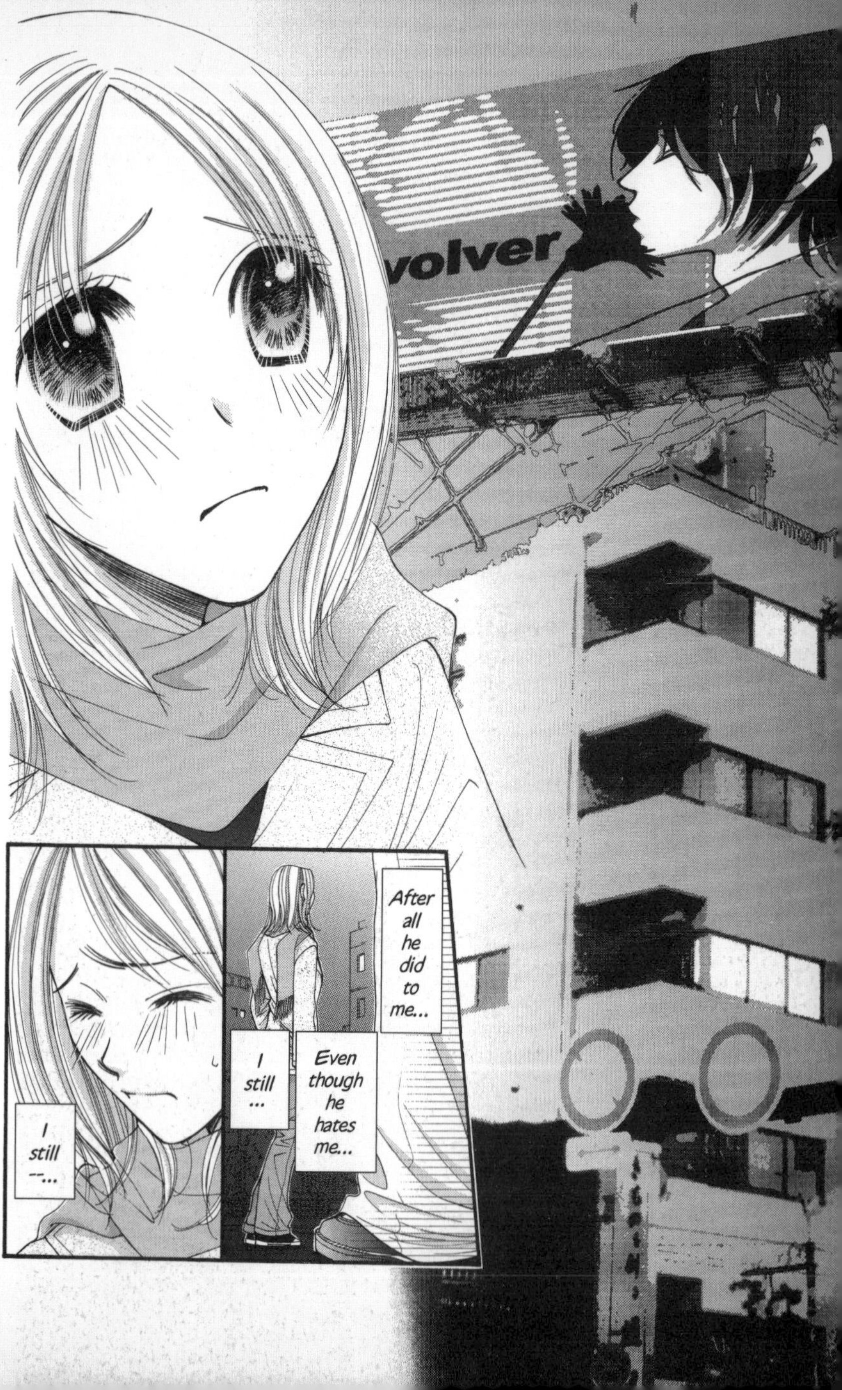
volver
After all he did to me...
Even though he hates me...
I still ...
I still --...

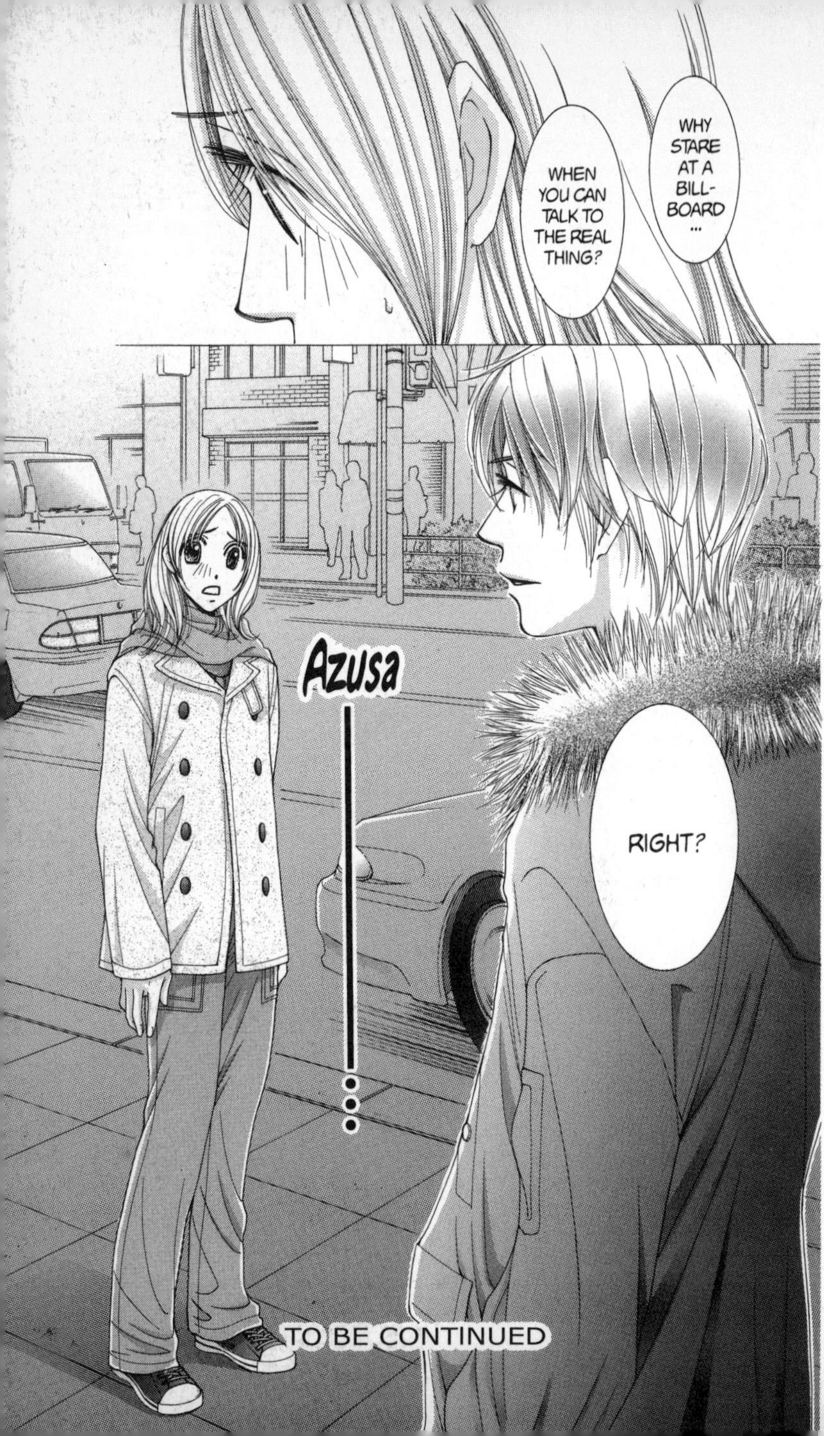
WHY STARE AT A BILL-BOARD ...
WHEN YOU CAN TALK TO THE REAL THING?
RIGHT?
Azusa
—...
TO BE CONTINUED

Hooray for animals!

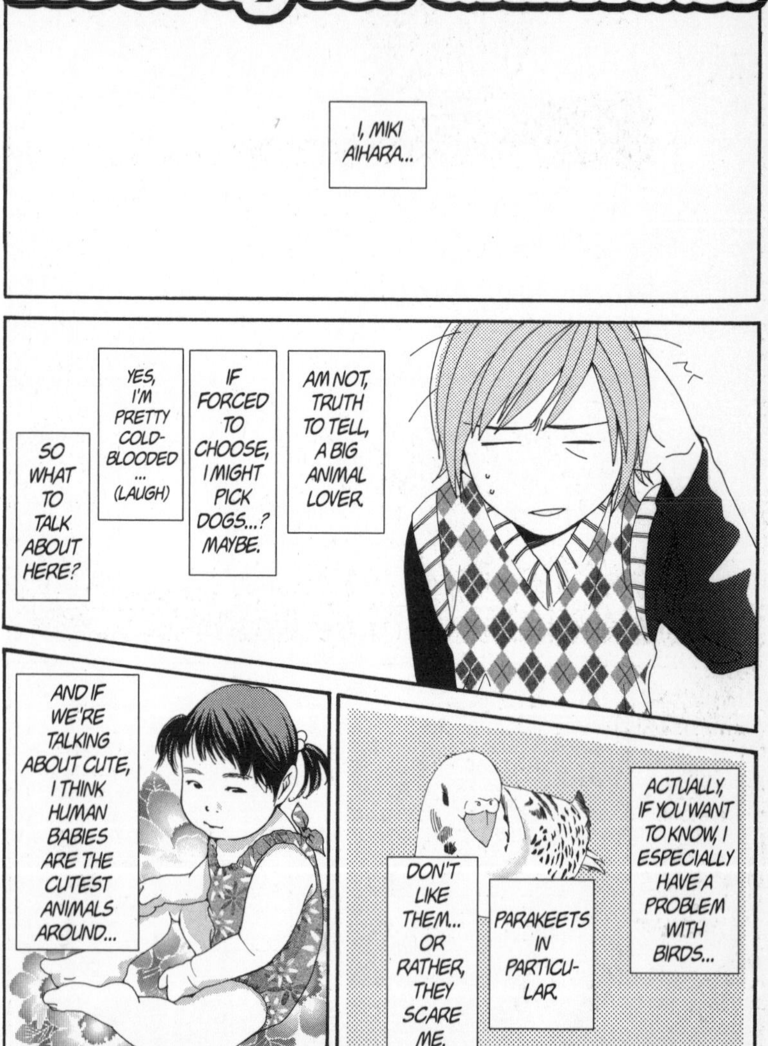
I, MIKI AIHARA...
AM NOT, TRUTH TO TELL, A BIG ANIMAL LOVER.
IF FORCED TO CHOOSE, I MIGHT PICK DOGS...? MAYBE.
YES, I'M PRETTY COLD-BLOODED ... (LAUGH)
SO WHAT TO TALK ABOUT HERE?
ACTUALLY, IF YOU WANT TO KNOW, I ESPECIALLY HAVE A PROBLEM WITH BIRDS...
PARAKEETS IN PARTICU-LAR.
DON'T LIKE THEM... OR RATHER, THEY SCARE ME.
AND IF WE'RE TALKING ABOUT CUTE, I THINK HUMAN BABIES ARE THE CUTEST ANIMALS AROUND...
MODEL: MY NIECE AH-CHAN, AGE 2

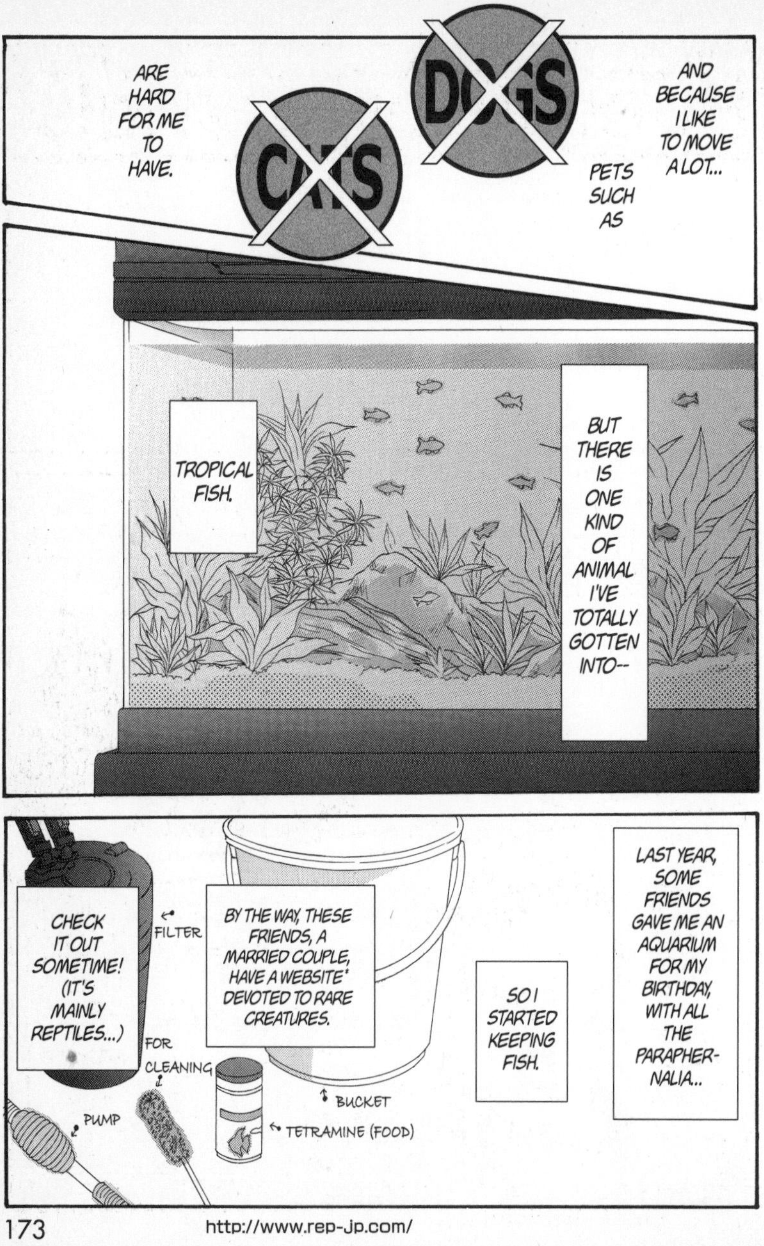
AND BECAUSE I LIKE TO MOVE A LOT...
PETS SUCH AS
DOGS
CATS
ARE HARD FOR ME TO HAVE.
BUT THERE IS ONE KIND OF ANIMAL I'VE TOTALLY GOTTEN INTO--
TROPICAL FISH.
LAST YEAR, SOME FRIENDS GAVE ME AN AQUARIUM FOR MY BIRTHDAY, WITH ALL THE PARAPHER-NALIA...
SO I STARTED KEEPING FISH.
BUCKET
TETRAMINE (FOOD)
BY THE WAY, THESE FRIENDS, A MARRIED COUPLE, HAVE A WEBSITE* DEVOTED TO RARE CREATURES.
FILTER
FOR CLEANING
PUMP
CHECK IT OUT SOMETIME! (IT'S MAINLY REPTILES...)

http://www.rep-jp.com/

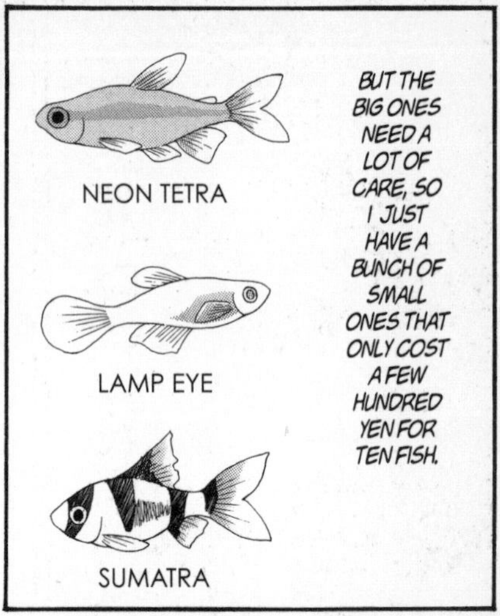
BUT THE BIG ONES NEED A LOT OF CARE, SO I JUST HAVE A BUNCH OF SMALL ONES THAT ONLY COST A FEW HUNDRED YEN FOR TEN FISH.
NEON TETRA
LAMP EYE
SUMATRA

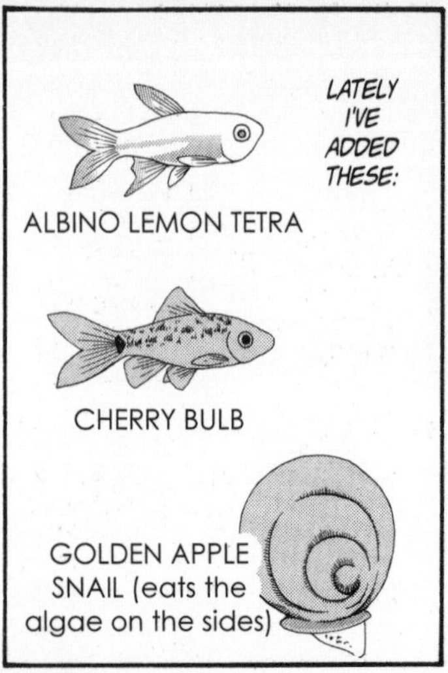
LATELY I'VE ADDED THESE:
ALBINO LEMON TETRA
CHERRY BULB
GOLDEN APPLE SNAIL (eats the algae on the sides)

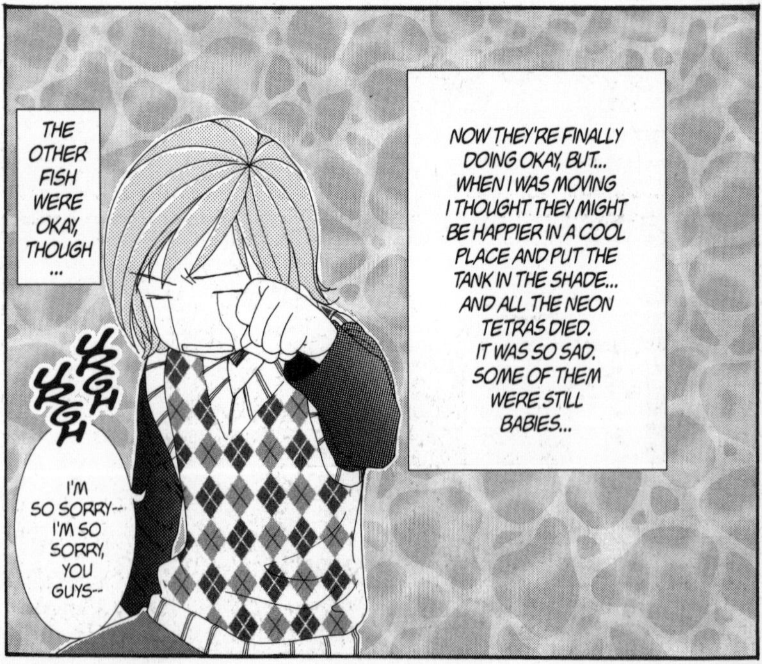
NOW THEY'RE FINALLY DOING OKAY, BUT... WHEN I WAS MOVING I THOUGHT THEY MIGHT BE HAPPIER IN A COOL PLACE AND PUT THE TANK IN THE SHADE... AND ALL THE NEON TETRAS DIED. IT WAS SO SAD. SOME OF THEM WERE STILL BABIES...
THE OTHER FISH WERE OKAY, THOUGH ...
URGH URGH
I'M SO SORRY-- I'M SO SORRY, YOU GUYS--

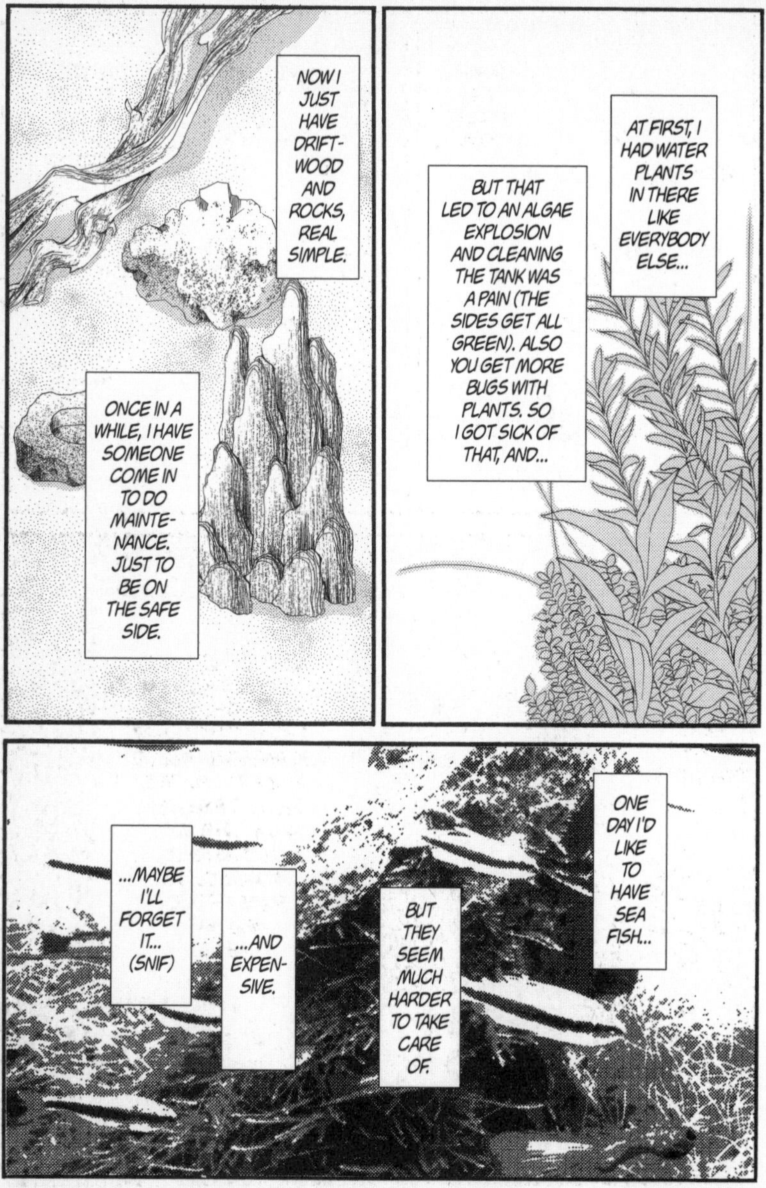
AT FIRST, I HAD WATER PLANTS IN THERE LIKE EVERYBODY ELSE...
BUT THAT LED TO AN ALGAE EXPLOSION AND CLEANING THE TANK WAS A PAIN (THE SIDES GET ALL GREEN). ALSO YOU GET MORE BUGS WITH PLANTS. SO I GOT SICK OF THAT, AND...
NOW I JUST HAVE DRIFT-WOOD AND ROCKS, REAL SIMPLE.
ONCE IN A WHILE, I HAVE SOMEONE COME IN TO DO MAINTE-NANCE. JUST TO BE ON THE SAFE SIDE.
ONE DAY I'D LIKE TO HAVE SEA FISH...
BUT THEY SEEM MUCH HARDER TO TAKE CARE OF.
...AND EXPEN-SIVE.
...MAYBE I'LL FORGET IT... (SNIF)

To be continued

EXTRA

GIMMICK

Thank you for buying Hot Gimmick Vol. 3.
My name is Miki Aihara.
Here, just for you graphic novel readers, is
more of that extra information that's so hard
to put into the actual story.
Read on!

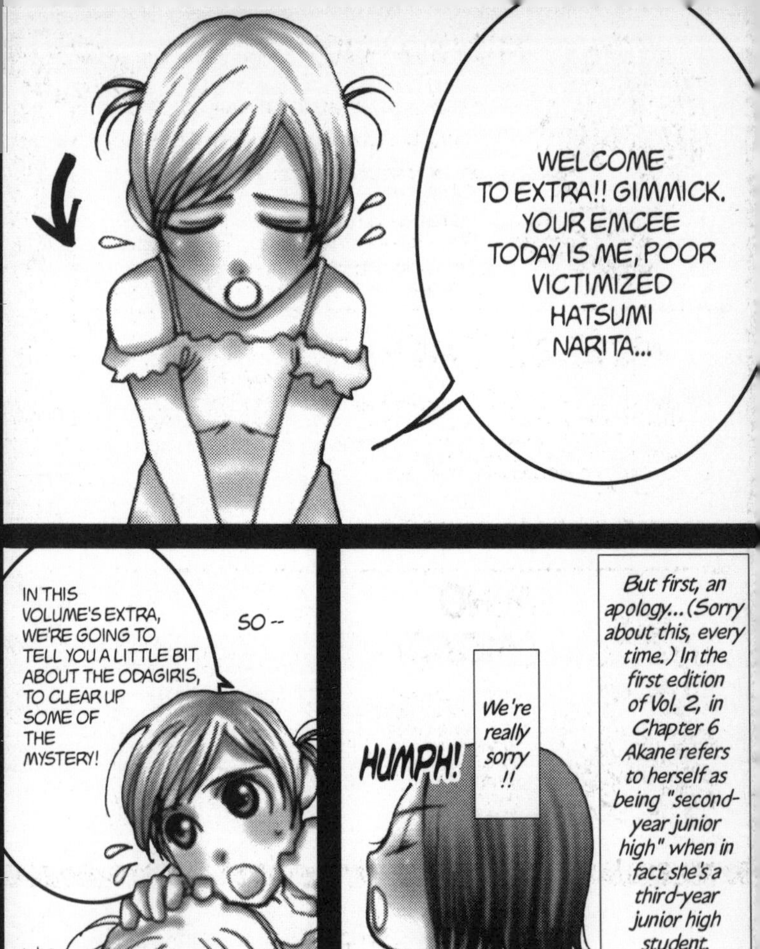
WELCOME TO EXTRA!! GIMMICK. YOUR EMCEE TODAY IS ME, POOR VICTIMIZED HATSUMI NARITA...
But first, an apology... (Sorry about this, every time.) In the first edition of Vol. 2, in Chapter 6 Akane refers to herself as being "second-year junior high" when in fact she's a third-year junior high student.
We're really sorry !!
HUMPH!
DON'T LOOK AT ME! THAT'S THE AUTHOR'S MISTAKE, NOT MINE, SO THERE!
SO --
IN THIS VOLUME'S EXTRA, WE'RE GOING TO TELL YOU A LITTLE BIT ABOUT THE ODAGIRIS, TO CLEAR UP SOME OF THE MYSTERY!
Yeah, for one thing, MY family is none of your business!

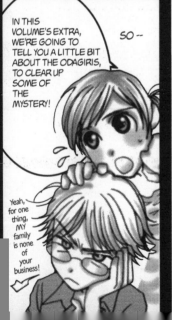

NO5 THE ODAGIRI FAMILY

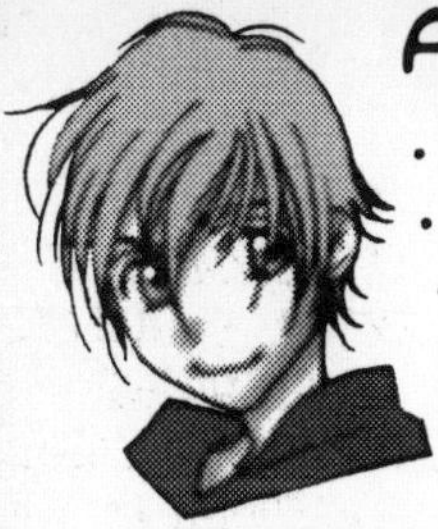

AZUSA (16)

- IN THE SAME CLASS AS HATSUMI AND SUBARU.
- 182 CM TALL (STILL GROWING), 60 kg (MORE OR LESS)
- POPULAR MODEL DOING MAGAZINE WORK AND TV COMMERCIALS.
- HOBBIES ARE FOLLOWING STYLISTS AROUND TO LEARN ABOUT CLOTHES, AND SLEEPING.
- ONLY LISTENS TO WESTERN MUSIC, NOT JAPANESE. GOOD COOK (BUT HARDLY EVER EATS HIS OWN FOOD).

MINORU (FATHER)

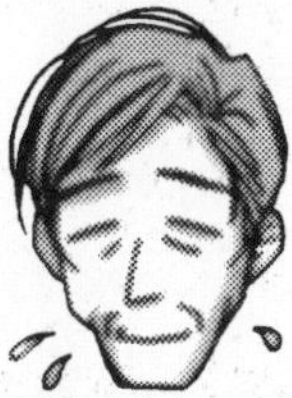

- WENT TO SAME UNIVERSITY AS HATSUMI'S DAD, BUT A YEAR OR TWO BEHIND HIM. RESPECTS HATSUMI'S DAD A LOT. WORKED OVERSEAS FOR ABOUT 5 YEARS, SO THIS IS THE FIRST TIME HE'S LIVED WITH AZUSA IN A LONG TIME. NICE GUY, VERY AFFABLE BUT A LITTLE TIMID.
- ABOUT TO REMARRY, AND WATCHING AZUSA TO SEE WHAT HE THINKS ABOUT IT.

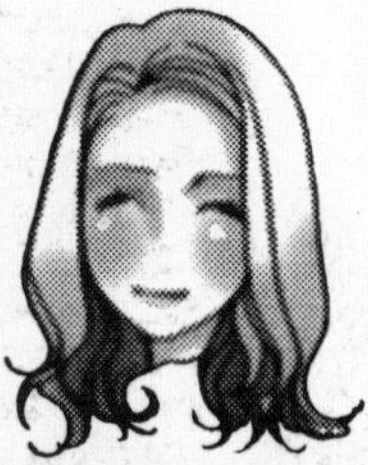

MIHO (MOM)

- DIED THREE YEARS AGO. A REAL BEAUTY. WENT TO COLLEGE WITH MINORU AND HATSUMI'S DAD. WHAT WAS HER RELATIONSHIP WITH ***HIM?!***

〈 OTHER AZUSA INFO 〉

- RAN AWAY FROM HIS MOM'S FAMILY WHEN HE WAS 13, AND MET RINA IN SHIBUYA. MOVED IN WITH HER.
- HAS MIXED FEELINGS ABOUT HIS FATHER'S REMARRIAGE, BUT PRETENDING TO BE MELLOW.

PLUS

IN RESPONSE TO REQUESTS FROM READERS OF VOLUME 2 -- SHINOGU IN HIS HIGH SCHOOL UNIFORM!! TURN THE PAGE, PLEASE!

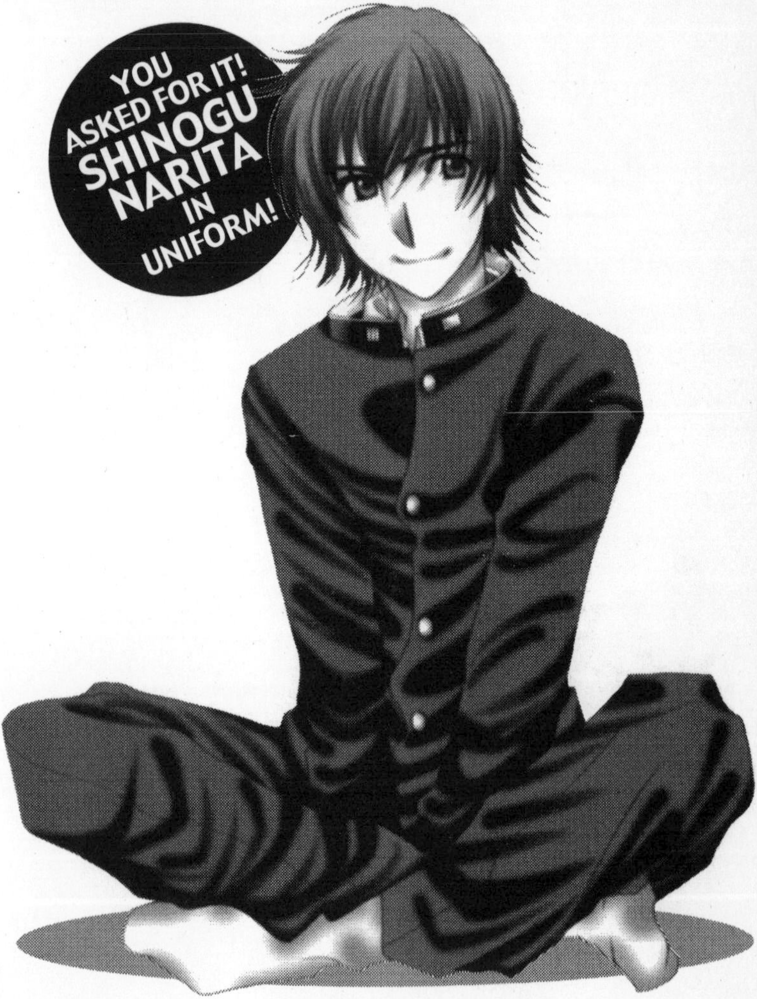
YOU ASKED FOR IT! SHINOGU NARITA IN UNIFORM!

HOT GIMMICK
Vol. 3

Shôjo Edition

STORY & ART BY MIKI AIHARA

ENGLISH ADAPTATION BY POOKIE ROLF

Touch-Up Art & Lettering/Rina Mapa
Design/Judi Roubideaux
Editorial Director/Alvin Lu

Managing Editor/Annette Roman
Director of Production/Noboru Watanabe
Sr. Director of Licensing and Acquisitions/Rika Inouye
VP of Sales & Marketing/Liza Coppola
Executive VP/Hyoe Narita
Publisher/Seiji Horibuchi

Printed in Canada

Published by VIZ, LLC, P.O. Box 77010, San Francisco, CA 94107

Shôjo Edition
10 9 8 7 6 5 4 3
First printing, February 2004
Second printing, May 2004
Third printing, October 2004

EDITOR'S RECOMMENDATIONS

More manga!
More manga!

If you enjoyed this volume of

Hot Gimmick

then here's some more manga you might be interested in.

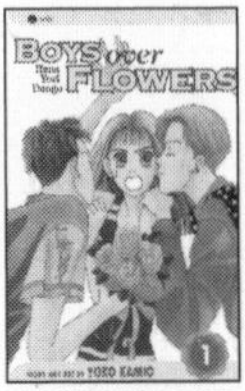
BOYS over FLOWERS
1
YOKO KAMIO

HANA-YORI DANGO © 1992 by Yoko Kamio/SHUEISHA Inc.

Boys over Flowers by Yoko Kamio: Meet Makino and Makiko Yuki–cute, popular high school girls whose lives take a turn for the worse when a gang of rich boys makes the whole school pick on them....

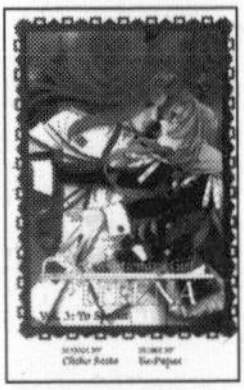

© 1996 SAITO CHIHO/ IKUHARA KUNIHIKO & BE PAPAS/Shogakukan, Inc.

Revolutionary Girl Utena by Chiho Saito: After being saved by a prince, Utena strives to grow up strong and noble–just like him! Now she's ready to revolutionize the world, if only it will lead her to her prince!

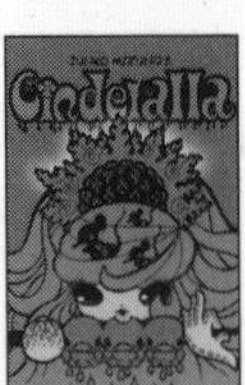
Cinderalla

© Junko Mizuno 2000

Junko Mizuno's Cinderalla by Junko Mizuno: The classic fairy tale re-told in psychedelic colors where Prince Charming is a... zombie?!

COMPLETE OUR SURVEY AND LET
US KNOW WHAT YOU THINK!

☐ Please do NOT send me information about VIZ products, news and events, special offers, or other information.

☐ Please do NOT send me information from VIZ's trusted business partners.

Name: _____

Address: _____

City: _____ **State:** _____ **Zip:** _____

E-mail: _____

☐ **Male** ☐ **Female** **Date of Birth** (mm/dd/yyyy): ___ / ___ / ___ (Under 13? Parental consent required)

What race/ethnicity do you consider yourself? (please check one)

☐ Asian/Pacific Islander ☐ Black/African American ☐ Hispanic/Latino

☐ Native American/Alaskan Native ☐ White/Caucasian ☐ Other: _____

What VIZ product did you purchase? (check all that apply and indicate title purchased)

☐ DVD/VHS _____

☐ Graphic Novel _____

☐ Magazines _____

☐ Merchandise _____

Reason for purchase: (check all that apply)

☐ Special offer ☐ Favorite title ☐ Gift

☐ Recommendation ☐ Other _____

Where did you make your purchase? (please check one)

☐ Comic store ☐ Bookstore ☐ Mass/Grocery Store

☐ Newsstand ☐ Video/Video Game Store ☐ Other: _____

☐ Online (site: _____)

What other VIZ properties have you purchased/own? _____

_____

How many anime and/or manga titles have you purchased in the last year? How many were VIZ titles? **(please check one from each column)**

ANIME	MANGA	VIZ
☐ None	☐ None	☐ None
☐ 1-4	☐ 1-4	☐ 1-4
☐ 5-10	☐ 5-10	☐ 5-10
☐ 11+	☐ 11+	☐ 11+

I find the pricing of VIZ products to be: **(please check one)**

☐ Cheap ☐ Reasonable ☐ Expensive

What genre of manga and anime would you like to see from VIZ? **(please check two)**

☐ Adventure ☐ Comic Strip ☐ Science Fiction ☐ Fighting

☐ Horror ☐ Romance ☐ Fantasy ☐ Sports

What do you think of VIZ's new look?

☐ Love It ☐ It's OK ☐ Hate It ☐ Didn't Notice ☐ No Opinion

Which do you prefer? **(please check one)**

☐ Reading right-to-left

☐ Reading left-to-right

Which do you prefer? **(please check one)**

☐ Sound effects in English

☐ Sound effects in Japanese with English captions

☐ Sound effects in Japanese only with a glossary at the back

THANK YOU! Please send the completed form to:

NJW Research
42 Catharine St.
Poughkeepsie, NY 12601

All information provided will be used for internal purposes only. We promise not to sell or otherwise divulge your information.